THE DEFENCE OF GREECE
490 – 479 BC

To my students –
past, present and, I hope, to come

ARIS AND PHILLIPS

The Defence of Greece

490–479 BC

J. F. Lazenby

Aris & Phillips is an imprint of Oxbow Books

First published in the United Kingdom in 1993. Reprinted 2007, 2015 by
OXBOW BOOKS
10 Hythe Bridge Street, Oxford OX1 2EW

and in the United States by
OXBOW BOOKS
908 Darby Road, Havertown, PA 19083

Paperback Edition: ISBN 978-0-85668-591-0

A CIP record for this book is available from the British Library

For a complete list of Aris & Phillips titles, please contact:

UNITED KINGDOM
Oxbow Books
Telephone (01865) 241249
Fax (01865) 794449
Email: oxbow@oxbowbooks.com
www.oxbowbooks.com

UNITED STATES OF AMERICA
Oxbow Books
Telephone (800) 791-9354
Fax (610) 853-9146
Email: queries@casemateacademic.com
www.casemateacademic.com/oxbow

Oxbow Books is part of the Casemate Group

Contents

List of Plates and List of Maps

List of Plates

Acknowledgements: for Plates 1 and 2, The Oriental Institute of the University of Chicago; for Plate 10, The Trustees of the National Museums of Scotland; for Plate 20, Times Newspapers Ltd.; and for Plates 3–6, 8, 11–14, 17, 19 and 21–4 Mr and Mrs N. Fields.

List of Maps

Preface

This book is the fruit of many years of teaching 'The Persian Wars' as a 'Special Subject' in the University of Newcastle upon Tyne. It is not that there are not already good books on the subject. On the contrary, there are at least three in English alone. Peter Green's *The Year of Salamis* is deservedly famous, combining scholarship and imagination with the ability to tell a stirring tale. Burn, too, has a way with words in *Persia and the Greeks*, and is, perhaps, stronger on scholarship. Above all, Hignett, whose lectures I must confess I abandoned at Oxford, contrived to write, in *Xerxes' Invasion of Greece*, a book which is methodologically the soundest of the lot, and should have been a powerful corrective to the folly of rejecting Herodotos in favour of secondary and inferior sources.

But even Hignett succumbs to the besetting sin not only of those who write about the Persian Wars, but about ancient military history in general – the assumption that (*mutatis mutandis*) ancient warfare was much the same as modern. In part this stems from a perfectly laudable desire to make the former intelligible and to bring it alive. But the moment one begins, for example, to call a *lochos*' a 'battalion', or a heterogeneous collection of three ships a 'reconnaissance unit', one inevitably begins to think in modern terms. That way lies the nonsense of 'principles of warfare' which hereditary kings of Sparta, Athenian aristocrats or Persian grandees, are supposed to have understood.

My first aim, then, has been to try to explain what happened in terms of what we know or can surmise about how wars were actually fought in the early fifth century BC. In particular, unless there is very good reason to think otherwise, I have assumed that the protagonists, at all levels, but especially at the highest, however innately intelligent, were wholly untrained, and often almost wholly inexperienced. Only thus, it seems to me, can one even begin to give an account that is at all likely to approximate to the truth.

Secondly, I have tried, as far as possible, to see things as much through Persian eyes as through Greek. I make no claim to any detailed or profound knowledge of the evidence from the Persian side, though I have made use of what is accessible to someone, like myself, brought up in the 'classical' tradition. Rather, I have tried to ask myself how the Persians might have looked at each situation. I may not thereby have dramatically altered received wisdom, except possibly in my assessment of Mardonios' strategy, but at least the war may no longer seem quite such a saga of the heroic resistance of a freedom-loving people against a mindless juggernaut.

Thirdly, and above all, I hope I have done something not so much to vindicate Herodotos, as to add to our understanding of the way he worked. I was, indeed, tempted to call my book 'Herodotos and the Defence of Greece', but I did not want people to think that it was yet another historiographical analysis of his work. As a historian of the Persian Wars my approach is necessarily somewhat different.

I started with what I suppose is a common opinion - that however great Herodotos may have been in other ways, as a military historian he left much to be desired. I believed that one could usually accept his facts, but that his assessment of motivation was largely pure imagination, and naive with it. But although I still think one must be careful to distinguish between his statements of fact and his statements of motive, I have become more and more impressed by the acuteness of his understanding of the way men think. He may not have had good evidence for believing that his protagonists behaved in the way they did for the reasons he gives, but increasingly my guess is that he was right more often than not.

The more I have worked with him, and wrestled not only to understand what he may have meant, but why he may have said the things he does, the more impressed I have become. Above all, I have been drawn to feel that we do not have to make *allowances* for him. Rather, we have to come to terms with the way he wrote history. It may not be our way, but it is a valid way. Thus, for example, though we may be right to dismiss his 'speeches' as unhistorical, we ignore them at our peril. There is often more insight in a pair of Herodotean orations than in a chapter of modern 'analysis'.

I may, finally, seem to have set out to denigrate the heroes of the Greek resistance, but nothing could be further from the truth. It is true that I do not think that Miltiades or Themistokles, for example, were the military geniuses they have been made out to be, and I do not believe that Greek soldiers and sailors were well-drilled professionals who won through superior training and discipline. But my admiration for Greek courage was given life by seeing, for instance, the scroll presented to a humble Cretan village by the government of New Zealand, for the shelter it provided to their soldiers in 1941, and I have come to believe that ancient Greek resistance to Persia was of a piece - quarrelsome, amateurish, ill-organized, but spontaneously courageous and irrespressible.

My thanks are due, as usual, to my colleagues at Newcastle for allowing me to pick their brains on a multiplicity of subjects. Any errors of which I am guilty – and I am sure there are many – are not for want of their trying. It is wonderful to belong to a department which is such a hot-bed of ideas, and, above all, such fun.

I am also very grateful to my students. I am not sure that they have often succeeded in making me change my views, or in drawing my attention to evidence and arguments I had not considered. But they have certainly compelled me to refine and clarify my thoughts, and, again, the errors that remain are due to my stubbornness, not their lack of interest.

In particular, I have enjoyed having a number of army officers, of one sort or another, in my classes. They have cheerfully and rapidly accepted that ancient warfare was not like what they were trained to do, but have still helped me to understand more about soldiers and their attitudes. The latest, Nic Fields, has added to my debt by taking many of the pictures, and his wife, Helen, by developing them.

My publishers have waited a long time, without nagging, as one would expect of friends, and once the typescript arrived, made some acute suggestions which in particular, I hope, will make the final product more accessible to non-specialist readers.

My children have now left home, so I no longer have to thank them for keeping out of the way. However, we still have four cats, and while Cato (the elder), Fabius and Marcellus have treated mere Greek history with their usual ineffable disdain, their sister, Klio - the Muse of History no less – has often kept me company, lying on the top of my

Amstrad, and, from time to time, looking at me with her fathomless, all-knowing, yellow eyes.

Finally, my thanks to my wife, who put up with my usually being just too late, for example, to lay the table, because I had to 'Finish Edit' or 'Save and Continue', and who found time, in the midst of reading for a Ph.D., to draw the maps and design the jacket.

J.F. Lazenby
Newcastle upon Tyne
September, 1992

CHAPTER 1

The Evidence

The Persian Wars are the first in European history that we can study in any detail, and form the subject of the earliest surviving prose work in European literature – the 'Histories' of Herodotos. But our dependence on Herodotos – the other evidence is negligible – makes the question of his reliabilty crucial. It might be possible to write an account of the conflict without using him, but it would look very strange, would be lacking in detail, and, above all, would be very dull. The Persian Wars without Herodotos would not so much be *Hamlet* without the prince, as *Hamlet* without Shakespeare.

Unfortunately we know all too little about Herodotos the man, apart from what can be gleaned from his own words.[1] The only connected ancient account of his life to have survived is contained in the Byzantine lexicon now usually known as 'the *Souda*' (*s.v.* 'Herodotos'). According to this, he was born in Halikarnassos of good parents, but emigrated to Samos to escape the hostility of the 'tyrant' Lygdamis. There he learnt Ionic and wrote his history. Later he returned to Halikarnassos and helped to expel the 'tyrant', but emigrated again, this time to Thouria in southern Italy, because of his unpopularity with his fellow-citizens. He died in Thouria and was buried in the main square, though another tradition was that he died in Pella, the capital of Macedonia. To this the *Souda* adds elsewhere (*s.v.* 'Panyasis') that he was the nephew or cousin of the Halikarnassian epic poet, Panyasis, who was executed by Lygdamis, and quotes his epitaph (*s.v.* 'Thourioi').

Apart from the *Souda*, Dionysios of Halikarnassos, writing in the first century,[2] says that he was born a little before the Persian Wars, and lived until the Peloponnesian War (*Thucydides* 5), and Aulus Gellius, writing in the second century AD, but on the authority of a certain Pamphila, a 'blue stocking' of the time of Nero, claims that he was born precisely in 484 (*Noctes Atticae* 15.23). Plutarch (*Moralia* 862b) quotes the fourth century Athenian historian, Diyllos, for the story that Herodotos once received an *honorarium* of ten talents from the people of Athens, and himself records that Sophokles wrote a poem to him (*Moralia* 785b).

This is not much, and some of it is unlikely to be true. The tradition that Herodotos learned Ionic on Samos, for instance, and wrote his history there, even that he was a Samian, is probably partly an attempt to explain why a man supposedly from a Doric-speaking city, came to write in Ionic, partly derived from the historian's evident interest in and predilection for all things Samian. But the former is almost certainly to be explained by the fact that Ionic was the established prose-medium of the day – Hippokrates of Doric Kos also wrote in Ionic. In any case, Halikarnassos, as the most northerly of the Dorian cities of south-west Asia Minor, may well have contained an

---

1 For Herodotos' life see, e.g., HW i 1ff.; T.S.Brown, *The Greek Historians* (Lexington, Mass., 1973). For proper names, technical terms etc., see the Glossary, 274ff.

2 Unless otherwise stated, all dates in this book are BC. All references to Herodotos will be just to book, chapter and verse, without his name; those to Plutarch are to the Loeb Classical Library edition of his works.

Ionian admixture. A contemporary inscription from the city (ML 32), now in the British Museum, which may refer to the 'tyrant' Lygdamis and Herodotos' uncle, Panyasis, is also in Ionic. The tradition that Herodotos was honoured by the Athenians may be true – he certainly admired them – but the figure of ten talents is beyond belief,[3] and some of the other stories about the enthusiasm evoked by his work – for example that Thucydides was moved to tears by it (*Souda* s.v. 'Thucydides') – look like later embroidery. One would, in any case, very much like to know whether Thucydides' tears were ones of enthusiasm or exasperation.

There is, however, no particular reason to doubt other parts of the tradition. That he had some connection with Thouria, for example, is implied by the description of him as 'the Thourian' in the text of his work known to Aristotle (*Rhetoric* 3.1409a, cf. Plutarch, *Moralia* 604f & 868a), and although the date of his birth might have been worked out by assuming that he was forty at the time of his emigration to Thouria,[4] it is equally arguable that he is hardly likely to have been under, say, twenty.

He certainly did live to see the outbreak of the Peloponnesian War, for he refers to incidents in its early years – the Theban attack on Plataia in March, 431 (7.233.2), the expulsion of the Aiginetans from Aigina at the end of that year (6.91.1), the sparing of Dekeleia in the ravaging of Attica by the Spartans, probably in 431 or 430 (9.73.3), and the execution of the Corinthian Aristeus and the Lakedaimonian envoys at the end of 430 (7.137.3). This last is the latest datable event to which he certainly refers, and although this does not necessarily mean that he died soon afterwards, it does suggest that he completed his work at about that time. It is possible, too, that the comical account of the origins of the Peloponnesian War in Aristophanes' *Acharnians* (515-39) is a parody of Herodotos' account of the mythical origins of the conflict between east and west (1.1-5.2), in which case the latter at least had in some sense been 'published' by 425. It is extremely improbable, finally, that Herodotos would not have mentioned the destruction of the Aiginetan refugees in the Thyreatis in 424 (cf. Thucydides 4.57.1-3), when he wrote of their expulsion from Aigina, had he still been writing his work at that time, or told the story of Chilon's warning to the Spartans about Kythera (7.235.2), without mentioning the Athenian occupation of the island, also in 424 (Thucydides 4.53ff.).

It is also probable that Herodotos was a native of Halikarnassos. In the opening words of all the surviving manuscripts of his work, he describes himself as 'Herodotos the Halikarnassian', and although the text known to Aristotle and Plutarch evidently had 'Herodotos the Thourian', this is readily explicable by his having become a citizen of that city, whereas the tradition preserves no explanation of the reading of our manuscripts other than that he was born in Halikarnassos. There is also the point that whereas he seems to know things about Halikarnassos which a stranger to that city might not have known, and obviously takes an almost malicious delight in the doings of its queen, Artemisia,[5] he never even mentions Thouria.

---

3 See Fornara, *Herodotos* (Oxford, 1971), 46; Hammond, 1988, 492, accepts the tradition.

4 Cf. Diels, *RhM* 31 (1876), 1ff.

5 E.g. the reasons for the exclusion of the Halikarnassians from the Triopian Games (1.144), or the story of Phanes' advice to Kambyses how to invade Egypt (3.4). For Artemisia see 7.99; 8.68-9, 87-8, 93, 101, 103, 107.

It is very likely that he was a man of good family – most, if not all, fifth century writers were – and as such he could well have incurred the hostility of Halikarnassos' 'tyrant', have fled to Samos and returned to help expel the 'tyrant'; nor is it improbable that he lived and worked for some time in Athens. He evidently disapproved of 'tyrants', knew Samos well, and had certainly heard stories which are not likely to have been told outside Athens (cf. 5.78, 8.85.2-3, 6.117.2-3); the tradition of his friendship with Sophokles is borne out by correspondences between their works.[6]

If we are to believe what he says,[7] he travelled extensively in the world known to the Greeks – another indication, perhaps, that he was a man of means – from the Ukraine (cf., e.g., 4.81) to Elephantine opposite Aswan, on the first cataract of the Nile (cf. 2.29), and from the 'heel' of Italy (cf. 4.99.5) to western Iran (6.119.4). The text of his work known to Aristotle confirms that he did take part in the colonisation of Thouria, but despite the tradition that he died and was buried there, his references to fairly obscure events that took place in mainland Greece in the opening years of the Peloponnesian War, may indicate that he returned to Greece at about that time, in which case the alternative tradition – that he died at Pella – may be true.

We have no means of checking most of this, and it is possible that the 'traditions' about his life are no more than a reconstruction based on his own words, in which case some of the above arguments are circular. It is also, of course, possible that what he says is untrue, in which case there is no possibility of recovering the truth about him. But what he says, and what is reported about him, hang together and make a plausible story.

If it is true, it would mean that although perhaps not even alive at the time of Marathon, and perhaps too young to remember much, if anything, about the stirring events of 480/79, he could have talked to participants in events as far back as the beginning of the century. But the operative words here are 'talked to': there would have been almost no documentary evidence to which he could have turned. There would have been a few monuments, some of which have survived, for example the bronze column representing three entwined snakes set up at Delphi (9.81.1, ML 27). It bears a list of thirty-one states which fought in the war against Xerxes, and Herodotos possibly consulted it, because he knew the Tenians were one of them (8.82.1, cf. ML 27, Coil 7).[8] However, some of the monuments which he saw, no longer survive, such as the stone lion commemorating Leonidas' death at Thermopylai (7.225.2), and the epitaphs he quotes (7.228.1-3).

---

6 Compare 3.119.6 with *Antigone* 904ff., 2.35.2 with *Oedipus Coloneus* 337-41, 1.32.5 with *Oedipus Tyrannus* 1530, 4.95.4 with *Electra* 62-4, 1.31.4 and 7.46.3-4 with *Oedipus Coloneus* 1225ff. Fehling, 243-5, argues that Herodotos was not a member of the upper classes.

7 But see, e.g., O.K.Armayor, *HSCPh* 82 (1978), 45ff.; *Journal of the American Research Center in Egypt* 15 (1980), 59ff.; *HSCPh* 84 (1980), 51ff.; *Herodotus' Autopsy of the Fayoum: Lake Moeris and the Labyrinth of Egypt* (Amsterdam, 1985).

8 It is possible that Herodotos had not seen the monument since he makes two mistakes about it: the names were not on the *tripod*, as he says (8.82.1), and the column supporting it was not merely *three-headed* (9.81.1). However, these – particularly the last – are mistakes which it would have been easy for someone to make, perhaps writing some years after seeing the monument.

One may suspect that a documentary source lay behind other passages, for instance the lists of the Greek forces at Thermopylai, Artemision, Salamis and Plataia (7.202-203.1; 8.1, 43-6; 9.28.2ff.), though even these could have been passed on by word of mouth. Persian documentary sources may lie behind the list of satrapies in Book 3 (89ff.), the account of the 'Royal Road' in Book 5 (52ff.), and, possibly, that of the Persian forces in Book 7 (61ff.), though it can hardly have been a list of the forces which actually accompanied Xerxes.[9] In any case, Herodotos was almost certainly incapable of reading Persian documents for himself, since, if he had been, he could hardly have claimed that all Persian names ended in 's'. Probably, too, he had access to a written collection of oracles, most of which he quotes in verse, though it is worth noting that he quotes in prose one of the most famous of them, the one that told Croesus that if he marched against the Persians, he would destroy a great empire (1.53.3).

The extent to which Herodotos made use of other written sources is a matter of controversy. Most of the authors he names were early poets, such as Homer, Hesiod, Archilochos and Alkaios. He does mention contemporaries, such as Aischylos (2.156.6), Pindar (3.38.4), Phrynichos (6.21.2) and Simonides (7.228.4), but it is odd that he does not quote, for example, Simonides' lost poem about Artemision, or the one in which Pindar mentioned it (quoted by Plutarch, *Themistokles* 8.2), or the First Pythian in which Pindar mentions both Artemision and Salamis. Even more oddly he does not mention Aischylos' play *The Persians*, which contains an account of the battle of Salamis, or the poems of Timokreon of Rhodes attacking Themistokles, which are again quoted by Plutarch (*Themistokles* 21.4-7).[10]

He only mentions one prose-writer by name, Hekataios of Miletos (2.143.1 & 3; 5.36.2, 125, 126.1; 6.137 1 & 4), and then only once refers specifically to his work (6.137.1), though one may suspect that this was also the source for the story of Hekataios' visit to Egypt (2.143). Whether or not he used Hekataios and other early prose-writers without acknowledgement is very difficult to determine. In antiquity he was accused of plagiarizing not only Hekataios, but also Xanthos of Lydia, Charon of Lampsakos and Hellanikos of Lesbos.[11] For our purposes it does not matter much whether these accusations are true or false, since we are only concerned with the truth or falsity of what Herodotos says, whatever his source. But the accusation is probably false in the case of Hellanikos of Lesbos, since he seems to have been a younger

---

9 Cf. A.T.Olmstead, *History of the Persian Empire* (Chicago, 1948), 237ff., for the possibility that Herodotos had access to an official roster of Xerxes' forces; cf., also, Cook, 77ff, 101ff., 108.

10 For Simonides' poems on the events of 480 see A.J.Podlecki, *Historia* 17 (1968), 257ff. The poem on the Persian wars by the late fifth century poet Choirilos of Samos, could have been published after Herodotos' work, even though the *Souda* alleges Choirilos was a friend of the historian: cf. G.L. Huxley, *GRBS* 10 (1969), 12ff.

11 Cf. HW i 22ff. Pollio (*ap*. Eusebius, *Praeparatio Evangelica,* 10.3.16 & 23) accused Herodotos of taking over descriptions of Egypt word for word from Hekataios, and modern writers have suggested, e.g., that he drew on Hekataios' map for his list of satrapies in 3.90-6 (F.Altheim & R. Stiehl, *Die aramaïsche Sprache unter den Achaimeniden* i, Frankfort am Main, 1963, 127ff.), and for his account of Xerxes' forces (O.K.Armayor, *TAPA* 108, 1978, 1ff.; D.M.Lewis, 'Persians in Herodotus', *The Greek Historians: Literature and History*, Stanford, 1985, 101ff.).

contemporary – he mentioned an event as late as 406 (*FGH* 323F25). Of the others, Charon is twice quoted by Plutarch to refute stories told by Herodotos (*Moralia* 859a-b, 861c-d), and Dionysios of Halikarnassos (*Roman Antiquities* 1.28) specifically says that Xanthos did not mention the alleged Lydian migration to Etruria, of which Herodotos tells in Book 1 (94.2ff.). None of this suggests that Herodotos slavishly followed such sources, if he used them at all.

As for Hekataios, he is unlikely to have given an account of the Ionian Revolt, let alone Xerxes' invasion of Greece,[12] and there is no good reason to believe that any prose-author earlier than Herodotos had written of these things. None of the extant fragments of Xanthos of Lydia suggests that he dealt with the Persian attacks on Greece, and although the fragments of Charon of Lampsakos indicate that he did deal, perhaps at length, with the Athenian help to the Ionians, the attack on Sardis and the ill-fated expedition of Mardonios in 492 (*FGH* 262), these episodes are quite unimportant in Herodotos, and Charon's work, far from being a source for Herodotos, may in fact be an abbreviation of his work. When discussing the numbers of Xerxes' forces, Herodotos says that he cannot say exactly how many men each nation furnished, 'for it is not stated by any men' (7.60.1: οὐ γὰρ λέγεται πρὸς οὐδαμῶν ἀνθρώπων), and this suggests that he knew of no written source for Xerxes' invasion.

Apart from Herodotos, there is not much evidence to consider. There is, of course, the landscape of Greece itself, which provides physical parameters for the events he describes, though even here one must be careful. Recent studies have suggested, for example, that the ground-level at Marathon may have risen considerably, and that the '*charadra*' which appears on modern maps, and which has excited so many modern scholars, simply did not exist in 490. The battle of Thermopylai, too, was possibly fought below the present surface, and it is, of course, obvious that there the sea has receded a long way since the fifth century;[13] elsewhere, for example in the Saronic Gulf, the sea level may have risen.[14] There may have been more water about at the time of Xerxes' invasion, judging by Herodotos' account of the 'island' near Plataia (9.51), and there may well have been changes in the *flora*.

The main problem, however, is not having to make allowances for such changes, but in trying to identify the locations Herodotos mentions. Obviously, when he wrote, it was easy to find such things as the *temenos* of Herakles, where the Athenians camped before Marathon (6.108.1), or that of Androkrates near Plataia (9.25.3), to say nothing of such more ephemeral locations as the 'Black Buttocks' rock above Thermopylai (7.216). Now one is often reduced to the 'eye of faith'. In other words, however careful a topographer Herodotos may have been, his care is largely lost on us. Nevertheless, the physical environment should always be taken into account, and can sometimes play a part in the argument. It is impossible, for example, for watchers on the hills of Euboia to have reported the wreck of the Persian fleet off Magnesia, as Herodotos says they did (7.192.1), because they could not have seen it.

---

12 Jacoby, *RE* vii 2668f.; Blamire, *CQ* 53 (1959), 148 n.1.

13 Pritchett, *AJA* 62 (1958), 203ff., and *GSW* iv (Berkeley & Los Angeles, 1985), 172f., quoting Professor J.C.Kraft, but see Hammond, 1988, 516 n.2.

14 Pritchett, *AJA* 63 (1959), 251ff.; Hammond, 1956, 32ff., revised in *Studies in Greek History* (Oxford, 1973), 251ff.

There is hardly any contemporary evidence in the form of inscriptions. There is an enigmatic memorial to the polemarch, Kallimachos, who was killed at Marathon (ML 18), fragments of Athenian epigrams on the wars (ML 26), and the dedication of 'first-fruits' from Marathon to Apollo at Delphi (ML 19). The serpent-column from Delphi survives in Istanbul, still bearing the names of the thirty-one states which 'warred the war' (ML 27), and fragments of the memorial to the Corinthians who died fighting for 'Holy Hellas' at Salamis, also survive (ML 24). But even if the so-called 'Themistokles Decree' from Trozen (ML 23) is a more or less true copy of a decree of 480, what we have is still a copy, inscribed over two centuries later, and the surviving Megarian epitaph is even later (Tod *GHI*1 20).

From the Persian side there are no surviving archives which refer to the invasions of Greece, though there is some archival material bearing upon the revolts in Egypt and elsewhere, in the 480s.[15] Reliefs at Sousa and Persepolis are of some help for the equipment of the Persian armed forces, but the main evidence here comes from Herodotos himself.[16]

Inscriptions apart, there is little other archaeological evidence. The grave mound of the Athenians killed at Marathon has been excavated, and arrow-heads picked up from round about it, but another grave recently found, which has been thought to be that of the Plataians, probably has nothing to do with the battle;[17] masses of bones, which might or might not be those of Persians killed in the rout, were seen by a German surveyor near the Mesosporitissa chapel.[18] Traces of the Athos canal have been discovered and are now being studied,[19] and parts of the Phokian wall may still be seen at Thermopylai, where the hillock upon which the Greeks made their last stand has also been excavated.[20] A possible grave mound of the Athenians killed at Salamis has been found on the island,[21] and at Plataia traces of graves and the altar of Zeus Eleutherios have possibly been found.[22]

---

15 Cook, 99f.

16 Cook, 101ff.

17 On the alleged grave-mound of the Plataians see *AAA* 3 (1970), 164ff., 357ff.; *Ergon* 1970, 5ff.; *PAE* 1970, 5ff. Hammond (1973, 198n), and Burn ('Thermopylae revisited and some topographical notes on Marathon and Plataiai', *Greece and the Eastern Mediterranean in Ancient History and Prehistory*, Festschrift for F.Shachermeyer, Berlin, 1977, 92) accept the identification, but it is questioned by Themelis (*ADelt* 29, 1974[1978] *Meletai*, 244) and rejected by Koumanoudis (*AAA* 11, 1978, 232ff.; cf. also K.-W.Welwei, 'Das sogennante Grab der Plataier in Vranatal bei Marathon', *Historia* 28 (1979), 101ff.

18 For these bones see *Topographische, archaeologische und militärische Betrachtungen auf dem Schlachtfelde von Marathon* (Berlin, 1886); E.Vanderpool, *Hesperia* 35 (1966), 101 n.15.

19 For the Athos canal see now B.S.J.Isserlin, *BSA* 86 (1991), 83ff. The canal was probably completed, as Herodotos says, despite the doubts expressed by Demetrios of Skepsis (*ap.* Strabo, frag. 35), and others (Isserlin, *op.cit.* 87-8).

20 For excavations of the hillock at Thermopylai see Marinatos, *JHS* 59 (1939), 199ff.; *AJA* 43 (1939), 699f.

21 See Pritchett, *Studies in Ancient Greek Topography* i (Berkeley & Los Angeles, 1965) 1.95-6; Tsiribakos, *ADelt* 22 (1967), Chr.146 & pl.110; G.R.Culley, *Hesperia* 44 (1975), 207ff., denies that this has anything to do with Salamis.

22 See *AAA* 6 (1973), 373ff.

The only contemporary literary evidence to have survived, apart from Herodotos himself, is Aischylos' *Persai* and Pindar's *First Pythian*, and the value of later literary sources is disputable. The only connected narratives are those of Ktesias – though only in the epitome of the 9th century AD Byzantine bishop, Photios – and of Diodoros of Sicily. Since the former, though a Greek, was court physician to Artaxerxes II, king of Persia from 405 to 359, and wrote a history of Persia, it might have been hoped that his account of the invasions of Greece would have been immensely valuable in reflecting something of the Persian point of view. In the event, however, although it is perhaps unfair to judge Ktesias by Photios' summary, his account of the Persian wars seems to be almost entirely worthless. Most notoriously, he appears to have placed Salamis after Plataia, though this may have been a literary device to complete the narrative of events on land before turning to the sea. However, he also appears to have omitted Artemision altogether, and to have given Pausanias Leonidas' army. In the light of this, it is difficult to accept his figure of 110 ships for the Athenians at Salamis, and his placing of Xerxes' attempt to construct a mole across to the island *before* the battle, though both these items are worth considering (see below, 163 & 172–3).[23]

Unfortunately Diodoros' account of the Marathon campaign and of the events leading up to Xerxes' invasion is almost entirely lost – all that remains are a few fragments of his tenth book. However, Book 11 has survived complete, and is sometimes thought to provide valuable evidence to supplement or even correct Herodotos, for example on Salamis. It has even been claimed[24] that through the lost fourth century historian Ephoros, who was one of his principal sources, Diodoros ultimately drew upon Dionysios of Miletos, an author alleged by the *Souda* to have been a contemporary of Hekataios, and to have written not only a history of Persia, but a work in five books on 'the things after Darius'. But there is considerable doubt whether Dionysios was so early, and it is difficult to believe that he was of much significance when he is not cited by either Dionysios of Halikarnassos in his list of fifth century historians (*Thucydides* 5), or by Plutarch in his essay '*On the Malice of Herodotos*' (*Moralia* 854e-874c).

Diodoros' principal source, Ephoros, is described by Polybios as one of 'the most learned of the ancients,' alongside Xenophon, Kallisthenes and Plato (6.45.1), and said (12.25f.) to have had 'some idea of naval tactics'. But his account of Salamis, which many seem to regard as superior to that of Herodotos, is in fact very confused (see below, 184–5). Polybios also says (*loc.cit.*) that Ephoros was 'quite unacquainted with fighting on shore', and Diodoros' absurd story of the alleged night raid on Xerxes' camp before the final day at Thermopylai (11.10.1-4), culminating, apparently, in the annihilation of Leonidas' forces in the camp itself, is sufficient evidence of Ephoros' shortcomings in this respect, if he was Diodoros' source; Diodoros' account of Plataia is also very confused.

Diodoros' contemporary, Cornelius Nepos, was possibly the author of a series of '*Lives of Outstanding Generals*' (*Vitae Excellentium Imperatorum*), which have survived in an apparently abridged form, ascribed by the MSS to one Aemilius Probus, probably of the 4th century AD. Of these the lives of Miltiades, Themistokles, Aristeides and

---

23 See Burn, 136 n.11, for a devastating appraisal of Ktesias.

24 Obst, 'Der Feldzug des Xerxes', *Klio*, Beiheft xii (1914), 27-30, etc.

Pausanias are relevant, though only that of Miltiades is at all important. It contains an account of the Marathon campaign which may help to locate the Athenian position, though the text is unfortunately dubious at the crucial point.

A younger contemporary of both Diodoros and Cornelius Nepos was the geographer Strabo. He helps to locate some of the places mentioned by Herodotos and other writers, but unfortunately does not solve any of the important topographical problems. He preserves some interesting details, for example about Xerxes' mole across to Salamis (9.1.13), and that a mass grave was still visible at Thermopylai in his day (9.5.16). But he also has some dubious stories, such as the one about the Boiotian, Salganeus, who allegedly guided the Persians down the Euripos, and was executed for leading them into a dead-end, just before the Persian admirals spotted the channel (9.2.9).

From the 1st century AD we have the '*Stratagems*' of Sextus Julius Frontinus, consul in 73 or 74, 98 and 100, but very few, if any, of these anecdotes are of much value. A younger contemporary of Frontinus was Plutarch of Chaironeia in Boiotia, whose lives of Themistokles and Aristeides both contain lengthy passages about their heroes' exploits in the Persian Wars, and there are scattered references in many of his minor works (*Moralia*). Although he lived over half a millenium after the Persian invasions of Greece, he was a learned man who consulted and cites a wide variety of sources, some of which were early, and most of which are lost to us. Thus he cites Hellanikos of Lesbos to the effect that there were six Naxian ships at Salamis, not four as Herodotos says, and quotes Simonides' epigram on their captain, Demokritos (*Moralia* 869a-c). Plutarch possibly also preserves some contemporary non-literary evidence, such as the decree providing for the sending of Athenian ambassadors to Sparta during the winter of 480/79 (*Aris*teides 10.8). But he also tells some absurd stories, such as that Leonidas' heart was found to be covered in hair, when his body was cut open after his death (*Moralia* 306c-d, citing Aristeides of Miletos), or that Agesilaos, brother of Themistokles, killed Mardonios by mistake for Xerxes off Artemision, dressed as a Persian (*Moralia* 305d-e, citing Agatharkidas of Samos).

These stories are obviously ridiculous, but they illustrate the lengths to which the secondary sources evidently went in embellishing the story of the Persian Wars, and call in question even ostensibly sober additions, let alone corrections, to Herodotos' narrative, unless quoted on very good authority. Thus Plutarch's life of Themistokles (14.2) contains the plausible story of the dawn wind at Salamis, which may be authentic,[25] and his figure for the number of marines on each Athenian trireme may be supported by the 'Themistokles Decree' (see below, 35–6). But doubt is cast on the whole passage by the story that Themistokles sacrificed three noble youths before the battle, given on the authority of Phanias of Lesbos (13.2-3), and by his reference to an apparently mythical Persian admiral, Ariamenes (14.3).[26] Thus, when, for example, Herodotos says that Ameinias, the first Greek to ram a ship at Salamis, came from the Attic deme of Pallene (8.84.1), whereas Plutarch describes him as 'the Dekeleian' (*Themistokles* 14.3), one should surely believe Herodotos.

Later even than Plutarch, from the second century AD, we have one or two relevant passages in the '*Stratagems*' of Polyainos, one of which, for example, has been claimed

---

25 Cf. Grundy, 208 n.28; Hammond, 1956, 46.

26 See Hignett, 10 and n.3, 233 and n.7.

to date Thermopylai, another to preserve an authentic detail of Leonidas' strategy (1.32.2-3). In the end, however, what Polyainos has to say about the Persian Wars is probably worthless. Far more important is Pausanias' '*Guidebook*' (*Periegesis*), which is sometimes invaluable in preserving a memory of contemporary or near-contemporary evidence, which has long since vanished. It is Pausanias, for example, who describes the painting of Marathon in the *Stoa Poikile* at Athens (1.15.4), which may, in a sense, be the earliest evidence for the battle to have survived. But Pausanias also shows how stories were embroidered in his tale (10.19.1) of 'Skyllis' the diver ('Skyllias' in Herodotos 8.8), and gives us a glimpse of the kind of information purveyed by local guides in his day. Anyone who has been to Greece more recently will know exactly what to make, for instance, of 'the stone troughs of Artaphernes' horses, and the marks of his tent in the rocks' (1.32.6).

There are many incidental references to the Persian wars in ancient literature, some of them, like the story of the cavalry's absence from Marathon in the *Souda* (*s.v.* 'χώρις ἱππεῖς'), worth considering, some, like Lucian's story of Philippides' exploits (*On Mistakes in Greeting*, 3), hardly worthy of notice. But even where later sources tell us something which does not contradict Herodotos, and which is in itself plausible, the question should be asked how such information managed to survive, sometimes for hundreds of years, when he knew nothing of it, even though he obviously took trouble to find out all he could, and loved a good story. In the end the extent to which we can reconstruct what happened and why depends on the extent to which we believe Herodotos, and it is clear that even in his own day he found both his credibility and his opinions under attack. For example, some of his contemporaries evidently disbelieved his account of the political debate in Persia at the time of Darius' accession (3.80.1 & 6.43.3), and in a famous passage praising Athens' part in the great war, he says he feels compelled to express an opinion jealously rejected by the majority (7.139.1). His great successor, Thucydides, in criticizing the Greeks for their ignorance of both the past and contemporary history, singles out as examples the belief that the kings of Sparta had two votes in the *gerousia* and that there was a Spartan military unit called the '*lochos* of Pitana' (1.20.3), the first of which Herodotos appears to say (6.57.5),[27] and the second of which he mentions in his account of Plataia (9.53.2-3). Plutarch, for his part, devoted a whole essay to the 'malice' (κακοήθεια) of Herodotos (*Moralia* 854e-874c).

As we have seen, there is almost no other evidence by which to check Herodotos, but in general, where there is, it tends to bear him out.[28] For example, the Persian 'Fortification Tablets',covering the years 510 to 493, confirm the accuracy of his knowledge of the names of Persian grandees and their marriage relations;[29] *ostraka* have confirmed the existence of such a minor character as Themistokles' friend,

27 Herodotos may have meant that each of the nearest relatives of the kings cast a proxy-vote for that king and one for himself, but what he actually says is that 'their nearest relatives amongst the *gerontes* have the rights of the kings, casting two votes, and a third for themselves' (τοὺς μάλιστα σφι τῶν γερόντων προσήκοντας ἔχειν τὰ τῶν βασιλέων γέρεα, δύο ψήφους τιθεμένους, τρίτην δὲ τὴν ἑωυτῶν: 6.57.5).

28 If Armayor is right – see n.7 above – the credibility of Herodotos' claims to have been to various places must come into question, and hence his credibility in general.

29 Cf. HW i 135.

Mnesiphilos (8.57.1, 58.2), whom one eminent commentator had dismissed as fiction,[30] and the name of the Tenians does, as he says (8.82.1), appear on the monument set up at Delphi, though not on the tripod. In the one case where we do have a contemporary account of a military event – Aischylos' description of Salamis in *The Persians* – there are no major discrepancies from Herodotos, despite what has been claimed.[31]

In the end, however, the credibility of Herodotos can only be assessed by reference to the kind of evidence he used, the way he used it and the plausibility of what he says. In a recent book[32] it is argued that in fact he invented his sources, and if this is true, it becomes very difficult to believe anything he says. To refute the argument in detail would require a book in itself, and would, indeed, be difficult since poor Herodotos is left in a 'no win' situation. For example, if he cites different accounts or declares himself unable to discover the truth, this is, in Pooh-Bah's immortal words, 'merely corroberative detail, intended to give artistic verisimilitude to a bald and unconvincing narrative.'

But the Herodotos this view asks us to imagine is far more incredible than some of the statements by his sources he asks us to believe. In effect, we are being asked to accept that the first historian was also the first historical novelist, inventing sources, even conflicting ones, before anyone had really tried to use real ones.[33] Nor does the view make nearly enough allowance for the almost infinite possibilities of misunderstanding and misremembering that can arise when one talks to people of different languages and culture, either directly, or, even worse, through interpreters, probably without even taking notes, let alone tape-recording what is said.[34] It will be assumed, therefore, in this book, that however Herodotos may have distorted what he was told, his claims to have used oral sources are genuine.

The one undoubted example of an eyewitness account used directly in the books relating to the two Persian invasions of Greece, is thus the story of the banquet at Thebes, shortly before Plataia, which Herodotos plainly states (9.16.1 & 5) he heard from Thersander of Orchomenos, who was present. Elsewhere he does not name his sources for contemporary events, but one may suspect that Arimnestos of Plataia, for example,

---

30 Cf. Macan (1908) i 2.444.

31 See J.F.Lazenby, *Hermes* 116 (1988), 168ff.

32 Detlev Fehling, *Die Quellenangaben bei Herodot* (Berlin & New York, 1971), now revised by the author and translated into English by J.G.Howie under the title '*Herodotus and his 'Sources': Citation, Invention and Narrative Art*' (Leeds, 1989). All my citations are from this latter version.

33 Cf. Oswyn Murray's remark: 'To postulate deliberate and wholesale deception (with Fehling, 1971), rather than faulty execution, requires an answer to the question, who invented the model which Herodotus is thought to have abused? It implies a proto-Herodotus before Herodotus' ('Herodotus and Oral History', *Achaemenid History II. The Greek Sources*. Proceedings of the Groningen 1984 Achaemenid History Workshop, ed. H.Sancini-Weerdenburg & A.Kurt, Leiden, 1987, 101 n.12).

34 I once met an old shepherd at Plataia, whose first words, on being told that we had come to see the place where the Greeks defeated the Persians, were, 'I remember when the barbarians came'! It soon became apparent that he was referring to a party of German officers whom he had met during the war, but this was the kind of situation which might well have led Herodotos to report apparently incredible oral evidence.

may have been his source for the story of the death of Kallikrates (9.72.1), and possibly Archias, whom he met in Pitana (3.55.2) for the story of Amompharetos, '*lochagos* of the Pitanate *lochos*' (9.53.2). The family of the exiled Spartan King Damaratos, descendants of whom were still living in western Asia Minor in Xenophon's day (cf. *Anabasis* 2.1.3 & *Hellenika* 3.1.6), are likely to have been the source of the many anecdotes about their ancestor.[35]

Examples of the indirect use of eyewitnesses are the stories of Philippides' encounter with Pan, which Herodotos says the runner told the Athenians (6.105.1), and of the blinding of Epizelos at Marathon, which he introduces with the words 'I heard that he himself told the following story about what happened to him' (6.117.3)). Something similar is perhaps implied by the story of the miracle witnessed by Dikaios in the Thriasian plain before Salamis, which is introduced by the statement 'Dikaios, son of Theokydes, a man of Athens, said ...' (8.65.1), though this might imply that Herodotos had heard the story from Dikaios himself.

Usually he refers to his sources in a more general way, sometimes specifying the people of a state or area – for example 'the Lakedaimonians' (6.52.3) or 'the Thessalians' (7.129.4), or, more loosely, 'the Greeks' (e.g. 6.134.1) or 'the Persians' (e.g. 7.12.1) – but more often using phrases such as 'it is said that ...' or 'they say'. Occasionally he indicates that he was not content simply to accept these second-hand reports, but had made his own enquiries (cf., e.g., 8.35.2, 8.79.1).

Obviously there are dangers in using this kind of evidence,[36] but, as we have seen, there was very little else, and Herodotos does seem to have been at least as aware of the dangers as Thucydides (1.22). If there was other evidence, he sometimes used it to check the stories told him. He says, for example, that the Spartans, in maintaining that it was the hero, Aristodemos, himself, who led their ancestors to Lakedaimon, were 'in agreement with no poet' (6.52.1), and he claims to have checked the Athenian version of the expulsion of the Pelasgians from Attica against Hekataios (6.137). These are examples of attempts to check legends, but it is surely safe to assume that he did the same for contemporary events, wherever possible. For example, he refers to the *stele* commemorating the eleven Samian trierarchs who did not desert at Lade (6.114.3), and in discussing who was responsible for betraying the Anopaia track to the Persians, he argues that it was Ephialtes upon whose head a reward was placed (7.214.2), suggesting that he had perhaps seen the name on an inscription or in some kind of official record.

In any case, he was clearly not just content to put down the first story he heard and leave it at that. He repeatedly gives conflicting accounts,[37] and obviously went to some trouble to find out as much as he could, judging by the occasions when he despairingly admits defeat[38] or doubt.[39] Occasionally he claims to know more than he is prepared to say, sometimes, presumably, because to have reproduced all he knew would have been tedious – for example the names of all the three hundred Spartans who fought at

---

35 Cf. 5.75, 6.50.3, 51, 61-7, 70-5; 7.3, 101-4, 209, 234, 237, 239; 8.65.

36 Cf. the article by Murray cited in n.33 above.

37 Cf. 6.52-3, 54, 75.3, 84.1, 134, 137; 7.55, 129.1ff., 150.1, 166, 167, 214.1, 230; 8.84.2, 94, 118; 9.74.

38 Cf. 6.118.1; 7.60.1, 153.3; 8.133; 9.32.2.

39 Cf. 8.8.2-3, 87.1-3, 112.2, 128.1; 9.16.2, 84.1.

Thermopylai (7.224.1) – sometimes because it might have caused resentment, for example the names of Greek 'collaborators' who captured Greek ships at Salamis (8.85.2); the two names he does give were presumably common knowledge. But he obviously thought it his duty to record what was told him, even if he did not believe it (cf. 7.153.3), and this should be a warning against assuming that he himself believed all the stories he tells. He was certainly no fool, and was perfectly capable of recognizing a tall story when he heard one. He rejects, for example, the story that Skyllias swam underwater from Aphetai to Artemision, a distance of about 16 kilometres (8.8.2), and if he had heard the story that the diver and his daughter loosened the anchors of Persian ships during the great storm (Pausanias 10.19.1), he presumably also rejected that – scepticism which some modern scholars would have done well to emulate.[40]

If Herodotos was gullible, it was perhaps where religion was concerned. He expresses approval, for example, of the Poteidaian claim (8.129.3) that the exceptionally high tide which destroyed a Persian besieging-force, was due to Poseidon's anger, and he appears to have believed the Delphic story of the shrine's miraculous preservation from Persian attack (8.37-9). He seems to have doubted some elements in it, however, and it is at least not totally inconceivable that an earthquake did send the two huge boulders still to be seen lying across the archaic temple of Athena Pronaia, crashing down on Persian heads. Elsewhere, after describing the wreck of Persian ships off the 'Hollows' of Euboia, he says 'everything was being done by the god that the Persian fleet might be made equal to the Greek and not be much larger' (8.13). But the Athenian claim that Boreas was responsible for the previous storm off Magnesia is treated with some scepticism (7.189.3), and in one passage he seems to try to rationalize the rôle of the the gods, where he argues that anyone who thinks that Poseidon is responsible for earthquakes, would say that he created the Tempe gorge, 'for the parting of the mountains is the work of an earthquake, as it seems to me' (7.129.4).

In general, Herodotos certainly does not allow his religious beliefs to distort his views about what happened. His analysis of the reasons for the Persian defeat at Plataia, for example, ascribes nothing to the agency of Hera, to whom Pausanias prayed before the advance, save the good omens that suddenly appeared (9.62.1), and miraculous phenomena play little part in the narrative of the war. In the account of Marathon, indeed, the giant phantom responsible for Epizelos' blinding is evidently fighting on the Persian side (6.117.3), whereas Pausanias, for example, has a story of how the rustic hero, Echetlaos, was seen killing innumerable barbarians with a ploughshare (1.32.4).

Herodotos may seem to show an over-credulous respect for oracles, prophecies and omens, in contrast to the common sense of Thucydides. He reports an earthquake on Delos, for example, and seems to accept that it was an omen of the things to come (6.98.1), whereas Thucydides, probably referring to the same earthquake, though he evidently connected it with the Peloponnesian War,[41] merely says it 'was said and thought to be a sign of events'. The latter also hints at what is surely the correct explanation of the apparent links between unusual natural phenomena and man-made

---

40 See F.Meijer, *A History of Seafaring in the Classical World* (London & Sydney, 1986), 50.

41 Cf. HW ii 104, Gomme, *HCT* ii 9, and *Essays in Greek History and Literature* (Oxford, 1937), n. on 122.

disasters, when he goes on to say that 'if anything of the same kind happened to occur, its meaning was always carefully examined' (2.8.3). Herodotos' work is full of oracles and omens in which he sometimes expresses defiant belief (e.g. 8.77), but he was perfectly well aware that some oracles were fraudulent – for example the Pythia's declaration that Damaratos was not Ariston's son (6.66) – and in so far as such things were part of the political and diplomatic scene in ancient Greece, he is quite correct to report them. There is no reason to doubt, for example, that the famous oracle referring to the 'wooden wall' (7.141.3-4) did play an important part in arguments about strategy.

In the end it is arguable that there is not much point in discussing the credibility of Herodotos, since, if what he says is not in general true, we might as well stop studying the Persian Wars. The ludicrous lengths to which 'reconstruction' of what 'really' happened can go, are exemplified by Delbrück's remark that 'certain portions of Herodotos' account [of Salamis] correspond so closely, it is true, to the nature of the matter, that we can well accept them'. This implies that the truth is somehow recoverable without reference to Herodotos, and that we can then compare his account with it. But even though this is impossible, it is of some comfort that Herodotos is as good a source as he is. He was evidently so nearly contemporary with the Persian invasions of Greece that he was able to talk to people who had taken part; he evidently checked their stories against what little other evidence existed, his own observations and each other; and he was evidently a man of wide knowledge, broad sympathies, sound common sense and considerable humour.

There is one aspect of his work particularly pertinent to our purposes, which has been singled out for special criticism – his ability as a military historian. Thus, in discussing the view just put forward – that we cannot really go beyond what Herodotos says – it has been argued that it 'can only be founded on the assumption that Herodotus was qualified not merely to record the acts of the men of the period of which he wrote, but to appreciate to the full the ideas and motives which produced the acts of those who were presumably the most skilled men of their day in special, departments of life.'[42]

This may be right in one particular sense. Even if Herodotos' account of at least Xerxes' invasion is based on the evidence of eye-witnesses, he is very much less likely to have talked to any of the Greek leaders. Some of them – Kallimachos, Miltiades, Leonidas – were certainly dead before he began his enquiries; others – Themistokles, Pausanias – probably were. In any case, if he had ever spoken to anyone more important than Thersander of Orchomenos or Arimnestos of Plataia, it is difficult to believe that he would not have said so, and the way he talks about his enquiries into Aristeides' character (8.79.1), for example, strongly suggests that he had never met him. In general, most of the higher-ranking officers would, presumably, have tended to be men of relatively mature years, and hence more likely to have died before Herodotos began his 'research' than the ordinary men who had taken part. Hence the information he gleaned from his eye-witnesses would have tended to be of a factual nature – *what* happened rather than *why* it happened. This may be why Herodotos' motivation may sometimes appear superficial, or even naive.

---

42 Grundy, 579. For a defence of Herodotos as a military historian see A.Ferrill, *American Historical Review* 72 (1966), 102ff.

But there is another possibility – that the strategy and tactics of the Greeks, at any rate, *were* naive, and that Herodotos accurately reflects the situation. The argument quoted above, after all, presumes that the Greek leaders *were* 'the most skilled men of their day in special departments of life;' in other words that Herodotos, who, as far as we know, had no military experience of his own, was incompetent to judge professional soldiers. But in what sense, if any, were the Greek leaders professionals? Such skills as they possessed would have had to derive from one or more of three things – innate intelligence, training and experience. The first is unquantifiable: all the Greek leaders may have been intelligent men, and in Themistokles' case we have Thucydides' word for it that he was (1.138.3). It is, however, most unlikely that any of them had had any formal training of any kind. There was no Sandhurst or Dartmouth at either Athens or Sparta, and no evidence that there was any attempt to study past campaigns or the theory of warfare, at that time. The earliest extant book which has any pretensions to being a military manual is Xenophon's '*Education of Cyrus*' (*Kyropaideia*), written probably over a century after Xerxes' defeat. As for experience, we do not *know* that any of the Greek leaders had had any real experience of warfare, and certainly none of them can have experienced warfare on the scale of what took place in 480/79.

Given this, it is likely that Herodotos *was* as well 'qualified to appreciate to the full the ideas and motives' of the leaders of both sides, as any of his contemporaries, since the military expertise of the early fifth century would have been really no more than what any intelligent man could readily grasp for himself. When one looks at what he says, or, more often, at what his protagonists say, about strategy and tactics, one can see that he perfectly well understood them at the level likely to have been normal among contemporary generals and admirals. He says little about them in his account of the Ionian Revolt, but he had evidently, for instance, grasped the importance of sea-power, if only from Hekataios (cf. 5.36.2), and if his view that Pixodoros, son of Mausolos, was right to advise the Carians to fight with the Maiander at their backs (5.118.2), may seem naive,[43] there is something to be said for the view that this would deter desertion – one thinks of Cortes' 'burning of the boats' – and, in any case, who are we to assume that the matter was not discussed in such terms?

Herodotos is most unlikely to have had any direct access to what was actually said by the 'High Command' on either side, though it is, presumably, possible that the descendants of Damaratos, for example, passed on to him family traditions about their ancestor's conversations with Xerxes. But his grasp of simple strategic and tactical ideas is perfectly sound, whether it represents the fruits of his own thinking, or what was generally thought by his contemporaries. The conversation between Xerxes and Artabanos, after the review at Abydos, for instance (7.46ff.), admirably sets out the dangers for the Persian forces, and the reasons why they none the less had some hopes of success, and Mardonios' contemptuous dismissal of Greek notions of warfare (7.9) contains a lot of truth. Equally Herodotos knew that the Greeks could not have hoped to win unless they matched the Persians at sea (7.139), and that their best chance, initially, lay in defending narrow passes and channels (7.173.1, 175.1ff.; 8.60). This is surely the

43 Cf. HW ii 64: 'Herodotus, as usual, shows complete ignorance of tactics; he really thinks that an army should fight where no retreat is possible'.

kind of consideration which governed the strategy of the Greeks, rather than the sophisticated notions which have been foisted upon them by modern scholars.

By modern standards, and even by the standard of a Thucydides or a Polybios, Herodotos may seem far from a good military historian. There are many things which we should like to know and which he does not tell us, and many things he does tell us – for example about Persian numbers – which seem very dubious. But the more one studies him, the more one comes to the conclusion that there is very little that he says about the two Persian invasions of Greece which can be proved to be wrong, and one is continually struck by the realisation that there is a lot more acute observation and analysis in what he says than at first one thinks. His technique is very different from that of later historians, but it is not so much a question of making allowances – why should not Herodotos write as he wants to do? – as of tuning in to his way of doing things. Once one makes the effort, it is surprising how much is there. He certainly tells us enough to enable us to see, in broad outline, and sometimes in some detail, what happened and why, and in some respects his seemingly primitive historical technique may be appropriate to the primitive nature of the warfare he describes. It is legitimate to query what he says, particularly about the motives of the protagonists, and to search elsewhere for evidence to supplement his narrative. But we should realise that if we reject what he says, whether or not we may think we have good reasons for doing so, we are cutting off the branch on which we sit, and that all we can hope for from a Diodoros or a Plutarch are some very thin twigs indeed.

Even with Herodotos it may seem an impossible task to determine exactly what happened, let alone why it happened. But this is unnecessarily despairing. It is true that we cannot analyse the Persian Wars to anything like the extent we can more modern conflicts, but ignorance of detail should not be confused with ignorance *per se*. If we accept Herodotos, we can give a worthwhile account of the campaigns of 490 and 480/79, and the onus is on the sceptics to prove that he is unreliable. So the principle of this book will be to accept his statements of fact, unless what he says is either impossible or wildly improbable, but not necessarily to accept his statements of motive. Even to these latter, however, we shall extend the respect due to their proximity in time and in attitude of mind to those whose motives he is purporting to explain.

On the other hand, it seems almost always legitimate to reject the secondary sources when they conflict with Herodotos, and even when they merely supplement his narrative, without direct contradiction, we must always ask ourselves how they came to know something which he did not – the *argumentum e silentio* is here not conclusive, but it is cogent. Above all, we must guard against the insidious argument that there 'may be some truth' in even the most absurd stories. Rather, we should accept that many of the stories recorded in later sources are simply untrue. No one, presumably, believes that Leonidas' heart really was hairy,[44] so why should one seek for the 'truth' behind such stories as that of the night raid on Xerxes' camp? Even in Herodotos' day it is clear that silly tales were being bandied about, which he did not believe, such as the one about Skyllias' underwater swim, and we should not always assume that there 'must' be some gold among the dross. If Ktesias forgets Artemision, and gives Pausanias

44 No doubt sooner or later someone will come up with a medical explanation of the condition, and use it to explain Leonidas' failure to retreat in time!

Leonidas' army, why should we believe his figure of 110 ships for the Athenian fleet at Salamis? If Plutarch believes fifth century Athenians' capable of human sacrifice, why should we believe his story of the dawn wind at Salamis? It is not the business of the historian to accept all evidence at its face-value and try to fit it all together, but to sift it according to rational principles, and reject what does not seem to be true. Respect for the evidence is all very well, but the evidence must be respectable.

Nevertheless, in the end, respect for the evidence is fundamental. Far too many modern accounts, particularly of ancient military history, appear to be written by people who seem to think that they know better than the ancient sources upon which they rely. But we should recognize that if we reject what the sources say, though this is perfectly legitimate, we cannot then go on to 'reconstruct' what happened and call it 'history'. If the evidence permits no conclusion, then we should say so, as Herodotos does, and if there is no evidence, we should also say so, as again Herodotos does. The alternative is to write a 'historical novel' rather than history, and while both are equally respectable, they are not the same thing.

CHAPTER 2

Greeks and Persians

The empire with which the mainland Greeks came into conflict in the early years of the fifth century, was probably the most extensive in the world at the time, for China, its only possible rival, was at the beginning of the period of the 'Warring States'. The Persian empire had been founded by Cyrus (Kurush) in the 550s, and by his death, almost certainly in 530, already embraced much of Asia Minor as far west as the Aegean coast, and most of what are now Syria, Irak, Iran and Afghanistan, in the east. To the south his sway extended down to Gaza, and in the north, according to Herodotos (1.204-14), he lost his life fighting the Massagetai in what used to be the Soviet Socialist Republic of Kazakhskaya.[1] His son and successor, Kambyses (Kabijiya) added Egypt, and after a brief interlude of disorder and revolt, Darius (Darayawaush), who came to the throne in the autumn of 522, conquered much of present-day Pakistan, west of the Indus, and then crossed the Bosporos into Europe about 513. This foray was foiled by the guerrilla tactics of the tribes beyond the Danube, but when Darius himself returned to Asia, he left an army behind him, which, in the years that followed, conquered Thrace as far west as the Strymon, and Macedonia, too, appears to have acknowledged Persian suzerainty.

Despite its huge size, the empire was efficiently organized. Contemporary records from Persepolis, for example, give details of the payment of salaries in kind to officials and workmen, from the highest to the lowest, and documents from Egypt enable us to catch a glimpse of the Persian attitude to at least one of their subject peoples.[2] From Asia Minor we have a Greek inscription of Roman times (ML 12) which probably reproduces an original in Aramaic of a rescript of Darius to Gadatas, perhaps satrap of Ionia, about the privileges of the priests of Apollo at Magnesia on the Maiander. 'Yauna' (i.e. 'Ionians', but probably meaning 'Greeks' in general) appear with 'Karka' (i.e. 'Carians' from southwest Asia Minor) helping to transport Lebanese timber from Babylonia to Sousa,[3] and working in the quarries near Persepolis.[4] Herodotos (3.90-7) tells us of the empire's division into twenty tributary satrapies,[5] and, in the case of the Greek states in western Asia Minor, of the land-survey on which the tribute was

---

1 See, e.g., Cook, 1ff., and T.Cuyler Young, *CAH*2 4ff., for an account of the rise of the Persian empire. Sources other than Herodotos (Ktesias, fr.9.7-8; Berossos, *FGH* 680F10) give different names for the tribe with whom Cyrus fought his last battle, but there seems no real reason to doubt Herodotos: see now H.-P.Francfort, 'Note sur la mort de Cyrus et les Dardes', *Orientalia Iosephi Tucci Memoriae Dicata* (Serie Orientale Roma 56), ed. G. Gnoli & L.Lanciotti (Rome, 1985), 395ff. For a historical summary, see 272ff. below.

2 See., e.g., R.T.Hallock, *Persepolis Fortification Tablets* (Chicago, 1969) and G.G.Cameron, *Persepolis Treasury Tablets* (Chicago, 1948). For Egypt see , e.g., A.H.Gardiner, *Journal of Egyptian Archaeology* 24 (1938), 159-79; *Sitzungsberichte der Akademie der Wissenschaften zu Berlin* 1928, 604-22; Cook, 49, 71, 99, 101-11; E.Bresciani, *Studi classici ed orientali* 7 (1958), 147-53.

3 See Cook, 238-9 n.3.

4 G.P.Carratelli, *East and West* 16 (1966), 31-6; G.Gullini, *PP* 142-4 (1972), 13-39.

5 For a defence of Herodotos' list see T.Cuyler Young, *CAH*^{2} iv 87ff.

assessed after the 490s revolt (6.42.2); Darius' introduction of a royal coinage may have been primarily to normalize payment of tribute (cf. 3.89.3).[6] Herodotos, too, tells of the couriers who passed to and from the king and his satraps (3.126ff., 5.32), and of the 'Royal Road' they travelled on from the Aegean coast to Sousa (5.52-4).

The chief instruments of Persian rule were the 'satraps', who probably had authority in both civil and military matters, and were responsible for collecting tribute, administering justice, internal security and raising levies when necessary; they were invariably Persians in the early fifth century. There is a possibility that some generals were responsible to the king rather than the local satrap, if we can trust what Herodotos says, for example Otanes (5.25.1, cf. Hydarnes – 7.135.1) and Mardonios (6.43.1-2). But the latter at least was clearly a special case, as were, surely, the generals who suppressed the Ionian revolt (5.116ff.), and satraps could also certainly command troops, according to Herodotos. Artaphernes, satrap of Sardis, did so during the Ionian revolt (5.123), and earlier appears to have appointed Megabates to command the expedition against Naxos (5.32). After the revolt was over, too, it was Artaphernes who surveyed Ionia and assessed the tribute each community was to pay (6.42.2).

The satraps were obviously extremely powerful, and, in the circumstances of the times, were bound to act with considerable independence. They were often relatives of the king. Artaphernes, for example, was Darius' brother (5.25.1), and Achaimenes, appointed satrap of Egypt after its revolt in the 480s, Xerxes' brother (7.7). Later, too, there was a tendency for the office to become hereditary in some satrapies. Pharnabazos, for example, satrap of Daskyleion in north-west Asia Minor in the late fifth and early fourth centuries, was a great-grandson of Artabazos, appointed by Xerxes in 478 (Thucydides 1.129.1). But however powerful a satrap might be, he was still, ultimately, subject to the king's authority, at least judging by what Herodotos says. Artaphernes, for example, put Aristagoras' plan to attack Naxos, to Darius (5.31.4ff.), and his predecessor, Oroites, although apparently able to get rid of Polykrates of Samos on his own, and even to dispose of his enemy, Mitrobates of Daskyleion, was easily dealt with by Darius. He sent an agent with sealed orders to Oroites' Persian guards, firstly to refuse to obey his orders, and then to execute him. Herodotos, who tells the story (3.120-8), says the letter was read out by the 'royal secretary', and that all satraps had such secretaries. Obviously such men might have acted as a check on over-mighty satraps,[7] and the 'King's Eye' so beloved of Greek writers (cf., e.g., Aristophanes, *Acharnians* 92ff.), may have been an official with a title such as '*spathaka*' ('he who spies');[8] a fifth century papyrus from Elephantine speaks of 'listeners' in Egypt.[9]

Even at the highest level, however, there was no uniformity about Persian rule. Cilicia, for example, was apparently ruled by a native king, and there were similar subordinate kings on the fringes of the empire, for instance in Macedonia. In Babylonia and Egypt, though satraps were put in charge, the Persians simply continued to use the already well-developed administrative systems which had existed before the conquest, and some of the highest officials were natives, though Persians also appear. Probably most of the

---

6 Cook, 69-71.

7 Though see Cook, 84-5.

8 H.H.Schaeder, *Iranica* I (Berlin, 1934), Abh. Göttingen No.10.

9 A.L.Oppenheim, 'The Eyes of the Lord', *JAOS* 88 (1968), 173ff.

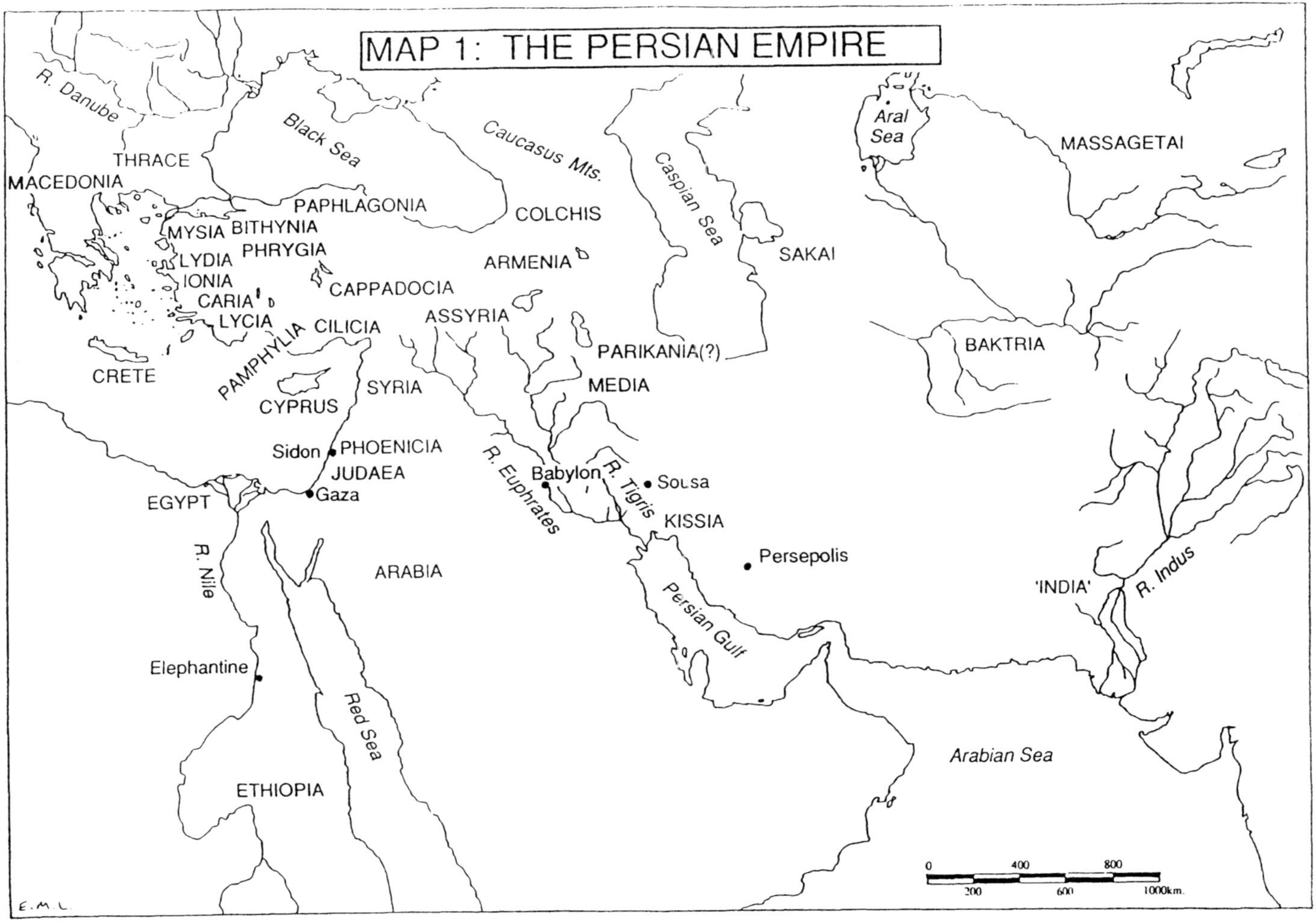
MAP 1: THE PERSIAN EMPIRE
R. Danube
THRACE
MACEDONIA
Black Sea
Caucasus Mts.
Caspian Sea
Aral Sea
MASSAGETAI
PAPHLAGONIA
COLCHIS
SAKAI
MYSIA
BITHYNIA
PHRYGIA
LYDIA
IONIA
CARIA
LYCIA
ARMENIA
CAPPADOCIA
ASSYRIA
CILICIA
PAMPHYLIA
PARIKANIA(?)
BAKTRIA
CRETE
SYRIA
MEDIA
CYPRUS
Sidon
PHOENICIA
JUDAEA
Gaza
EGYPT
R. Euphrates
Babylon
R. Tigris
Sousa
KISSIA
Persepolis
R. Nile
ARABIA
Persian Gulf
'INDIA'
R. Indus
Elephantine
Red Sea
Arabian Sea
ETHIOPIA
0
200
400
600
800
1000km.
E.M.L.

MAP 2: MAINLAND GREECE

Greek states in the empire continued to administer their own affairs, under the despots the Greeks called 'tyrants' (τυράννοι) down to the Ionian revolt (cf. 4.138, 5.37.1), though after the revolt, Herodotos insists (6.42.3), Mardonios installed 'democracies' in their places. From the military point of view it is interesting that Persian grandees, and probably more humble veterans, seem to have received estates from the king, perhaps in return for military service. The evidence mainly comes from the end of the fifth century onwards, but as early as the 490s Herodotos tells of a Persian called Harpagos who 'happened to be' in the region of Atarneus, in command of a large enough force to defeat Histiaios' raiders and capture him alive (6.28.2ff.), and the Persians who held '*nomoi* within the river Halys', and who rallied to the defence of Sardis, earlier in the revolt (5.102.1), may not have been the Persian governors of western Asia Minor, as used to be thought, but holders of fiefs in the area.[10]

But whatever the degree of independence enjoyed by satraps or other rulers in the Persian empire, and however diverse the ways of administering its vast territories, one potential military advantage the Persians enjoyed, in comparison with Greece, was unity of command. Even if Herodotos' account of the size of Xerxes' army and navy is greatly exaggerated, there is no reason to doubt that they contained contingents from an immense variety of peoples, and yet, in the ultimate resort, they all obeyed the king's command. Similarly, Darius had been able to order ships and horse-transports to be built by all his maritime subjects (6.48.2), and to launch a mixed force at Athens, even if the alleged Athenian claim that it was made up of forty-six nations (9.27.5) in fact refers to Xerxes' invasion. Obviously the king could at any time call upon nobles, courtiers and officers for advice (cf., e.g., 3.127; 8.8, 67-9), but there does not seem to have been anything resembling a regular council of ministers,[11] and the informal gatherings obviously bore no resemblance to the meetings of representatives of Greek states, of which Herodotos also speaks (e.g. 7.145, 172, 175). In the Persian case, the king's word was law.

Greece, in contrast, was a land of dozens of independent, sovereign states, whose peoples clearly regarded themselves as Athenians, Corinthians or Spartans, for example, first, and as Greeks only second. It is worth remembering that in their own 'national epics', the poems of Homer, there was no single name for 'Greece' or 'Greeks', and that 'Hellas' then meant an area south of the river Spercheios, in the vicinity of Thermopylai, and 'Hellenes' a people divided between Achilles and the lesser Ajax.[12] In 490 only one other state – Plataia – helped Athens, though Sparta sent a force which arrived too late. In 480/79 there were many states which sided with Persia, sooner or later, including at least one, Argos, in the Peloponnese,[13] and it is clear that even among those states which did resist, there were sharp divisions which more than once threatened to shatter

---

10 Cook, 178.

11 D.M.Lewis, *Sparta and Persia* (Leiden, 1977), 22f.

12 See R.Hope Simpson & J.F.Lazenby, *The Catalogue of the Ships in Homer's Iliad* (Oxford, 1970), 128-9.

13 Vegetius (1.2-4) records a tradition that Karyiai also 'medized', and that this was the origin of 'Karyatids', but although this is accepted by some scholars – e.g. G.L.Huxley, *GRBS* 8 (1976), 29ff.; P.Cartledge, *Sparta and Lakonia* (London, 1979), 205, 216, 297; M.Vickers, *RA* 1985, 3ff. – it is extremely unlikely to be true: see p. 217 n.2 below.

their fragile unity. Significantly the first decision of those determined to resist was to try to end their quarrels (7.145.1).

Luckily for Greece, the loose alliance modern scholars call the 'Peloponnesian League', but which the ancient Greeks called more simply and more accurately 'the Lakedaimonians and their allies', provided a core of unity round which those determined to resist could coalesce, though in fact there were precious few of them. The Spartans and their allies had also worked out an embryonic machinery both for deciding upon a common policy and for carrying it out. After the fiasco at Eleusis, in the last years of the sixth century (5.75), it was decided that Sparta should summon a conference of her allies, before embarking on any operation involving them (cf. 5.91ff.), and that the decision of such a conference should be binding (cf. 5.93.2). This no doubt provided the model for the conferences of the new alliance of those prepared to fight Xerxes (7.145, etc.).[14]

The nature of the Spartan alliance, in which Sparta was acknowledged as the leading state, also provided an embryonic unity of command, since it would usually be assumed by her existing allies that a Spartan – normally a king – would command any allied forces, and this was accepted by her new allies, such as the Athenians. Thus the Athenian member of the delegation sent to ask Gelon of Syracuse for help, in response to Gelon's demand that he command the Greek navy, if Sparta insisted on commanding the army, told him that the Athenians were prepared to obey a Spartan commander at sea, but no other (7.161.2). But this by no means meant that Spartan commanders, even kings, could command the absolute obedience the kings of Persia exacted. Leonidas clearly had trouble with some of the allies at Thermopylai (7.207, 219.2), Eurybiadas could hardly control his fellow-admirals at Salamis (8.56, 59ff.), and at Plataia twenty-one of the twenty-four contingents allegedly disobeyed orders the night before the battle (9.52).

In the end, perhaps, this did not matter very much, since arguably the correct decision was forced upon the Greeks at Salamis, and the defection of the centre at Plataia made no difference. But the latter could have been disastrous, and it is arguable that the lack of a unified central authority was responsible for the disaster at Thermopylai. Once the decision to defend the pass had been taken, it should not have been left to individual states to decide how many troops they were prepared to contribute. Indeed, if Greece had been a unified state, it would not have been up to each state to decide whether to fight or to 'medize'. As it was, the Greeks who did decide to resist, had to balance the obvious desirability of trying to hold the enemy as far north as possible, against the natural reluctance of the majority of them to commit their forces too far from home. The Tempe episode well illustrates the dilemma: should the more southern states risk sending a force to Thessaly in order to secure the adherence of the Thessalians (cf. 7.172)? Once there, should they risk remaining, after they had been warned of the huge size of the enemy forces, and had learned that the pass could be turned (7.173.3-4)? The decision to try to hold Thermopylai, similarly, though perhaps primarily dictated by the belief that this was the traditional gateway to central and southern Greece, was also, surely, due to the desire to try to hold the loyalty of the Boiotians, above all, but also of Phokis and Lokris, to say nothing of protecting Athens

14 For the new alliance see p. 105 n.10 below.

and Megara. These were the kind of complications which the Persians simply did not have to face.

The armed forces of the two sides were also very different, at least on land. Our knowledge of the Persian army and navy comes almost exclusively from Herodotos, and he was probably wrong to believe that all the forces he describes in his account of the review Xerxes' allegedly held at Doriskos (7.59.3ff.), actually accompanied the king to Greece. Certainly his army cannot have been as large as the historian thought, and one wonders whether it even contained as many contingents (see below, 92). But there is no reason to doubt the accuracy of his description of the dress and equipment of the various contingents, whether he got it from some kind of official Persian source, from an earlier Greek source, such as Hekataios, or from general Greek and Persian tradition.[15]

He is also likely to have been right to believe that Persian field-armies always had a core of Persian troops. At Marathon, for example, he says they formed the centre (6.113.1), and according to him Xerxes' army contained both Persian infantry (7.61) and cavalry (7.84), apart from the 12,000 infantry, including the so-called 'Immortals', and 12,000 cavalry, who formed the royal guards (7.40.2ff.). Thus, too, Mardonios is said to have retained the Persian 'corslet-wearers' (θωρηκοφόροι), after Xerxes' retreat, in addition to the Immortals, and apparently one of the two guards cavalry regiments, 1000 strong (8.113.2, cf. 7.40.2 & 41.1). Elsewhere Herodotos mentions units of 10,000, 1000, 100 and 10 (7.81), and Persian records confirm that there were at least officers called 'commanders of ten' and 'commanders of a hundred', and although the '*azarapates*' (in Persian, '*hazarapatish*', i.e 'commander of a thousand'), mentioned by Ktesias and others, seems to have been a court official, there cannot be much doubt that the Persian army was organized on a decimal basis.

Herodotos (7.61.1) describes the Persians in Xerxes' army as wearing 'tiaras' (originally a Persian word) of unstiffened felt, sleeved tunics of many colours, and trousers. Their military equipment consisted of cuirasses of iron scales looking like those of a fish,[16] wicker shields with quivers hanging below, short spears, long bows with reed arrows, and short swords hanging from their belts on the right. In his account of Plataia the historian stresses that the Persian troops were 'unarmoured' (ἄνοπλοι: 9.62.3) and 'without protective clothing' (γυμνῆτες, literally 'naked': 9.63.2), compared with Greek hoplites, though if they wore scale-corslets, these would probably have afforded them at least as good protection as the jerkins made of leather or strips of glued linen worn by Greek hoplites,[17] as the difficulty the latter had in killing Mardonios'

15 See, e.g., HW i 27; A.T.Olmstead, *History of the Persian Empire* (Chicago, 1948), 237ff.; Hammond, 1988, 533; H.Bengston and others, *The Greeks and the Persians: from the Sixth to the Fourth Centuries* (London & New York, 1969); O.K.Armayor, *TAPA* 108 (1978), 1ff.; D.M.Lewis, 'Persians in Herodotus', *The Greek Historians: Literature and History* (Stanford, 1985), 101ff. T.Cuyler Young, *CAH*² iv 93 n.75, notes that it is difficult to match Herodotos' description of the clothing of his contingents with the dress of peoples on the Apadana reliefs. He also suggests that the very multiplicity of armour, weapons, etc., to say nothing of languages, might have been a serious weakness in Xerxes' army.

16 See HW ii 152 *ad loc.*

17 Cf. Snodgrass, *Arms and Armour of the Greeks* (London, 1967), 90f.; Peter Connolly, *Greece and Rome at War* (London, 1981), 54ff.; Cook, 102, is quite wrong to talk of 'the bronze panoply of the Greek hoplites' at this date.

cavalry commander at Plataia would seem to demonstrate (9.22.2). Perhaps, however, not all Persian infantry wore such a corslet, or Herodotos may have been thinking primarily of the heavy, wooden, bronze-faced and leather-backed shield of the hoplites, and of their bronze helmets.

Reliefs at Sousa and Persepolis confirm that Persian guardsmen, at least, carried bows and spears, though no corslets are visible – Masistios, the cavalry general mentioned above, wore his under his tunic. The spears of the guardsmen on the reliefs appear to be about 2.2 metres long, compared with the 2-2.5 metres of the average Greek spear, so again there may not have been much difference, though Herodotos says that the Immortals' spears were shorter than those of the Greeks at Thermopylai (7.211.2). Their bows, too, appear to be about 1.2 metres long, and so were certainly not 'long bows' in the mediaeval sense, but were longer than contemporary Greek bows, judging from vase-paintings. Persian bows were almost certainly of the 'composite' or 'Asiatic' type, probably with an 'effective' range of 160-175 metres, and a maximum range of 200-300.[18]

In Herodotos account of Xerxes' army (7.61ff.), the Persians naturally come first, and nine of the next ten infantry contingents, together with the last (the 29th), are said or implied to be similarly equipped, with minor variations in head-gear, though one doubts whether they all had scale-corslets, even if the Persians did (see Pls 1 &2). Other passages suggest that of these the Medes, Kissians, Baktrians and Sakai (forming the 2nd. 3rd and 6th of Herodotos' infantry contingents), were, with the Persians, the best of the empire's infantry. The Sakai, for example, probably from what is now Russian Turkestan, who wore stiff, upright caps, rising to a point – Persian documents call them '*Saka* of the pointed caps'[19] – formed the centre at Marathon with the Persians, according to Herodotos (6.113.1), and with the Medes and Persians provided extra marines for the fleet (7.184.2). Medes and Kissians, from central Iran, were the first to assault Thermopylai (7.210.1), and Medes, Sakai and Baktrians were chosen by Mardonios to stay behind with him, when Xerxes left (8.113.2).

The main differences between these troops and Greek hoplites were that none wore helmets or greaves, possibly none wore body-armour, and all carried wicker shields, if they really were all equipped like the Persians, as is implied. For offence they were armed with bows, unlike hoplites, but, like them, carried spears and short-swords (ἐγχειρίδια) for hand-to-hand fighting. It was presumably such troops Aristagoras had in mind, when, according to Herodotos (5.49.3), he summed up Persian equipment as 'bows, short spears, trousers and turbans,' and remarked (5.97.1) that they had 'neither shield (ἀσπίς) nor spear (δόρυ),' using the normal Greek terms for the hoplite shield and spear.

The only other contingent of troops mentioned elsewhere than in the main description of Xerxes' army, are what Herodotos calls the 'Indians', who, he says (8.113.2), were also chosen to stay behind by Mardonios. This is odd, because they

18 See W.Mcleod, *Phoenix* 19 (1965), 1-4, and 26 (1972), 78-82.

19 Cook, 195-6. It is noticeable that on the Apadana staircase the Saka are one of only three peoples shown entering the palace carrying weapons, which may indicate how much they were trusted: see A.D.H.Bivar, 'The Indus Lands', *CAH*^{2} iv 209. For Saka scale armour see S.P.Tolstov, *Po drevnim del'tam Oksa i Yaksarta* (Moscow, 1962), 148ff.

Pl. 1: Persian and Median guardsmen on the Apadana Reliefs at Persepolis; the men with the 'fluted' hats are Persians, the others Medes. (Photo courtesy of The Oriental Institute, The University of Chicago).

Pl. 2: 'Saka of the pointed hats' on the Apadana Reliefs at Persepolis. (*Photo courtesy of The Oriental Institute, The University of Chicago*).

were allegedly only dressed in cotton garments (7.65), and apparently had no other weapons than their 'reed' (bamboo?) bows and iron-tipped arrows. They probably came from the Indus valley, south of the Salt range, i.e. from what the Persians called '*Hindush*', the new province conquered by Darius. They were accompanied, according to Herodotos (7.70.1), by people he calls 'Ethiopians from the rising of the sun', who, he says, were no different from the Ethiopians of Africa, except in language and hair. These eastern 'Ethiopians' had straight hair, and were possibly an earlier Dravidian strain of people in the Indus valley.[20]

Herodotos' 12th to 16th infantry contingents, in the review at Doriskos, were composed of peoples who mostly seem to have come from south-eastern Iran, Afghanistan and north-eastern Pakistan (7.67.8),[21] but since none of them are ever mentioned again, one suspects that few if any such troops actually accompanied Xerxes. It is noticeable that although all carried bows, and had a variety of hand-to-hand weapons, apparently none carried shields or wore protective clothing – they mostly wore skins. Of even less account, one suspects, were the Arabians – probably from eastern Egypt, between the Nile and the Red Sea, since they are grouped with the 'Ethiopians living beyond Egypt' (7.69).[22] They apparently already wore a kind of *burnous* and carried long, composite bows, slung, unusually, on the right. The Ethiopians were dressed in the skins of leopards and lions, and had bows 'not less than four cubits long' (i.e. about two metres), made from the stem of a palm-frond, but short, reed arrows, tipped with flint. Of little account, too, surely, were the Libyans of the 18th contingent, dressed in skins and armed merely with javelins with fire-hardened points (7.71).

It is surprising, however, that more was not made of the people Herodotos calls 'Assyrians', comprising his 5th infantry contingent, and probably including most of the peoples of what is now Irak.[23] In addition to linen corslets, which were, presumably, like the Greek, they wore bronze helmets made in a way Herodotos found difficult to describe, and carried shields for which he uses the usual term for hoplite-shields (ἀσπίδες). For offensive purposes, in addition to spears and short-swords, they had wooden clubs, studded with iron, but Herodotos, curiously, does not say that they carried bows, though these are conspicuous on Assyrian monuments of an earlier day. Perhaps this was why they did not form part of the front-line infantry.

Also not armed with bows were the men of the 19th to 28th infantry contingents (7.72-9), mostly from what is now Turkey, though the Mares and Colchians of the 27th contingent came rather from Georgia. Instead of bows, most of these carried throwing-spears, the exceptions being the men of the 25th and 26th contingents, from north-east Anatolia, who carried short spears with long heads, though Xenophon says that in his day the Mossynoichoi, at least, carried nine-foot pikes (*Anabasis* 5.4.12-3). None of

20 Cook, 61-2, 190. Bivar (*loc.cit.* n.19 above) notes that the Indians also carry weapons on the Apadana staircase.

21 This seems to be true of the Sarangai (Cook, 78), Outioi (Cook, 87), Mykoi and Parikanioi (Cook 79 & 190). The Kaspioi of the 12th contingent and the Paktyes of the 14th may have come from the Caucasus region.

22 See Rawlinson on Herodotos 2.8.

23 Cook, 79.

these peoples wore protective clothing, unless we assume that this is implied for the Lydians by the statement (7.74.1) that they had 'arms (ὅπλα) very like the Greek'. On the other hand, unlike the Persians and the other front-line troops, these Anatolians mostly had helmets of a kind – plaited in some cases (7.72), bronze (7.76), leather (7.77) or wooden (7.78 & 79) in others – and all carried shields, though most are designated as 'small' (σμικραί: 7.72.1, 74.1, 76.1, 78, 79). The Bithynians, originally from Thrace, carried the '*pelta*', which was later to give the troops the Greeks called 'peltasts' their name (7.75.1).

Herodotos claims (7.84) that all the nations which supplied infantry, also had cavalry, but that only a few sent cavalry contingents on this occasion. These were the Persians themselves, whose cavalrymen were equipped like their infantry, but some of whom apparently wore bronze or iron helmets, or at least ones strengthened with bronze or iron. Brigaded with them were the nomad Sagartians, armed with lassoes. These were one of the ten 'clans' (γένεα) who formed the Persian people, according to Herodotos (1.125); they came from the area called '*Asargata*' by the Persians. Cavalry was also supplied by the Medes, Kissians, Indians, Baktrians, Kaspians, Sakai[24] and Parikanians, but some of the Indians drove chariots drawn by horses or wild asses, and all the Libyans drove chariots (7.86). The Arabians were mounted on camels (7.87). The chariots are not mentioned elsewhere, and camels appear only as pack-animals. They were attacked by lions in lower Macedonia (7.125).

At first sight it may seem surprising that the Persians did not make use of infantry from the Greek states under their rule, since this would have given them the solid core of 'heavy' troops they needed, if their tactics were to succeed (see below, 92, 256). As it was, the Lydians were, in Herodotos' view (7.74.1), the nearest thing to Greek hoplites the Persians had. Perhaps they could see no place for hoplites in their tactics, and were convinced that they had nothing to fear from them by their string of victories in Egypt (cf. 3.11) and in the Ionian revolt. If so, Marathon must have come as a rude shock, though perhaps they dismissed this as a side-show.[25] On the other hand, none of the other coastal peoples of the empire, not even the Egyptians, were apparently required to supply troops for Xerxes' army, and naval service may have been thought to be a sufficient burden. The Greeks seem to have served at sea from the first. The presence of a Mytilenean ship in the fleet Kambyses took to Egypt (3.13), suggests that the Ionians and Aiolians he took with him (3.1.1), served in his fleet, and the Greeks who served in Darius' Scythian expedition also served in the fleet (4.89.1).

Certainly, if we are to believe Herodotos' figures (7.89ff.), naval service would have been a burden, but here at least the Persians had every reason for confidence. They had beaten the Asiatic Greeks at Lade, and although they may have owed this victory to treachery, they now had these tough opponents on their side. Nor is there any evidence of disloyalty – the Ionians fought particularly well at Salamis (8.85.1-2). Apart from these Greeks, the Persians had in the Phoenicians some of the most experienced sailors

24 The MSS. of Herodotos repeat 'Κάσπιοι' here (7.86.1), but this is probably a mistake for 'Σάκαι', since otherwise there would be no mention of the Sakai in this list of cavalry, although they are said to have been the best of the cavalry at Plataia (9.71.1), and in the infantry list they are brigaded with the Baktrians: see Munro, 1902, 297.

25 Cf. the poem by Robert Graves quoted on 248 below.,

in the Mediterranean. They furnished the 'best sailing' (ἄριστα πλεούσας) ships, according to Herodotos (7.96.1), and the Persians as a whole had 'better sailing' (ἄμεινον πλεούσας: 8.10.1) ships than the Greeks. The Egyptians, too, showed themselves to be formidable fighters at Artemision, where they captured five Greek ships with their crews (8.17).

In general, it would be a great mistake to underestimate the armed forces the Persians had at their disposal, despite their failures in 490 and 480/79. In three generations they had conquered an empire which stretched from the Strymon to the Indus, and from the shores of the Black Sea to Aswan. They had suffered some setbacks, but on the whole they had been enormously successful. What, then, were their strengths and weaknesses?

First, intelligence: in ancient times, little or no attempt was made to prevent an enemy from gathering information, but not all belligerents made equal use of the information available, and the Persians seem to have been exceptional. Cyrus, for example, evidently knew of the potential hostility of the Asiatic Greeks to Lydian rule, and tried to stir them to revolt – in vain, as it turned out (1.141.3). Later he made full use of Babylonian religious susceptibilities and Jewish nationalist aspirations.[26] Kambyses made good use of the information and advice of Amasis of Egypt's mercenary captain, Phanes, when he deserted (3.4), and had obviously realised the desirability of having Arabian aid to cross the deserts into Egypt (3.4 & 9). Later he sent spies into 'Ethiopia' (i.e. the northern Sudan: 3.15.2), though, if we are to believe Herodotos (3.25.1), he took little notice of their report. Darius sent ships to reconnoitre the Indus, on one of which was Skylax of Karyanda, before his conquest of '*Hindush*' (4.44), and sent the Greek doctor, Demokedes, and fifteen Persians to reconnoitre Greece (3.135ff.).[27] If Ktesias is to be trusted, he also sent a reconnaissance force across the Black Sea before his Scythian expedition, and his generals obviously made good use of Hippias' advice in landing at Marathon (6.102).

Xerxes' generals presumably planned the details of the march through Thrace on the basis of knowledge gained from previous commanders (e.g. Mardonios) and Persian governors already in the area (cf. 7.105 & 106.1). The division of the army between three routes from Doriskos to Akanthos (7.121.2-3), for example, was probably designed to ease the problem of supply. The route from Macedonia to Thessaly, too, seems to have been planned well in advance (cf. 7.128.1 & 131). The story of how Pammon of Skyros showed the captains of scouting ships the Myrmex reef between Skiathos and the mainland (7.183.3), shows vividly what good use the Persians made of even the most detailed intelligence.

Another area in which the Persians excelled was diplomatic warfare. We have already seen how Cyrus tried to make use of the Ionians against Croesus, and won Babylonians and Jews to his side by sympathetic treatment. Herodotos alleges that Kambyses sacrilegiously wounded the Apis-bull (3.27ff.), but the granite sarcophagus

---

26 Cook, 31-2.

27 For doubts about the story see A.Griffiths, 'Democedes of Croton: a Greek doctor at the Court of Darius', in *Achaemenid History II. The Greek Sources* (Proceedings of the Gröningen 1984 Achaemenid History Workshop), ed. H.Sancisi-Weerdenburg & A.Kurt (Leiden, 1987), 37-51.

in which the bull that died in August, 525, was interred, was dedicated by Kambyses himself,[28] and, unlike the Assyrian kings, Kambyses also had himself crowned as a legitimate pharaoh. Lade was virtually won by the Persians' success in causing desertion from the Ionian fleet (6.13-4), and Mardonios' suppression of Ionian tyrants in favour of democratic regimes, after the collapse of the Ionian Revolt, was presumably partly a response to the evident distaste for tyranny which the Ionians had expressed at the revolt's beginning (cf. 5.37-8). Darius' diplomatic campaign before Marathon had considerable success (6.48-49.1), and although force was used against such places as Naxos, Karystos, Eretria and, of course, Athens, it is noticeable that care was taken to avoid attacking Delos (6.97).

Xerxes, for his part, obviously succeeded in detaching much of northern and central Greece from the Greek cause, and, in the Peloponnese, Argos remained neutral throughout 480 and 479, allegedly even warning Mardonios that the Spartans were on the move before Plataia (9.12). Some of this was due not so much to Persian diplomacy as to age-old hatreds among the Greeks themselves. Herodotos remarks, for example, that in his opinion the Phokians only remained loyal to the Greek cause out of hatred for the Thessalians, and would have 'medized' if the Thessalians had taken the Greek side (8.30). However, the way in which Mardonios prodded away at Athens during the winter of 480/79 (9.140ff., 9.4-5) shows the kind of pressure the Persians will have exerted on Greek states both before and during the invasion.

Good intelligence and diplomatic warfare were backed up by meticulous planning. Cyrus' lightning strike at Sardis – so fast that he was his own messenger, in Herodotos' words (1.79.2) – would not have been possible without careful attention to logistics, and Herodotos mentions, for example, the use of camels as pack-animals (1.80.2). The sea-borne expedition which led to Marathon is another good example of what the Persians could achieve (cf. 6.48.2 & 95), and the story of Xerxes' invasion is full of evidence that there was nothing wrong with Persian 'staff work'. It was a great achievement in itself to get an army and fleet from the Hellespont to Athens in three months (8.51.1), despite resistance, and here and there Herodotos gives us a glimpse of how it was done. Preparation, he says (7.20.1), took four years, though he should probably have said three (see below, 97), and involved not only the mustering of infantry and cavalry, but the requisitioning of ships both for bridges and for battle, and the gathering of stores (7.21.2). The cutting of the canal through the isthmus joining Athos to the mainland took three years (7.22.1), and those responsible went on to construct a bridge over the Strymon (7.24). Careful enquiries were made about the most suitable places for food-dumps in Thrace and Macedonia, and the supplies were carried by sea to the selected sites (7.25.2). No doubt routes for the army were also carefully chosen, for example when it divided into three from Doriskos to Akanthos (7.121.2-3), and perhaps passes were surveyed, for example in Macedonia (cf. 7.128.1 & 131). Above all, of course, the two bridges of boats were constructed across the Hellespont (7.33ff.).

Much of this planning involved engineering expertise of a high order. The Greeks were obviously most impressed by the Hellespont bridges and the Athos canal, though Herodotos thought that the latter was for show rather than for practical purposes (cf. 7.24). The road taken by the army from the Strymon to Akanthos was, according to him

---

28 K.M.T.Atkinson, *JAOS* 76 (1956), 166ff.

(7.115.3), so revered by the natives that they never ploughed it up or sowed seeds on it, though one suspects, in fact, that they found it too useful. It was still in use nearly three hundred years later, according to Livy (39.27). We hear, too, of the clearing of tracks in Macedonia (7.131), and plans for constructing a mole across from the mainland of Attica to Salamis (8.97.1), as well as of purely military projects like the huge palisaded camp, each side approximately two kilometres long, built for Mardonios' army near Plataia (9.15.3).

Persian engineers were also past-masters in siege-works, their technique being to raise a mound against the wall, as they did against Phokaia, Teos and other Asiatic Greek towns (cf. 1.162.2, 168, etc.). The siege-mound they used to capture Paphos in Cyprus, in the 490s, has been excavated, and there is even evidence to suggest that the Persians may already have been using stone-throwing catapults.[29] In their two invasions of Greece they were never really called upon to demonstrate their skill in siege-warfare, though in 490 Karystos is said to have surrendered after a siege (6.99.2), and Eretria was betrayed after six days of fierce assaults on its walls (6.101.2). In 480 the Persians assaulting the acropolis of Athens showed their ingenuity in wrapping tow round their arrows and setting light to it, to destroy the Athenians' wooden barricade, but they were baffled by the continued defence – presumably the approaches were too rocky for the construction of a siege-mound – until some soldiers managed to climb up by way of a cleft about seventy metres east of the main entrance (8.53.1).[30] In the winter of 480/79 Artabazos swiftly took Olynthos (8.127), though he failed to take Poteidaia (8.128-9).

In ordinary land operations the Persians were equally proficient, as their many victories demonstrated. Croesus' army was first fought to a standstill in Cappadocia (1.76.4), and then defeated outside Sardis, despite its formidable reputation (1.79.3). Kambyses destroyed the Egyptian army at Pelousion, despite the presence of Greek and Carian mercenaries – years later Herodotos was shown the bones of the dead (3.12). In the Ionian revolt, the Persians won four of the five land battles recorded – the only one they lost was when the Carians ambushed their army at night near Pedasos (5.121). Clearly their great strengths were their flexibility and their ability to call upon different types of troops for different tasks, as when Mardonios, for example, was able to halt the retreating Spartans and Tegeates by the use of cavalry, on the final day at Plataia, and then bring up his infantry to finish the job – as he hoped (cf. 9.57.3). This flexibility enabled the Persians to respond correctly to changing situations, and to stick to the task in hand, as when the 'Immortals' were sent off to make use of the path bypassing Thermopylai, and simply ignored the Phokians when they failed to bar the way (7.218.3).

It is, however, very difficult to see exactly how the Persians won their battles, except where some odd detail was handed down in the tradition, for example the use of camels by Cyrus to disconcert the Lydian cavalry (1.80.2ff.). Herodotos does not tell us how Kambyses defeated the Egyptians, and the only explanations he gives of the Persian victories in the Ionian revolt are that the Carians on the Marsyas were defeated by

---

29 *JHS* 99 (1979), 206. But it is more likely that the balls were thrown down by the defenders: see E.Erdmann, *Nordosttor und Persische Belagerungsrampe, Waffen und Kleinfunde*, in *Ausgrabungen in Alt-Paphos auf Cypern*, I, ed. F.G.Maier (Konstanz, 1977).

30 See G.Dontas, *Hesperia* 52 (1983), 48ff.

numbers (διὰ πλῆθος: 5.119.1), and that it was the late arrival of the Persian cavalry, when the infantry of both sides were locked in combat, which tipped the balance at Malene (6.29.1). Nevertheless, what he says about the battles the Persians lost in Greece, enables us to see something of their tactics. At Marathon, he says (6.112.2), they thought the Athenians mad to be attacking without cavalry or bows, so presumably he thought the Persians normally used both. Their attack on the Greeks at the foot of Kithairon shows how Persian cavalry operated. It attacked in squadrons, not *en masse* (9.20 & 22.1), charging in to let missiles fly (9.49.2), and then retiring to wheel back and charge again (9.22.3). Clearly it did not attempt to ride infantry down, using lances or sabres, but to wear it down with repeated missile attacks – since it consisted of horse-archers, it was difficult to deal with, as Herodotos says (9.49.2), particularly for hoplites.

Persian foot-soldiers, too, were mostly armed with the bow and presumably their tactics were also to wear opponents down with volleys of arrows, as they attempted to do against the Spartans, *perioikoi* and Tegeates at Plataia (9.61.3). If an enemy stood to receive their fire, presumably they hoped to cause such losses that the enemy line would begin to disintegrate, whereupon they could close in with stabbing-spear and sword. It is worth noting that the spear seems to have been regarded as highly as the bow. Darius, for example, claimed to be equally adept with bow or spear, on horse or on foot, in his tomb inscription. If the enemy line advanced, presumably they hoped to inflict so many casualties that it ground to a halt, or was so reduced as to be in no state to hold its own when it came to hand-to-hand fighting. Thus, at Marathon, for example, the Persian and Sakai infantry broke the Athenian centre and drove it back (6.113.1). Alternatively, as possibly happened at Malene, they may have hoped to pin the enemy infantry with their own, until the cavalry could finish it off, perhaps by attacking flanks and rear (6.29.1).

Whatever tactics the Persians used, they certainly seem to have been effective, for until they came up against the mainland Greeks, they had suffered only two serious defeats. The one against the Massagetai, in which Cyrus lost his life, was a battle in which both sides used the same tactics – archery-fire until the arrows were all spent, then hand-to-hand combat with spear and sword, if we can believe Herodotos (1.214.2). The second was the night ambush by the Carians near Pedasos (5.121), which hardly counts. It must also be emphasised that the Persians won four victories against armies which presumably at least included hoplites. It is true that the Egyptian army defeated near Pelousion many not have included many, but it certainly included some (3.11), and the Ionian army defeated outside Ephesos (5.102.2-3) was presumably predominantly composed of hoplites, including Eretrians and, probably, Athenians, from the mainland. The Carians, defeated at the White Pillars on the Marsyas (5.119.1), were, strictly speaking, not Greeks, but Herodotos believed that it was they who had first fitted shields with handles (ὄχανα), instead of straps, and thus had invented the typical hoplite shield, and Anakreon described the '*ochanon*' as 'of Carian workmanship' (Καρικοεργὲς' *ap.* Strabo 14.11.27). Even if this is not true, Carians certainly figured prominently as mercenaries, probably from the 7th century. They are already in Archilochos (fr.24), and the 'bronze men' who aided Psammetichos I throw off the Assyrian yoke c.660 (2.152.3ff.), included Carians. In the third battle of the Ionian revolt, fought in or near the sacred grove of plane trees at Labraunda, the Carians were aided by the Milesians (1.119.2-120), and these would almost certainly have included hoplites.

It has been suggested[31] that these rebel hoplites would have consisted of hastily raised levies, since the Greeks of Asia Minor had been under Persian rule for more than a generation, and even at the time of Darius' Scythian expedition had only been used to guard the bridge over the Danube (4.97-8). However, the probable reason for Darius' leaving the Greeks to guard the bridge was that it was an appropriate task for the naval forces, whereas chasing Scythians about the Ukraine was hardly a job for hoplites, as Herodotos' Koes of Mytilene hints (4.97.3-4). In any case, Spartans apart, it is doubtful whether any hoplites were 'trained' in any proper sense, at this date. Some mainland hoplites might have had some experience of straightforward, hand-to-hand encounters with other hoplites – for example, the Athenians had fought both Boiotians and Chalkidians (5.77) – but even the Spartans would have had no experience of fighting troops like the Persians.

In the wider aspects of warfare in which the Persians excelled, the Greeks would also have been at a disadvantage, since their wars tended to be between neighbours and on a small scale (cf. Thucydides 1.13.2). The Spartans, however, had had some comparatively recent experience of mounting operations at a distance. In c.525 they had sent a sea-borne expedition to Samos (3.39.1, 44-6, 54-6), and in the last fifteen years of the sixth century had invaded Attica four times, once by sea (5.63.2ff., 70-2, 73-5). These operations would not only have given them some experience in logistics, but may also have improved their tactical expertise. The sea-borne expedition against Athens, for example, had been defeated by Thessalian cavalry serving the 'tyrant' Hippias, after he had cleared the plain near Phaleron of trees (5.63.4). But the second expedition, by land, had apparently driven the Thessalians off with some ease (5.64.2), perhaps because trees were cut down to form an *abattis*, though the evidence for this is late (Frontinus, *Strategemata* 2.2.9). The last of the invasions involved a multi-national force, and a certain amount of co-ordination with Boiotian and Chalkidian attacks on Athens' borders (5.74). The behaviour of their Corinthian allies and of their two kings (5.75) will have given the Spartans a taste of the problems of commanding allied troops and having a divided command. The campaign against Argos which culminated at Sepeia, probably in 494 (6.76-81), although probably on a smaller scale, again gave rise to fairly complicated logistic and strategic problems, and involved at least two of Sparta's allies, Aigina and Sikyon, though Herodotos believed the former's help was involuntary (6.92.1-2).

The Spartans will thus have found no difficulty in sending help to Athens at the time of Marathon, and they will have known something about planning, organizing, transporting and maintaining long-distance expeditions, which perhaps explains how the Greeks were able to cope with the operations of 480 and 479. The only thing they perhaps failed fully to grasp was the sheer scale of the enemy forces, hence the mere 10,000 hoplites sent to Tempe (7.173.2), and, possibly, the small size of Leonidas' force. According to Herodotos (7.207), when the Persians drew near the pass, most of Leonidas' troops were for abandoning the enterprise, and he immediately sent for reinforcements. By the time of Plataia the Greeks had realised that they would need a

31 See Grundy, 186 & 535.

much bigger army if they were going to stand a chance, but their inexperience in handling such an army was shown up by the chaos of the Plataia campaign.

Some of Sparta's recent campaigns had involved the use of sea-power – the attack on Polykrates of Samos, the first, abortive attempt to oust Hippias from Athens, and the Sepeia campaign – and Athens and Eretria, too, had had experience of mounting an overseas operation when they sent help to the Ionians (5.97.3, 99ff.); more recently Athens had been embroiled in naval warfare with Aigina (5.81.2-3, 6.87-93). But none of this will have prepared the Greeks for naval operations on the scale of those of 480. The Athenian contribution to the Ionian cause, for example, had been 20 ships, that of Eretria five (5.99), though there may have been more Eretrian ships than Herodotos allows.[32] In order to match Aigina at sea, Athens had had to hire 20 ships from Corinth, giving her a fleet of 70 against 70 of Aigina (6.89 & 92.1), and after Marathon Miltiades commanded a fleet of 70 against Paros (6.132). But if Herodotos' figures are accurate, some 324 ships took part in the operations off Artemision (8.2.1 & 14.1), and 366 at Salamis (see below, 172–3). It is surprising that the Greeks were able to muster and maintain such large fleets in 480, and it is unlikely that they thought in more sophisticated terms than of getting the ships to the right place and fighting any enemy fleet that came their way.

It is less easy to see what tactics were usually employed at sea by either Greeks or Persians, at this time. Herodotos claims (6.12.1) that the Asiatic Greeks were already practising the *diekplous* at the time of Lade, but he also says that the Chiot ships, which, he claims, actually carried out the manoeuvre in the battle (6.15.2), each had 40 marines on board, and this suggests that boarding was still the order of the day (cf. Thucydides 1.49.1-3). The *diekplous* was almost certainly a manoeuvre in which single ships in line abreast tried to row through the gaps between the ships of an opposing line, and then turn to ram in side or stern.[33] As such, it was a manoeuvre which required speed and manoeuvrability – it was, as Thucydides says (2.98.8), one of the actions of 'better sailing ships' – and would have been hampered by the weight of too many marines (20 fully-armed men would have weighed something like two metric tons), to say nothing of the effect on the stability of the vessel.[34]

At Artemision, Herodotos implies (8.9), it was the Persians who were thought to be able to use the *diekplous*, and consistently with this he says (8.10.1) that they had the 'better sailing ships', and that the Greeks first formed a circle, if that is what he meant by saying, 'they drew their sterns together towards the middle' (ἐς τὸ μέσον τὰς πρύμνας συνήγαγον: 8.11.1). This was later a formation adopted by inferior ships against the *diekplous* (cf. Thucydides 2.83.5 & 3.78.2), though here it may have been

---

32 Plutarch, referring to Lysanias of Mallos, appears to say that the Eretrians defeated the Cypriots in the Pamphylian sea (*Moralia* 861b-c), which would imply a considerable fleet. But there is clearly something wrong with Plutarch's text here – see P.J.Stylianou, 'The Age of the Kingdoms', *Meletai kai Hypomnêmata* 2 (Leukôsia, 1989), 375ff. – I am very grateful to the author for sending me an offprint. I suspect confusion with the *Ionian* victory over the Persians off the 'Keys' of Cyprus (5.108.2 & 115.1). The 'Keys' were probably the small islands off Cape Apostolos Andreas – cf. Strabo 14.6.3.

33 See J.F.Lazenby, *Greece & Rome* 34 (1987), 169ff.

34 Private communication from I.M.Whitehead, who acted as official recorder of the first trials of *Olympias*.

mainly to counter the Persian numbers (see below, 138–40). However, Herodotos also says (7.184.2) that each Persian warship carried thirty extra marines, Persians, Medes and Sakai, in addition to native marines, and although it has been suggested that this was primarily to enforce discipline and prevent desertion,[35] it is more likely that the extra marines were there because boarding was anticipated, after the experience of fighting the Chiots at Lade. The calculation of the total numbers serving in the Persian fleet, apart from the thirty extra marines, implies that each ship normally carried two hundred men, and this may imply fourteen marines (see below).

Unfortunately Herodotos never says how many marines each ship on the Greek side carried in 480, but he implies that the normal complement of a Greek warship, at about this time, like that of the Persian ships, was 200 men. Thus this is the case with the ships from the Greek states of Thrace and its off-shore islands which joined Xerxes' fleet (7.185.1), and with the command of the Athenian, Kleinias, at Artemision (8.17; cf. also 3.14.4-5). Assuming that these complements were made up in the same way as the crews of later Athenian warships, they would only have included fourteen marines,[36] and it is argued that this is borne out by both the 'Themistokles Decree' and Plutarch (*Themistokles* 14.1).[37]

It is possible that at least the new Athenian warships constructed in the 480s at Themistokles' instigation (cf. 7.144.1), were built with a view to employing ramming rather than boarding tactics. Plutarch says that Themistokles' ships were 'very well constructed for speed and manoeuvrability' (πρὸς ... τάχος ... καὶ περιαγωγήν: *Kimon* 12.2), and implies that they were not decked right across from side to side – it was, he alleges, Kimon who did this for the Eurymedon campaign.[38] Similarly, in his account of Salamis, he contrasts the Greek ships, which were 'low in the water' (ἁλιτενεῖς) and 'somewhat squat' (ταπεινοτέραι), with the barbarian ships, 'with their towering poops, lofty decks and heavy movement' (ταῖς τε πρύμναις ἀνεστώσας καὶ τοῖς καταστρώμασιν ὑψορόφους καὶ βαρείας ἐπιφερομένας: *Themistokles* 14.2).

However, although it will be argued later (see below, 196–7) that the Greeks won Salamis by ramming rather than boarding, this does not by any means prove that they had the faster, lighter and more manoeuvrable vessels, and Herodotos evidently thought that it was the Greek ships which were the heavier (βαρυτέρας). There is no way in which Plutarch and Herodotos can be reconciled here,[39] but Plutarch's account of Salamis is dubious on other grounds (see below, 194–5) and Herodotos is surely to be preferred.[40] Salamis was fought in a very confined space, where lighter ships would not

35 Morrison & Coates, 110.

36 Morrison & Coates, 107ff.: 170 rowers, 10 hoplites, 4 archers, six 'officers', and two parties of five seamen at bow and stern to manage sails, etc.

37 Plutarch actually *says* that each Athenian ship carried four archers and *fourteen* hoplites, but this is usually thought to be a mistake for four archers and *ten* hoplites, as on Athenian vessels of the later 5th century.

38 Cf. Morrison & Coates, 154ff.

39 Morrison and Coates, 152ff., suggest the Greek ships were 'heavier' because they had not been dried out, as the Persian ships had been at Doriskos (cf. 7.59.2-3), but this is very forced.

40 Cf. Tarn, 1908, 208 & n.28. The presence or absence of decks by itself does not indicate how many marines were on board. Athenian triremes of the later 5th century undoubtedly had

have been able to make any real use of their speed and manoeuvrability, and heavier, perhaps more stoutly-built, vessels, would for once have had an advantage.

In view of the fact that some Greeks were still fighting sea-battles in the old-fashioned way in the 430s (cf. Thucydides 1.49.1-3), it seems unlikely that even the Athenians had adopted the new tactics by 480. It is possible that the *diekplous* was already in use, and the Persians may, indeed, have learnt it from the Ionians, if the latter were the first to practise it, as Herodotos implies (6.12.1, 15.1), for they were now in the Persian navy. Rumours of the new manoeuvre may also have crossed the Aegean, and hence the Greek desire, on the first day at Artemision, to 'make trial of the Persian style of fighting and *diekplous*' (8.9). But both sides will have been aware that even the fastest and most manoeuvrable ships were, sooner or later, going to find themselves locked in the press of battle, and there marines would be at a premium. Thus tactics are likely to have been at a transitional stage, and the new ones never entirely replaced the old, in any case, as the Athenians were to find to their cost at Syracuse.

Probably, then, even Athenian triremes had many more than fourteen marines on board in 480, and this would explain why there was not even a token force of Athenian hoplites at Thermopylai. With 180 ships to man, the Athenians would have needed all their hoplites at sea, if each carried as many as the Chiot ships at Lade (40: 6.15.1), or Xerxes' ships. In view of the importance of the defence of Thermopylai to Athens, it would be difficult to explain why there were no Athenians there, if there were only 1800 hoplites aboard the fleet. When Herodotos assigns crews of two hundred to the ships in Xerxes' fleet and to the one commanded by Kleinias, he may either be making an anachronistic mistake, or, possibly, triremes may normally have carried fewer marines unless battle was anticipated, as was the case with Roman quinqueremes, for example, at the time of the First Punic War.

The Persians, then, had the advantage because their ships were 'better sailing' (8.10.1), probably primarily because their crews were better trained.[41] This would have helped any captain who tried a *diekplous*, though it seems unlikely that the Persian fleet as a whole relied on such tactics. Conversely, the Greek ships were 'heavier' (8.60α), but this did not preclude a captain from trying a *diekplous*, if the opportunity arose. In any case, speed and manoeuvrability were not the only advantages the Persians enjoyed. In both passages (8.10.1 & 60α), Herodotos also stresses their numerical superiority, and this would probably have had a greater influence on the tactical thinking of the two sides than any differences in ship-design or number of marines.

As for the question whether the Greek or the Persian forces were the more highly trained, it is possible that there was some kind of rudimentary military training in many Greek states, as there certainly was in Sparta, but this would have been largely, if not exclusively, at the level of what the British army calls 'square bashing'. At most it would have included a few essential drills, such as for forming line-of-battle – the kind of thing described by the author of *The Constitution of the Lakedaimonians*, attributed

---

decks, but only carried ten hoplites and four archers. When Thucydides (1.14.3) says that the triremes Themistokles built 'did not yet have decks throughout' (διὰ πάσης), he probably means that the decks did not run right across the ship from side to side throughout its length, not that the decks at bow and stern were not connected (cf. Morrison & Coates, 160-1).

41 Cf. Morrison & Coates, Appendix I, 230ff. esp. 232-3.

to Xenophon (11-13). But it is noticeable that the treatise implies that even these simple manoeuvres were virtually unique to Sparta, and Thucydides' account of the battle of Mantineia in 418 (5.65ff.) implies that even such obvious things as a proper chain-of-command, organization into sub-units and marching in step were peculiar to Sparta. The Spartans may already have had such a system in 480/79, but it is most unlikely that other Greek states did – the first evidence for any kind of 'National Service' in Athens, for example, comes from the 4th century.[42] In any case, even Spartan drills were designed with hoplite opponents in mind, and one may doubt whether any mainland Greeks had given much thought to the problems of dealing with archers or cavalry, though the Athenians who fought in the battle of Ephesos (5.102.2-3), some years before Marathon, might have done.

At a higher level, it often seems to be forgotten that Greek generals and admirals owed their positions primarily, if not exclusively, to factors other than military ability, and above all to social prestige. Miltiades, for example, belonged to a family which had been prominent in Athens for three generations, powerful enough to incur the suspicion of 'tyrants', and wealthy enough to win chariot races at the Olympic Games (6.34ff.). Themistokles, though possibly of a less distinguished family, was socially acceptable enough to have held the prestigious office of 'archon' in 493/2, and was at least connected with the aristocratic clan of the Lykomidai.[43] Leonidas, of course, was King of Sparta, and Pausanias was his nephew and regent for his young son, Pleistarchos.

As for experience, Miltiades may have had some in winning control of the Chersonese (6.39.2) and capturing Lemnos (6.137ff.), but his service under Darius had been confined to guarding the bridge over the Danube (4.137.1ff.), and thereafter he had done nothing but flee ignominiously first from the Skythians and then from the Persians (6.40 & 41). Nothing in his previous experience as recorded by Herodotos would have prepared him for a full-scale confrontation between several thousand hoplites and a probably even more numerous Persian army, such as he faced at Marathon. In any case, in the end, it was possibly the polemarch, Kallimachos, who was responsiblle for the Athenian tactics there, and we do not know that he had ever before commanded an army. He might have fought Boiotians and Chalkidians (cf. 5.77), and possibly even Persians, in the Ionian Revolt (cf. 5.102), but he may well have been a youngish man when he held the *polemarchia* in 490, and might never before have even seen a battle.

Of Leonidas and Pausanias we know nothing prior to their commands at Thermopylai and Plataia. Leonidas could well have had experience of war stretching back to the 520s, but, as far as we know, it could only have been against Athenians in the last fifteen years of the sixth century, against Argives in c.494, and, possibly, against helots in 490; Pausanias was probably still a young man at the time of Plataia.[44] Among their subordinates, Aristeides, who commanded the Athenian contingent at Plataia, is said by Plutarch (*Aristeides* 5.2ff.) to have been one of the ten *stratêgoi* at Marathon, and the Plataian Arimnestos, who fought at Plataia (9.72), might also have fought at Marathon (Pausanias 9.4.1).

---

42 See P.J.Rhodes, 1981, 494f. 502f.
43 See Podlecki, 1f.; Lenardon, 18ff.
44 See M.E.White, *JHS* 84 (1964), 149ff.

But of all these men it can safely be said that they had never experienced war on such a scale as they saw in 480/79, even if Marathon was within their comprehension, and the attempts they made to stop the Persians with 10,000 hoplites at Tempe, and with 6-7000 at Thermopylai, may well indicate their total lack of understanding of what faced them. There is no hint that any of them had made any kind of study of the Ionian revolt, though there were, probably, some refugees from that conflict in Greece, and Athenians and Eretrians, at least, had taken part (5.99ff.).

At sea, the mainland Greeks' lack of experience was, if anything, even worse. It was only natural that Athens should make no attempt to meet the Persian threat at sea in 490, since, even if Herodotos' figure of 600 triremes for the Persian fleet (6.95.2) is exaggerated, it presumably still outnumbered the 70 or so that Athens could probably muster at the time (cf. 6.89 & 132). Ten years later, thanks to Themistokles (cf. 7.144.1), Athens had become the greatest naval power in Greece, with some 200 triremes at least at her disposal. But although her sailors may have had some experience fighting Aiginetans in this last decade (cf. 6.92.1, 93), this was on a small scale, in both numerical and geographical terms. One doubts whether anyone in Athens had bothered to study the one great sea-battle there had been between Greeks and Persians – off Lade (cf. 6.7-15): as Thucydides has Hermokrates of Syracuse argue (7.21.3), naval skill was not 'native' (πάτριον) to Athenians – 'they had been compelled by the Medes to become sailors'. It may be of significance, as we have seen, that on the first day at Artemision, according to Herodotos (8.9), the Greeks deliberately provoked a fight late in the afternoon, 'wishing to make trial of their [the Persians'] way of fighting and their *diekplous*' (8.9). It is possible that some thought had been given to the problem of how to fight more numerous and 'better sailing' ships (see below, 138–40), but at a strategic level it is unlikely that any Greeks had considered the advantages and limitations of sea-power, when they had only really had enough ships to begin to think in these terms, for two or three years. Thus any notion that the Greek strategy in 480 was based on the idea of holding or delaying the Persians on land, while the fleet won a decisive victory, is unlikely to be correct (see below, 117–8).

All this means that we should be extremely wary of any arguments about what did or did not happen in 490 and 480/79 which depend on assumptions about the expertise of Greek officers. We can believe that they were, on the whole, intelligent men, and that many of them may have had some experience of fighting fellow-Greeks, some few even of fighting Persians. But they were not like the officers of modern armies, and their commanders had not won their way to the top on merit, after years of training and service. Thus, for example, contrary to what has been claimed,[45] there is *every* difficulty in supposing that the principle of 'limiting the movements of a hostile fleet by taking up a position flanking its advance was understood and acted upon by Themistokles,' and we must beware of fancies that Miltiades was a fifth century Hannibal, applying to Marathon the principle of 'double-envelopment', or that Pausanias deliberately split his army at Plataia to lure Mardonios to destruction. Let us not forget, after all, that men like Themistokles and Miltiades would have been expected to command Athenian forces on land or sea, as circumstances dictated, as if Wellington were to have been given command at Trafalgar, and Nelson at Waterloo.

45 Hignett, 208.

We must even try to avoid terms like 'intelligence officer', 'administrative staff', 'reconnaissance unit', 'staff commanders', 'staff planning', 'commando force', 'shock-troops' and 'pioneer corps',[46] which convey the impression that the Greek armed forces of the early fifth century were rather like those of the Second World War. The Greek victory must be understood in 5th century terms.

Nevertheless it is arguable that this lack of training and experience among the Greek commanders, at any rate on land, made little or no difference in the ultimate resort. The one priceless asset the Greeks had was the hoplite phalanx itself, and it required little skill in its commanders. All they had to do was to find it a suitable battlefield and choose the right moment to attack. Driving forward, it was extremely formidable, as the Persians were to learn to their cost at Marathon and Plataia: Xenophon's descriptions of the charge of himself and his comrades in the review before their employer and his mistress, and at Kounaxa (*Anabasis* 1.2.14ff. & 1.8.17ff.) give some idea of how frightening it could be. It could, of course, be beaten by other troops if caught in unsuitable terrain, as the Aitolians showed in 426 (Thucydides 3.97-8), or if not properly formed, as happened to the Megarians and Phleiasians at Plataia (9.69.2). But, in normal circumstances, it required either overwhelming numbers, or immense skill, for 'light' troops like the Persians, armed with missile weapons, to defeat hoplites. Thus it took something like 10,000 Athenian troops to deal with 420 Spartan hoplites on Sphakteria (Thucydides 4.31-32), and the skill of an Iphikrates to bring about the defeat of a Spartan *mora* of 600 men near Lechaion in 390 (Xenophon, *Hellenika* 4,5.11ff.). Above all, on both these occasions, the light troops were backed up by hoplites of their own – about 800 Athenians on Sphakteria, and an unknown, but probably considerable number, on the later occasion. In neither case did the hoplites take part in the fighting, except right at the end near Lechaion, but their presence would have inhibited the hoplites from pursuing light troops too far. Hoplites, as we have seen, were the one thing the Persian army conspicuosly lacked.

Persian officers, too, are unlikely to have had any formal training, and they also owed their positions to social standing. Datis may have been something of a Greek expert, and, as a Mede, may have owed his command partly to merit,[47] but his colleague at Marathon, Artaphernes, was Darius' nephew (6.94.2), and many of the top commanders in 480/79 were relatives of the king. Of the six generals in overall command of the infantry, Mardonios, Tritanaichmes and, possibly, Smerdomenes,[48] were Xerxes' cousins (7.5.1 & 82), Masistes his full brother, while of the twenty-nine infantry contingents at least fourteen were commanded by members of the royal family by blood or marriage (7.61ff.). Similarly, of the three admirals in command of the fleet, one was Xerxes' full brother, another his half-brother.

But although it is most unlikely that any of the Persian generals or admirals in any sense 'rose from the ranks', at least they, unlike their Greek counterparts, are likely to have had some experience of warfare on an appropriate scale. The Ionian Revolt, for example, was directly relevant to the invasion of Greece, in many respects, and after that there had been fighting in Thrace, where Mardonios had certainly served (6.43-5),

46 All used by Peter Green in *The Year of Salamis* (62, 103, 111, 112. 163, 234, 246, 261).

47 Cook, 97ff.

48 See HW ii 158 *ad loc.*

Egypt (7.3 & 7), and, possibly, Babylonia and Judaea.[49] At sea, too, even if Herodotos' figure of 600 ships for Darius' Scythian expedition (4.87.1), Lade (6.9.1) and the Marathon campaign (6.95.2) is conventional and too high, at least it suggests that the Persians had become accustomed to operating with fleets of this order of magnitude. Above all, they seem to have grasped something of the value of sea-power. They evidently realised, for example, that it was necessary to crush the Ionians, and that it was also desirable to support operations against Greece with a naval force, as Mardonios did (6.43-5). The Marathon campaign had shown that – in the absence of a Greek fleet – the whole seaboard of Greece became a potential beach-head. At the same time these campaigns are likely to have taught the Persians invaluable lessons in logistics, and given them the experience in providing the back-up necessary for distant operations. Their success in reaching Athens within three months of crossing the Hellespont (7.51.1), is a sufficient demonstration of their expertise in large-scale warfare.

Nevertheless, even with the Persians, we should beware arguments which depend on the underlying assumption that they 'understood and acted upon' alleged principles of warfare. It has been argued, for example,[50] that the Athenians must have used the main road to Marathon because otherwise Persian patrols would soon have discovered that it lay open. But although the conclusion is probably right (see below, 54), the argument is not a good one, since it presupposes that the Persians would have sent out such patrols. Worse still is the notion that Datis and Artaphernes 'must have known all about those Spartan reinforcements, and the alleged reason for their delay'[51] – arguments which include the word 'must' are nearly always suspect. Similarly, it is highly dubious whether the reason for the cavalry attack on the Greek army when it came down from Kithairon in 479, was the strategic principle that the best way to defend a mountain chain is not to occupy the passes, but to attack as the enemy emerges from them.[52] Mardonios was an experienced general, but he had never read any Prussian military manuals.

Before the fifth century there had been no conflict between the Persians and the mainland Greeks, but there had been contacts between them for a generation. The first recorded contact, at a state level, resulted from an embassy to Sparta from a number of Ionian and Aiolian communities, which had tried and failed to obtain the same terms from Cyrus that they had enjoyed under the Lydians (1.141ff.). The spokesman for the party, Pythermos of Phokaia, seeking to impress his audience by the splendour of his clothes – or perhaps to dress like the Spartans themselves – chose to wear crimson for the occasion, but the Spartans refused the request for aid. They did, however, send a pentekonter to Ionia – presumably the Spartans as yet had no triremes – and a distinguished member of its crew, one Lakrines, went to Sardis to deliver an ultimatum to Cyrus , warning him 'to commit no wanton aggression against any city of Greece, for they [the Spartans] would not overlook it' (1.152.3). Cyrus' immediate response,

49 Cf. Cook, 99-100.
50 Green, 32 (note at bottom of page).
51 Green, 34.
52 Cf. Delbrück, 92ff., 114; Macan (1908) i 2.630; Munro, 1904, 157.

Herodotos reports (1.153.1), was to ask 'who of the Greeks the Spartans were and how many in number that they should speak to him like this'.[53]

There is a certain fairy-tale air about the story, but there is no particular reason to doubt that some appeal was sent to Sparta – Croesus, too, is alleged to have made one before his disastrous war with Persia (1.69.1ff.) – or that Sparta may have responded in such a naive manner. Mutual ignorance is, after all, likely at the time. Some scholars have seen a response to the Persian threat in much of Sparta's foreign policy in the last quarter of the sixth century,[54] and although this is far-fetched, it is by no means improbable that Sparta's growing power attracted the attention of those who had cause to fear Persian aggression.

Foolishly, however, the Asiatic Greeks joined in the Lydian revolt soon after Cyrus' departure, and were rapidly subdued (1.154ff.). Even some of the islands submitted (cf. 1.169), and by the time of Kambyses' invasion of Egypt, as we have seen, a Mytilenean ship was serving with his fleet (3.13.1). Herodotos' story of Polykrates' offer of support to Kambyses (3.44ff.), suggests that Samos still enjoyed a measure of independence, but, if so, it was short-lived. Polykrates himself was lured to his death by Oroites, satrap of Sardis, 'at about the time of Kambyses' illness' (3.120.1), i.e. in late spring or early summer, 522, and after Darius had removed Oroites, he helped Polykrates' brother, Syloson, to win control of Samos (3.139ff.). Thus, by the time of Darius' Skythian expedition (c.513), the Greeks of Asia Minor and the off-shore islands, even the Athenian ruler of the Chersonese, Miltiades, had passed under Persian control (cf. 4.89.1, 137-8), though Herodotos implies that Byzantion and Chalkedon were then in revolt (5.26). After Darius had returned to Asia, his generals had gone on to conquer Thrace (4.143-4, 5.1-2), the Propontine coast, the Troad and even Lemnos and Imbros (5.26-7).

The mainland Greeks could not have failed to be aware of all this, and there are traditions of contacts between them and the Persians at this time. Hippias of Athens, for example, when he felt his position threatened, married his daughter to the son of the 'tyrant' of Lampsakos on the Hellespont, because he knew that the Lampsakenes enjoyed Darius' favour (Thucydides 6.59.2-3), and after his expulsion from Athens, the Athenians sent two embassies to Sardis (5.73 & 96.2). The Spartan expedition against Polykrates of Samos, which failed, and the successful one against Lygdamis of Naxos, if it is historical (cf. Plutarch, *Moralia* 859d, etc.), may have been partly intended to prevent the Persians from winning control of the Aegean, but one cannot help but feel that the Greeks could have done more to preserve the independence of at least the Greek islands: 230 of the 353 Greek ships which fought at Lade, after all, came from them.

Early in the fifth century came the revolt of the Asiatic Greeks against Persian rule, which was the prelude to the Persian attempts to conquer Greece. Herodotos' account of what is usually called the 'Ionian' revolt, though it spread far beyond the confines of

---

53 One is reminded of Stalin's alleged remark when asked to conciliate the Pope (Churchill, *The Second World War*, vol. i Ch.8): 'The Pope! How many divisions does he have?".

54 Cf., e.g., Burn, 173-6; *contra*: K.H.Waters, *Historia* 19 (1970), 504-8; G.A.R.Chapman, *Historia* 21 (1972), 553-5. For Achaemenid policy towards the Greeks from 513 onwards see A.T.Olmstead, *CP* (1939), 305ff.

Ionia, has come in for much criticism,[55] but we are only concerned with the revolt's bearing on the invasions of Greece. Obviously the aid given to the rebels by Athens and Eretria was the first clash between Persia and mainland Greece, and, from the Persian point of view, the actions of the two states will have seemed unprovoked aggression. The action of Athens, indeed, may have seemed something worse, for at least once in the not too distant past, Athenian envoys had made formal submission to the king of Persia (5.73). Thus, although, according to Herodotos (5.73.3), the envoys had been blamed for this on their return, and Athens had subsequently refused to bow to demands to take Hippias back (5.96), the Persian attitude is likely to have been that the Athenians were already subjects of their king.

Equally clearly, the Athenians did not think so, and one of their motives for giving support to the Ionians may have been the desire to remove a potential source of support for Hippias. They may have been somewhat suspicious of the antecedents of the spokesman for the Ionians, Aristagoras of Miletos, for he was the cousin and son-in-law of Histiaios, 'tyrant' of Miletos, and had been left in charge of the city while Histiaios was at the Persian capital (5.30.2). But perhaps Aristagoras' ostentatious repudiation of tyranny and introduction of '*isonomia*' ('equality of rights') at Miletos, at the beginning of the revolt (5.37.2), had been reassuring, and it may well be that hatred of Persian-backed 'tyranny' had been one of the causes of the revolt, in the first place.

Sentiment also undoubtedly played a part in the Athenian decision to help the Ionians. The Athenians believed that the majority of the original colonists of Ionia had come from Attica (9.106.3; Thucydides 1.1.6, 12.4), and, according to Herodotos (5.97.2), Aristagoras reminded them that the Milesians, in particular, were their colonists. He also reminded them, as he had done the Spartans (cf. 5.49.3-4), of the riches of Asia, and of the poor quality of Persian troops. These may seem crude arguments to use in persuading people to embark on a war with the greatest empire in the world, but although Herodotos is unlikely to have known precisely what Aristagoras said to the Athenian assembly, and obviously got his information from a source which disapproved of the Athenian decision to help (cf. 5.97.2), this may have been the kind of argument that won the Athenians over.[56] It would also be in keeping with a mood of ignorant optimism that the first set-back outside Ephesos should have caused the Athenians to withdraw their forces and take no further part (5.103.1).

By then, of course, it was too late. It is not likely that Darius' first response to the news of the burning of Sardis was to ask who the Athenians were (5.105.1) – this is reminiscent of Cyrus' enquiry about the Spartans, and by then Darius had presumably met at least one Athenian, Miltiades (4.137.1). Nor is it likely that the king had to be reminded of the Athenians each day at dinner, by a slave specially appointed for the

---

55 Cf., e.g., HW ii 66; Grundy, 79-80, 559-61; Burn, 197; R.Meiggs, *The Athenian Empire* (Oxford, 1972), 24; A.Blamire, *CQ* (NS) 9 (1959),142ff.; Mabel Lang, *Historia* 17 (1968), 24ff.; but see J.A.S.Evans, *Historia* 25 (1976), 31ff., for the view that Herodotos' assessment of the revolt can be justified by what happened.

56 For a similar appeal mingling sentiment, greed and feelings of military superiority see the kind of arguments allegedly used to persuade the Athenian assembly to vote for the Sicilian Expedition: Thucydides 6.1.1, 6, 8ff.; note also the argument that Syracuse might help Athens' enemies (6.6.2).

purpose (5.105.2). But it is quite likely that the king sent for his bow, set an arrow to the string, and fired it into the sky, calling on his god to grant him that the Athenians should pay (5.105.1).[57]

For the time being, however, any attempt to exact revenge from the Athenians had to be postponed. It took five years of hard fighting to crush the rebellion in Asia Minor (cf. 6.18), which spread to Byzantion in the north and to Cyprus in the south-east (5.103.2). The decisive battle of Lade was probably not fought until 496 or 495, and was followed by the capture of Miletos, and extensive mopping-up operations. It was, thus, probably not until the spring of 492 that the new commander-in-chief in the west, Darius' son-in-law, Mardonios, mustered a large army and fleet in Cilicia, and, after setting up 'democracies' in the Greek cities of Asia Minor,[58] crossed the Hellespont and marched through Thrace as far as Macedonia (6.43-4).

Herodotos believed (6.43.4) that Mardonios' ultimate objectives were Eretria and Athens, and although, in the event, after suffering disastrous losses to his fleet off Mt. Athos, and to his army in Macedonia, he returned to Asia without getting anywhere near Eretria or Athens, it is by no means impossible that his operations were intended to be the prelude to an invasion of Greece. Herodotos actually says (3.134ff.) that Darius' queen, Atossa, had urged him to conquer Greece twenty years before, and that he had sent the doctor, Demokedes of Kroton, to reconnoitre the coasts (3.135.1), and even if this is untrue (see above, 29), it is not impossible that the idea of conquering Greece had been in Persian minds since they first made contact with the Greeks in Cyrus' time. The demand of the satrap at Sardis, in about 510, that the Athenians give 'earth and water' to Darius, in return for alliance (5.73), is, after all, suggestive, and even the Spartan ultimatum to Cyrus, if it is historical, may have caused the Persians to think that their rule over Asia Minor would never be secure while mainland Greece remained independent, a view which the Spartan expedition to Samos (c.525), even though it failed, will have reinforced.

Thus the Athenian and Eretrian aid to Ionia may well only have served to confirm a long-cherished object, and one based on sound strategy, rather than megalomaniac dreams of world conquest. Nor will the experience of war against the Greeks of Asia Minor have done anything to weaken Persian resolve to deal with their mainland cousins. They had managed to operate on a large scale, in difficult terrain and on several different fronts (cf. 5.116-123), without any apparent breakdown in organization, commissariat or communications, and they had won all the set-piece battles. They had successfully transported an army to Cyprus and crushed the rebellion there within a year, despite defeat at sea (5.108-116). They had raised a fleet from their

57 The bow was clearly a royal symbol, as Darius' coins show (Cook, 70 and Pl.35 between 164 and 165), and the king's bow-bearer was an important official, appearing in reliefs behind him (e.g. that of Darius at Behistun – Cook, pl.7). There may have been some kind of ceremony, involving the king shooting an arrow, to symbolize the declaration of war.

58 Ostwald, *Nomos and the Beginnings of Athenian Democracy* (Oxford, 1969), 109, suggests that Mardonios' motive for establishing 'democracies' in Asia Minor was to protect his rear when he left for Thrace. H.Wood ('The Histories of Herodotus', *De Proprietatibus Litterarum*, Series Practici 21, 1922, 124-5 n.20) thinks democracy was safer: the revolt had been engineered by 'tyrants'. On Persian policy in Thrace see now J.M.Balcer, *Historia* 37 (1988), 1ff.

maritime subjects,and although defeated off the 'Keys' of Cyprus they had gone on to win the decisive battle of Lade. They had taken walled towns in Cyprus (5.115.2), on the Hellespont (5.117), in Ionia (6.18 & 31.2), in Caria (6.25.2), in the Chersonese and on the coast of the sea of Marmara (6.35). They had, no doubt, been surprised by the degree of unity which their quarrelsome subjects had achieved, and by the size of the forces they had mobilized (cf. 6.9), but they had also seen how easy it was to divide them by a mixture of promises and threats (cf. 6.9.2-4 & 13-14). Thus it will have been with high hopes that they embarked on the preparations which were to lead to the first invasion of Greece, and to Marathon.

CHAPTER 3

The Mountains Look on Marathon

It was probably in 491 (cf. 6.95.1) that Darius began his preparations for the first real Persian attack on Greece. Envoys were sent to the Greek states to test their attitude, demanding the symbolical 'earth and water', while others went to the maritime states under Persian rule to order the construction of warships and horse-transports (6.48). If Herodotos is right that the ultimate objective of Mardonios' operations in Thrace and Macedonia had been Eretria and Athens (cf. 6.43.4), these new preparations indicate a change of strategy from an invasion by land to one by sea. Either, then, the disaster off Mt. Athos had not cast doubts on the feasibility of sea-borne operations, and it was the difficulties which Mardonios had encountered in Macedonia which brought about the change, or Herodotos misrepresents the objective of Mardonios' operations. In fact it seems likely that these had never had anywhere in Greece south of Macedonia as their objective, but had merely been intended to round off Megabazos' earlier operations, and, in particular, to secure the submission of Macedonia.[1]

Presumably the Persians were aware of the distances and difficulties involved in trying to invade Greece from the north, even if Herodotos' story (3.135-8) of the reconnaissance led by the doctor, Demokedes of Kroton, is unhistorical (see above, 29). Conversely, the expedition to Naxos may well have shown how easy it would be to attack Greece by sea. Naxos is, after all, halfway across the Aegean, and a natural stepping-stone to Euboia, as Aristagoras of Miletos is supposed to have told the satrap at Sardis, in proposing the Naxos expedition (5.31.3). Aristagoras had asked the satrap for 100 ships, but in the event had been given 200, and had managed not only to reach the island safely, but to maintain a siege of its main town for four months. Herodotos believed the only reason the expedition had failed was because the Persian commander had informed the Naxians of its coming, after a quarrel with Aristagoras (5.31.3-34). The only difference between the Naxian expedition and the one prepared in 491, except possibly their size (see below, 46–7), was the addition of horse-transports in 491, and this is readily understandable: cavalry would not have been of much use on Naxos.

According to Herodotos, Darius' diplomatic offensive in 491 had considerable success, both in mainland Greece and in the islands (6.49.1). The historian is, however, principally concerned with the 'medism' of Aigina, which gives him an opportunity for a long digression on previous relations between Aigina and Athens, and on the history of Sparta in the 490s (6.49.2-93). Thus he omits to tell us here that the Athenians brusquely rejected the Persian demands, and threw the envoys into the *barathron*, the pit in the deme *Keiriadai* reserved for those condemned to death (7.133.1, Bekker, *Anecdota* 219). Nor does he tell us that the Spartans, similarly, flung the Persian envoys down a well, telling them to get their earth and water for the king from there (*loc.cit*).[2]

---

1 Grundy argues (151-2) that Mardonios' large fleet – he is reported to have lost about 300 ships off Athos (6.44.3) – indicates that his objective was more than Thrace and Macedonia. But see Beloch ii 2 84ff., and Macan (1895) ii 74.

2 Hignett, 87, argues that the story of the heralds in 491 is unhistorical, the murder of the heralds at Sparta, in particular, belonging to 481, but see R.Sealey, *CJ* 72 (1976), 13-20.

However, he does imply that there was now an understanding between Athens and Sparta, even if, as yet, there was no formal alliance. He says that the Athenians denounced the Aiginetans to the Spartans, and that eventually the Spartans arrested those responsible, and handed them over to Athens (6.73.2).

These diplomatic moves suggest that Darius was ultimately thinking in terms of the conquest of Greece, not just of punishing Eretria and Athens, but his objective was clearly limited in the first instance. Unfortunately, Herodotos does not tell us how large a force was sent, beyond saying that there were 600 triremes, and this seems to have been a 'conventional' number for a Persian fleet. It is also said to have been the number of Persian ships which accompanied Darius' Skythian expedition (4.87.1) and which fought at Lade (6.9.1). Plato (*Menexenos* 240a) says the Persian fleet in 490 numbered 300 ships, but since he also gives the total number of men involved as 500,000, his figures can probably be discounted. The contemporary poet, Simonides (frag. 90 Bergk) gives 90,000 as the number of men on the Persian side, but this seems too high for the actual fighting men, too low for the total of troops and crews combined.[3]

If the Persian losses at Marathon were really about 6400 (6.117.1), assuming that they came mostly from the centre, and that the centre was about a third of the army, something like 25,000 men took part in the battle on the Persian side. This may not have been the total Persian force, but if it was (as will be argued below), then it is not impossible that Herodotos' figure for the number of triremes is about right. At Lade Chiot triremes each carried 40 marines (6.15.1), and Xerxes' triremes 30 Persians and Sakai in addition to natives (7.184.2), who probably numbered about 14 (see above, 35). Thus 600 triremes could well have carried some 24,000 soldiers. Assuming that the horse-transports were additional, and that they were converted triremes, between thirty and forty would probably have been needed to carry 1000 cavalry. An army of about 24,000 foot and 1000 horse was clearly not large enough to conquer Greece, but it

3 Cf., e.g., Grundy, 160 & n.; Burn, 237. Hammond, 1988, 504, accepts Plato's 300 ships, and by juggling figures for troops and crews is able to arrive at Simonides' figure of 90,000. But since so much is hypothetical, what is the point? We can, presumably, ignore the huge totals given by later sources like Lysias (500,000: *Epitaphios* 2), Plato (*Menexenos* – above), Nepos (200,000 foot, of whom 100,000 took part in the battle: *Miltiades* 4.1 & 5.6), Justin (600,000: 2.9), Pausanias (300,000 killed: 4.25.4) and the *Souda* (200,000).

I do not understand where Van der Veer (*Mnemosyne* 35, 1982, 309n.78, referring to Herodotos 7.184) gets his notion that there were 80 marines on each Persian ship in 490. The Herodotos passage actually says there were 30 Persians and Sakai, in addition to native marines, aboard each of Xerxes' warships, and it is clear from his calculations that their total complements were thus 230, which probably means there were only some 14 native marines. For the troop-carrying capacities of triremes see Morrison & Coates, 225-6; for horse-transports, 226-8.

J.A.S. Evans, (*CJ* 82, 1986/7, 101-2) argues that the Persian horse-transports in 490 were not converted triremes, but probably smaller vessels. However, as he points out (102 n.47), according to the MSS reading, Herodotos describes Xerxes' horse-transports as 'long ships' (πλοῖα μακρά: 7.97), and although he accepts the emendation 'σμικρά') ('small'), this is arbitrary. In any case, I do not see what horse-transports were doing in Xerxes' fleet, and they may have been smaller vessels than those of 490. Incidentally, Evans, 97 and n.4, refers to Diodoros '11.5.9' as saying that there were 850 horse-transports in 490, but the reference should be to 11.*3*.9, and Diodoros is there referring to Xerxes' expedition.

would have seemed large enough to settle the score with Naxos, punish Eretria and reinstate the 'tyrant' Hippias in Athens, probably the three primary objectives of the expedition.

Operations began with the arrival in Cilicia of the two new Persian commanders, Datis and Artaphernes, with their land forces, presumably in the spring of 490.[4] Here they were met by the fleet and horse-transports, and, having embarked their forces, proceeded to Ionia, where they presumably picked up the Ionian and Aiolian contingents they are later said to have had (6.98.1). Thence they proceeded by way of Samos and Ikaros to their first objective, Naxos. Here the inhabitants had fled to the hills, and the Persians had to be content with a few prisoners and with burning shrines and city. The treatment of Naxos was presumably in revenge for the island's earlier resistance, and may also have been intended to demonstrate the fate that would befall anyone who resisted. But Datis, on the orders of the king, was careful to try to reassure the inhabitants of nearby Delos, who had fled to Tenos (6.97), and this may have been intended to show that the Persians were prepared to respect the Greek way of life, provided that they submitted. Delos was by tradition the birthplace of Apollo and his sister, Artemis, and a sacred island to all Ionians in particular.

Herodotos goes on to say (6.98) that after Datis' departure there occurred the only earthquake on Delos recorded up to his time, and this appears to be contradicted by Thucydides' statement (2.8.3) that the only recorded earthquake on the island occurred shortly before the *Peloponnesian* War. However, Herodotos does imply (6.98.2) that the disasters forboded by the earthquake occurred in the reigns of Darius, Xerxes and Artaxerxes, and the last did not die until 424. Thus it is possible that there was only one earthquake, and that it was connected with the Persian or Peloponnesian Wars, as circumstances dictated.[5]

The 'stick-and-carrot' policy pursued by Datis may have had some success, for when the Persian fleet visited other islands, there seems to have been no resistance. Though hostages were taken as a precaution, troops were also levied – for example the Parian trireme mentioned later by Herodotos (6.133.1). The first resistance came from Karystos at the southern tip of Euboia, for, to their credit, the Karystians declined to give hostages or to fight neighbouring cities – a most remarkable sentiment for Greeks! But a brief siege and the ravaging of their land soon induced a change of mind.

Meanwhile the Eretrians, aware that they were one of the principal targets of the expedition, asked the Athenians for help. They were offered the support of the four thousand Athenians settled on land confiscated from Chalkis, Eretria's neighbour to the north, some fifteen years earlier (6.100.1, cf. 5.77.2). But as might have been expected, there were differences of opinion among the Eretrians, some advocating flight to the hills, some, with a view to personal gain, plotting treachery. Luckily the Athenians were warned by a prominent sympathiser, Aischines, son of Nothon, and crossed safely to Oropos, in north-eastern Attica. The warning was timely, for although the Eretrians resisted fiercely for six days, on the seventh the city was betrayed to the enemy (6.101.2). It was sacked and burned, including its temples, and its inhabitants enslaved,

4 For the date see T.J.Cadoux, *JHS* 68 (1948), 117, n.253.

5 Cf. HW ii 104-5; Gomme, *HCT* ii 9 & *Essays in Greek History and Literature* (Oxford, 1937), 122 n., and see now H.Y.McCulloch, Jr., *SO* 57 (1982), 37-8.

according to Darius' instructions (6.101.3). Then, after waiting a few days, the Persians crossed to Marathon.

The reasons Herodotos gives for the choice of Marathon are that it was the most suitable place for cavalry in Attica and also the nearest to Eretria. As they stand, neither of these statements is true. The plain south of Athens itself would have been at least as suitable for cavalry, as Hippias knew, since his Thessalian allies had destroyed a Spartan force there (5.63.3-4), and Oropos, for example, is nearer Eretria than Marathon. What Herodotos may have meant is that Marathon was the best place for cavalry near Eretria, but there may also have been other reasons for the choice. Firstly, Herodotos' statement that it was Hippias who led the Persians there (6.102), suggests that there may have been a political motive. Hippias' ancestral home was in the deme by then called *Philaïdai*, about twenty-five kilometres to the south (Plutarch, *Solon* 10.2), and he may have been remembering the day, over half a century before, when he had landed at Marathon with his father, Peisistratos, and they had gone on to win the battle of Pallene against their aristocratic rivals, and to seize power in Athens. Herodotos says that on that occasion they had been joined not only by partisans from the city, but also supporters 'from the demes' (1.62.1), which presumably means primarily from the country districts of eastern Attica. It is true that much had changed in Attica since the mid-6th century, but it is not unlikely[6] that Hippias was under the illusion that he would be greeted just as enthusiastically now, as he and his father had been all those years ago. He was an old man, perhaps in his dotage – he lost one of his teeth, Herodotos tells us (6.107.3), when he landed at Marathon, to a violent fit of sneezing and coughing.

It is also worth remembering that Hippias may not have been entirely deluded if he thought that he and his Persian allies might have supporters in Attica. Even if the story of the shield-signal is untrue (see below, 72–3), or if the Alkmaionidai had nothing to do with it, the fact that such stories could be told indicates that treachery was not inconceivable, and Herodotos also has Miltiades hint at the possibility in his speech to Kallimachos (6.109.5: see below, 57). At the very least there were probably many Athenians who were in favour of what would now be called 'appeasement'. It was presumably such men who had secured the withdrawal of aid to Ionia, and possibly the condemnation of Phrynichos for his play '*The Capture of Miletos*' (cf. 6.21.2). Athens would have been almost unique among Greek states if her citizens had been completely unanimous, and the example of Eretria will have reinforced Persian convictions that they would find allies in all Greek cities.[7]

Some modern commentators have seen a clever strategy behind the choice of Marathon as a landing-place. The Persians, we are told, had no intention either of marching on Athens, or of fighting the Athenians at Marathon. Their sole purpose was to draw the Athenian army out as far as possible from the city, so that treachery might have a free hand there, or that part of the Persian force might be transported there by

6 *Pace* HW ii 358; see Burn, 238-9; McCulloch, *op.cit.*, 38.

7 Cf. G.W.Williams, 'The Curse of the Alkmaionidai, II. Kleisthenes and the Persian Wars,' *Hermathena* 79 (1952), 18-9; Grundy, 166-71; HW ii 359-60; Burn, 238-9; G.Shrimpton, *Phoenix* 34 (1980), 27-8 and n.17.

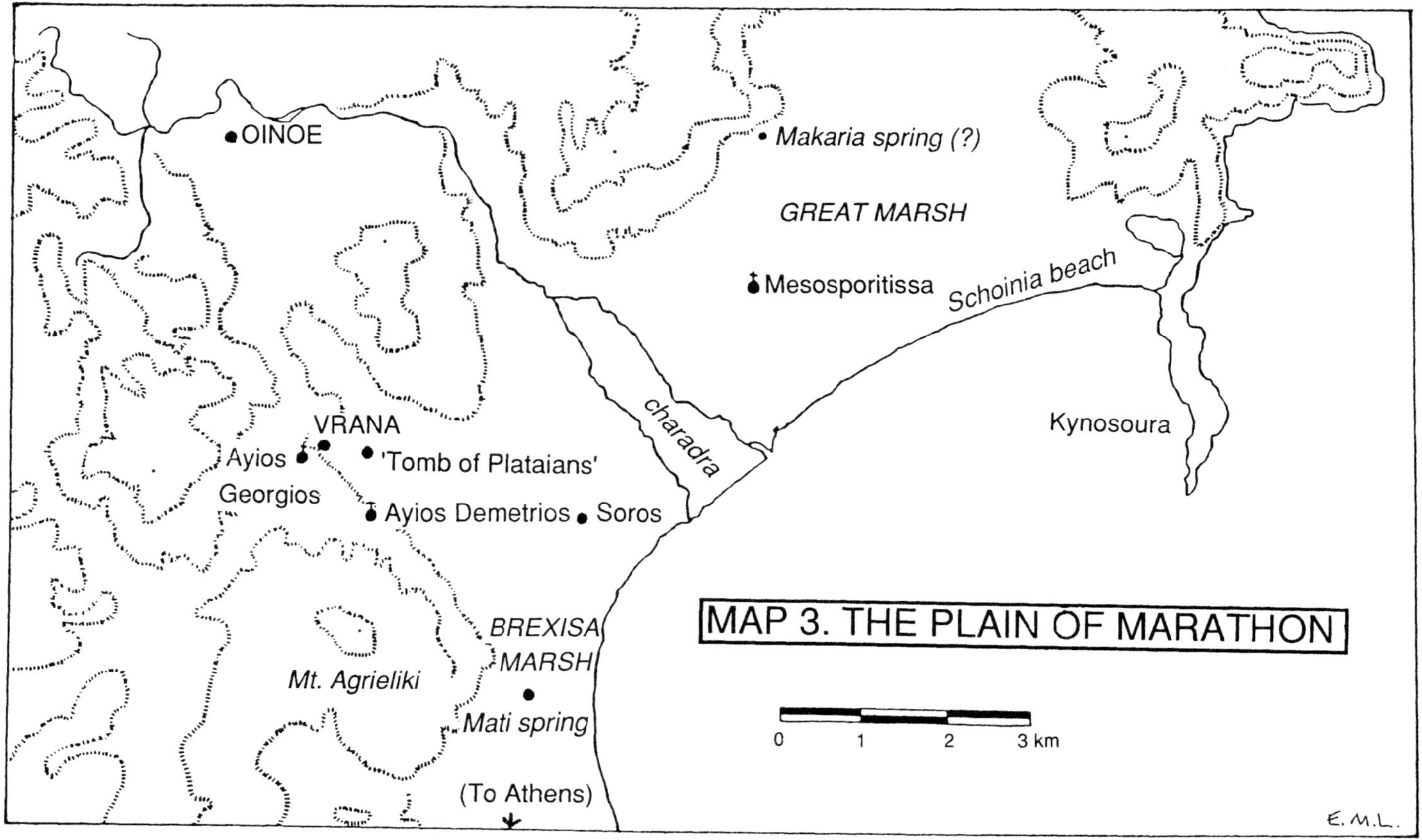

MAP 3. THE PLAIN OF MARATHON
OINOE
Makaria spring (?)
GREAT MARSH
Mesosporitissa
Schoinia beach
Kynosoura
charadra
VRANA
Ayios
Georgios
'Tomb of Plataians'
Ayios Demetrios
Soros
BREXISA
MARSH
Mt. Agrieliki
Mati spring
(To Athens)
0
1
2
3 km
E.M.L.

sea, while the rest pinned the Athenians down at Marathon.[8] But it is unnecessary to look for such sophistication in what the Persians did, and *a priori* unlikely that they thought in such terms (see above, 39–40).

Even if Hippias was under no illusions about the support he was likely to attract, he might well have suggested Marathon as a suitable place for a landing simply because he and his father had landed there before their successful march on Athens. After all, what were the alternatives? A landing at Oropos, the nearest point in Attica to Eretria, would have left the Persians with a comparatively long and difficult route to Athens. A landing at Phaleron would have been nearest to Athens, but it was a long way from Euboia or any other place of safety should things go wrong, and although the Persians probably did not fear that a landing there would be contested, it was bound to have led to a battle within a short time. A landing at Rafina (the ancient Araphen), finally, though nearer to Athens, would not have provided a terrain which suited Persian strengths as well as Marathon, in the event of a battle. Marathon was, thus, probably the best place for a beach-head for anyone coming from Euboia, and wishing to take Athens, as Peisistratos, too, seems to have thought.[9]

Where exactly the Persians landed and established their camp is uncertain. The only evidence, if 'evidence' it can be called, is Pausanias' statement (1.32.6) that 'beyond (i.e. 'north of') the meer (i.e. the marsh in the northern part of the plain) are the stone troughs of the horses of Artaphernes, and the marks of a tent in the rocks'. One can imagine the kind of phenomena which Pausanias' tourist-guide may have shown him to lead him to write like this. But there is a good spring (now called Megalo Mati) at Kato Souli (the ancient Trikorinthos) (see Pl. 3), which might be the ancient spring 'Makaria', mentioned by Pausanias (1.32.5), and the fringes of the marsh might have provided better grazing for the Persian horses, towards the end of a Greek summer, than the plain to the south-west. The beach immediately west of the promontory of Kynosoura, at the north-eastern end of the bay, would have provided a good, sheltered anchorage for the ships (see Pl. 4).[10]

Later sources ([Demosthenes] 59.94; Plutarch, *Moralia* 305) refer to Persian ravaging, and although not mentioned by Herodotos, it is not unlikely at least that parties were sent out to forage the immediate neighbourhood. So presumably the news of the Persian landing reached Athens in a matter of hours, and Herodotos implies (6.103.1) that the Athenian army almost immediately marched to Marathon.[11] Nepos, however, (*Miltiades* 4.4) implies that it was only after considerable debate about whether to confront the Persians where they had landed or to defend the walls, that it

8 Cf. Munro, 1899, 188; Grundy, 171-2, 182; HW ii 358-9, etc.

9 See Hignett, 66-8. For the disadvantages of landing at Rafina see Burn, 245.

10 Shrimpton, *op.cit.* n.7 above, 30, seems to envisage the Persian camp as near the *Soros*, and has a long and interesting note – n.23 on 31 – about the problems of feeding and watering horses, and see also Evans, *op.cit.* n.3 above, 102-3. For a clear restatement of the case for locating the Persian base beyond the Great Marsh, at the northern end of the plain, see Van der Veer, *op.cit.* n.3 above, 297-9. For the ravaging see Hammond, 1988, 507.

11 It seems unnecessary to discuss the theory of Munro in *CAH*[1] iv, 234ff., that the Athenian army was marching to aid Eretria when a detachment of Persians landed at Marathon. As Burn argues (238 n.5), the Athenians can never have seriously contemplated sending their forces to Euboia, in the face of Persian naval superiority.

Pl. 3 (top): The modern spring-chamber at Kato Souli, possibly the ancient spring 'Makaria' mentioned by Pausanias, and used by the Persians. (Photo: N. Fields) Pl. 4 (bottom): Marathon – the Schoinia beach. (Photo: N. Fields)

was decided, on the motion of Miltiades, to march out, and there may be something in this tradition. It goes back at least to the fourth century, when Demosthenes and Aristotle, for example, evidently knew of a decree of Miltiades to 'take provisions and march' (Demosthenes 19.303; Aristotle, *Rhetoric* 1411a).

But this presupposes that the defence of the city would have been considered a practical alternative, and this is dubious. Athens probably did have walls by this time, as Thucydides implies (6.57.3, cf. 1.89.3ff.),[12] but how long could they have been held? The Persians were famed for their expertise in siege-warfare, and it had been amply demonstrated again by the capture of Miletos (6.18), the subject of a famous tragedy by Phrynichos, which had been recently staged in Athens (6.21.2). The fate of Eretria was a more recent reminder of the possibility of treachery. Even if the walls could be held, it would probably have been impossible to accomodate the entire population of Attica within them, and with no possibility of supplying the city by sea, at this date, the greatly increased numbers who could have found refuge, would rapidly have faced starvation. The only hope would have been to hold out until the Spartans arrived, but there was no guarantee that the Spartans would send help, or that it would be in sufficient strength to raise a siege.

It is also worth noting that the normal Athenian response to invasion, down to 480, was to confront the enemy in the field. Peisistratos' opponents had done so c.546 (1.62.2ff.), Hippias had done so against Anchimolios c.513 (5.63.2ff.), and the Athenians as a whole had done so against Kleomenes and his Boiotian and Chalkidian allies c.506 (5.74-7). The only sieges of which we hear, were when the defenders were few enough to congregate on the acropolis – Kylon and his supporters (5.71, Thucydides 1.126.3ff.), Hippias and his (5.64.2ff.), and Kleomenes and Isagoras and theirs (5.72.2).

Before their departure from Athens, the Athenian generals sent a runner to Sparta with a message asking for help. Although the best manuscripts of Herodotos give his name as 'Pheidippides' (6.105.1 & 2, 106.1), it was probably 'Philippides', as one manuscript spells it, and as Plutarch (*Mor*alia 862a) and Pausanias (1.28.4, 8.54.6) read it in their texts of Herodotos.[13] Herodotos says that the runner reached Sparta the day after leaving Athens (δευτεραῖος ἐκ τοῦ 'Αθηναίων ἄστεος: 6.106.1), and this has now been shown to be perfectly feasible. In 1982 a Flight-Lieutenant in the RAF ran the distance in 34 hours, and a Wing-Commander of fifty-six in 35$^{1}/_{2}$.[14] Thus, even if

12 See R.E.Wycherley, *The Stones of Athens* (Princeton, 1978), 7ff. For an excellent analysis of the possible reasons why the Athenians marched to Marathon see R.M.Berthold, *REA* 78-9 (1976-7), 85-7.

13 But see Burn, 239-40, n.7.

14 See *The Times* for 11 October, 1982. Hammond, 1988, 507, apparently thinks that Philippides returned to Athens three days later, but it is difficult to believe in *two* 140-mile runs in a week. It is, of course, the supposed run of the messenger bringing the news of victory from Marathon to Athens that is commemorated by the modern Marathon race, though there have been some recent attempts to revive the idea of a race from Athens to Sparta, following the feat of the RAF team referred to above. Both Plutarch and Lucian say that the use of the word 'χαίρετε' as a form of greeting resulted from its use by the bringer of the news of victory, and although this is very unlikely to be true, it is nice to think that – just possibly – when one uses or hears the word in Greece to-day, one is harking back to Marathon.

modern training-methods, diet and so on, are held to be superior, there is surely no difficulty about believing that an experienced ancient runner could have achieved the feat.

Obviously it is less likely that Philippides met Pan on Mt. Parthenion, above Tegea, though exhaustion might have produced some kind of hallucination. Herodotos tells the story on the authority of Philippides himself (6.105), and in the euphoria of victory probably few cared to dispute the tale. But it is a far cry from this to the tall stories evidently later told about Philippides. In the second century AD, for example, Lucian (*On Mistakes in Greeting*, 3) said that he returned to Athens in time to take part in the battle of Marathon, and to bring the news of the victory from Marathon to Athens. Plutarch (*Moralia* 347c) reports that Herakleides of Pontos gave this honour to one Thersippos, though 'most writers' said it was Eukles.

Philippides' message to Sparta, as recorded by Herodotos (6.106.2), contained the information that Eretria had been captured, but not that the Persians had landed at Marathon, and from this it has been deduced that it was sent before the Persian landing.[15] This may be the case, for the Athenians, after all, had presumably been expecting a Persian attack for months. Once the Persians had reached Euboia, they would have assumed that it could not be long delayed, and it would have made sense to ask Sparta for help before the blow fell. But it is unwise to place too much reliance on the exact wording of the message as recorded by Herodotos.

The Spartan reply, he says (6.103.3), was that although willing to help, they could not do so without breaking their law, 'for it was the ninth of the month just beginning, and on the ninth, they said, they could not go out unless the circle of the moon was full.' As it stands this reply does not make sense, since the moon could never be full on the ninth day of a lunar month, but presumably what Herodotos meant is that the Spartans could not march on the ninth or any day until the moon was full. He also implies that the rule applied to all months, and this is how some ancient writers understood him (e.g. Pausanias 1.28.4). Plutarch (*Moralia* 861e) castigated him on the grounds that the Spartans had fought innumerable campaigns and battles at the beginning of the month. However, although it is odd that he does not mention the *Karneia* here as he does later in the case of Thermopylai (7.206.1), Herodotos almost certainly meant that military action was precluded before the moon was full in this particular month, in which the *Karneia* fell. These indications of time in the narrative have been used by some scholars to work out a precise chronology for the Marathon campaign, but unfortunately it is not certain whether August or September, in our terms, is the month in question.[16]

At first sight it may seem that the Spartans were just making excuses,[17] but the evidence of Thucydides (cf., e.g., 5.54.2-3, 75.2, 76.1) and Xenophon (cf., especially,

15 Grundy, 173; Hignett, 55-7.

16 Burn, 240-1, n.10. For a recent attempt at an exact chronology see, e.g., Hammond, 1988, 506ff., based on arguments in 1973, 170ff., but, in the end, this is as hypothetical as all the others.

17 Grundy, e.g. (n. on 173) says 'it is impossible to say how far this excuse for delay was genuine'; Hignett, 63, thinks that the tradition recorded by Plato (*Laws* 698e & 692d) was invented by a 4th century apologist to whom Herodotos' 'excuse ... must have seemed unconvincing'; Green, too, is sceptical (31). HW ii 109 comment that the speed of the Spartan march 'seems to show that their desire to help Athens was genuine,' and cf. W.G.Forrest,

Hellenika 4.7.2-3) shows that the Spartans were still scrupulous about such taboos in the late fifth and early fourth centuries, and the speed with which they eventually marched in 490, reaching Athens 'on the third day', if Herodotos is to be believed (τριταῖοι ἐκ Σπάρτης: 6.120), surely indicates that they were in earnest, for they were not to know when the battle would be fought. The later tradition that they were delayed by trouble with the helots rests on poor authority (Plato, *Laws* 692e, 698d), and is implausible in itself. Even if there was trouble with the helots at the time,[18] it is unlikely that the Spartans would one moment have been unable to move because of it, and the next – within a week or two – have been able to do so. Scepticism about Sparta's attitude is belied by Herodotos' narrative, which is at least consistent. Darius' demands were brusquely rejected (7.133.1), Aiginetan 'medizers' were arrested, though there was some opposition here (6.49ff.), and now 2000 troops were sent, perhaps a quarter of the army (cf. 7.234.2).

Meanwhile, however, the Athenians were on their own. They probably marched by the normal route to Marathon, *via* the gap between Pentelikon and Hymettos – the alternative routes west-about round Pentelikon are not really suitable for an army[19] – and took up a position at a *temenos* of Herakles. Here they were joined by the full force of the small town of Plataia in south-western Boiotia, which had been allied to them for some thirty years (6.108, cf. Thucydides 3.68.5). According to Pausanias (9.4.2), the Plataians were commanded by a man called Arimnestos, but this may be an invention based on Herodotos' reference to a Plataian of that name in the later Plataia campaign (9.72.2).

Unfortunately Herodotos does not give any numbers for the Athenian and Plataian forces, but Nepos (*Miltiades* 5.1) says that with the addition of 1000 Plataians, the Greeks numbered 10,000, and Plutarch (*Moralia* 305b), Pausanias (10.20.2, cf. 4.25.5) and the *Souda* (s.v. *Hippias*) all seem to have the same tradition; Justin (2.9) gives 1000 Plataians and 10,000 Athenians. Although these numbers rest on dubious authority, they are likely to be approximately right, for Herodotos says there were 8000 Athenian and 600 Plataian hoplites at Plataia (9.28.6). At Marathon the Athenians are likely to have been, if anything, in larger numbers, the Plataians, perhaps, somewhat fewer.

The location of the *temenos* of Herakles at which the Athenians encamped has also long been the subject of controversy.[20] Basically there are two alternatives: either it was

---

Phoenix 38 (1984), 8: 'We are told that the Spartans turned up late for Marathon because they were celebrating a festival (6.106 and 120). We have to be told so because that is what happened. ... It is only modern historians who impute cowardice or selfishness or deceit.'

18 Cf. *The Minnesota Messenia Expedition*, ed. W.A.McDonald & G.R.Rapp, Jr. (Minneapolis, 1972), 86-7.

19 See R.M.Berthold, *op.cit.* n.12 above, 84-5, for some sound arguments for thinking the Athenians would have gone by way of Pallene. More recently – 1988, 507 – Hammond has the Athenians use *both* routes, but why should they have divided their army like this? For an interesting suggestion that the painting in the *Stoa Poikile* which Pausanias believed depicted a 'battle of Oinoe' (1.15.2), actually depicted the arrival of the Plataians at Marathon, by way of Oinoe in Attica, see E.D.Francis and M.Vickers, *BSA* 80 (1985), 99ff.

20 The alternatives are clearly set out by Berthold, *op.cit.*, 87-91, and Van der Veer, *op.cit* n.3 above, 294-7, though they disagree. I agree with Van der Veer: in particular, Berthold is, surely, wrong to claim that 'what evidence there is' and 'all the evidence' (91) points to the

somewhere in the south-western part of the plain – for example, on the slopes of Agrieliki near the chapels of Ayios Demetrios or Ayios Georgios, or near Vrana – or it was to the south-east, covering the southern exit from the plain. In favour of the former are the contemporary Pindar's reference to games in honour of Herakles being held 'in the nook of Marathon' (μυχῷ τ' ἐν Μαραθῶνος: *Pythian* 8.79), Herodotos' description of how the Athenian centre was later driven back 'inland' (ἐς τὴν μεσόγαιαν: 6.113.1), and the good, defensive nature of most of the proposed locations. On the other hand, Herodotos says that 'no less than eight stades' (i.e. probably just under 1600 metres) separated the two armies before the Greeks began their advance (6.112.1), and although we may allow that they had moved some distance from their camp before deploying, and that we cannot be certain where the Persian battle-line stood, some of the locations for the Greek camp in this part of the plain seem too far away: it is, for example, over three kilometres from Vrana to the *Soros*. The proposed location at the southern entrance to the plain is much nearer the *Soros*, which probably marks roughly where the battle was fought. Also in favour of this view are the two inscriptions referring to Herakles that have now been found in the vicinity,[21] and the fact that such a position would better cover the main route to Athens.

Certainty is not possible, but, on balance, one should, perhaps, go for the location for which there is now the evidence of the inscriptions, since none of the other evidence actually precludes it. Pindar, for example, may have been thinking of the secluded position of the plain of Marathon as a whole, rather than that of the *temenos* in particular, and a Greek camp at the southern exit from the plain would not prevent the Greeks' deploying in such a way on the day of battle that their centre could be driven 'inland' (see below, 65–6).[22] Although such a position may seem more exposed than one to the north-west, there is in fact less than a kilometre and a half between the lower slopes of Agrieliki and the sea, even if the so called 'little marsh' (Brexisa) did not exist in 490.[23] In any case, the Athenians may not have been so much concerned to find a

---

Vrana valley, and is far too cavalier in thinking that an Athenian camp near Vrana would still cover the southern exit from the plain. It is also nearly twice as far from Vrana to the *Soros* as Herodotos' 'eight stades'. For the length of the stade see O.Broneer, *Isthmia* I (Princeton, 1971), Appendix I: he reckons it was 195.6 metres.

21 E.Vanderpool, *Hesperia* 11 (1942), 329ff., cf. *AJA* 70 (1966), 319ff.; S.Marinatos, *PAE* 1972, 6; P.Themelis, *ADelt* 29 (1974), 236. Burn accepts the location at the southern exit from the plain, arguing that this best blocked the main road to Athens, in *Studies presented to F.Schachermeyr* (München, 1977), 90-1.

22 This seems better than Van der Veer's explanation (*op.cit.* n.3 above, 313 and see his excellent map on 291) that 'the valley of Nea Makri-Dionysos ... may have served as a route of escape for the Greek centre flying inland (ἐς τῆν μεσόγαιαν, Hdt. VI 113)'. Green's suggestion (37) that the words mean 'towards the Mesogaia' is far-fetched: Herodotos, who even explains, e.g., who Solon was, the first time he mentions him (1.29.1), would hardly have used an Athenian technical term like 'Mesogaia' without explanation.

23 It still appears in some modern discussions (e.g. Hignett, 60, and map on 56; Green, 32, and map on 33; Hammond, 1988, 43, fig.43), but see G.Soteriades, *PAE* 1935, 121; Pritchett, *University of California Publications in Classical Archaeology* IV 2 (1960), 154; Themelis, *ADelt* 29 (1974), 239-41, 298; Van der Veer, *op.cit.* n.3 above, 306. Another feature of the plain nowadays, the absence of which from Herodotos' narrative has aroused criticism, is the *charadra*, but this, too, was possibly not there in antiquity: Pritchett, *op.cit.*, 156ff., but cf.

defensive position, as to stop the Persians advancing on Athens: advocates of locations elsewhere are rather cavalier in supposing that their 'good, defensive positions' nevertheless covered the main exit from the plain to the south. There is, in addition, a good water supply here, at Mati.

It has also been suggested that the Athenians protected their camp with an *abattis* of felled trees,[24] but the evidence for this is very weak. Cornelius Nepos (*Miltiades* 5.3) says that there were 'scattered trees' (*arbores ... rarae*) in the area where they eventually deployed for battle, and that their plan was that 'the enemy cavalry might be impeded by a line (or 'area') of trees' (*arborum tractu*). But this does not necessarily mean that the trees were to be felled and dragged into position, and the only other evidence for there being trees near the Greek camp is the enigmatic reference in the *Souda* to the Ionians 'climbing up on,' or 'coming up to, the trees' (ἀνελθόντας ἐπὶ τᾶ δένδρα), to signal to the Greeks that 'the cavalry was away' (see below, 59). There may well have been a grove near the *temenos* of Herakles, for Aischylos' epitaph, quoted in the ancient life attached to the manuscripts of his tragedies, called upon the 'grove of Marathon' (Μαραθώνιον ἄλσος) to bear witness to his valour. But this would have been a *sacred* grove, and the Athenians would not have dared to fell its trees. The use of an *abattis* to impede cavalry may seem obvious to us, but the only evidence for such tactics in the archaic and classical periods is Frontinus' reference (*Strategemata* 2.2.9) to Kleomenes' use of trees to protect his army from Hippias' Thessalian cavalry, and although this episode is close in time to 490, the evidence for it is very late.

The Persian failure to occupy the entrances to the plain, to attack the Athenians or to move rapidly on Athens after landing, has seemed a problem to some,[25] and some ingenious explanations have been advanced, including, as we have seen (above, 48–50), that the intention was to lure the Athenian army to Marathon, where it could be pinned down, while treachery delivered the city into Persian hands. Alternatively it has been suggested that the Persians did not have sufficient troops to secure all the entrances, or that they actually wanted the Athenians to try to fight them in the plain, or that their cavalry was in fact absent, and thus that they dared not try conclusions with the hoplites until it came. But all these surmises probably presuppose too high a degree of sophistication in Persian military thinking. Even if getting their army ashore was a comparatively simple exercise,[26] they may well have felt the need for a period of rest and recuperation after the operations at Eretria, and may simply have neglected to

---

Van der Veer, *op.cit.*, 304-6, and Hammond, 1988, 516 n.2. Hammond raises the point about the exposed position of the Greeks if the Herakleion lay where Vanderpool proposes in 1968, n.96. Van der Veer, 297, suggests that Pindar's description of the Herakleion as 'μυχῷ ἐν Μαραθῶνος' may refer to 'the oblong southern entrance into which the narrowing plain leads'.

24 Cf., e.g., Burn, 243; Hammond, 1968, 38, and 1988, 508; Green, 32. Hammond even has a 'creeping abattis' (1988, 511)! The words '*arborum tractu*' surely just mean 'by a tract (i.e. area) of trees', cf. Cicero, *Pro Plancio*, 9.22, and the emendation '*stratae*' for the '*rarae*' of the MSS (*Corn. Nepotis vitae cum Augusti Buchneri commentario*, Francot. a. Lipsiae, 1721), accepted by, e.g., Hammond, *locc.cit.*, is quite arbitrary – see Caspari, 1911, n.13. Van der Veer, *op.cit.* n.3 above, 307, accepts the 'scattered trees'; Shrimpton, *op.cit.* n.7 above, 21, interestingly suggests that Nepos may have got his 'trees' from the painting in the *Stoa Poikile*.

25 Berthold, *op.cit.* n.12 above, 92 and nn.55-6.

26 Cf. Berthold, *op.cit.*, 91-2.

secure the entrances to the plain through carelessness.[27] Even if the Athenians entered the plain and moved west along the foot of Agrieliki to a position on its slopes or at Vrana, the Persians may have ignored them, not so much for strategic or tactical reasons as through sheer inertia, particularly if their own main camp was some six or seven kilometres away, near the Great Marsh, in the north-eastern part of the plain.

Once the Athenians had taken up their position, wherever it was, Herodotos says (6.109), there was a division of opinion among their generals, half arguing that they should not engage the enemy because they were too few, the others, including Miltiades, that they should. In the end, he says, the argument was resolved by Miltiades' appealing to the polemarch, Kallimachos, who gave his casting-vote in favour of fighting. It is possible that this argument among the generals, or some part of it, has been misplaced from the debate in Athens whether to confront the enemy in the field or to defend the city,[28] but we have seen reason to doubt whether there was such a debate in Athens, and, in any case, the question at issue now was different. If the Athenian army was camped astride the main route to Athens, or even if its position only threatened any force attempting to use that route, it was arguable that it need do nothing until the Persians made a move. It is perhaps significant that in Herodotos' version of Miltiades' appeal to Kallimachos (6.109.3-6), his main argument is not a military one, though he does say that 'if the gods give us a fair chance, we are capable of winning the battle.' The main argument is political: 'if we do not engage now, I expect some great dissension will fall upon the Athenians and so shake their spirits that they will medize.'

There are other doubts, however, about this council-of-war. It is possible, for example, that Herodotos is anachronistic in saying that the polemarch merely had an equal vote with the *stratêgoi* at this time, and wrong to describe him as 'chosen by lot' (6.109.2). The Aristotelian *Constitution of the Athenians* (22.5) implies that the archons, of whom the polemarch was one, were still directly elected, and that the latter still had overriding authority. On the other hand, it may be the case that although the nine archons were still directly elected, they drew lots to determine which particular post each was to hold, and that the polemarch's function as 'leader' (ἡγεμών) of the army was largely ceremonial. Herodotos is, after all, consistent in giving the *stratêgoi* the major rôle throughout his account of the campaign, for it is they who are said to have sent Philippides to Sparta (6.105.1, 106.1). Even Kallimachos' post on the right

27 N.Whatley, *JHS* 84 (1964), 138-9; Hignett, 67.

28 For the possibility that Herodotos misplaced at least part of the argument, see Gomme, *Phoenix* 6 (1953), 77ff.; Burn, 241 n.12; but see Shrimpton, *op.cit.* n.7 above, 24 n.11. Hignett, 57 n.1, argues that since Herodotos says 'the worse of the views was prevailing' (ἐνίκα ἡ χείρων τῶν γνωμέων: 6.109.2), there must have been a majority in favour of not fighting. But the words 'ἐγίνοντο δίχα αἱ γνῶμαι' and 'ὡς δὲ δίχα τε ἐγίνοντο' surely imply that the views were *equally* divided, and since this produced stalemate, the worse view *was* prevailing – see Hammond, 1988, 508. Shrimpton, *op.cit.*, 25-6, suggests that it was really the arrival of the Plataians which tipped the balance in favour of fighting, but this seems unlikely. Francis and Vickers, *op. cit.* n.19 above, esp. 110ff., accepting this, suggest that the Oinoe painting somehow indicated the role of Miltiades in getting the decision to fight taken, but it is difficult to see how a painting could have done this.

wing (6.111.1), which was the traditional position for the commander-in-chief, may not be significant for his actual powers.[29]

It is, indeed, likely that there was controversy soon after the battle about who had been principally responsible for the victory. No doubt Miltiades' family and supporters made much of his part at his trial after his failure at Paros (6.132-7: see below), and Kallimachos' family may have countered with the enigmatic dedication to Athena on the acropolis, parts of which have survived (ML 18). Argument will also have continued to rage into the next generation, for Perikles' father, Xanthippos, was Miltiades' accuser (6.136.1), and Perikles was later an opponent of Miltiades' son, Kimon, who paid his father's fine (cf. 6.136.3; Plutarch, *Kimon* 14.5, etc.). But although Kimon also eventually fell from grace, and was ostracized at the end of the 460s, by then his immense popularity and influence may well have secured his father's niche in the hall of fame forever. On the other hand, even if the polemarch did still exercise an overriding authority, and should, therefore, in the end, be regarded as responsible for the victory, he would have been a fool not to listen to the advice of his ten most senior officers, and although Herodotos is probably wrong to imply (6.103.1) that Miltiades had some kind of superior position, it may well be the case that he was the most influential of the *stratêgoi*.[30]

Even after the polemarch had given his casting-vote for fighting, Herodotos implies (6.110), there was a delay of several days, since each of the *stratêgoi* in favour of fighting surrendered his day-of-command to Miltiades, and he chose to fight on the day his own came round. Presumably we are to understand, too, that if any of the generals who were *not* in favour of fighting, had a day of command in the meantime, they also refused to fight. Thus the maximum delay would have been nine days, if Miltiades' previous day of command had been that of the day before the war-council. This is a most implausible story, if only because there is no good evidence that when later more than one *stratêgos* commanded an Athenian force, they took it in turns to exercise overall command.[31] Nevertheless, there is no compelling reason to doubt that there was a delay of

29 See Rhodes, 1981, 264f. & 273. E.B.Harrison, *GRBS* 12 (1971), 21 and n.42, following Hammond, 1969, 111ff., argues that all that *AP* 22.2 means is that Kallimachos had some ceremonial and traditional function as 'leader' (ἡγεμών) of the army, but this is, plainly, *not* what is meant. For a criticism of Hammond's views on the command-structure, and the controversies about who was responsible for the victory see P.J.Bicknell, *AC* 39 (1970), 427ff. On the Kallimachos epigrams see ML 18; B.B.Shefton, *BSA* 45 (1950), 140-64, 47 (1952), 278; P.Amandry, 'Sur les "épigrammes de Marathon"', in *Θεωρία: Festschrift für W.-H.Schuchhardt* (ed. F.Eckstein, Baden-Baden, 1960), 1ff.; and E.B.Harrison, *op.cit.*

30 Herodotos uses the phrase 'of whom Miltiades was the tenth' (τῶν ὁ δέκατος ἦν Μιλτιάδης: 6.103.1) which, it has been claimed, implies that Miltiades had some kind of overriding authority as in the case of similar phrases in Thucydides (1.116.1, 2.13.1) – cf. Hignett, *History of the Athenian Constitution* (Oxford, 1952), 353. But K.J. Dover (*JHS* 80, 1960, 61-77) argues that such phrases do not mean that the *stratêgos* so designated was superior to his colleagues.

31 Diodoros (13.97.6 and 106.1) implies it happened at Arginousai and Aigospotamoi, but Xenophon says nothing of this, and there is no hint of it in Thucydides, e.g., when Alkibiades Nikias and Lamachos could not agree about the strategy to be adopted in Sicily (cf. 6.47ff.). Hammond, 1968, 11ff., and 1988, 508, accepts the story. Shrimpton, *op.cit.* n.7 above, 25-6,

several days between the arrival of the Athenians at Marathon and the battle. Admittedly the secondary sources have the battle take place either on the day the Athenians arrived (Isokrates 4.87; *Souda* s.v. Hippias), or the next day (Nepos, *Miltiades* 5.3; Plutarch, *Moralia* 350e). But this is probably due to the rhetorical tradition which came to infect so much ancient historical writing, and cannot really stand against Herodotos' *factual* testimony, however absurd his motivation may seem to be.

Even if we believe Herodotos to the extent of accepting that the Greeks had decided to take the offensive – which is by no means certain (see below, 61–2) – it is still not hard to find reasons why they should have waited. It may, for example, have been due to simple inertia, as was perhaps the case with the Persians, or the Greeks may have been wary of trying conclusions with an enemy strong in cavalry and missile-troops on an open plain,[32] though in the end this is almost certainly what they did (see below). But there is a far more obvious explanation, namely that they were waiting for the Spartans. Although it seems unlikely that Philippides himself had returned with the news that the Spartans would march after the full moon, despite what later legend said,[33] one would have thought that some means of getting so vital a piece of information to the Athenians could have been contrived. In any case, there was everything to be said for waiting until either they heard the Spartans were not coming, or the latter arrived, and little or no point in fighting in the meantime, unless it became absolutely necessary.

In the end, of course, the battle did take place before the Spartans arrived, and it is difficult to see why, if, as Herodotos implies, it was the Athenians who took the offensive. The theory that has gained most favour in recent years is that the Persian cavalry, or a substantial part of the Persian army including the cavalry, was, for some reason, removed from the scene of operations, and that when the Greeks learned of this, they decided to attack.[34]

The only explicit evidence for this is the comment by the *Souda* on the phrase 'the horsemen are away' (χωρὶς ἱππεῖς), that 'when Datis invaded Attica, they say the Ionians, on his setting off, climbing up on (or 'coming up to: ἀνελθόντας) the trees, informed the Athenians that the horsemen were away, and that Miltiades, realising their departure, thereupon engaged and won the victory; whence, [they say] the proverb is used of those who break ranks.' It is held that this is supported by the absence of any reference to cavalry in Herodotos' account of the battle, despite his insistence that it was because of the suitability of Marathon for cavalry operations that Hippias had guided the Persians there in the first place (6.102). It is sometimes also argued that the Persians

suggests that the four *stratêgoi* who agreed with Miltiades just co-operated with him and hence appeared to have handed their commands over to him.

32 Creasy, *The Fifteen Decisive Battles of the World* (London & New York, 1911, reprint), 11, and Munro, 1899, 189.

33 Hammond, 1988, 508, assumes that the Athenians knew from Philippides that the Spartans would not be there for several days, but this is most implausible – see n.14 above.

34 The variations on these arguments are too numerous to mention, but see, e.g., Munro, 1899, 189ff.; Grundy, 183ff.; HW ii 360ff.; Caspari, 100ff.; Burn, 246ff. (n.28 on 247f., points out that the *Souda* is nearer our time than Marathon); Hammond, 1968, 13ff., and now 1988, 511; Pritchett, *Studies in Ancient Greek Topography 2 (Battlefields)* (Berkeley, 1969), 8-9; Green, 34f. Hignett, 66ff., produces some strong counter-arguments.

could hardly have got away after their defeat, with the loss of only seven ships, unless a large part of their forces had already been re-embarked.

Exciting as this story is, however, it rests on dubious grounds. In the first place, the *Souda* is a very late source. It seems to be a compilation which refers to people of possibly as late as the end of the eleventh century AD, and most of it can certainly not be earlier than the tenth century. Thus it is nearer our own time than the battle, and the question should be asked, though it is usually avoided, how so vital a piece of evidence came to be preserved for something like fifteen hundred years, when it was apparently not known to any of the writers who referred to the battle in the intervening centuries. Unless and until some convincing explanation of this miracle is produced, this 'evidence' should be viewed with the greatest suspicion, and it is not even at all clear what it means. There is the problem of how exactly the Ionians are supposed to have conveyed the information, and there is the final, enigmatic remark which suggests that the saying had something to do with 'desertion in the face of the enemy', rather than a piece of tactical manoeuvring.[35]

There is also some positive evidence that the Persian cavalry did take part in the battle. Pausanias says that at night you could hear horses whinnying at Marathon (1.32.3), which at least implies that in the second century AD local legend held that the Persian cavalry had been there, and Pausanias' contemporary, the orator Aristeides, claims that the Athenians captured some horses (*Panathenaïkos* 106-8 Behr). It is even possible that Persian horsemen were depicted in the painting of the battle put up in the *Stoa Poikile*, probably within some thirty years of the battle, for a case has been made out for believing that the surviving 'Brescia Relief' derives from that painting.[36]

As for the arguments drawn from Herodotos, they are not nearly as cogent as they may seem. He himself clearly did believe that the Persian cavalry was present at least up to the point when the Greeks began their advance, for otherwise there is no sense in his remark that the Persians thought them mad to be attacking *without* cavalry and archers (6.112.2).[37] This holds good whether he derived his information from a good source (see below, 67), or if, as seems more likely, he simply tried to *imagine* what the Persians might have thought. He could hardly have suggested they thought the Greeks mad to attack without cavalry, if he believed they had no cavalry themselves. The most probable explanation for the absence of the cavalry from his account of the battle is that

---

35 Shrimpton, *op.cit.* n.7 above, 20-2 & 37, has, I think, the best explanation of the *Souda*-passage. J.A.S.Evans, *Florilegium* 6 (1984), 1ff., suggests that the cavalry was absent securing the road to Athens, but this is impossible if the Greek camp was astride the road, and unlikely in any case.

36 For the view that the Brescia Relief derives from the painting in the Stoa Poikile see E.G.Pemberton, *AJA* 76 (1972), 303ff., and E.B.Harrison, *op.cit.* n.29 above, 353ff.

37 See Macan (1895) i 370, & ii 161; Whatley, *op.cit.* n.27 above, 135; and *pace* H.C.Avery, *TAPA* 103 (1972), 15ff. Avery's ingenious argument that the Persian failure to attack the Greeks was due to the absence of their cavalry – falls to the ground if it was in fact the Persians who by advancing down the road to Athens made the battle virtually inevitable, and, incidentally, Herodotos 9.59.1 does not prove, as he claims (21), that 'the Persians could attack the Greeks on the run': the passage refers to the Persian advance across the Asopos on the morning of Plataia; when they eventually caught up with the Greeks, they planted their shields and fought a static battle (9.61.3).

it actually played no part. The speed of the Greek advance would have precluded its usual hit-and-run tactics, which required a static target to be effective, and there was certainly no place for such cavalry in a hand-to-hand encounter. At Plataia, similarly, the Persian cavalry plays a part in the pursuit of the retreating Greeks (9.57.3), and reappears to protect the fugitives (9.68). But Herodotos makes no reference to it in his account of the actual battle: the only cavalry there consists of the thousand picked Persians around Mardonios himself, on his white horse (9.63.1), who are, presumably, the thousand horsemen he had chosen at the end of 480 (8.113.2).

The fact that the Greeks only captured seven Persian ships also does not prove that a substantial part of the army had been re-embarked before the battle. As we shall see, the way the battle went and the route the fugitives will have taken back to the ships, provide a perfectly adequate explanation of why so few ships were taken. They were probably not beached, but moored stern-first, close off shore – Kynegeiros lost his life clutching the stern of one of them (6.114) – and could easily have escaped once they had taken up as many soldiers as were able to clamber on board. Obviously it would have been difficult, if not impossible, to reload horses once the Athenians reached the beach. But if, as seems likely, the cavalry had been stationed on the flanks of the infantry, it presumably fled with, or was carried away by, the fleeing infantry wings, and would have had plenty of time to re-embark while the Athenians dealt with the infantry in the centre, and then fought their way to the beach-head. The horses Aristeides claims the Athenians captured could well have been found straying on the beach, abandoned by their riders.

There is a much simpler explanation for the fact that the battle eventually took place before the Spartans arrived than the elaborate hypotheses put forward by modern commentators, and that is that the Persians at last began to make a move. Because of Herodotos' story about the Athenian war-council, and because his account of the battle has the Greeks famously advance to the attack, we have become accustomed to assuming that it was the Greeks who took the initiative. But, as we have seen, the story of the war-council is dubious at several points, and we should remember that there is a distinction between taking the initiative at a strategic level, and taking it at a tactical level.

Strategically speaking it was the Persians who were on the offensive. They may have waited to see whether Hippias would, after all, attract the local support he had no doubt promised; they may possibly have been waiting for some message from Athens, though the shield-signal shown after the battle – if, indeed, there was such a signal – can hardly have been what they were expecting (see below, 72–3); possibly they even knew or guessed that the Spartans would soon be on their way, and decided to make their move before they arrived, as Cornelius Nepos says (*Miltiades* 5.4), and Diodoros evidently implied (see the fragment of 11.27.3). However, modern commentators have been too prone to assume that the Persians knew all about the Spartans. Why should they have known that the Athenians had asked for Spartan help in the first place, let alone that the Spartans had agreed to give it? After all, the last time the Spartans had had any dealings with Hippias, it had been *they* who had been proposing to restore him (5.91)! But, sooner or later, whatever reasons they may have had for delaying, it was the Persians who had to make a move if they were to accomplish their objective of bringing Athens under their control.

The Athenians, on the other hand, had little or nothing to gain by risking battle, so long as the enemy was confined to a comparatively remote corner of their land, and, strategically, they were on the defensive. But this need not have prevented them from seizing the tactical initiative once battle was forced upon them. Later, at any rate, Greek armies normally advanced to fight, once they were committed to battle, and at Plataia, in 479, both the Tegeates and the Lakedaimonians were to advance on the final morning (9.62.1). At that battle it was the Persians who fought from behind a static hedge of shields (9.61.3 & 62.20), though it was certainly they who had taken the initiative at the strategic level, and it may well be the case that they fought like this at Marathon, though Herodotos gives no such details.

There are two further reasons for believing that it was the Persians who, strategically speaking, made the first move at Marathon. Firstly, if it is true that their base-camp was near the 'Great Marsh' at the north-eastern end of the plain, and that the battle was fought in the vicinity of the *Soros* (see below, 65), they would have had to advance some four or five kilometres before battle was joined. In other words, it would have appeared to the Greeks that the enemy was finally on the move, and, if so, they really had to fight. The alternatives were either to retreat, harassed all the way by cavalry and archers, if they were to cover the route to Athens, or, if their position was not on that route, to allow the enemy to march on the city unopposed.

The second reason for believing that it was the Persians who took the strategic initiative comes from Herodotos himself. He says that on the day of battle, the Athenian centre was formed few ranks deep 'in order to make the army equal to the Median army' (τὸ στρατόπεδον ἐξισούμενον τῷ Μηδικῷ στρατοπέδῳ: 6.11.3), and this surely implies that it was the Persians who were 'first in the field'. It has been argued that the Persians were unprepared for the Greek attack on the ground that Herodotos says that when they saw them 'coming at the run, they prepared to receive them' (ὁρῶντες δρόμῳ ἐπίοντας παρεσκευάζοντο ὡς δεξόμενοι: 6.112.2).[38] But this does not mean that it was only then that the Persians began to don their armour and grab their weapons, but that they readied themselves – dressed ranks, put arrow to string and so on – to receive the Greek attack.

It was probably, then, when they saw the Persians moving south towards the southern exit from the plain that the Athenians and Plataians began to prepare for battle. If their camp was somewhere near Vrana, they presumably advanced eastwards as quickly as possible so as to bring the enemy to battle before he could reach the exit; if their camp was at the exit, they would only have needed to move far enough to deploy their battle line. As was the custom at the time, Herodotos says (6.111.1), the polemarch, Kallimachos, commanded the right wing, and 'with him leading, the *phylai* took station successively as they were numbered' (ἡγεόμενου δὲ τούτου ἐξεδέκοντο ὡς ἀριθμέοντο αἱ φυλαί: *ibid.*). This possibly means that after the polemarch had taken his position, the *phylai* deployed to his left, which was the way the Spartan army

38 Shrimpton, *op.cit.* n.7 above, 28ff., has the most elaborate explanation for the Persian cavalry's failure to affect the outcome, despite its presence, but his whole reconstruction depends on the belief that the Persians were unprepared for the Greek attack (26-7). This is belied by Herodotos' statement (6.111.3) that the Athenians adjusted the length of their line in order to make it as long as that of the Persians.

deployed in the 4th century (*LP* 11.8). It may also mean that the ten regiments (later called '*taxeis*'), based on the ten groups or *phylai* into which the adult, male citizens of Athens were divided, took station in the fixed order, known from later inscriptions (e.g. *CIA* i 443, 446, 447): *Erectheïs, Aigeïs, Pandionis, Leontis, Akamantis, Oineïs, Kekropis, Hippothoöntis, Aiantis* and *Antiochis*. However, Plutarch (*Moralia* 628d), referring to the 'elegies of Aischylos', says that *Aiantis*, to which Kallimachos belonged, was on the right, and not only is Aischylos good evidence, if he took part in the battle, as his epitaph and tradition claimed (cf. Pausanias 1.21.2), but it might seem natural for the polemarch's *phylê* to have the post of honour.

An easy way to resolve the discrepancy would be to suppose that *Aiantis* was placed on the right in this instance, out of order, but that the other *phylai* followed in the normal order. Elsewhere, however, Plutarch also claims (*Aristeides* 5.3) that *Leontis* and *Antiochis* were in the centre, and although this would have been true of *Leontis* if it was preceded by *Aiantis, Erectheïs, Aigeïs* and *Pandionis*, it would not have been true of *Antiochis*, which should have been on the extreme left. An ingenious suggestion to get round this is that the ten *phylai* first advanced in two columns – *Aiantis, Erechtheïs, Aigeïs, Pandionis* and *Leontis* on the right, *Akamantis, Oineïs, Kekropis, Hippothoöntis and Antiochis* on the left – and that each column then swung outwards, so that *Leontis* and *Antiochis* ended up in the centre.[39]

But this presupposes a level of training which was still regarded as beyond most Greek armies in Xenophon's time (cf. *LP* 11.5-10), and, in any case, the passage in which Plutarch claims that *Leontis* and *Antiochis* were in the centre, is highly rhetorical and cannot be literally true. In it Plutarch states that Aristeides, who belonged to *Antiochis*, and Themistokles, who belonged to *Leontis*, fought side by side. Even Herodotos' statement that the *phylai* 'succeeded as they were numbered' may be anachronistic, for he was writing fifty or sixty years after the battle, when the order of *phylai* had become fixed. But at least there is no reason to doubt him when he says that the Plataians were on the left of the line (6.111.1).[40] He adds that from that time onwards, 'whenever the Athenians perform sacrifices at their quadrennial festivals, the Athenian herald prays that blessings may fall upon the Plataians at the same time as upon the Athenians' (6.111.2).

Although it is not mentioned by Herodotos, there is no particular reason to doubt Plutarch's statement (*Aristeides* 5.1-2) that Aristeides was one of the *stratêgoi* at Marathon. He was a prominent man who was archon in 489/88 and ostracized in 483 – the ultimate cachet for an Athenian. Themistokles, too, may have been a colleague, as the story of his fighting alongside Aristeides perhaps implies. He was also one of the most prominent men in Athens at the time, having almost certainly already been archon in 493/2. Herodotos provides us with the name of one of the other *stratêgoi*, Stesilaos, son of Thrasylaos, who was killed in the battle (6.114), so that, with Miltiades, we may know the names of four of the ten. But Plutarch's statement (*Moralia* 305b-c) that Kynegeiros and Polyzelos were also *stratêgoi*, is obviously not to be trusted. 'Polyzelos' is probably a mistake for 'Epizelos', the man who was blinded in the battle, and that he

39 Cf. Munro *CAH*[1] iv, 246.

40 There is no evidence for the view of H.Stein, *Herodotos* (Berlin, 1893-1908), ch.103 n., that Miltiades' *phyle*, *Oineïs* (cf. Plutarch, *Kimon* 18.4) was on the left of the Athenian line.

and Kynegeiros were *stratêgoi* is probably just embroidery of the stories Herodotos tells about them (6.117.2-3 & 114).[41]

Later in the fifth century Athenian hoplites seem normally to have been drawn up eight deep, where their depth is specified (cf., e.g., Thucydides 4.94.1 & 6.67.1). But at Marathon, Herodotos says (6.111.3), 'in order to make their army equal in length to the Median army, its centre was formed few ranks deep, and there the army was weakest, but each wing was strong in number'. Unfortunately, he does not give details, but it might be the case, for example, that the wings remained eight deep, while the centre was thinned to four deep. Even then we do not know how many *phylai* constituted the centre and each wing, but presumably there were something like two *phylai* together with the Plataians on the left wing, five *phylai* in the centre, and the remaining three *phylai* on the right. If the figures given by most of the secondary sources for the Greek army are roughly correct (i.e. 9000 Athenians and 1000 Plataians), and we allow about 90 centimetres per man, we would get the following frontages: left wing 315 metres, centre c.1000, right wing c.300, total c.1615 metres.[42]

Modern commentators have see in this last-minute thinning of the centre a brilliant piece of tactical thinking, and Miltiades is usually held responsible.[43] But if Herodotos is to be believed, the move was purely defensive, and, incidentally, he says nothing of Miltiades here. The Athenians, in other words, were not thinking in terms of smashing the enemy wings and going on to crush their centre by a 'double envelopment', but purely of preventing their own line from being outflanked. The phrase translated 'each wing was strong in mumber' above (τὸ δὲ κέρας ἑκάτερον ἔρρωτο πλήθει), does *not* mean that each wing was *strengthened*, but merely that it 'was strong' in comparison with the now weakened centre. It is even possible, though Herodotos does not say so, that an additional step was taken to protect the flanks of the hoplites. Pausanias (1.32.3, cf.7.15.7) says that there was a grave at Marathon said to be that of the slaves who had fallen in the battle, and it is possible that the soldier-servants, probably mostly slaves, who will have accompanied the hoplites, were deployed on either flank, though their military value was probably not very great.[44]

---

41 For the *stratêgoi* of 490 see Bicknell, *op.cit.* n.29 above; for Themistokles' archonship Podlecki, 196; Lenardon, 35f. It is not certain whether the *stratêgoi* actually commanded the *taxeis* at this time. From the time of the Peloponnesian War at the latest they were commanded by *taxiarchoi* (cf., e.g., Aristophanes, *Acharnians* 569; Thucydides 4.4.1, 7.60.2, 8.92.4), but perhaps before the diminution of the polemarch's powers brought about by the use of the lot for their selection, the *stratêgoi* were simply the commanders of the *taxeis* – cf. Wilamowitz, *Aristoteles und Athen*, ii (Berlin, 1893), 88, 108, and B.Jordan, *University of California Classical Studies* 13 (1975), 240 and n.79; *contra*: P.J.Rhodes, 1981, 684-5, on *AP* 61.3.

42 Cf. Macan (1895) i 369; Pritchett, *University of California Publications in Classical Archaeology* IV, 2 (1960), 144-5, allows 36 inches per man; cf. Van der Veer, *op.cit.* n.3 above, 310.

43 Cf., e.g., Caspari, 103; HW ii 112; Burn, 249; Green, 37; Shrimpton, *op.cit.* n.7 above, *passim*.

44 Cf. Hauvette, 247 and n.5; Delbrück, 77 and 81 n.3. Pausanias (7.15.7) says that in 146 Diaios imitated Miltiades in setting slaves free, after the (2nd) battle of Chaironeia.

Unfortunately, Herodotos gives even fewer details for the Persian deployment, beyond saying that the Persians themselves and the Sakai were in the centre (6.113.1). But were these infantry or cavalry, or a mixture of both? Were there other infantry and cavalry to left and right, and where were the Greeks from Asia Minor and the islands, or were they left to guard the ships? It has been argued that the Sakai at least were cavalry,[45] but this is not necessarily the case: although Sakaian cavalry was highly regarded (cf. 9.71.1), they certainly also provided infantry in 480 (7.64.2), and some of them served as marines on Persian warships (7.184.2), which suggests that their infantry, too, were highly regarded. On the whole, it is probably best to assume that the Persian cavalry was on the flanks of the infantry line, as was normal in ancient warfare.

The battle was almost certainly fought in the vicinity of the *Soros*, the ancient mound which still dominates the southern half of the plain. This is where the ashes of the Athenian dead were deposited, and it seems likely that the bodies were burned near where most of the dead had fallen, that is, presumably, where the Athenian centre had broken. Moreover, arrow-heads of an Asiatic type have been picked up in the vicinity of the mound.[46] But it is not possible to be certain how the two armies were aligned.[47] Herodotos' statement that the victorious Persian centre pursued the Athenian centre 'inland' (ἐς τὴν μεσόγαιαν: 6.113.1) would naturally mean that the Persians had their backs to the sea. However, Pausanias (1.32.6) says that when they fled, they stumbled into the marsh, and this is confirmed by his description of the picture of the battle in the *Stoa Poikile* (1.15.4). This rather implies that the Persians had their backs to the marsh, and therefore their left flank to the sea. Another way of approaching the problem – which, unfortunately, produces the same opposite results! – is from the point of view of where one thinks the Greek camp was. If it was in the vicinity of Vrana, it would be natural to imagine the Greeks advancing from there towards the sea; if their camp was at the southern exit from the plain, however, it would be more natural to imagine them advancing with their right flank towards the sea. There is also, for what it is worth, Cornelius Nepos' description of the Athenian position as 'below the mountain's spurs' (*sub montis radicibus: Miltiades* 5.3), though unfortunately the text of the rest of the passage is dubious.

Certainty is not possible, but if, as seems likely, the Greek camp was at the southern exit from the plain, it is not impossible that they deployed to their left, in the normal way, with the lower slopes of Agrieliki at their backs, particularly if, as is possible, the Brexisa marsh did exist in 490. This has the merit of conforming with what Cornelius Nepos says: they would be 'below the mountain's spurs' and would be protected – at the

---

45 D.Gillis, *Collaboration with the Persians* (*Historia* Einzelschriften 34), 27, argues that if the Ionians had actually fought at Marathon, Herodotos would have said how well or how badly, but this seems a weak *argumentum e silentio*. It is Kromayer's view (*Abhandlung des Sächs. Akad.* 34, 1921, 15-9; cf. *AS* iv (Berlin, 1924-31), 13-6) that the Persians and Sakai in the centre were cavalry. Burn, 250, suggests, and Shrimpton (*op.cit.* n.7 above, 29-30) argues, that the Sakai, at least, were cavalry.

46 That the *Soros* was where the cremated remains of the Athenian dead were buried was first shown by Staes, *ADelt* 1890, 65-7, 123-32; 1891, 34, 67 & 97; *AM* 18 (1893), 46-63 and plates 2-5. For the arrow-heads cf. Staes, *locc.cit.*, and Hammond, 1973, 172ff.

47 For a very clear exposition of the alternative alignments of the battle-lines see Van der Veer, *op.cit.* n.3 above, 310-8. I prefer his 'Battle Position B', 313-5.

rear – 'by the height of the mountains' (cf. '*ut et montium altitudine tegerentur*'). What Nepos means by saying that their plan was 'also that the enemy's cavalry might be impeded by a line (or 'area') of trees' (*et arborum tractu equitatus hostium impediretur*) is more problematical. But if the reading '*namque arbores multis locis erant rarae*' ('for there were scattered trees in many places'), just before, is correct, it seems more likely that the author is talking about trees growing naturally, not about some kind of artificial *abattis*, as we have seen (above, 56). If so, there is obviously no means of telling where such trees might have been growing in antiquity.

To locate the Greek line at the foot of Agrieliki also has the merit of putting it almost exactly 1600 metres from the *Soros*, which is the distance Herodotos says separated the two armies (6.112.1). Finally, it would mean that the Greeks were facing north-east, the Persians south-west, so that when the Greek centre was driven back, it could be said to be driven 'inland', at least in the sense that it was driven away from the sea, and when the Persians fled, they would have fled in the direction of the marsh.

After reorganizing their centre, the Greeks performed the usual sacrifice before battle, and then launched themselves at the enemy. A late source (Schol. Aristeides 3.566 ed. Dindorf) has Miltiades give the command, and the fourth century orator, Aischines, says that in the Marathon-painting Miltiades was shown urging on his countrymen (3.186). But this may be part of the Miltiades-legend: in reality, why should we doubt that the polemarch, Kallimachos, gave the order to advance? Herodotos insists that the advance was 'at the double' (δρόμῳ), although there were no less than eight stades (c.1600 metres) between the armies, and this statement has caused some controversy. One eminent German authority, for example, has stated categorically that 'such a run is a physical impossibility: a heavily equipped unit can cover at most 400 to 500 feet (120 to 150 metres) at a run without completely exhausting its strength and falling into disorder,' and more recent experiments carried out in America have tended to confirm his view.[48] Others have suggested that 'δρόμῳ' was simply a technical term for 'quick march', as opposed to 'βάδην' for 'slow march', or even that the whole story of the charge is a myth arising from the festival of the *Boedromia*.[49]

But there really is no need either to reject entirely what Herodotos says, or to resort to forced interpretations of what he might mean. Presumably there was a strong tradition that at least some part of the charge was 'at the double', and by the time Herodotos heard the story, it might well have been extended to the full 'eight stades' in the popular imagination, whereas, in reality, it had only been over the last part of the distance. Alternatively Herodotos, hearing that the charge had been 'at the double' and that the distance separating the two armies had been eight stades when the advance began, may himself have mistakenly assumed the Greeks had run the full distance.

---

48 Delbrück, 74 – on 86 he quotes the Prussian *Vorschriften über des Turnen der Infanterie* – and see now W.Donlan & J.Thompson, *CJ* 71 (1976), 339ff., and *CW* 72 (1979), 419f. Delbrück, whose 'reconstruction' of the battle relies on Nepos, departs too far from Herodotos to be worth serious consideration. He has the Persians attack the Athenians deployed across the mouth of the Vrana valley, and thinks that the 'eight stades' was the distance over which the Athenians pursued the defeated enemy, with the *Soros* marking the place where the last of them fell in the pursuit (76, and *Klio* 17, 1917, 221ff.).

49 Grundy, n. on 188; Kromayer, *AS*, 11 and n.1; Gomme, *HCT* iii, 544f.; Burn, 249. But see W.W.How, *CQ* 13 (1919), 40-2.

There was, of course, a very good reason why they should have begun to break into a double as they approached the Persian line. Probably at anything from between 300 and 200 metres, they would have begun to come under fire from the Persian archers, firing at extreme range, and this fire would probably have begun to get increasingly effective from about 175 metres.[50] Before one of the innumerable skirmishes fought by Xenophon and his comrades on the long march home from Kounaxa, Xenophon ordered his men to break into a double when the first sling-stones rattled against their shields (*Anabasis* 4.3.39), but we do not even have to assume that any such orders were issued at Marathon. At Kounaxa some of Xenophon's fellow mercenaries – far more experienced troops than the citizen-militia at Marathon – had difficulty in restraining themselves from getting ahead of the line, and had to be told that they were not running a race (*Anabasis* 1.8.18-9), so it is quite likely that the Greeks at Marathon spontaneously broke into a double as the first arrows began to fall among them.

Herodotos says that this was the first occasion he knew on which Greeks had charged at the double, and although later it became quite normal – Thucydides implies that the slow advance of the Spartans at Mantineia, in 418, was unusual (5.70) – it may be the case that the Greeks at Marathon were the first known to have done it. After all, although archers and slingers were almost certainly already employed by Greek armies, it is clear that they were of little importance. This may well have been the first time that mainland hoplites, apart from the few that had fought the Persians outside Ephesos during the Ionian revolt, had faced an army largely composed of archers. But Herodotos does not give the Asiatic Greeks their due when he also claims that the Greeks at Marathon were the first to 'endure seeing the Median dress and the men clad in it' (6.112.3), though he may well be right to say that 'until then, even the name of the Medes was a thing of dread to hear.'

Herodotos also claims that the Persians thought the Athenians mad and doomed to destruction, 'seeing that they were few and those coming on at the double with no cavalry in support nor archers' (6.112.2). It has been suggested that he got this ultimately from Persian prisoners, or from Greeks who had been present on the Persian side.[51] But although it is more likely that he merely imagined what the Persians might have felt, at least what he says surely proves that he himself assumed that the Persian cavalry was present (see above, 60). In reality, moreover, the Persians may well have been disconcerted by the Greek advance, though it is going too far to suggest, as one modern commentator does, that what Herodotos says about their reaction derives from

---

50 Cf. Grundy, n. on 188; F.Schachermeyr, *Historische Zeitschrift* 172 (1951), 28. W.M.McLeod, *Phoenix* 19 (1965), 1ff., concludes (8) that the effective range of Persian bows would have been 160-175 metres, but that the Athenians would have come under fire from between 200 and 300 yards away (13). Hammond, 1968, n.27 on 17, argues that this is too far, and thinks 150 metres about right for the 'effective range', but see McLeod's reply in *JHS* 90 (1970), 197-8.

51 Whatley, *loc.cit.* n.27 above, suggests Herodotos' remarks came from a Persian prisoner. Avery, who thinks they may have come from one of the Greeks with Hippias (*op.cit.* n.37 above, 15 n.2), too readily assumes that the Persians really did think as Herodotos says they did - cf., e.g., 'The *Persians* [my italics] use very strong language in their comments on the Greek attack' (18), and 'when the *Persians* [again, my italics] enumerate the reasons why the Greeks exhibit a complete and destructive madness ...' (21).

what Athenian participants had seen on their faces and that it was really alarm![52] Their tactics, as we have seen, probably depended on their being able to pour arrow-fire into an enemy until he disintegrated, whereupon they could close and finish the job with spear and sword. But here, perhaps for the first time, as Herodotos says, was an enemy coming on at the double, giving the archers time for possibly only 10-20 volleys, before the hoplites were on them.[53]

The fighting, Herodotos says (6.113.1), lasted a long time, though Aristophanes surely exaggerates when he implies it went on until evening (*Wasps* 1085: see below). In the centre, where the Persians themselves and the Sakai were positioned, and where the Greek line was thin, the barbarians got the upper hand, and, 'breaking through, pursued [the Athenians] inland'. Both the Persians and the Sakai were armed with bows, whether they were cavalry or infantry (7.61.1, cf. 84; 7.64.2, cf. 86.2), so the arrow-fire is likely to have been heaviest here. Presumably the Athenians, perhaps only four deep, ground to a halt and broke before the spears of the Persians and axes (cf. 'σαγάρις': 7.64.2) of the Sakai, when they closed. We do not know how far the Greek centre was driven back, but sooner or later the survivors would have found themselves on the slopes of Agrieliki, if they had started with that hill at their backs, and here they might have found some measure of safety.

But meanwhile, on the wings, the Athenians and Plataians had been victorious (6.113.1). This was possibly because the Persian wings consisted of less reliable troops, perhaps even partly of Greeks whose hearts were not really in the business, and who, being without bows, and armed more or less like their opponents, had no means of slowing their advance. If the Persian cavalry had been stationed on the flanks of the infantry line, it may have been carried away in the rout. One might have expected it to have slowed the enemy advance by its usual harassing tactics (cf. 9.18.1, 22 & 49.3), but it, too, may have been disconcerted by the speed of the Greek charge, and since it consisted of mounted archers and javelineers, it could not close with hoplites and hope to win.

Normally such a success would have been followed by the hoplites' streaming off in pursuit,[54] but on this occasion, Herodotos says (6.113.2), the victorious Athenians and Plataians 'let the defeated part of the barbarians run away, and, having gathered the wings together (συναγαγόντες τὰ κέρεα), continued the fight against those who had broken through their centre'. It is sometimes assumed that this means that the wings pivoted round to join up in the rear of the Persian centre,[55] but this seems to be belied by

---

52 Shrimpton, *op.cit.* n.7 above, 27.

53 This is the answer to Delbrück's argument (73) that if the battle had been fought in the open plain, the Greeks would have been defeated. Donlan and Thompson, *op.cit.* n.48 above, 342, estimate that the Athenians would have been under fire 'for considerably less than two minutes'; for speed of fire see Robert Hardy, *Longbow* (Cambridge, 1976), 68.

54 Cf., e.g., the 1000 Argives and the Mantineians at 1st Mantineia in 418 (Thucydides 5.72.3), and the Thebans at 2nd Koroneia (Xenophon, *Hellenika* 4.3.18).

55 Liddell & Scott[9] *s.v.* συνάγω II 2, for the passage in question, give the meaning '*draw together*, so as to make the extremities meet,' and cf. Hammond, 1988, 512. Burn, 250, says 'the two wings converged and attacked those who had broken through their centre,' Van der Veer (*op.cit.* n.3 above, 319) that 'both Greek wings ... drew together into a single unit. They closed in on the Persian centre ... so as to enclose it as it were in a pincer movement.'

Herodotos' statement that after the victorious Greek wings had defeated the Persian centre in turn, 'they pursued the fleeing Persians, cutting them down until reaching the sea ...' (φεύγουσι δὲ τοῖσι Πέρσῃσι εἵποντο κόπτοντες, ἐς ὃ ἐπὶ τὴν θάλασσαν ἀπικόμενοι...: *ibid.*). If the Persian centre had been taken in the rear, it is difficult to see how any of them could have got away, particularly in the direction of the sea. A second, theoretical possibility is that the Greek wings pivoted *back* to form a line behind their own defeated centre. This would have meant that the Persian centre, when it in turn was defeated, could have escaped, but it seems improbable that citizen-militia could have carried out so complicated a manoeuvre.[56] Other commentators seem to dodge the issue, sometimes by apparently ignoring what Herodotos says about 'gathering the wings together'.[57]

Perhaps the closest parallel to what he says here is a passage in which he describes how two rivers' 'bring their ends together' (συνάγουσι ... τὰ τέρματα: 4.52.4), but the nearest *military* parallel is the passage where he says the Greeks at Artemision 'brought their sterns together' (τὰς πρύμνας συνήγαγον: 8.11.1), and, whatever this means (see below, 139), it can hardly mean that they literally 'joined their sterns together'. Elsewhere (3.150.2, cf. 2.111.3, 8.59), Herodotos uses the aorist participle 'συναγαγόντες' of bringing individuals together, but 'συναγαγόντες ἐς ἕνα χῶρον μυριάδα ἀνθρώπων' at 7.60.2 means 'having gathered together a myriad of men into one place,' and this might be the kind of meaning we want in the Marathon passage. In short, what he may have meant is that the Greeks 'gathered the wings together' in the sense of *rallying* them, not of combining them together into a single line.

But this is not the end of the problem. The Persian centre had, presumably, pursued the broken Athenian centre some distance 'inland', and if the Greek wings did not fall upon its rear, they presumably fell upon its flanks. But, on the face of it, this would have involved about-facing, and marching back to where the Persian centre then was,[58] and it seems improbable that untrained militia could have carried out a manoeuvre even as comparatively simple as this. A clue to what may have happened is provided by later battles in which sections of armies which had won in their part of the field, were taken in flank by an undefeated part of the enemy army. In two cases – 1st Mantineia and the Nemea (cf. Thucydides 5.73 and Xenophon, *Hellenika* 4.2.22-3) –what happened was that the victorious right wing of one army, having gone off in pursuit, as the Persian centre had done at Marathon, was caught in flank *as it returned across the battlefield* by the undefeated wing of the other army. At Marathon it is possible that the Persian centre, realising that its wings had broken and fled, also tried to return across the battlefield, and was thus taken in *both* flanks by the victorious Greek wings.

Even this may seem remarkable enough, but it is not necessary to assume, as most modern commentators do, that the whole thing was planned, even down to what becomes, according to one view, the 'falling back' of the Athenian centre.[59] It is more

56 This would have involved a double *anastrophe* – for this manoeuvre see J.F.Lazenby, 'Hoplite warfare' in *Warfare in the Ancient World*, ed. Sir John Hackett (London, 1989), 65-6 and diagram on 65.

57 Shrimpton, *op.cit.* n.7 above, 25, seems to me to dodge the issue.

58 Green, 37, seems to have realised this, although it is not totally clear what he means.

59 Cf. Grundy, 186; Burn, 250; Green, 36-7; Shrimpton, *op.cit.* n.7 above, 23ff.

likely, given the nature of the Greek army and its officers, that what happened was almost, if not entirely, accidental. If it is true that the phalanx had 'doubled' some hundred metres or two, before coming to grips with the enemy, the men on its victorious wings would probably not have been capable of pursuit, in any case, and would simply have ground to a halt as the enemy wings melted away in front of them. But, given the defeat of their centre, and the comparative ease of their own victory, there would almost inevitably have been a tendency for the wings to 'hinge' on the centre. The nearer the centre, presumably, the harder the fighting would have become, whereas at the two extremes of the enemy line, the cavalry may have fled very rapidly, if that is where it had been stationed. In this way, the hoplites to either end of the Greek line may well have got ahead of their fellows, and, in effect, this would have been the beginning of the turning movement. As the enemy centre swung round, and headed back the way it had come, the Greek wings would have found themselves in position to take it in both flanks, with the Athenians from the original right, in particular, being presented with the always tempting target of a shieldless flank.

At all events, whatever precisely the Greek wings did, it was decisive. Now the Persian centre, too, broke and ran, and at last the Greeks set off in pursuit. Herodotos merely says that they 'followed the fleeing Persians, cutting them down, until, reaching the sea, they called for fire and tried to seize hold of the ships' (6.113.2), and this suggests that he envisaged the Persians simply being driven back to the shore where there ships were. However, if the battle was really fought in the vicinity of the *Soros*, and if the Persian fleet was moored in the shelter of Kynosoura, the fleeing Persians would have had some five kilometres to go before they reached the safety of their ships, for there is no evidence for the suggestion that the latter had moved down the coast before or during the battle.[60] Moreover, in the painting of the battle in the *Stoa Poikile* at Athens, probably put up within thirty years and described by Pausanias (1.15.4),[61] there was evidently a scene in which the Persians were in flight and pushing each other into a marsh, between the scene of the battle itself and that of the attempted burning of the ships. This may also be the basis for the tradition, recorded by Pausanias in his description of the topography of Marathon, that the Persians suffered their greatest losses through stumbling into the marsh in ignorance of the paths through it (1.32.6). This evidence might have been dismissed – after all, the painting of the battle, however close in time to the event, may have borne about as much resemblance to reality as pictures of more recent battles sometimes do, and the story of the losses in the marsh may derive from local tradition, and be on a par with the trough for Artaphernes' horses and the marks of his tent in the rocks (Pausanias *loc.cit.*). But a German officer who surveyed Marathon for the *Karten von Attika*, reports seeing masses of bones in the area of the chapel of the Panaghia Mesosporitissa, not far from the marsh, and traces of

60 Grundy, 187, assumes that part of the Persian fleet had moved south-westwards down the coast to take up a position adjacent to where the battle was fought.

61 See R.E.Wycherly, *PCPhS* 198, (NS) 18 (1972), 78. Francis and Vickers, *op.cit.* n.19 above, think that Herodotos relied on the paintings in the *Stoa* for his account of the battle, but nowhere explain why, in that case, he made no reference to the marsh.

Pl. 5 (top): Marathon – the Mesosporitissa chapel, near which masses of bones were found, possibly the ramains of Persians trapped in the marsh. (Photo: N. Fields). Pl. 6 (bottom): Marathon – column-capital, possibly part of Pausanias' 'trophy of white marble'. (Photo: N. Fields).

Pausanias' monument of white marble (1.32.4) have also been found in the vicinity (see Pls. 5& 6).[62]

It is possible, then, that as the fugitives from the battle streamed north-eastwards, they found themselves up against the marsh. If they were trying to make their way to ships still moored under the lee of Kynosoura, they would have crowded into the bottleneck formed by the narrow strip of beach – the *Schoinia* – between the marsh and the sea, and many of them, in their panic, may have tried to get through the marsh instead. Alternatively, if the main Persian camp had been near Kato Souli, some may have made for that, or tried to work their way round to the ships by taking this route – the chapel of the Panaghia Mesosporitissa is about 2.5 kilometres south of Kato Souli. The press of fugitives, particularly along the *Schoinia* beach, would also have held up the pursuit, and although this may have been when the slaughter was greatest, as Pausanias suggests, the fighting may well have been some of the fiercest of the whole battle, for the Persians will have fought with the ferocity of desperation. The inability of the Greeks to break through the bottleneck may also explain why so few ships were taken, and even when they did reach the ships, they still evidently encountered stiff resistance. It was only now, Herodotos implies (6.114), that Kallimachos and the *stratêgos*, Stesilaos, fell, as well as Aischylos' brother, Kynegeiros, his hand severed by an axe – perhaps a Sakaian *sagaris* – as he clutched at the stern of a ship.[63]

Despite the Greek victory, moreover, the Persians were by no means finished, for their fleet eventually pushed off with the loss of only seven ships, and, according to Herodotos (6.115), having picked up the Eretrian prisoners from the island where they had been left, made off round Sounion, 'wishing to reach the city [i.e. Athens] before the Athenians.' Herodotos goes on to say that 'among the Athenians a common charge was that they [the Persians] hit upon this idea as a result of a device of the Alkmaionidai, for the latter, by agreement, raised a shield as a signal to the Persians when they were already aboard their ships.' This story was already controversial in Herodotos' day – he devotes eleven whole chapters (6.121-31) to a defence of the Alkmaionidai and to a history of the family – and it has remained so ever since.[64]

There are really three interlinked problems. Firstly, *was* such a signal given? Secondly, what was its nature and meaning? Thirdly, who was responsible? Herodotos is categorical that a signal was given (6.124.2), but his very vehemence suggests that this was denied, and it is difficult to see how it was given and what its meaning could have been. It is often assumed that Herodotos is talking about signalling by flashing a shield in the sun, but this is not necessarily what he means. The words he uses – various forms of the verb 'ἀναδείκνυμι' (6.115, 121.1, 123.1, 124.2) – mean, literally, to 'lift up and show' or 'show by lifting', and this probably means that the raising of the shield was

---

62 Captain von Eschenburg, 'Das Schlachtfeld und die Schlacht von Marathon,' *Wochen-schr. f. klass. Phil.* 1887, col.156; A.Milchöfer, *Karten von Attika, Erläuternder Text*, Heft III-VI (Berlin, 1889), 53; Vanderpool, *Hesperia* 11 (1942), 101 n.15. For the monument of white marble see Leake, *The Demi of Attica*[2] (London, 1841), 103; E.Vanderpool, *Hesperia* 35 (1966), 93-106.

63 Anyone wishing to see how basically sober a historian Herodotos is, should read Justin on this episode. In his account Kynegeiros has both arms severed, one after the other, and then tries to hold onto the enemy ship with his teeth!

64 See D.Gillis, *op.cit.* n. 45 above, 45-6 and nn.2-5, for a selection of the literature up to 1979.

itself the signal, nothing more. If so, the signal would have had to be given from near enough to the Persian ships for it to be seen, and that means that it is unlikely to have been given from as far away as Mt. Pentelikon, for example.[65] But with hundreds of Greek troops milling around near the shore from which the Persian ships had departed, how could the signaller have escaped detection, or, more particularly, how could the Persians have picked out the one significant raised shield from the hundreds that were no doubt being waved around at the time?

This raises a second point. Assuming that we are not dealing with a primitive heliograph, the message can only have been a very simple one, and one preconcerted between the parties – something like 'if you see a shield raised, do x,' or 'do not do x'. Here, since the Persian fleet proceeded round Sounion to Phaleron, the implication is that the signal meant 'proceed to Phaleron', unless we are to imagine that they ignored the signal.[66] A further implication is that there was some reason for the Persians to do this, and presumably this was, as Herodotos implies (6.121.1), that the signal suggested at least the possibility that Athens would be betrayed to them; indeed, after their shattering defeat, it is arguable that they would have needed some very positive reason for carrying on with the campaign.

But when had the traitors concerted plans with the Persians? If before or during the campaign, why was it only now that the signal was given, and why resort to so chancy a method, when one would have thought a message could have been delivered to the Persian camp one dark night before the battle? Indeed, the method used suggests that no other one was possible, and that its use was forced by the unexpected outcome of the battle. But, if so, given that its meaning had to be preconcerted, it can only have meant something like, 'if you fight and lose, but it still seems worthwhile your making an attempt on Athens, we will show a shield,' and this seems somewhat improbable. It would have taken very sanguine traitors to think that they could still succeed, after what had happened.

All in all, it seems unlikely that there was such a signal,[67] and that it was one of the rumours used to discredit the Alkmaionidai and their associates in the early 480s, when several of them were ostracized, probably primarily for alleged 'medism' (see below, 81–2). The best reason for believing in the signal is the fact that the Persians did sail round Sounion, but we do not need the signal to explain why they did this. Even if they had no reason to believe that treachery would deliver Athens into their hands, they may still have felt that it was worthwhile to try to seize the city by a *coup de main*, before the Athenian army could return, and they may have been encouraged to try by their comparatively small loss of ships.

---

65 Burn, 251, has the signal made by flashing the polished surface of a shield from Pentelikon; Green, 38, has it 'flashed from the mountains above Marathon'; Macan (1895) ii 166 suggests it may have been sent from Agrieliki; Hammond, 1988, 512, even goes so far as to suggest that the object giving the signal was not a shield at all, but a 'signalling disk'; Hignett, 73, rightly says that there is no evidence that the signal was given from Pentelikon, which means that modern attempts to time it, based on the position of the sun, are worthless.

66 For the view that the signal meant 'abort' see Baillie Reynolds in *JHS* 49 (1929), 100ff., but cf. Hignett, 73.

67 Cf. Wilamowitz, *Aristoteles und Athen* II (Berlin, 1893), 85-6 and n.24.

At all events, presumably it is true that the Persians did sail round Sounion to Phaleron, and there is no good reason to doubt that they picked up the Eretrian prisoners on the way, or that they hoped to get to Athens before the Athenian army. These statements by Herodotos (6.115) have been used to support the hypothesis that the Persians had divided their forces before the battle,[68] but they do no such thing. One might think that a fleet about to make a dash on Athens would not have gone out of its way to pick up the prisoners, but ships could have been detached for this purpose,[69] and it is probably not true that the fleet was bound to take longer to reach Phaleron than the Athenian army. The distance by sea is about 100 kilometres, and the latest opinions on trireme speeds suggest that the fleet could have done this in about ten hours.[70] A famously fast walker, using the shortest route from Marathon to Athens *via* Vrana and Kephisia, reckons that an army would have taken eight or nine hours[71] and the route *via* Pallene, which is much more likely, would have taken an hour or two longer. The fact that the Athenians did reach Phaleron first, according to Herodotos (6.116), does not prove that the Persians could not have thought it worth a try.

The Athenian response to the sight of the enemy fleet streaming south was to march, 'as fast as their legs would carry them' (6.116), back to Athens, where, by one of those coincidences Herodotos loved, they camped at another sanctuary of Herakles, in the suburb of Kynosarges. Plutarch (*Aristeides* 5.5) says that Aristeides was left at Marathon, with his own division, to guard the prisoners and booty, and although this may be an invention to exemplify the reputation for honesty Aristeides enjoyed, it could be true, especially if *Antiochis* had been in the centre of the Athenian line, and had suffered heavy losses. On the other hand, one might have thought the surviving *stratêgoi* would have wanted to take every available man back with them to Athens. However, with or without *Antiochis*, the Athenian army was sufficient to deter the Persians from attempting to land. 'Having lain off Phaleron ... with their ships at anchor,' Herodotos says (6.116), 'they sailed away back to Asia.'

Soon after the battle, two thousand Spartan hoplites arrived, having marched from Sparta to Athens in three days, but just too late. They demanded to see the dead Persians, and having done so, and praised the work of the Athenians, they tramped home again. Herodotos gives the losses as 6400 Persian and 192 Athenian dead. The latter figure we can surely accept. The number is likely to have been accurately remembered, and it is even possible, though unlikely, that the Parthenon frieze is a mute witness to it.[72] The number of Persian dead may seem out of all proportion, but the losing side in ancient warfare often seems to have lost far more heavily than the

---

68 E.g. Grundy, 190-2. As against those like Munro (1899, 193 and n.1) and Macan (1895 ii 166f.), who think the signal originally had something to do with the alleged embarkation of part of the Persian army *before* the battle, Hignett, 72-3, rightly argues that if any such thing had happened, the Athenian army could hardly have reached Athens in time.

69 As Burn suggests, 252.

70 See especially Morrison & Coates, 103-6.

71 Hammond, 1953, 216 n.2.

72 See J.Boardman, *Festschrift for F.Brommer*, ed. U.Hoeckmann & A.Krug (Mainz von Zabern, 1977), 39ff.

victors,[73] and we have Xenophon's word for it (*Anabasis* 3.2.12) that the Athenians had vowed a she-goat to Artemis Agrotera for every enemy killed, and that they had to ask the goddess to let them off with 500 a year![74] Thus there was every reason for them to have counted the enemy dead as accurately as possible. According to Ktesias (18), Datis himself was among the dead, and according to Cicero (*ad Atticum* 9.10.3, cf. Justin 2.9), Hippias, though Ktesias (*loc.cit.*) and the *Souda* (*s.v.* 'Hippias') say he died at Lemnos on the way back to Asia.

Pausanias says (1.32.4) he was unable to find any Persian grave, though the Athenians claimed to have buried the Persian dead. The Athenian dead were cremated on the field, and the *Soros* undoubtedly marks the spot where their ashes were buried (see Pl 7).[75] When Pausanias saw it, the marble slabs containing the names of the fallen, listed *phylê* by *phylê*, could still be seen (1.32.3), but they have long since vanished. Pausanias also says that he saw another grave, that of the Plataians and slaves, and this has been identified, almost certainly wrongly,[76] with a grave in the Vrana valley, excavated in 1970 (see Pl 8). This grave is about 2.5 kilometres west of the *Soros*, whereas Pausanias implies that the one he was talking about was near the *Soros*, and, if anything, north of it. The grave of the 'Plataians and slaves' was more likely the tumulus near the *Soros* seen by earlier travellers, which has since disappeared.[77] Other possible relics of the battle which have survived include a helmet found at Olympia in 1961, with an inscription recording that the Athenians took it from the Medes; the helmet dedicated by a 'Miltiades', also from Olympia,[78] and the enigmatic monument referring to Kallimachos (see above, 58).

Marathon was a famous victory, but a much misunderstood one. Scholars have praised the strategy of the Athenians in 'containing the beach-head',[79] though they would almost certainly not have understood the concept, and probably had no notion other than to confront the enemy, wherever he was; they have praised the Athenian

---

73 See H.C.Avery, *Historia* 22 (1973), 757, and W.F.Wyatt, *Historia* 25 (1976), 483-4, for the far-fetched view that the number of Persian dead was arrived at by assuming that ten of them were killed for every three Athenians. But why on earth should anyone ever have assumed any such thing?

74 A scholiast on Aristophanes *Knights* 658ff. says Kallimachos himself made the vow, and this is probably right. The vow may have been made at a sacrifice to Artemis Agrotera as the advance began – cf. Xenophon, *Hellenika* 4.2.20.

75 See the references in n.46 above.

76 The identification is accepted by Hammond, 1973, 198n., and Burn (*Greece and the Eastern Mediterranean*, Festschrift for F.Schachermeyr, Berlin 1977, 92), but questioned by Themelis *ADelt* 29 (1974[1978], *Meletai* 244), and rejected by Koumanoudis, *AAA* 11 (1978), 232-7; cf. also K.-W.Welwei, *Historia* 28 (1979), and Van der Veer, *op.cit.* n.3 above, 301-4. For the excavations by Marinatos see *AAA* 3 (1970), 164-6, 357-63; *Ergon* 1970, 5-13, and *PAE* 1970, 5-28.

77 See E.D.Clarke, *Travels in Various Countries*^{4} (London, 1818), 27-8; Leake, *op.cit.* n.62 above, 101.

78 Cf. Snodgrass, *Arms and Armour of the Greeks* (London, 1967), 100 and 141 n.16. Snodgrass says that the first of these helmets was 'probably worn by a cavalryman'. If so, and if it was 'taken from the Medes' at Marathon, this would be another proof that Persian cavalry took part.

79 Cf. Green, 31-2.

Pl. 7 (top): Marathon – the Soros, *looking towards Agrieliki. (Photo: the Author). Pl. 8 (bottom): Marathon – the so-called 'Tomb of the Plataians'. (Photo: N. Fields).*

Pl. 9: Hoplites arming, from a cup, signed by Douris (c. 500–460 BC), now in Vienna (Photo: Audio-Visual Centre, University of Newcastle upon Tyne, after Furtwängler-Reichold, pl. 53).

Pl. 10: Hoplite killing a Persian from the tondo of a cup by the 'Triptolemos Painter' (c. 480–470 BC), now in Edinburgh. (Photo: courtesy of the Trustees of the National Museums of Scotland).

choice of position,[80] though we cannot be sure where it was, and if it was really near Vrana, it left the main road to Athens open; if it was astride the main road, as it probably was, it was the obvious position to take. Finally, scholars have praised the Athenian tactics, which appear to have led to the envelopment of the Persian flanks,[81] though Herodotos evidently thought that the formation they adopted was forced upon them by the length of the Persian line, and that the repulse of their centre was certainly not part of any plan. Miltiades, too, has come in for extravagant praise,[82] though it is worth noting that Herodotos does not mention him after stating that the other *stratêgoi* handed over their days of command to him, which is almost certainly untrue. It may well be the case that Miltiades received the principal credit for the victory, as Herodotos implies (6.132) – after all, Kallimachos was dead – but to regard all that happened as the result of a brilliant tactical plan based on Miltiades' 'experience of Persian arms and methods'[83] is to go far beyond the evidence. As far as we know, Miltiades had actually had very little experience of Persian tactics and methods (see above, 37).

Nor was the victory due to the superiority of Greek discipline or to the fact that 'they were not imperial conscripts, but free men fighting to preserve their freedom'.[84] If anything, one suspects, the Persian troops would have been better disciplined than highly individualistic, quarrelsome middle-class Athenians, who were already, by now, coming to think that they were the equal of anyone, and 'imperial conscripts' can fight courageously for their 'emperor', as Indian soldiers repeatedly demonstrated in the days of the Raj. Even the notion that Greek troops were better armed than their opponents, at this date, needs to be carefully examined. It is, for example, almost certainly untrue that Athenian hoplites any longer wore bronze armour, as has often been claimed.[85] Contemporary vase-paintings rather depict some kind of leather or linen jerkins (see Pls 9 & 10).[86]

These kinds of explanations for the Greek victory in many ways do the victors an injustice. They may not have been the first Greeks to endure the sight of Median dress and the men clad in it, as Herodotos claims (6.112.3), but it certainly took collective

80 Cf., e.g., Grundy, 181.

81 Cf., e.g., Burn, 249-50, and, more recently, Shrimpton, *op.cit.* n.7 above, 23ff., Van der Veer, *op.cit.* n.3 above, 319-20. But, as Green says, 37, though he believes the Athenians did plan their battle, 'the tactical skill which this complex movement implies is quite extraordinary'

82 E.g. Delbrück, 80, says: 'the figure of Miltiades as a field-commander stands giant-like in the early annals of world military history'; Delbrück thought the battle began with a Persian assault on the Greek position. Cf. also Grundy, 193; Burn, 248-50.

83 The words are Burn's, 249.

84 As Green, 36, claims.

85 Thus Burn, 252, talks of the Greeks' 'corselet of solid bronze', Green, 36, of their 'bronze-lapped cuirasses', and Cook, 102, of the 'bronze panoply' of Greek hoplites. Hammond, 1988, 510, says 'the hoplites or 'the bronze men', as they were called (II.152.4), had helmet, cuirass, greaves and shield of that metal', but that is the point: the 'bronze men' of Herodotos 2.152.4 were seventh century hoplites. Even they had never carried *bronze* shields, only shields *faced* with bronze, and later hoplites mostly also discarded the bronze cuirass – see n.86 below.

86 Cf. A.M.Snodgrass, *Arms and Armour of the Greeks* (London, 1967), 90f.; Peter Connolly, *Greece and Rome at War* (London, 1981), 54ff.

courage of a high order to decide to resist, in the first place, then to march out – this is particularly true of the Plataians – and finally to fight an enemy army perhaps twice as numerous or more. We should remember that whatever kind of a regime there may have been in Plataia, and however much Athens may still have been dominated by the rich and powerful, these decisions were still not those of a despot, like the king of Persia, but of a group of men, perhaps several thousand in the case of Athens, who probably knew or guessed something of the fate of Eretria, and certainly knew what had happened to Miletos. Surrender, after all, would have meant little but the reimposition of the 'tyrant', Hippias, and, for the future, the payment of tribute, and, no doubt, service in the imperial army or navy. To argue that the battle was not won by highly trained and disciplined 'professionals' through brilliant strategy or tactics, but by militiamen through sheer guts and chance, enhances the quality of the victory, and makes it all the more astonishing.

By Herodotos' time it had already taken on the quality of legend. There was the story of Philippides' meeting with Pan, and of Epizelos, son of Kouphagoras, blinded in the battle by the vision of a huge warrior, his beard covering his shield (6.117.3), who slew the man at his side. Later came the inevitable embroidery. Philippides had to return to take part in the battle, and to bring the news to Athens, and there was the man of rustic appearance who had killed numbers of barbarians with a ploughshare, and vanished after the battle: on enquiring who he was, the Athenians were told to worship the hero Echetlaos (Pausanias 1.32.4). If you went to Marathon, you could not only see the trough where Artaphernes' horses had fed and drunk, and the marks of his tent in the rocks (Pausanias 1.32.6), but if you spent the night on the plain, you could hear the whinnying of horses, and the sounds of battle, though woe betide you if you went there specifically to hear this (Pausanias 1.32.3)!

Those who had taken part in the battle no doubt remembered the day 'with advantages' ever afterwards. Thus in Aristophanes' *Wasps* the old men who form the chorus, reminisce about how once, 'when the barbarian came,' they ran out with spear and shield, though you could not see the sky for arrows, and still shoved them back 'towards evening', and then pursued them, 'stabbing them like tunny in their trousers' (1078ff.).[87] No doubt old soldiers became something of a bore on the subject, but to this day there is something very special about the sight of that mound at the end of its avenue of cypress trees, with the blue sea beyond, and the hills of Euboia grey in the distance.[88]

---

87 It is from evidence like this that J.H.Schreiner, *PCPhS*, (NS) 16, (1970), 97ff., conjures up his *two* battles of Marathon. But cf. Shakespeare's Henry V before Harfleur, exhorting his men not to shame their fathers -

> 'Fathers that, like so many Alexanders,
> Have in these parts from morn till even fought
> And sheathed their swords for lack of argument.'

88 I shall always remember the slight catch of the heart as I asked, for the first time, for a ticket to the 'σωρὸς Μαραθῶνος', on the bus from Athens. Byron, of course, in the poem from which the title of this chapter is taken (*Don Juan*, 3rd Canto, lxxxvi), apparently thought the *Soros* was 'the *Persian's* grave'.

CHAPTER 4

Between the Wars

Herodotos follows his account of Marathon and excursus on the Alkmaionidai with the story of Miltiades' disastrous attack on Paros (6.132-6), prompted, he says, by the presence of a Parian trireme at Marathon (6.133.1). The secondary sources (Nepos, *Miltiades* 7.1-2; Stephanos of Byzantion *s.v.* 'Paros') make the attack part of a general campaign against islands which had aided the Persians, and they may be right. In any case, revenge is a more likely motive than a desire to acquire bases for the Athenian fleet.[1] The campaign possibly explains why many of the islands – Keos, Naxos, Kythnos, Seriphos, Siphnos and Melos (8.46.2-4) – subsequently sided with the Greeks, but it should be remembered that the Persian fleet did not visit the Cyclades in 480.

The failure of the attack on Paros led to the prosecution of Miltiades by Xanthippos on the capital charge of 'deceit of the Athenians' (6.136.1). Herodotos says Miltiades was unable to plead because a wound in his thigh, received at Paros, had turned gangrenous, and that his friends pleaded for him, as he lay on a litter, reminding the Athenians of his services at Marathon and his earlier capture of Lemnos. The people reduced the penalty from death to the colossal fine of fifty talents, but Miltiades soon died, and it was his son, Kimon, who paid the fine (6.136.2-3). Later sources (Nepos, *Miltiades* 7.6; Diodoros 10.30; Plutarch, *Kimon* 4) have the hero of Marathon actually die in prison, but Herodotos does not necessarily imply that this is what happened.

The detail that Xanthippos was the prosecutor is interesting, for he had married Agariste, niece of the lawgiver, Kleisthenes, and so an Alkmaionid (6.131), and it is possible that the prosecution of Miltiades was an attempt by members of the family to get back at those who were spreading stories about their 'medism'. It is also possibly relevant that Aristeides was almost certainly archon in 489/8,[2] for he had been a close friend of Kleisthenes, according to Plutarch (*Aristeides* 2.1). However, if the Alkmaionidai did thus succeed in making something of a come-back, it was shortlived, for their enemies turned the weapon of 'ostracism' against them. The first man to be 'ostracized', in 487, was Hipparchos, son of Charmos, certainly a member of the 'tyrant' Hippias' family, and probably his grandson.[3] But in 486 it was the turn of Megakles, Xanthippos' brother-in-law, and probably head of the Alkmaionidai, and in 485 that of Xanthippos himself (*AP* 22.5-6). There is no definite evidence that these men were regarded as 'medizers', and the author of the *Constitution of the Athenians* distinguishes Xanthippos from the first *ostracisés*, whom he stigmatizes as 'friends of the tyrants'.[4] But this at least leaves Megakles as a 'friend of the tyrants', and some measure of the hostility felt for him may be gauged from the fact that more *ostraka* bearing his name have been found – 4662 to date! – than that of any other man; that the Alkmaionidai as a whole were regarded as traitors is suggested by the *ostraka* bearing the name

1 As suggested by Burn, 258.
2 Cf. Rhodes, 1981, 280.
3 J.Kirchner, *Prosopographia Attica*, 7600; J.K.Davies, *Athenian Propertied Families*, 451.
4 Cf. W.G.Forrest, *CQ* (NS) 10 (1960), 233-4; but see P.J.Bicknell, *Historia* Einzelschriften 19 (1972), 73-4, 81-2, and *AC* 44 (1975), 172ff.

'Kallixenos', one of which describes him as 'of the Alkmaionidai', another as 'traitor' (προδότης).[5]

Perhaps also connected with the Marathon campaign was the change to the use of the lot in the method of choosing archons, 'in the archonship of Telesinos' (487/6: *AP* 22.5). Some have seen in this reform a deliberate attempt to enhance the position of the *stratêgoi* at the expense of the archons, and particularly that of the polemarch.[6] But this is far-fetched – too Machiavellian, one feels, even for Themistokles, who is usually credited with the reform. In reality, it may be the case that the archonship was already becoming a largely honorary post held by young men of the upper classes at the beginning of their careers,[7] and that by the time of Marathon the *stratêgoi* held the real power, as Herodotos implies. In this case the reform of 487/6 will only have been a recognition of an existing situation. If the reform had any significance, one suspects that it was political rather than military – i.e. that it was a further step in the development of Athens towards democracy – though even then it is going too far to see the hand of Themistokles behind it, preparing the way for Ephialtes' attack on the Areiopagos a quarter of a century later.[8] If one has to put a name to the author of the reform, a better guess might be that it was Xanthippos. It may be significant that whereas Themistokles and Aristeides both held the archonship, Xanthippos never did.

Much more important for the future development of Athens was the war with Aigina, which either broke out in the 480s, or continued into them, for it was this that led to a huge increase in the size of the Athenian navy. Herodotos puts the beginning of the war before Marathon (6.94.1), but his chronology here is notoriously difficult, since it is almost impossible to believe that everything he relates, from the arrival of Darius' envoys (6.48.2) to the beginnings of the Marathon campaign (6.94.1), can really have taken place between the spring of 491 and that of 490.[9] One solution is to split the war between Athens and Aigina into two,[10] but this is rather drastic. Despite its anomalies, Herodotos' account of the war can be accepted as it stands. It began with the Aiginetan seizure of an Athenian ship carrying leading citizens on their way to a quadrennial festival at Sounion, clearly with a view to using them as hostages to secure the release of the Aiginetans handed over to Athens by King Kleomenes of Sparta. Athens responded by supporting an Aiginetan democrat, Nikodromos, with a fleet of seventy ships, twenty hired from Corinth. Nikodromos' attempted *coup* was premature by one day – operations which involved co-ordination of timing, always seem to have been difficult in antiquity (cf. Thucydides 4.76-77, 89) – but the Athenians defeated the

5 Cf. ML 21, 40-2; J.M.Balcer, 'Athenian politics: the ten years after Marathon', in *Panathenaia: Studies in Athenian Life and Thought in the Classical Age* (ed. T.E.Gregory & A.J.Podlecki; Lawrence, 1979), 27ff.

6 E.g. Hignett, *A History of the Athenian Constitution* (Oxford, 1952), 183ff.; Burn, 283-6; Green, 46-7.

7 F.J.Frost,*CSCA* 1 (1968), 114-5; E.Badian, *Antichthon* 5 (1971), 1-34.

8 Cf. R.J.Buck, *CP* 60 (1963), 96-101; E.Badian, *op.cit.* Note that the archon of 479/8 – 'Xanthippos' in *Marmor Parium* 52, 'Xanthippides' in Diodoros 11.27.1 – is not the famous Xanthippos.

9 Hammond, *Historia* 4 (1955), p.406ff., argues that Herodotos can be believed, but cf. HW ii 101-2; A.Andrewes, *BSA* 37 (1937), 4, and Burn, 267-73.

10 This is Andrewes' suggestion, *op.cit.*

Aiginetan fleet, and seem initially to have had the better of the fighting on the island. Later, however, the Aiginetan fleet managed to catch the Athenian ships in disorder, and appears to have won a decisive victory, capturing four ships with their crews (6.87-93).

Herodotos gives no more details about the war, but it was apparently still going on in 481, when news of Xerxes' preparations first began to reach Greece (7.145.1), and it was ostensibly to defeat Aigina that when, in 483/2, the question arose of what to do with the profits from the silver mines owned by the Athenian state at Laureion, Themistokles was able to persuade his fellow-citizens to use them for building warships, rather than for distribution to all the citizens at ten *drachmai* a head (7.144.1). Herodotos says the number of warships he proposed was 200 (*ibid.*), but it is more likely that the *Constitution of the Athenians* is right to say (22.7) that the money – 100 talents – was handed over to a hundred of the richest citizens on condition that they saw to the building of 100 ships, though the story that Themistokles asked that he should not have to reveal the purpose of the distribution, is absurd. Herodotos was probably misled by the tradition that the Athenians had at least 200 ships in 480 (cf. 8.1 & 14.1, 44.1 & 46.2) into thinking that these were all built under Themistokles' aegis, whereas Athens already had at least 50 during the war with Aigina (6.89).[11] In any case, whatever the exact figures or the mechanics of the building programme, there can be no doubt that it was now that Athens began to become the greatest sea power in the Greek world.

The question also arises whether the new ships built in the late 480s were of some new design, as Plutarch seems to imply in his life of Kimon (12.2). This is sometimes accepted,[12] but the evidence is weak, and, as it stands, nonsensical. Kimon could not literally have modified the *hulls* of Themistokles' warships, as Plutarch implies – this would have meant rebuilding the ships from the keels up. All he could have done was to extend the *decks* to accomodate more hoplites, and even this depends on the unsatisfactory view that Themistokles' triremes only carried 14 *epibatai* (see above, 35–6). What Plutarch says about the speed and manoeuvrability of Themistokles' ships contradicts what Herodotos says about the Persians' having the 'better sailing ships' (8.10.1), and the Greeks the 'heavier' (8.60α), and should be rejected. The Athenians may have had the 'best sailing ships' in the Greek fleet, as Herodotos claims (8.42.2), but this does not mean that they were better than the best of the Persian ships. In any case, any superiority enjoyed by either Persian or Athenian ships was probably due more to having better rowers than to superior ship-design.[13]

It is often assumed that it was opposition to Themistokles' naval building programme which led to Aristeides' 'ostracism' in 483/2 (*AP* 22.7), though there is no evidence for the view.[14] However, the successive elimination of Xanthippos and

---

11 Cf. Burn, 292-3. The story was a famous one – cf., e.g., Thucydides 1.14.3, Nepos, *Themistocles* 2.2; Plutarch, *Themistokles* 4.1-3; Polyainos 1.30.6 – and the modern literature is voluminous. The most comprehensive treatment is by J.Labarbe, *La Loi navale de Thémistocle* (Paris, 1957), but this is marred by an attempt to squeeze all the evidence into a coherent story, which is impossible (cf. also *BCH* 70, 1952, 407ff.). See also Podlecki, 1975, Appendix B, 201-3; Lenardon, 1978, 51-6.

12 See most recently Morrison & Coates, 52, 60, 154-7, 160-1.

13 *Op.cit.*, 232.

14 Originally suggested by Beloch, ii 2 142, but nowhere stated in the ancient sources. Plutarch (*Themistokles* 4.3) quotes Stesimbrotos as saying that it was Miltiades who opposed

Aristeides by 'ostracism' probably did leave Themistokles in a position of unrivalled influence, and this may be why Herodotos introduces him, in his story of the 'wooden wall' oracle of 481 or 480, as a man 'recently come to the first rank' (7.143.1). On the face of it, this is an odd way to describe someone who had been archon in 493/2, assuming that the 'Themistokles' who was archon in that year (Dionysios of Halikarnassos, *Roman Antiquities* 6.34.1), was the great Themistokles.[15] But Herodotos uses the word 'recently' (νεωστί) vaguely elsewhere, as when, in the context of 481, he describes the battle of Sepeia, fought c.494, as having taken place 'recently'.[16] Alternatively, as was argued above, the holding of the archonship may have meant little at this date, though in Themistokles' case we have Thucydides' word for it that the fortification of the Peiraeus was begun in his archonship,[17] which suggests that he already enjoyed considerable influence, if he was responsible for it. It would also be striking evidence for the foresight which Thucydides regarded as his chief quality (1.138.3), for the fortifications were only finally completed after Xerxes' invasion (Thucydides 1.93.3ff.).

In view of Thucydides' testimony to Themistokles' foresight, there is little reason to doubt that when he persuaded the Athenians to build such a huge fleet, he was primarily thinking of the possibility of a renewed Persian attack. Herodotos does not actually say this, merely that Themistokles referred to the war with Aigina (7.144.1), but Thucydides thought that he was also thinking of the expected Persian attack (1.14.3), and Plutarch is probably right (*Themistokles* 4.1-2) that he deliberately concentrated on the war with Aigina in his speeches, knowing that his fellow-citizens would not so easily be persuaded if he dwelt on the more remote danger from Persia. But it is probably a mistake to credit Themistokles with too much foresight. Almost certainly, for example, he had little or no inkling of what the political effect of the creation of a large navy might be, despite the view of Plato (*Laws* 4.706, quoted by Plutarch, *Themistokles* 4.3). Still less is it likely that he wanted to bring about the radical democracy which was certainly one of the results of the navy's creation (cf. 'Old Oligarch' 1.2). Although some of the sources regard Themistokles as a 'democrat', as opposed to Aristeides, there is no real reason to believe this was the case.[18]

Themistokles on this issue. This is obviously wrong, but Stesimbrotos might have been referring to opposition to the building of the Peiraeus fortifications in 493/2.

15 Argued by Busolt, 642-3, n.1. The alternative is that some other Themistokles was archon in 493/2 – e.g. the eponymous uncle in one of the spurious 'Letters of Themistokles' (Ep. 8, p.749 Hercher) – or that Dionysios' date is wrong – cf., e.g., W.H.Plommer, *CR* (NS) 19 (1969), 126-9 – and that Themistokles was in fact archon in 482/1, the only year for which we do not have a name.

16 Rhodes, 1981, 279; R.J.Lenardon, *Historia* (5 (1956), 412, n.57, argues that 'Herodotos merely states that Themistokles had recently come to the front with the proposal concerning the fleet,' but this is surely not what Herodotos means.

17 Despite Gomme, *HCT* 1, 262-3, C.W.Fornara, *Historia* 20 (1971), 534ff., and now A.A.Mosshammer, *Hermes* 103 (1975), 227-34, Thucydides almost certainly meant that Themistokles was eponymous archon when the construction of the Peiraeus fortifications began – cf. Thucydides 6.54.6 & Podlecki, 196 n.7; D.M.Lewis, *Historia* 22 (1973), 757-8; W.W.Dickie, *Historia* 22 (1973), 758-9.

18 Cf. Plutarch, *Aristeides* 2-3, 7.1; Burn, 279ff.; Frost, *op.cit.* n.7 above, 111f.

If, however, in advocating the building of the fleet, he was looking to Persia in the long-term, it is worth asking how he contemplated using the fleet. Did he, for example, think in terms of winning the war at sea, as some have thought?[19] This is not impossible, for he might have learnt a lesson from the Ionian revolt, where sea power had clearly, in the end, proved decisive, as Hekataios is supposed to have thought it would be (cf. 5.36.2, 6.6ff.). But it is perhaps going too far to think that any Athenian, however far-sighted, could have thought in such terms so soon after the creation of the navy, and it is worth considering whether Themistokles did not rather think in defensive terms.

If the Persian came again in greater force, it did not require any great foresight, after all, to realise that Athens and Attica were themselves indefensible, despite Marathon, and that it was unwise to rely on the enemy's being stopped before he reached Attica. In other words, the Athenians would in all probability be faced with the stark alternatives of submission or evacuation, as in the event they were, and the latter depended upon sea power, as the whole history of Greek colonisation taught. More recently the people of Phokaia had fled to the west to escape the Persians c.540 (1.163ff.), and those of Teos to Abdera (1.168). If Herodotos is to be believed, Bias of Priene had even advocated Ionian emigration *en masse* to Sardinia (1.170), and Aristagoras of Miletos had contemplated flight to the same island (5.124.2), while Hekataios had suggested Leros as an alternative (5.125). In 480, after the evacuation of the Athenian populace to Trozen, Aigina and Salamis, Themistokles, when faced with Peloponnesian reluctance to fight at Salamis, is supposed to have threatened to take his fellow-countrymen to Siris in southern Italy (8.62.2), as well as warning Adeimantos of Corinth that 'they had a city and a country greater than theirs [the Corinthians'], whilst they had two hundred ships manned, for none of the Greeks could resist an attack by them' (8.61.2). Thus, although there is no reason to doubt that Themistokles was already thinking of fighting the Persians at sea, when he advocated the building of the fleet, there is no reason to believe that he thought that the war could be *won* at sea, and, if he did, he was wrong (see below, 197).

There can be little doubt that the Athens which faced Xerxes in 480 was more united than it had been in 490. There seems now to have been no 'appeasement party', and the unfortunate Lykidas, who, in late spring 479, proposed that Mardonios' terms be accepted and put to the people was stoned to death as a result, with his wife and children (9.5). Nor is there even a hint of treachery, except for the story Plutarch tells (*Aristeides* 13) of an oligarchic conspiracy at the time of Plataia, which is very difficult to believe (see below, 229). It is interesting, in any case, that both these pieces of evidence refer to 479. The unity and resolution with which the Athenians initially faced the invasion, despite the terrifying prognostications of Delphi (cf. 7.140-1), presumably owe much to the peaceful expulsion of potential trouble-makers like Hipparchos and Megakles, the transition to a more democratic executive in the board of ten *stratêgoi*, and, perhaps, to the employment provided by not only the building, but the manning, of the new ships.

Unfortunately we know very little about what was going on in the rest of Greece in the decade after Marathon. In Sparta, the reign of Kleomenes ended in mystery and scandal. According to Herodotos (6.74ff.), after his success in arresting the Aiginetans

19 See, e.g., Burn 352ff., 361ff.

held responsible for giving 'earth and water' to Darius, the falsity of his allegation of illegitimacy against his fellow-king, Damaratos, became known, and he fled to Thessaly. Thence he returned to Arcadia and began to stir its people up against Sparta, binding them to him by an oath on the waters of the river Styx. In alarm, the Spartans recalled him, but he went mad, and started to assault anyone he met, hitting them in the face with his sceptre. His relatives then confined him in stocks, but by threatening his helot guard, he secured a knife and began to mutilate himself until he reached a vital part. After telling this extraordinary story, Herodotos then proceeds (6.75.3ff.) to give four possible explanations for the king's affliction, three ascribing it to divine punishment for one reason or another, the fourth – that of the Spartans – to his having developed a taste for drinking wine neat, after carousing with Skythian ambassadors.[20]

It has been suggested that Kleomenes' mysterious demise is to be connected with the trouble he had stirred up in Arcadia, and the helot revolt said to have occurred at the time of Marathon (Plato *Laws* 698e).[21] The evidence for a helot revolt is not very good, but one possible effect of Kleomenes' activities in Arcadia may have been the apparent reluctance of Mantineia to honour its obligations to Sparta, in 479, when its contingent arrived too late to take part in the battle of Plataia (9.77). At some point in these years, too, Tegea was hostile (9.37.4), and although in the end its hoplites proved the staunchest of Sparta's allies at Plataia, Herodotos' story of their objection to the Athenians' being posted on the left wing (9.26-28.1), may reflect the beginnings of the disaffection which was to lead to overt hostility in the 470s (cf. 9.35.2).

It has sometimes been suggested that behind much of Sparta's foreign policy in the last half of the sixth century can be discerned a growing awareness of the threat from Persia, and Kleomenes has even been credited with far-reaching schemes to create a coalition against her.[22] This is far-fetched, and if anything Kleomenes' heavy-handed policies had potentially disastrous consequences. Crucial to the defence of Greece north of the isthmus was the attitude of Boiotia, and one would very much like to know why, in the event, with the exception of Plataia and Thespiai, Boiotia chose to 'medize'. The Spartans had had some dealings with the area, possibly as early as 519/8,[23] when, according to Herodotos (6.108.2ff.), the Plataians, hard-pressed by Thebes, had placed themselves in the hands of Kleomenes and the Lakedaimonians who 'happened to be in the area',[24] and had been advised to seek an alliance with Athens instead. Herodotos maintains that this was not out of goodwill for the Plataians, but simply to embroil Athens and Boiotia, and his view is borne out by the co-operation of Boiotia in Kleomenes' third invasion of Attica (5.74.2ff.).

---

20 For the view that Herodotos' statement that Kleomenes fled to 'Thessaly' is a mistake for 'to Sellasia', see D.Hereward, *CR* 1 (1951), 146. On the question of Kleomenes' madness, some years ago when sitting on an appointments board for a lectureship in psychiatry, I asked candidates to diagnose Kleomenes' mental state from what Herodotos tells us about his behaviour. Remarkably, one candidate said that he would hazard the guess that the king was a heavy drinker.

21 See W.P. Wallace, *JHS* 74 (1954), 32-6.

22 See, e.g., Burn, 173ff.

23 For the date see Thucydides. 3.68.5 and HW ii, 109-10 *ad* Hdt. 6.108.1.

24 Not necessarily an army as in the Penguin translation (2nd ed.), 426.

In 480, according to Plutarch (*Moralia* 864e), possibly on the authority of the lost writings of Aristophanes of Boiotia (cf. *op.cit.* 864d), Thebes sent 500 hoplites under one Mnamias to join the expedition to Tempe (see below, 109), and although Herodotos says nothing of this, he does record the presence of a Theban contingent at Thermopylai (7.202). Even if what Plutarch says is true, 500 hoplites would not seem to be much of a contribution to an army of 10,000 men (cf. 7.173.2), and although the size of the contingent at Thermopylai – 400 hoplites – compares favourably with some of the others, if little Thespiai could produce 700, it is obvious that Thebes was not really trying. However, this does not necessarily mean that Thebes' attitude to Sparta had changed as a result of the death of Kleomenes or anything else. Co-operation against Athens was one thing, co-operation against the Persians something quite different, especially in view of Sparta's own reluctance to commit large forces at least to the initial defence of Thermopylai. As it was, the Theban contingent was commanded by a man from a family which may have provided the hereditary *proxenoi* ('consuls') of Sparta at Thebes,[25] and probably included many men who were opposed to the idea of 'medism'. Here, too, old antagonisms may have played a part, for Athens was the most powerful of Sparta's allies against Persia, and the Thebans would naturally have been suspicious of Athenian relations with both Plataia and Thespiai.

In the Peloponnese, Sparta's great rival, Argos, had been crippled for a generation by Kleomenes' victory at Sepeia in c.494, and the subsequent massacre of fugitives from the battle who had sought sanctuary in a sacred grove (6.75.3-83, 7.148.2) – Herodotos says that there was even some kind of 'slave' revolt, which left the 'slaves' in power until the sons of those slain at Sepeia grew to manhood (6.83).[26] However, even in her crippled state, Argos was able to maintain her independence, and, in effect, rejected the attempt by Sparta and her allies to draw her in against Persia, by making what she must have known would be unacceptable demands (see below, 106–7). Whether or not Argos would have sided with Sparta and her allies against Persia, but for Sepeia, we can never know, but Kleomenes' treacherous massacre of the fugitives can have done nothing to endear Sparta to the Argives while he was still on the throne. In the end, the only concrete advantage Sparta derived from their defeat, when it came to resisting Persia, was the adherence of two of the small towns in the Argolid, which were normally under Argive control, the Bronze Age fortresses of Mykenai and Tiryns (7.202 & 9.31.3), though it is, of course, possible that Argos might have played a more active part on Persia's side, but for her weakness.

Relations between Sparta and Athens evidently improved after Kleomenes' attempts to overthrow the infant democracy, if it is true that it was at Athens' prompting that he intervened to arrest the 'medizing' leaders of Aigina (6.49ff.). But here again, though it is arguable that the friendship of Athens was more important than that of Aigina, Kleomenes' manner of dealing with the islanders risked antagonizing one of the most important of Greek naval powers, and certainly had the effect of escalating the hostility between Aigina and Athens into open war.

Another area with which Kleomenes had dealings was Thessaly, if it is true, as Herodotos says (6.74.1), that he fled there when his machinations against Damaratos

---

25 Cf J.Buckler, *The Theban Hegemony* (Cambridge, Mass., 1980), 42.

26 Cf. W.G.Forrest, *CQ* (NS) 10 (1960), 221ff.

became known. The Thessalians, too, had been on friendly terms with Athens in the days of the 'tyrants', and Thessalian horsemen had defeated Sparta's first attempt to oust Hippias in about 513 (5.63.3-4). Subsequently, however, Herodotos says nothing about Thessalian aid for Hippias against Kleomenes' first, full-scale invasion of Attica, and unless the Thessalian horsemen were simply rendered ineffective by Kleomenes' use of *chevaux de frise*, as Frontinus alleges (*Strategemata* 2.2.9), this suggests that Thessaly may have reached some understanding with the Spartan king. If so, this would explain his choice of Thessaly as a place of refuge. Unfortunately the MSS of Herodotos are probably corrupt in describing the 'king' who led Hippias' Thessalian allies as a 'Koniaian' (ἄνδρα Κονιαῖον: 5.63.3), since the only known Konion is in Phrygia (Pliny, *Natural History* 5.32). But if the true reading is 'Gonnaian' (i.e from Gonnos – ἄνδρα Γοννaῖον),[27] it is possible that it was leading men from that area of Thessaly who appealed to the Greeks for help, in 480, against the influence of the 'medizing' Aleuadai of Larisa (cf. 7.172), for Gonnos commands the mouth of the Tempe pass. Here for once, Kleomenes' activities may have borne potentially useful fruit.

One other state which was to play some part in attempts to mould resistance to Xerxes, and whose relations with the leaders of that resistance may have taken a new turn after Marathon, was Kerkyra (Corfu). In 480 she agreed to send 60 ships to aid her fellow-Greeks, which would have been the largest contingent after that of Athens, as Herodotos reminds us (7.168.3). Although they never arrived, we do not necessarily have to be as cynical as Herodotos (7.168.4) in dismissing their claim that bad weather had prevented their rounding Cape Malea – there was plenty of bad weather about in the summer of 480, as the Persians were to find to their cost, though ships from Ambrakia and Leukas managed to make it in time for Salamis (8.45). At all events, it is possible that the initially favourable response of Kerkyra was due to Athenian intervention on her behalf in a quarrel with Corinth (Plutarch, *Themistokles* 24, cf. Thucydides 1.136.1), and this may also lie behind Cornelius Nepos' otherwise nonsensical story (*Themistocles* 2) that Themistokles first employed the new Athenian fleet in a war in which he defeated Kerkyra and cleared the sea of pirates.[28] Themistokles' interest in the west is indicated by the names of his daughters, Sybaris and Italia (Plutarch, *Themistokles* 32), and by his threat to take the Athenians to Siris, before Salamis (8.62.2).

Thus, here and there, despite the lack of evidence, we can discern something of the background that helped to determine the attitudes of various Greek states in 481-0. The threat of invasion added a new dimension, and states would by no means necessarily have adhered to traditional friendships or alliances as the threat developed. But it is possible, for example, that but for the bitterness roused by Sepeia, Argos might have joined the resistance, despite her age-old hostility to Sparta, and that but for suspicions of Athens' relations with Plataia, Sparta's friends in Thebes might have swung their fellow-countrymen behind Sparta. Down to his death in about 490, Kleomenes had perhaps been the most powerful man in Greece, and his heavy-handed policies, however

---

27 As HW suggest, ii 30.

28 Burn, 293-6. The Athenian interest in the west may have been prompted by the necessity to find an alternative source of timber, now that Macedonia was under Persian control – see R.Meiggs, *Trees and Timber in the Ancient Mediterranean World* (Oxford, 1982), 123ff.

well-intentioned, had clearly had potentially disastrous effects. His death was in this sense, if no other, a blessing in disguise, though it was too late to mend all the damage.

The Persians, too, had their internal problems, though these were largely resolved by the time of Xerxes' invasion. Herodotos says (7.1.1-2), and we can well believe him, that the defeat at Marathon served only to increase Darius' determination to conquer Greece, and that immediate preparations were made for a new campaign. If his language is to be pressed, there was one significant addition to the preparations (cf. 6.48.2 & 95.1) – grain (σῖτος: 7.1.2) – which may indicate that a lengthier campaign was now contemplated, not merely a punitive expedition with limited objectives. However, the preparations were interrupted, according to Herodotos (7.1ff.), first by a revolt in Egypt, then by a dispute about the succession amongst Darius' sons, and finally by Darius' death (7.1.3ff.). We know that the latter event occurred shortly before 1 December, 486, but although there is some slight evidence that there was already trouble in Egypt in October, in general the documents surviving from the last year of Darius' reign hardly suggest that there was as yet a real rebellion.[29] In any case, it certainly fell to Darius' son, Xerxes, to crush the rebellion, and it does not appear to have taken long, for there is documentary evidence from quarries that the Persians were back firmly in control by early in 484.[30] However, there was also trouble in Judaea, and later in Babylonia.[31]

Herodotos, as usual, does not attempt to analyse the reasons for Xerxes' decision to invade Greece, as a modern historian might do. But the anecdotes he retails about advice from various people, prophecies and dreams, enable us to see at least what the Greeks believed to have been the Persians' motivation, and they were probably not far wrong. Thus we can well believe that Mardonios' ambition was a factor, and that he used both revenge and profit as arguments for invading Europe (7.5.2-3). We can also believe that the urgings of Greek 'quislings' like the Aleuadai of Thessaly and the Peisistratidai of Athens, to say nothing of the oracle-monger, Onomakritos, may have had an effect (7.6.2-5). It is also very likely that Xerxes, whose accession had not gone unchallenged,[32] would have wanted to emulate his ancestors' conquests, as Herodotos makes him say (7.8.1ff.), and in particular to show that he was as good a man as his father by not abandoning the enterprise for which the latter had begun to prepare before his death (cf. 7.11.2). We may doubt Herodotos' stories of the dreams of Xerxes and Artabanos (7.12-19), but there is no reason why there should not have been those who,

---

29 *SB Berl.* 1928, 614-22; Cook, 99-100.

30 G.Posener, *La première domination Perse en Egypte* (Cairo, 1936), nos.. 43-77; A.T.Olmstead, *History of the Persian Empire* (Chicago, 1948), 235-7; Couyat & Montet, *Inscriptions du Ouadi H.* nos. 52, 74, 91, 118.

31 On events in Judaea see Ezra 4.6; J.M.Myers, *The Anchor Bible: Ezra, Nehemiah* (Garden City, 1965, 36-7; J.Mogenstern, *HUCA* 27 (1956), 100-79; 28 (1957), 15-47; 31 (1960), 1-29; 37 (1966), 1-28. For doubts about Morgenstern's views see J.Bright, *History of Israel* (Philadelphia, 1959), 360; see also P.R.Ackroyd,, *Israel under Babylon and Persia* (Oxford, 1970), 173. On events in Babylonia see G.G.Cameron, *AJSL* 58 (1941), 314-25; Olmstead, *op.cit.* n.30 above, 237 and n.23; F.M. de Liagre Böhl, *Bibliotheca Orientalis* 19 (1962), 110-14; J.M.Bigwood, *AJAH* 3 (1978), 32-51.

32 Cf. Cook, 74-5; for Xerxes' desire to emulate his predecessors see J.M.Balcer, *Historia* 38 (1989), 133-4.

like Artabanos in Herodotos, were doubtful of the wisdom of the enterprise, and Xerxes himself may well have got 'cold feet' from time to time.

Though the invasion soon became the stuff of legend, and the Greeks tended to exaggerate everything about it, there is no reason to doubt that the preparations were on a grand scale. How far the exaggeration went is an intractable problem, and one of the odd things about it is that the numbers, for example, seem to be largest in the earliest sources, and then to decrease. Thus by the time the epitaph for the Peloponnesians who fell at Thermopylai was composed, the enemy strength was already put at 3,000,000 (7.228.1), which makes even Herodotos' estimate of 1,800,000 (cf. 7.184.4), seem comparatively modest. Ktesias further reduced the total to 800,000, excluding charioteers (23), and this may ultimately be where Diodoros, using Ephoros, got his figure of 800,000 apparently including charioteers (11.3.7, cf.5.2); Isokrates (6.100, 12.49) and Justin (2.10.18), remarkably, give the lowest total, at 700,000.

All these figures are clearly unacceptable, and it is worth noting that Herodotos specifically says that he could not give totals for individual contingents, because 'it is not said by any men' (7.60.1), though earlier he does give totals for the Persian troops who preceded and followed the king when he left Sardis (7.40.2-41). His story of how the total of 1,700,000 for the infantry was arrived at, though not impossible, does not seem very likely. He says a group of 10,000 men was assembled – perhaps the 'Immortals', who were allegedly always kept at this strength (7.83.1) – the area they had occupied marked off with a wall reaching to the height of a man's navel, and then the rest of the army was herded into the same space, batch by batch (7.60.2-3). But in view of his evident inability to find detailed figures, it seems unlikely that the later sources can have had access to any more reliable evidence. In any case, their totals are also far too high. The problem is, however, that although the figures must clearly be reduced, once one starts, it is difficult to know where to stop. One modern scholar, for example, considers that the Persian forces may not have been much, if at all, larger than the Greek, another would put their total as high as 300,000.[33]

There are two ways of approaching the problem, neither wholly satisfactory, though it may be of some comfort that estimates derived from both tend to be somewhat similar. The first way is, in effect, to juggle Herodotos' figures. Thus one hypothesis is that he mistakenly believed that his twenty-nine generals in command of infantry contingents were *superior* to 'myriarchs' (i.e. commanders of 10,000), whereas in reality they *were* 'myriarchs', as was Hydarnes, who commanded the 10,000 'Immortals'. This gives a paper-strength of 300,000 for the infantry, and since Herodotos says there were six generals in overall command of it (7.82), we may presume that five infantry 'divisions' were brigaded together to form an 'infantry corps'.[34] Herodotos' figure of 80,000 cavalry is then reduced to 60,000, also supposed to be divided into 'myriads', and by attaching one of these to each 'infantry corps', we get 'army corps' of 60,000.

This arrangement, it is held, is confirmed by Herodotos' references to the commands of Artabazos and Tigranes, which are each said, at one point, to be 60,000 strong

33 For the lower estimate see T.Cuyler Young, Jnr., *Iranica Antiqua*, 15 (1980), 237 – his arguments are mainly logistical, but we, perhaps, lack sufficient hard data for such an analysis; for the higher estimate see Cook, 113-5.

34 Cf. Munro, 1902, 294ff.

(8.126.1, 9.96.2). The overall strength of 360,000 is also held to be confirmed by adding Mardonios' 300,000 (8.113.3) to Tigranes' 60,000 at Mykale, and even by the story that Cyrus separated his army into 360 divisions to divide the river Gyndes into separate channels (1.189.3)! Finally, it is argued, the figure of 360,000 men actually represents the total paper-strength of the Persian armed forces, all of which the Greeks assumed Xerxes brought with him, whereas in fact he only brought half. Thus, after leaving Akanthos, his army marched in *three* divisions, each commanded by *two* of the six generals in overall command (7.121.2-3).

The main difficulty with any such hypothesis is that – in the end – it rests on too many arbitrary assumptions – for example that the 'correct' figure for the cavalry is 60,000, and that the 'Immortals' formed part of the ordinary establishment, whereas Herodotos specifically says that they did not (7.83.1). It is also very difficult to believe that all Herodotos' infantry contingents were of the same size. The same applies to the theory that the Greeks habitually misinterpreted a Persian unit of 1000 as one of 10,000, so that all figures derived from Persian sources should be divided by ten.[35]

An alternative way of tackling the problem is effectively to ignore the figures given by the sources, and to try to work out how many men Xerxes' had by what German scholars term '*Sachkritik*' (criticism based on facts), i.e. considerations of such things as time, space and supply. Again the main difficulty is that this method involves too many arbitrary assumptions, for instance that 30,000 Persians on the march would have occupied the same space as 30,000 Prussians.[36] The most interesting example of this method is one based on a detailed examination of the water-supply available along Xerxes' route from the Skamander to Doriskos.[37] The conclusion is that the forces from Asia numbered not more than 210,000 of whom 60,000 were non-combatants. However this, too, involves assumptions such as that the water-supply was the same in 480 BC as it was when the Allies were operating in that area in the first World War, and, indeed, that the Persian army's needs would have been the same as those of modern armies.

Perhaps the best way of arriving at a true approximation of the numbers involved is by a combination of these two methods. The Greeks believed (cf. 8.100.5, 113.2ff.; Aischylos, *Persai* 804; Thucydides 1.73.5) that Xerxes took the bulk of the army back to Asia with him after Salamis, but this is belied by the apparent necessity for Artabazos to escort him as far as the Hellespont (8.126.1). Tigranes' army at Mykale might have been largely made up of troops which had formed part of Xerxes' army, but, if we are to believe Herodotos (8.113.2), Mardonios had retained the Medes Tigranes had originally commanded (7.62.1), and the troops at Mykale were probably gathered from local sources. Thus, if Mardonios in fact retained most of Xerxes' army, we may be able to work out how large it was on the basis of the alleged size of his stockaded camp on the Asopos. Herodotos says that this was ten stades square (i.e. c.400 hectares or c.1000

35 Attributed to 'an Oxford scholar' by Hignett, 351, and picked up by Green, 58.

36 Delbrück, 35. Delbrück does, however, concede that an ancient army, unaccompanied by artillery and ammunition caissons (!), would require less space than the Prussian army.

37 F. Maurice, *JHS* 50 (1930), 210-35. A recent attempt to calculate the size of Xerxes' forces on the basis of their food and water requirements comes to the conclusion that they were about equal to those of the Greeks: see T.Cuyler Young, Jr., *Iranica Antiqua* 15 (1980), 213ff.

acres in area: 9.15.3), and it has been estimated that this would have held something like 60-70,000 men, including about 10,000 cavalry.[38] Assuming that the stockade was meant for the troops from Asia, and not also for Mardonios' Greek allies, we would arrive at a total of something like 70-80,000 men for Xerxes' Asiatic army, to which we could perhaps add 10-20,000 for Thracian and Greek allies picked up after he crossed the Hellespont.

A further question is whether Herodotos' description of the army accurately reflects its composition, or whether here, too, he has mistakenly supposed that representatives from all the peoples in the empire were present. One modern scholar has curtly dismissed Herodotos' account as 'a complete fabrication', based on Hekataios' alleged enumeration of all the forces available in the empire (cf. 5.36.2),[39] though it is not clear why Herodotos should be believed when he tells us about Hekataios' survey, but not when he claims to be describing Xerxes' army. On the face of it it does seem unlikely that some of the more outlandish contingents actually went to Greece, but another modern scholar has argued that the picturesque details Herodotos supplies, are the kind of thing men who saw them might have remembered,[40] and it is true that they are not likely to have occurred in an official list. On the other hand, they are the kind of detail which could have been included in a work such as Hekataios is supposed to have written.

Certainty is not possible, but we may perhaps allow that Xerxes' army did at least include contingents which are mentioned elsewhere than in the general description of the army as it was at Doriskos. This would mean that it included Persians – as one would have expected – Medes, Kissians, Sakai, Baktrians and Indians, in each case both infantry and cavalry (7.210.1, 8.113.2, 9.31.1-4). In addition, there may have been smaller detachments of Phrygians, Mysians, Thracians, Paionians, Ethiopians and others, such as are alleged to have been included in Mardonios' army at Plataia (9.32.1). As such the army would have been strong in cavalry, missile troops and light infantry, but weak in infantry capable of withstanding the shock of a hoplite attack. If the hoplites available to them from their Greek subjects were too few or unreliable, or most of them were committed to the fleet, they should, perhaps, have thought of hiring mercenaries. But they may have felt that what had happened at Marathon would not recur, and assumed that what they had done against hoplites in Egypt and in the Ionian revolt, they could do again.

The numbers given in the sources for the size of Xerxes' fleet also present a problem. According to Herodotos (7.89-95, 184.1) there were originally 1207 triremes from Asia, and this figure almost certainly lies behind what Aischylos says in the *Persai* (341-3). His language is slightly equivocal, but although he could mean that Xerxes'

---

38 Burn, 511; Connolly, *Greece and Rome at War* (London, 1981), 29, suggests 120,000 for the whole army, including cavalry.

39 N. Sekunda, 'The Persians' in *Warfare in the Ancient World*, ed. Sir John Hackett (London, 1989), 88. Sekunda seems to imply that he accepts Ktesias' figure of 800,000 men, on the grounds that Ktesias 'used Persian sources'!

40 Cook, 104, cf. 114. Olmstead, *History of the Persian Empire* (Chicago, 1948), 237ff., thinks Herodotos may have secured some kind of roster of Xerxes' army from Persian sources, but this seems unlikely.

fleet consisted of 1000 ships, of which 207 were particularly fast, it is more likely that he means that it consisted of 1000 ordinary ships, *plus* 207 particularly fast ones.[41] Aischylos' figures apply to Salamis, but there is, strictly speaking, no discrepancy from Herodotos here for the latter claimed that 120 further ships had been added to Xerxes' fleet from Thrace and its off-shore islands (7.185.1), and that the losses which occurred during the Artemision campaign, were made up before Salamis (8.66). Even if this is unbelievable, it seems clear that there was a strong and early tradition that there had once been 1207 triremes in the Persian fleet, and, for what it is worth, Diodoros more or less agrees with Herodotos. He first says that there were 'more than' 1200 triremes (11.2.1, 3.7), though he then gives numbers for the individual contingents which differ slightly from those of Herodotos, and which in fact add up to exactly 1200 (11.3.7-8). Ktesias (23), perhaps misinterpreting Aischylos, gives the total as 1000. Herodotos also says that there were at least 3000 other craft, of one kind or another (7.97, cf. 184.3), possibly more (cf. 7.186.1), though Diodoros (11.3.9) gives the number of triakonters alone as 3000. Both Herodotos (7.97) and Diodoros (loc.cit.) also mention horse-transports, the latter giving their number as 850, though quite what they were doing is unclear, since one would have thought even the spare horses would have accompanied the army.

It is often claimed[42] that Herodotos was perhaps subconsciously aware that his figures for the Persian fleet were far too high, and he is accused of trying, in effect, to reduce them by exaggerating the losses in storms off Magnesia and Euboia, as though, as he says (8.13), 'everything was being done by God that the Persian forces might be made equal to the Greek and not be much larger.' This, however, not only conjures up a strange picture of the historian's mentality, but is nonsense in any case, since in the end he evidently believed, or at least affected to believe, that any losses inflicted by God, were made up by man before Salamis (8.66).

Moreover, one of the passages which is sometimes cited as indicating an awareness that the Persian fleet was not really as large as he said, is in fact consistent with his figures. In it (7.236.2) Achaimenes warns Xerxes that if, after losing 400 ships by shipwreck, he detaches another 300 to attack the Peloponnese, the Greeks will be equal in number. As it stands this means that the Persian fleet had originally been at least 1000-1100 ships strong, assuming that Achaimenes estimated the Greeks at between 300 and 400. In fact, however, according to Herodotos, the Persians had lost not 400, but 600, in storms (cf. 7.190, 8.7.1 & 13), and more than 45 by enemy action (cf. 7.194.1, 8.11.2, 14.2, 16.3). Thus detaching a further 300 would have meant that the

41 Tarn, (*JHS* 28, 1908, 203) suggested that the 207 should be included in the 1000, but the grammar of the passage suggests Aischylos intended to contrast the 1000 with the 207: cf. Beloch, ii 2 67; Macan (1908) ii 150, n.5; Hignett, 344. Fehling, 233, following Beloch, typically argues that 'Aeschylus' figure is based on the assumption that Xerxes had as many ships as Agamemnon in the *Iliad*,' which would come to around 1200, (cf. Thucydides 1.10.4), and that Aischylos then added seven because he 'needed an irregular number'. This seems to me to be carrying criticism to absurdity, and as Fehling himself points out (233, n.4), Aischylos himself actually describes Agamemnon's fleet as 1000-strong (στόλον χιλιοναύταν: *Agamemnon* 45).

42 Cf., e.g., Burn, 331; Hignett, 209 & 347; Green, 61.

remainder would only have numbered between 300 and 400, precisely as Achaimenes implies.

It may be argued that in relating what Achaimenes allegedly said, Herodotos appears to forget the destruction of the 200 ships sent round Euboia, to say nothing of the losses in battle. But although it is just conceivable that the historian derived the story from the descendants of Damaratos, who was also allegedly present, it is more likely that what we have here is a typical example of Herodotos' method of discussing strategic alternatives through the medium of a discussion between some of the participants in his story. He himself knew, or believed he knew, that the Persian fleet had by now lost more than 645 vessels to storm and enemy action. But he could not have Achaimenes refer to the losses in the second storm, or in the fighting, either because he thought that at that point they would not have been known to the land forces, or because he had not himself mentioned them in his narrative.[43] So he can only have Achaimenes refer to the loss of 400 ships in the first storm, but the point he himself is making really depends on his own knowledge of what had happened. Thus the passage can certainly not be used to prove that the Persian fleet was really much smaller than Herodotos says.

As usual, we are left with probabilities, and some scholars are prepared to accept Herodotos' figures.[44] The existence, as early as 472, of a tradition that the Persian fleet had at one time numbered 1207 ships, is one good reason to believe what the historian says, and it is worth remembering that ships are much easier to count than men. On the other hand, this would be by far the largest fleet ever recorded, and the logistic problems would have been horrific, with well over a quarter of a million mouths to feed on the triremes alone, to say nothing of those on smaller craft of one kind or another. However, the Greeks clearly consistently believed that they were heavily outnumbered by the Persians at sea, and if Herodotos' account of the tactics employed by the Persians on the first and last days of the fighting at Artemision is accurate, these also confirm that the Persians had a much larger fleet (see below, 138–40, 148–9). In what follows it will be assumed that there were originally at least something of the order of 12-1300 triremes in the Persian fleet, that this number was whittled down by losses in storms and by enemy action to something like 5-600, but that the numbers were not significantly made up before Salamis.

Even if both the land and sea forces were much less numerous than Herodotos believed, there is no reason to doubt that the preparations for the invasion were on a

---

43 Cf. G.Giannelli, *La spedizione di Serse da Terme a Salamina* (Milan, 1924), 25.

44 E.g. Grundy, 219. Hammond, 1988, 532, even accepts Aischylos' figure of 1207 for Salamis, and then goes on to add *another* 200 on the basis of Plutarch, *Themistokles* 12.5. But what Plutarch says here is surely based on Aischylos, whom he quotes at 14.1, and does not mean that the 200 were in addition to the 1207. Hammond goes on to say that Herodotos recorded a figure 'in excess of 1200 ships', referring to 8.66.1, compared with 7.184.1 & 185.1. But in 8.66.1 he merely says that the ships which arrived at Athens were 'no fewer' (οὐκ ἐλάσσονες) than those with which the Persians had reached Sepias, because the numbers lost in storm and battle had been made up from medizing states! Wallinga, *Actus. Studies in Honour of H.L.W.Nelson* (ed. J. den Boeft & A.H.M.Kessels (Utrecht,1982), 463-5, suggests that it may not so much be the figures for Xerxes' *ships* which are at fault, as the assumption made already by Herodotos in his calculations that each ship had a crew of 200. But this is to fly in the face of too much evidence that triremes normally had something like 170 rowers.

Pl. 11 (top): the Western end of Xerxes' canal across the isthmus of Mt. Athos. (Photo: N. Fields). Pl. 12 (bottom): possibly one of the last traces of the western end of the canal from the sea. (Photo: N. Fields).

colossal scale, in comparison with anything to which the Greeks were accustomed. An army of 70,000 men, for example, would be seven times as numerous as the largest contingent fielded by a single city state, on the Greek side, if we count the 5000 *perioikoi* as part of the same contingent as the Spartiates, nearly nine times as numerous as the 8000 hoplites fielded by Athens; if the fleet was only 6-800 triremes strong, as many scholars believe, it was three to four times as large as the Athenian fleet. The organizational skills required to assemble, feed amd move forces of this magnitude from Sardis to Athens alone would tax the resources of most modern states, and it says wonders for the sheer 'professionalism' of the Persians that they were able to get their forces to Attica more or less intact.

We know about such feats as the construction of bridges across the Hellespont and Strymon (7.36ff. & 24), the cutting of the canal through the Athos-isthmus (7.22-4) (see Pls 11 & 12), the building of a road through Thrace (7.115.3), and the establishment of food-dumps along the Thracian coast (7.25), but we can only really guess at how the army and navy was fed, once it had passed beyond Persian-controlled territory. It is usually assumed that the army depended upon sea-borne supplies,[45] but there is no evidence that this was the case, and it is extremely unlikely. From the moment when the army departed from Therma, it was out of contact with the fleet for at least eighteen days, and possibly a day or two more (see below, 119–23), yet it did not starve, and when, after Salamis, the fleet returned to Asia Minor, Mardonios was clearly still able to operate effectively, possibly with the bulk of the army still under his command. Herodotos says that the supplies for the food-dumps were transported to them by sea (7.25.2), but there is no suggestion in the passage that the army would continue to be supplied by sea, and some slight implication that it would not be.

There is evidence that there were supply-ships with the fleet (7.184.5, 186.1 & 191.1), but these would surely have been carrying supplies for the *fleet*, not the army. Even if we assume that the fleet was as small as 600 triremes, they would have contained 138,000 men, and the crews of other vessels, including those of the supply-ships themselves, would also have had to be fed. In other words, the chances are that there were more men serving at sea than on land, and triremes at least were not designed to carry food for more than a day or two at most. Thus every ounce of food transported by sea would have been needed for the fleet.

In addition to the food-dumps in Thrace, Herodotos clearly implies that the army was fed in two ways – by carrying supplies with it and by living off the land. Thus, in the conversation at Abydos between Xerxes and Artabanos he reports (7.46-53), in response to Artabanos' gloomy prognostication that the army was bound to starve, even if no resistance was encountered, Xerxes declares that 'in the first place we march carrying quantities of supplies with us, and in the second, whatever land and people we come to, we shall have their food, for we are marching against men who are farmers, not nomads' (7.50.4). 'Draught animals' (ὑποζύγια: 7.25.2), a term which Xenophon says included oxen, mules and horses (*Economics* 18.4), are mentioned several times. The food-dumps are said to have been established partly to feed them (7.25.1), and they

45 Cf., e.g., Delbrück, 91; Custance, *War at Sea* (Edinburgh & London, 1919), 26f.; Grundy, 269, 368-9; Hignett, 208; Burn, 318-9; Green, 110 & 171. For the difficulties of supplying the fleet see T.Cuyler Young, Jnr., *op.cit.* n.37 above, 224ff.

turn up again at the departure from Sardis and at the crossing of the Hellespont (7.40.1, 55.1); even Herodotos was not prepared to try to estimate their number (7.187.2). We learn later that they included camels, for these were allegedly attacked by lions on the march through Paionia and Krestonia (7.125). Some food may also have been carried by human porters, though the word Herodotos uses (σκευόφοροι: 7.40.1) rather implies that they carried equipment.

In any case, the army could not possibly have carried all the food it needed, since, apart from anything else, draught-animals themselves need to be fed, as the passage about the food-dumps indicates, and almost certainly it mainly lived off the land, as Xerxes implies in his reply to Artabanos. Herodotos describes vividly how ruinous it was even for the king's subjects in Thrace (7.118-120), to feed him and his men. The cost to the Thasians, for example, was allegedly 400 talents (7.118), and Megakreon of Abdera advised his fellow-citizens to thank the gods that Xerxes did not dine twice a day (7.120.1). Presumably those regarded as hostile would have been even more harshly treated.

Herodotos says (7.20.1) that preparations for the expedition took four full years from the subjugation of Egypt, and that the march began as the fifth was coming to an end. In fact, the Egyptian rebellion can hardly have ended earlier than late in 485, and Xerxes certainly set out for Sardis before the end of 481, since he spent the winter of 481/0 there, setting out for Abydos in spring 480 (cf. 7.37.1). Thus the preparations can only have taken three full years at most. We can possibly date the departure for the west precisely to the day. Herodotos says that there was an eclipse of the sun when the army left Sardis (7.37.2), but there was no eclipse visible at Sardis in 480, save that of 2 October. This is the one Herodotos mentions (9.10.3) as taking place shortly after Salamis. It is possible that the annular eclipse of 16 February, 478, was predated to connect it with the expedition, but in fact this would almost certainly have been too early a date for the army to have left Sardis. There was, however, a total eclipse of the sun visible at Sousa on 18 April, 481, and it is possible that Herodotos or his source transferred this one to the departure from Sardis. According to Herodotos, Xerxes consulted the Magi about its significance, but was assured that since it was the Greeks to whom the sun gave warning, the omen foretold the eclipse of their cities (7.37.2). In the light of what happened, one would very much like to know what happened to these forecasters.[46]

46 Cf. HW ii, 144-5 *ad* 7.37.2.

CHAPTER 5

Phoney War

Herodotos says (7.138.1) that the Greeks had long been aware that the Persian preparations were directed at the whole of Greece, though Athens was the ostensible target. He even says that the Spartans were informed by their exiled king, Damaratos, before Xerxes left Sousa: to escape detection, he scraped the wax off a folded tablet, wrote his message on the wood, and then covered it again with wax – it took all the ingenuity of Leonidas' wife, Gorgo, to discover the secret (7.239). This is a tall story, for it is difficult to believe that Persian 'roadguards' (7.239.3) would have been prepared to pass apparently blank tablets – their very blankness would surely have made the guards deeply suspicious. Probably the story ultimately derives from Damaratos' descendants, and was an attempt to exonerate him, though Herodotos himself says that it was open to conjecture whether the ex-king did it out of good will or malicious pleasure. Nevertheless, there can be little doubt that there would have been a swelling flood of rumours reaching Greece from the moment preparations began in the Persian empire.

In a situation like this, modern states would resort to diplomacy and begin to put themselves on a war footing, but probably the first thing most Greeks would have thought of doing would have been to consult the oracle at Delphi, as Herodotos implies. Thus, he says that the Argives consulted Delphi as soon as they learned of the Persian preparations against Greece (7.148.2), and that they received their response before the arrival of the envoys sent by the Greeks who decided to resist, at their first meeting (7.148.3). He also says that there was a story current in Greece that Xerxes actually sent an envoy to Argos, before he started on his march, asking the Argives to remain neutral, on the grounds of the relationship between 'Perses', the eponymous ancestor of the Persians, and the Argive hero Perseus.

This may seem an absurd story to us, but diplomacy based on such mythological claims was by no means uncommon in the ancient Greek world, and, as Herodotos says (7.151), the story may be borne out by subsequent Argive attempts to renew the friendly relations they had established with Xerxes, with his son, Artaxerxes. Of course, these relations could have been established later, after Argos had decided to remain neutral, but in view of the known hostility between Argos and Sparta, there is nothing unlikely about a Persian attempt to win Argos over at an early stage. If this is the case, the Argives could well have been among the first Greek states to consult Delphi. Similarly, the Spartans are said to have consulted the oracle 'right at the beginning of the war' (7.220.3), and although the Cretans are alleged to have sent to Delphi only when envoys from the Greek patriots arrived (7.169), it seems improbable that the envoys would have been kept waiting in this way.

The most important of the oracles Herodotos records are the ones supposedly delivered to the Athenians, and they have been the subject of endless controversy.[1] Unfortunately Herodotos does not make it as clear as he does in the cases of Argos and Sparta, when Athens consulted the oracle, but although it has been argued that the consultation or consultations took place at some point in 480, usually after the Tempe expedition, there is really no reason to doubt the implication of Herodotos' narrative that they actually took place in 481. The Athenians are likely to have heard the rumours of Persian preparations as soon as any, and it would have been obvious to all that Athens would be a primary target. Thus even if Herodotos did not clearly imply that the Athenians sent to Delphi before the first meeting of the Greeks determined to resist, i.e. in the autumn of 481, it would be likely that they did.

More intractable are the questions whether Herodotos' versions of the oracles accurately reproduce what was actually said, what Delphi may have originally intended them to mean, and, more particularly, how the Athenians responded. According to Herodotos, when their official representatives, the *theopropoi*, had performed the customary sacrifices and taken their seats in the temple, the priestess of Apollo first delivered a doom-laden response advising flight to the 'ends of the earth' and foretelling utter destruction (7.140.2-3). Thereupon, however, on the advice of a Delphian well-wisher, the *theopropoi* approached the god a second time as suppliants, and were given the immortal response (7.141.3-4):

> Pallas cannot wholly win round Olympian Zeus
> Though beseeching him with many words and deep guile.
> But to you I will speak again this word, making it like adamant.
> Though the rest is taken, such as the bound of Kekrops
> Keeps within and the sacred nook of holy Kithairon,
> The wooden wall to the Triton-born grants far-seeing Zeus
> Shall alone be untaken, and will help you and your children.
> But do not you await the horse and foot advancing
> In vast host from the continent, without moving, but withdraw,
> Turning your back: yet I tell you one day you will be face to face.
> O divine Salamis, you will be the death of women's sons,
> Either when Demeter is scattered or when she is gathered in.

This response the envoys duly wrote down and reported to the Athenian people, whereupon there was considerable debate about its meaning, and, in particular, that of the phrase 'the wooden wall' and of the reference to Salamis. In the end, perhaps, it does not really matter what the oracle was originally intended to convey[2] – what matters

---

1 On the oracles see Hignett, Appendix XIII, 439-47; and, more recently, e.g., A.R.Hands, *JHS* 85 (1965), 55ff.; J.A.S.Evans, *CJ* 78 (1982/3), 24ff.; N.Robertson, *CPh* 82 (1987), 1ff.; Hammond, 1988, 540ff.

2 Robertson's hypothesis (*op.cit.*) is the most radical – that Delphi was advising the Athenians to withdraw to the Peloponnese, and not even fight at Salamis, the 'wooden wall' being the Isthmus wall. But why should Delphi have referred to this as a '*wooden*' wall? When built, though timber was used, it was mainly of stone, brick and sand (8.71.2), as Greek walls

is how the Athenians eventually interpreted the meaning. Delphi may have meant, for example, that although the advice to flee stood, and in particular not to try to resist by land, the Athenians would at least be safe if they took to their ships and emigrated. This is, after all, what Herodotos implies he thought was meant, since he says (7.139.6) that the Athenians were *not* persuaded by 'fearful oracles' to leave Greece, but decided to stay and await the invasion. Nor does it really matter, at least as far as the question of the 'wooden wall' is concerned, whether Herodotos' version of the response exactly reproduces what the priestess of Apollo said and the *theopropoi* wrote down. There can be no doubt that some such phrase figured in the discussion of the oracle, and that the Athenians eventually accepted that it meant 'ships'.

According to Herodotos (7.142.1ff.), amongst the various views in Athens about the oracle's meaning, there were two extremes (7.142.1). Some of the older men maintained that by 'the wooden wall' the oracle meant the acropolis, which had been fenced about with a palisade in ancient times. How they thought this might save the bulk of the population is not clear, but in any case it was the alternative view that prevailed. However, those who argued that 'ships ' was the meaning, Herodotos says, were worried by the reference to Salamis, since those skilled in the interpretation of oracles took this to mean that they would be defeated off Salamis, if they tried to fight at sea. At this point, Themistokles came forward and argued that if the oracle had meant this, it would have described Salamis as 'cruel', not 'divine', and that the prophecy was one of disaster to the enemy, not the Athenians. This interpretation the Athenians accepted (7.143), and after a digression on Themistokles' previous advice about using the silver from the Laureion mines for building a fleet, Herodotos concludes by saying that the result of the debate was that the Athenians decided 'to await the barbarian coming against Greece with their ships in full force, in obedience to the god, with those Greeks who wished' (7.144.3).

There is obviously some suggestion here that the arguments may have gone on for a considerable time, but it is hardly implied that it took months, rather than weeks or even days, for the Athenians to make up their minds. In any case, since Herodotos goes on to describe the first meeting of the Greeks determined to resist (7.145.1ff.), the implication is, clearly, that the Athenians had decided before the meeting. The only difficulties about accepting this implication would seem to be that to do so requires us to believe that the Athenians made up their minds to make their effort at sea from the first, and that the prospect of fighting at Salamis was also present in their minds from the beginning.

About the first of these suppositions, however, there really is no difficulty. Once the Athenians had made up their minds to resist, they could hardly have done anything else but decide to make their main effort at sea. They had been building ships for some three years, and, if we are to believe Herodotos (7.144.2), already had two hundred, with more planned. Although the ostensible purpose of the fleet was to fight Aigina (7.144.1), it is hardly possible to believe that anyone of any sense would not have

---

usually were. Moreover, if 'the *rest*' that lay within Kekrops' bound and Kithairon was to be taken (7.141.3, lines 4-5), does not this imply that the 'wooden wall' was also, in some sense, in *Attica*? Finally, if, as early as 481, Athens wanted to fight at Salamis (14ff.), and Sparta only for the Peloponnese, even if the Thessalian appeal could not be ignored, why fight at Thermopylai and Artemision? Robertson's answer to this (17), is very weak.

realised that so huge a fleet was not just needed against Aigina, and it did not need a Themistokles to realise that the Persians were likely to seek revenge for Marathon. We do not have to suppose that at this stage the Athenians had worked out any detailed strategy, or even thought about where to try to make a stand – all that would depend on which other states joined them. But even if Herodotos is right that no formal contact with other potential resisters had yet been made, there is no reason to doubt that the Athenians would have assumed that at least Sparta and her allies would resist, and that their main contribution would be land forces. The best contribution Athens could make was obviously at sea, if only because there was no point in having a large fleet and then not using it.

The reference to Salamis is more difficult. In the first place it fits rather oddly into the context of the oracle as a whole. Despite the concession about the 'wooden wall', whatever that may have been intended to mean, right down to the third line from the end, the advice is to flee. Then suddenly, in line 10, comes the first hint of the possibility of resistance – 'Yet I tell you one day you will be face to face' – and, finally, comes the reference to Salamis, which, despite Themistokles' ingenious argument, is still full of foreboding. A more likely context for a discussion about the suitability of Salamis for a confrontation would seem to be the many arguments that took place there after the Greek fleet had returned from Artemision. One could well imagine one of those who advocated withdrawal to the Isthmus, seizing upon the prophecy about Salamis to reinforce his point, and it would certainly then have taken all Themistokles' ingenuity to argue that it was not disaster, but victory, that was foretold.

But far more serious is the degree of prescience we are required to assume in the Delphic priesthood, if Salamis was mentioned as the scene of confrontation as early as the autumn of 481. It has been argued that it would not have required much intelligence to assume that a confrontation between the Persian and Athenian navies was eventually likely to take place in the Saronic Gulf,[3] but one wonders. It would mean that Delphi would have had to assume either that no attempt would be made to stop the Persians before they reached that point, or that any such attempt would fail.

This is not inconceivable, but it seems implausible. Delphi may have been aware in advance of the attitude of many of the states of northern and central Greece, since they were well represented on the Amphictyonic Council which managed the shrine, and Herodotos does say that when faced with Xerxes' demands for 'earth and water', most of the north-eastern Greeks, and all the Boiotians save the peoples of Thespiai and Plataia, acquiesced (7.132.1). But, even so, why should Delphi assume that if the Athenians were prepared to resist at all, and that by sea, they would only do so at Salamis? Even if it could be assumed that the majority of any allies they acquired would be likely to be Peloponnesians, and that the latter would naturally think in terms of defending the Isthmus, was it plausible, at this stage, to assume that the Athenians would make no attempt to hold the enemy north of Attica? If Delphi was prepared to accept the possibility of resistance at all, it would, surely, have assumed that the Athenians would do their best to defend their land, not that they would be prepared to evacuate it, and still carry on the fight. Because, with the benefit of hindsight, we know that this is what

3 Hammond, 1982, 80 n.24.

the Athenians were prepared to do, we should not forget what an extraordinary decision it was.

The problem of the 'wooden wall' oracle has been further complicated by the discovery of the 'Themistokles Decree' at Trozen (ML 23). This purports to contain the actual text of the decree that is implied by Herodotos' use of the technical term for a decision of the Athenian people – ('ἔδοξε', literally 'it seemed good': 7.144.3) – in reporting the result of the debate on the oracle. Controversy about the authenticity of the decree has continued to rage since it was first published, and it is difficult to imagine how the question can ever finally be settled.[4] However, it is now generally agreed that the inscription itself dates from the mid-3rd century, and few would argue that it is an accurate copy in every detail – for example, most commentators accept that some of the terminology of the preamble is anachronistic, and that the gods to whom the trierarchs are required to sacrifice are inappropriate for early-5th century Athens.

If genuine, the decree clearly antedates the Artemision campaign, since it provides for the sending there of 100 ships (lines 41-2), but by how long? It has been argued that some of the decree's provisions do indeed fit the situation in the autumn of 481, which is the implied date of Herodotos' decree, as we have seen. For example, the places to which the evacuees from Athens are to be taken do not include Aigina, and this might suggest that Athens was still at war with the island, whereas one of the outcomes of the first conference of the Greek resisters was the ending of this war (7.145.1); the provision that 100 ships are to be based 'off Salamis and the rest of Attica and guard the land' (lines 42-4), might also indicate that Athens still feared Aiginetan attacks.[5]

But is it really plausible to suppose that as soon as the Athenians decided to resist, they thought of sending part of their fleet to Artemision? This place was later chosen for the fleet's position because it tied in with the defence of Thermopylai (see below, 117–8), but that would require help from allies, and at this point *ex hypothesi*, the Athenians had none, since the first meeting of those determined to resist had not yet taken place. It is true that the decree assumes that the Spartans and others will 'share the danger' (lines 16-8), though unfortunately the other names are not clear on the stone.[6] But would the Athenians have assumed that the others would accept Athenian strategy? Indeed, would they publicly have named potential allies, before any alliance had been concluded?

Secondly, one wonders whether the Athenians would already have been planning the evacuation of Attica as early as the autumn of 481. It will be argued below that the decision to evacuate was taken long before Herodotos seems to imply – certainly before the Artemision campaign, and possibly before the abortive expedition to Tempe. But in the autumn of 481 the important thing, surely, was to unite all Athenians behind the

---

4 The bibliography on this subject is now vast – see the bibliography to the present volume. For an excellent introduction to the problems see ML 23, pp.50-2. For an illuminating discussion of the question why the Trozen inscription may have been set up when it was see N.Robertson, *Phoenix* 36 (1982), 1ff.: to my mind, this virtually proves that the decree is not authentic. I use the spelling 'Trozen' out of respect and affection for my old tutor, W.S.Barrett – see his edition of the *Hippolytos* of Euripides (Oxford, 1964), 157, *ad* line 12.

5 Hammond, 1982, 84f.

6 ML 23 restore the name 'Aiginetans' (Αἰγινητῶν), but any nine-letter name will do: 'Sikyonians' (Σικυωνίων) was suggested by A.M.Prestianni, *Umanità e Storia: Scritti in onore di A.Attisani* (Messina, 1971); 'Chalkidians' (Χαλκιδέων) by Hammond, 1982, 85-6.

decision to resist, and to resist at sea. This was no time for spelling out the possibly alarming consequences of such a decision, even if there were those prescient enough to appreciate what those consequences might be.

One even wonders, finally, whether this was an appropriate time for deciding in detail how to mobilize the fleet. Nobody, surely, expected the Persians to arrive before the following spring, and although there might have been something to be said for allocating trierarchs and crews to their ships as soon as possible, so that they could begin to train together, the fleet would presumably have had to be stood down during the winter. These provisions, like the allocation of half the fleet to Artemision, the assumption that Athens will have allies, and the planning of evacuation, really fit the context of the spring, or even early summer, of 480, much better than the autumn of 481. It is the general, but decisive, terms of Herodotos' decree which are right for the autumn of 481. Thus, even if the Trozen decree is an authentic copy of one passed at the time of Xerxes' invasion, it is very unlikely to be the one to which Herodotos refers.

Other apparent discrepancies with Herodotos need not detain us – for example, even those who believe in the authenticity of the decree are prepared to accept that it was 'modified in execution', and that two hundred Athenian ships eventually fought at Artemision – twenty manned by 'Chalkidians' – whereas the decree provides for only one hundred to go there, while the rest remained 'off Salamis and the rest of Attica' (lines 41-4). But can we accept the detailed provisions for mobilization, and, in particular, the number of marines for each vessel? Obviously when the Athenians did mobilize their fleet in 481 or 480 they would have had to make detailed arrangements in something like the way the decree envisages, but one wonders whether the details would ever have been embodied in a full-blown decree of the assembly, and some do not ring true – for example, the apparent implication (lines 30-2) that the 'foreigners' (ξένοι), living in Athens, are to provide half the crews.[7]

It is also odd that the ships are apparently to be assigned to their trierarchs by lot (lines 22-3). We do not, of course, known how such things were done in 481/0, but it was later practice for the state to assign hulls to trierarchs to equip, and there was great rivalry between them to do this on a lavish scale (cf. e.g., Thucydides 6.31). Herodotos tells us that at least one trierarch at Artemision, Kleinias, son of Alkibiades, served at his own expense and with his own ship (8.17), and this may be a loose way of describing the later system. For what it is worth the author of *The Constitution of the Athenians* (22.7) implies that the way Themistokles' new triremes had been built was that the state lent the richest men in Athens a talent each, on the understanding that they would use it to build ships, and although he differs from Herodotos on the number of ships so built, the mechanism for building them makes sense.[8] If so, men like Kleinias would surely have been extremely disgruntled if their ships and crews had then been alloted to someone else!

As for the manning of the ships, the decree says ten '*epibatai*' (i.e. hoplites) between the ages of twenty and thirty, and four archers, are to be assigned to each (lines 23-5),

---

7 It is Jameson himself who admits that his decree may have been 'modified in execution,' *Hesperia* 29 (1960), 205. For doubts about the details of how crews are to be assigned see Robertson, *op.cit.* n.1 above, 34ff., though cf. N.G.L.Hammond, *Phoenix* 40 (1986), 143ff.

8 See Podlecki, Appendix B, 201ff.; Rhodes, *ad loc.*

and this too is odd. The numbers are consistent with what Herodotos appears to have thought was the normal complement of Greek warships at this time (cf. 3.14.4-5, 7.185.1, 8.17), but both he and the decree may be anachronistic here. As we have seen (above, 35–6), in view of what he says about the number of marines on Chiot ships at Lade (6.15.2), and on those in Xerxes' fleet (7.184.1), it is likely that the Greek ships at Artemision and Salamis had more than the decree allows. One also wonders why the hoplites assigned to ships are to be under thirty years of age, and what those over thirty were to do. There were no Athenian hoplites at Thermopylai, so are we to imagine that those over thirty simply stayed in Attica when the fleet went north?

There are also problems with what the decree says about the rest of the crews. Thus the '*hyperesiai*' are to be allotted to ships at the same time as the trierarchs (lines 26-7), and not only is the use of the lot here as odd as it is in the case of the trierarchs, but it is not at all clear what is meant by '*hyperesiai*'. Later the term usually refers to deck-crews apart from marines and archers, but if this is the meaning here, we are not told how the latter are to be assigned. Hence it has been conjectured that here the term either refers to marines and archers, or includes them. But this would be an unparalleled usage, and perhaps again betrays the hand of a later forger. There is also, finally, the problem of the number of men to be assigned to each crew, apart from marines, archers and '*hyperesiai*'. On the face of it, the decree appears to assign 100 men to each crew (line 32), and this is too few, if these triremes were similar to later ones, and were to be fully manned.[9]

All in all, then, it seems less and less likely that the decree can be a true copy of an actual decree of 480, and, if the truth were known, the survival of anything like an authentic text has always seemed too good to be true. It is more likely that what we have is basically a patriotic fabrication of the fourth century, put in its final form in the third, and, again, Herodotos' shorter, vaguer version (7.144.3) looks much more like what could have been remembered.

We now return, then, to the autumn of 481, when the Athenians had received the response from Delphi, and had decided, in general terms, to ignore the advice to flee, and to resist the invasion by sea. After consulting the oracle, the Greek states began to behave much as their modern counterparts would behave. Those 'thinking the better about Greece' (τῶν περὶ τὴν Ἑλλάδα τὰ ἀμείνω φρονεόντων: 7.145.1, cf.172.1), to use Herodotos' odd but impressive formulation, met to discuss what to do. The meeting took place, he implies (7.145.2), at about the time the news of Xerxes' arrival at Sardis reached Greece, i.e. in the autumn of 481. He does not say where it took place, and it is usually assumed that it was at the Isthmus of Corinth, the venue for subsequent

9 For the size of later trireme crews see Morrison & Coates, 111; for the meaning of *hyperesia* Morrison, *JHS* 104 (1984), 48ff. Jameson (*Hesperia* 12, 1963, 385ff.) suggests it means marines and archers in the decree, Morrison (*op.cit.*, 50) that it includes them. Meiggs and Lewis (ML 23, p.51) argue that this usage would have been 'impossible for a fourth century forger', but their 'less convincing' explanation – that 'the details of the mobilization are not logically worked out, *thus betraying the hand of the forger* [my italics],' – seems more convincing! They also comment that they 'see no escape from the conclusion' that the decree only assigns 100 rowers to each trireme. For various attempts to 'escape' see Morrison & Coates, 114; Robertson and Hammond, *locc.cit.* n.1 above. Wallinga, *op.cit.* 94 n.44 above, 465, argues that the ships were undermanned.

meetings (cf. 7.172.1, 175.1). However, Pausanias says that there was a place called the 'Hellenion' in Sparta, where the Greeks planned their defence against Xerxes (3.12.6), and it is not impossible that the first meeting was held at Sparta, since she and her allies formed the core of the resistance.[10]

It is also not certain who was represented at this meeting. Presumably there were delegates from Sparta and her allies and from Athens, but the rest is guesswork. Assuming that Mykenai was an ally of Sparta at this time (see above, 87), the additional states represented at Thermopylai and Artemision were Thespiai, Thebes, Opountian Lokris and Phokis, at the former (7.202-203.1), and Chalkis, Eretria, Styra and Keos at the latter (8.1.1-2). Of these one may guess that the Opountian Lokrians and Phokians only joined when the alliance sent forces to occupy Thermopylai, as indeed Herodotos' language rather implies (7.203.1).[11] One suspects, too, that the 400 Thebans at Thermopylai represented the pro-Spartan element in an otherwise at least equivocal community, despite Herodotos' scathing account of their behaviour (7.222 & 233), and that they, too, only joined Leonidas on his march north. But delegates from Plataia and Thespiai may well have attended the first conference, and the same may be true of the three Euboian states – Chalkis, Eretria and Styra – which sent ships to Artemision, and of the island of Keos.

At this first conference, Herodotos says, the Greeks gave each other verbal pledges (cf. 'διδόντων σφίσι λόγον καὶ πίστιν: 7.145.1), and he subsequently refers to 'those of the Greeks who had sworn together against the Persian' (οἱ δὲ συνωμόται Ἑλλήνων ἐπὶ τῷ Πέρσῃ: 7.148.1). This indicates the setting up of a new alliance, in Greek terms a '*symmachia*', as Herodotos suggests by using the term '*symmachoi*' of those who resisted (e.g. 8.2-3), and when he says that the Samians, Chiots and Lesbians were admitted 'to the alliance' ('ἐς τὸ συμμαχικόν': 9.106.4) after Mykale. The latter passage also indicates that the oath included a promise not to desert the alliance. There was evidently some discussion at first about assigning command at sea to the Athenians, but seeing the reluctance of the other allies, the Athenians gave way, and Spartans commanded the forces of the alliance on both elements, from the beginning (8.2-3, cf. 7.160.2f.). Plutarch (*Themistokles* 7.3-4) says that it was Themistokles who persuaded the Athenians to give way on the point, but although this may be true, it smacks a little too much of attempts by later writers to fill in the blanks left by Herodotos, and to assign Themistokles a role wherever possible.

According to Herodotos (7.145.1-2), the conference took three decisions – to patch up quarrels between members of the alliance, of which the most serious was the one between Athens and Aigina, to send spies to Asia, and to send envoys to Argos, Syracuse, Kerkyra and Crete, to ask for help. Possibly it was also at this first conference that the allies swore to tithe all Greek states which submitted to the Persians,

10 For this conference and the alliance then formed see P.Brunt, *Historia* 2 (1953/4), 135ff.; Hammond, 1973, 379ff. Hignett, 98 n.1, says the tradition about the Hellenion at Sparta was 'probably a later invention', but see Brunt, *op.cit.*, 148 and n.2, cf. 156. A.Tronson, *Acta Classica* 34 (1991), 93ff., argues that no new 'Hellenic League' was formed – the alliance was merely 'The Spartans and their Allies'.

11 Brunt, *op.cit.*, 143, thinks Phokis and Lokris were in the alliance from the start, but overlooks 7.203.1.

except under compulsion. Herodotos only mentions this in connexion with a list of states which gave 'earth and water' to the invader, allegedly when Xerxes had reached Therma (7.132.1), and since the list includes the Lokrians and Boiotians who only submitted after Thermopylai, the implication is that the oath to tithe them was only taken then. However, it may originally have been couched in general terms, and may have been intended to warn uncommitted states of the possible consequences of submission. Since the tithe was promised to 'the god at Delphi' (7.132.2), it may also have been an attempt to win Delphi's support, perhaps in the light of the gloomy warnings the oracle had already issued to states like Athens.[12]

The three spies sent to Sardis were caught, but Xerxes ordered that they be shown everything they wanted to see and then released, calculating that their report would only serve to spread alarm in Greece (7.146.1–47.1). It has sometimes been argued that the Greeks would thus have had an accurate idea of the size of Xerxes' forces, but this is to underestimate the capacity of such 'spies' to exaggerate, and, indeed, of those spied upon to employ deliberate deceit, as Herodotos implies may have happened here.[13] Similarly, Xerxes ordered ships carrying provisions to Greece to be allowed to proceed, on the grounds that since the Persians were headed for the same destination, the ships were simply carrying their food for them (7.147.2-3)!

The missions to seek further allies were also an almost complete failure. The Argives demanded a thirty-year peace with Sparta and a share in the command of the alliance's forces, but although the Spartan members of the embassy agreed to refer the former to Sparta, they turned the latter down flat. Herodotos, who seems anxious to excuse the Argive attitude, says that they claimed they had been warned by Delphi to remain neutral (7.148.2ff.), though, as we saw (above, 98), he reports another story current in Greece (7.150-1) that Xerxes sent an envoy to Argos claiming kinship with its people, and asking that they remain neutral. Herodotos refuses to vouch for the truth of any of this – it is here that he reminds his readers that although he felt obliged to record what was said, he did not feel at all obliged to believe it, and that this should be held to apply to all he wrote (7.152.3). Then, as if to assert his impartiality, he reports yet another tradition, that the Argives actually *invited* the Persians to invade Greece because their war with the Spartans was going badly for them (*ibid.*).

Presumably he was thinking mainly of the disastrous battle of Sepeia, but although it has been claimed that 'Argos really had very little choice,'[14] this goes too far. If Herodotos is to be believed, the alliance's overtures in fact offered Argos an honourable way out of her difficulties, for since it was the alliance's declared policy to patch up quarrels between Greek states, presumably Argos would have got her thirty-year peace. It was Argive 'presumption', not, as they claimed, that of the Spartans (7.149.3), which really led to the break-down of the negotiations, since Sparta could hardly be expected

12 Cf. Brunt, *op.cit*, 137; Hignett, 99. Hammond, 1982, 75-9, through a most interesting analysis of Herodotos' style, makes out a good case for thinking that the historian does not really mean to imply that the heralds only returned to Xerxes when he had reached southern Macedonia.

13 N.Robertson, *JHS* 96 (1976), 118, says 'however we regard the story of the spies, details would infallibly reach Greece,' but if the Greeks relied on rumour, they would probably have been even more deceived.

14 Gillis, 'Collaboration with the Persians', *Historia* Einzelschriften 34 (1979), 62.

to concede to Argos what she had not conceded to Athens. Whether the Spartans and their allies really had hopes of winning the Argives to their side, we can never know, nor whether the Spartans secretly hoped to assert their authority over Argos by these round-about means, as, according to Herodotos, the Argives claimed (7.149.3). But in view of the desperate situation facing Greece, there is no compelling reason not to take the alliance's overtures at face-value.

The embassy to Gelon of Syracuse also foundered, according to Herodotos (7.157-62), on Gelon's claim to command either by land or sea. But again he also dutifully reports the Sicilian view that Gelon would have swallowed his pride had he not been faced with a Carthaginian invasion (7.165-7), and whether or not this was true, there can be no doubt that the Carthaginian invasion would have prevented help from being sent to Greece. Later tradition (Ephoros 70F186, Diodoros 11.1.4-5) even claimed that the Carthaginians concerted plans with the Persians. Herodotos, however, though he records the Sicilian tradition that Gelon's victory in Sicily took place on the same day as Salamis (7.166), says nothing of any joint-planning with the Persians, and Aristotle cites the fact that the decisive battles in Greece and Sicily took place at about the same time – not on the same day as in Herodotos – as an example of pure coincidence (*Poetics* 1459a). Some modern scholars are inclined to accept the Ephoros tradition, but, on the whole, it seems unlikely, even though Carthage and Persia will probably have been aware of each other's preparations.[15]

There is, however, no reason to doubt that the Greeks did send an embassy to Gelon, and presumably they had serious hopes that he might help them.[16] Herodotos' account of the forces the tyrant said he could provide (7.158.4), is no doubt exaggerated, but Syracuse was a powerful state at this time, and even fifty or so ships would have been a valuable contribution. Nor is there any reason to doubt the general outline of the exchanges between the Greek representatives and the tyrant, and one would like to believe that the Athenian representative did say that 'Greece did not send us to ask for a leader, but for an army' (7.161.1), and that Gelon responded by saying that it looked likely that they would have commanders, but no one to command.

It is less easy to see what the tyrant meant by saying that the envoys had better go home and tell Greece that the spring had gone out of the year (7.162.1). According to Aristotle (*Rhetoric* 1.7, 1365b31, cf. 3.10), Perikles used the same striking metaphor in a funeral oration – possibly the one for those who fell in the war against Samos in 440/39 – with reference to the dead, where it would seem far more appropriate. Herodotos may have taken it from Perikles, though this is by no means necessarily the case, and it would still be unclear why he gave it to Gelon. Perhaps he intended the tyrant to be comparing the youthful vigour of Syracuse with the declining strength of

---

15 Meyer, n. on 335; Burn, 306 and n.30; Green, 83; P.J.Stylianou, *Meletai kai Hypomnêmata* 2 (Leukôsia, 1989), 423-4. Burn's argument that 'it would scarcely be conceivable, even with no evidence whatever, that Persia and Carthage were not in communication,' is beside the point: communication is one thing, concerting plans quite another. For sceptical views see K.Meister, *Historia* 19 (1970), 607ff., and D.Asheri, *CAH*^{2} iv, 773-4.

16 P.Treves, *CP* 36 (1941), 321ff., denies the historicity of the mission to Gelon, but on inadequate grounds, see Brunt, *op.cit.* n.10 above, 158ff. For the meaning of Gelon's remark about the spring going out of the year see HW ii 198 *ad loc.*

old Greece, or more generally suggesting that by refusing his demands, the Greeks had lost their chance. Finally, it is entirely possible that when he learned that Xerxes had crossed the Hellespont, Gelon sent an envoy, with a considerable sum of money, to Delphi, with instructions to wait and see how the war went: if the Persians won, he was to give the money, together with 'earth and water', to Xerxes, if the Greeks won, to bring it back (7.163.2).

Herodotos says (7.168) that the envoys sent to Gelon, also called in at Kerkyra (Corfu) with the same request, and that the Kerkyraians responded in appropriately patriotic terms. In the event, however, he believed that although they fitted out a fleet of sixty ships, they were deliberately dilatory about sending it to sea, and that it then delayed 'about Pylos and Tainaron' to see what the outcome of events in Greece would be. Again he reports (7.168.4) the Kerkyraian claim that their ships were prevented from rounding Cape Malea by the Etesian winds, but he evidently did not believe it, and, as we have seen (above, 88), if ships from Ambrakia, Leukas and even Kroton in southern Italy (though see below, 173) could arrive in time for Salamis (8.45 & 47), there seems no reason why Kerkyraian ships should not also have done so. Sixty ships would have been the largest contingent in the Greek fleet after that of Athens, and Kerkyraian naval power in the 430s (cf. Thucydides 1.25.4) suggests that they could have provided such a fleet in 480.

The final embassy went to Crete, but was brusquely rejected on Delphi's advice, according to Herodotos (7.169). One wonders why the allies even bothered to send envoys to an island which, as far as we know, had few if any hoplites, and no naval power. Possibly it was felt that Cretan archers would be valuable in the coming fight with the Persians,[17] and Ktesias (26) actually alleges that some were hired by Themistokles and Aristeides to deal with Xerxes' mole at Salamis. But this is an absurd story, as it stands, since there would not have been time. It may have been, rather, for sentimental reasons that appeal was made to Crete. After all, in the *Iliad* the Cretans had, with Diomedes, contributed the third largest contingent to the Greek fleet against Troy, and the Spartans believed Lykourgos had brought their constitution from the island (1.65.4).

Herodotos implies that it was only at the second meeting of those determined to resist that there was any consideration of how to do it, and however improbable this may seem to us, it is not impossible in the context of the early fifth century. This second meeting, he says, took place at the Isthmus (7.172.1), and although he does not say when, we can probably assume it was in the spring of 480, the various measures decided on at the first conference having taken up the winter of 481/0. We do not know what might have been decided at this second conference if the delegates had been left to their own devices, but in the event the situation was completely altered by an appeal from Thessaly.

This was made Herodotos says (7.172.1), when the Thessalians learned that Xerxes was just about to cross the Hellespont, i.e. about the end of May or the beginning of June (see below, 114). According to the historian, the Thessalians were not pleased by the machinations of the Aleuadai of Larisa, who, he says in an earlier passage (7.6.2),

17 Cf. Macan (1908) ii 225.

had been instrumental in urging Xerxes to undertake the invasion.[18] Their envoys suggested that the Greeks should defend the Tempe pass, and what they go on to say in Herodotos, even if it is the historian's own invention, is so likely to have reflected not only the Thessalian viewpoint, but that of other Greeks in a similar situation, like the Boiotians later, that it is worth quoting in full: 'Now we are ready to guard the pass with you, but you, too, must send a substantial force, since if you do not send one, be sure that we shall reach an agreement with the Persian. There is no reason why we, situated as we are far in advance of the rest of Greece, should perish alone on your behalf. If you are unwilling to help, you will not be able to bring any compulsion to bear upon us, for no compulsion is stronger than inability. We will try to work out some means of salvation for ourselves' (7.172.2-3). The response was the sending of an army by sea, through the Euripos, to Halos in Achaia Phthiotis, whence it marched through Thessaly to the pass. The army consisted of 10,000 hoplites under the command of one of the polemarchs of Sparta, Euainetos, the Athenian contingent being under the command of Themistokles (7.173.1-2).

Herodotos only mentions Spartans and Athenians but it is very unlikely that these states were the only ones represented, and we can probably assume that there were also contingents from at least some of Sparta's Peloponnesian allies. Plutarch, in his essay on *The Malice of Herodotos*, possibly drawing on Aristophanes of Boiotia, says that Thebes also sent a contingent of 500 men under Mnamias (*Moralia* 864e), but despite the apparently circumstantial detail, this is not necessarily true. If Plutarch's story of Leonidas' dream, in which he foresaw the future power and sudden decline of Thebes (*Moralia* 865f), also comes from Aristophanes, the latter was still writing after the collapse of the Theban hegemony in the 350s, and so long after the war.[19] In any case, he may have distorted the truth just as much because of pro-Theban bias, as Herodotos allegedly did because of antipathy towards Thebes. It is even possible that the reason for transporting the army to Thessaly by sea was distrust of the Theban attitude.[20]

When the Greek forces reached Tempe, they were duly joined by the Thessalian cavalry, as promised, but only remained in the pass for a few days, before returning to their ships and retiring to the Isthmus.[21] Herodotos says (7.173.3) that messengers arrived from Alexander, King of Macedonia, advising them to withdraw and indicating the size of the forces arrayed against them. But he adds his own opinion that what

---

18 For Thessalian politics at this time see now N.Robertson, *op.cit.* n.13 above, 102-8.

19 Robertson, *op.cit.*, 101, dates Aristophanes of Boiotia to the late fifth/early fourth century, but makes no mention of Leonidas' dream.

20 *pace* Grundy, 228. Robertson, *op.cit.*, 111, says that 'Herodotos does not say or imply that all 10,000 hoplites went by sea,' and suggests that some of the central Greeks went by land. But 'ὡς δὲ συνελέχθη ὁ στρατός, ἔπλεε δι' Εὐρίπου' (7.173.1) surely at least *implies* that the army went by sea, and it would have been easy to pick Boiotians up at, say, Larymna.

21 Robertson, *op.cit.*, 101-2, 113ff., following a fragment of Damastes of Sigeion (*ap.* Speusippos, *Letter to Philip* 30 = *FGH* 5F4), suggests that the Greek position was actually at Herakleion, and this is accepted by, e.g., Hammond, 1982, 76 n.5, 91 n.63, though in 1988, 545, he merely says the Greeks 'probed as far as Heracleum'. But although Robertson claims, 116, that 'the allied army stationed at Heracleium [*sic*] could also prevent a sea-borne landing on the open beaches to north and *south* [my italics],' it is doubtful whether it could have interfered with a landing to its rear, if it was already pinned by a frontal assault.

persuaded them was fear that their position might be 'turned', 'when they learned that there was also another pass into Thessaly by way of upper Macedonia through the Perrhaiboi, by way of the city of Gonnos, the pass which Xerxes' army actually used to invade' (7.173.4).

Some scholars have found Herodotos' explanation for the abandoning of the defence of Tempe unconvincing, and it has even been suggested that there was no expedition on a scale such as he describes.[22] But such doubts will only occur to those who imagine that the Greeks fought wars like a modern state, with all the intelligence apparatus that modern armies can command. If, on the other hand, we assume that the geographical knowledge of Thessaly among southern Greeks was slight, and that they had little or no idea when Xerxes was going to reach Thessaly, or of the likely reaction of the Thessalians, beyond what they had gleaned from the envoys who made the appeal at the Isthmus, there is no problem. The Thessalian envoys may well have been less than frank about other possible routes into their country, and given the southerners the impression that Tempe was another Thermopylai.[23]

Assuming that the expedition to Tempe is historical, and on the scale suggested by Herodotos, several things are worth noting. Firstly, it perhaps indicates the naive way in which the Greeks approached this war, which was so far beyond their normal comprehension. Herodotos says nothing about any Thessalian infantry, and even if they joined the Greek army with all the cavalry they could muster – perhaps 6000 men (cf. Xenophon, *Hellenika* 6.1.8) – the Greeks would still have been assuming that a force of some 16,000 men would be enough to stop the Persians. Such a force no doubt seemed colossal to them, but even if they did not believe the no-doubt already grossly exaggerated rumours of the size of Xerxes' forces, they ought to have had some idea that he probably had at least three or four times as many men as they had at Tempe. Although the terrain may have seemed to be markedly in favour of the defence, they seem to have had no conception of how sheer numbers could be made to tell in the end, nor do they appear to have appreciated that the Persians might not choose just to fling themselves at their lines. Alexander's information, if it is historical, may have begun to give them some inkling of what lay ahead of them, but it is worth considering that a possible explanation for the small size of Leonidas' army at Thermopylai is that the Greeks still thought something of the order of 10,000 men was sufficient.

Nevertheless, although the army sent to Tempe was not nearly as large as the one that could have been raised, judging by the numbers at Plataia (9.29.10), it is larger than the one that fought at Thermopylai (see below, 134–5). This gives the lie to any notion

22 For the view that Herodotos misunderstood the nature and purpose of the Tempe expedition see, e.g., E.Obst, 'Der Feldzug des Xerxes', *Klio* Beiheft xii (1914), 52-5; Munro, *CAH*[1] iv 281-2; de Sanctis, *RFIC* 18 (1930), 339ff.; M.Sordi, *La Lega Tessala fino ad Allessandro Magno* (Rome, 1958), 92ff.; Hignett, 103; F.Schachermeyr, *JöAI* 46 (1963), 169; M.R.Cataudella, *Athenaeum* 43 (1965), 389f.; J.A.O.Larsen, *Greek Federal States* (Oxford, 1968), 117; V.Ehrenberg, *From Solon to Socrates* (2nd edition, London, 1973), 153f.

23 Robertson, *op.cit.*, 114-5, argues that the Greeks need not have worried about the two passes round Olympus to the west, because they would have been defended by the Thessalians, and that the modern view – cf. HW ii 370, Burn, 342f. – that the defenders of Tempe suddenly took alarm at learning of the existence of such passes, is 'naive'. However, I am not so sure that it is not 'naive' to assume this level of military intelligence in the Greeks of 480.

that the Greeks were still not fully prepared at the time of the latter campaign (see below, 136). The Tempe expedition, moreover though it came to nothing, surely indicates that even the Peloponnesians were prepared to fight as far north as possible, given the right political climate. There is no hint in Herodotos' narrative of opposition to the idea of sending an army to Thessaly, or of any lack of will to try to defend central or even northern Greece. The Peloponnesians were evidently not yet thinking just of defending the Isthmus.

The fact that the army intended for Tempe was conveyed by sea as far as Halos in Achaia Phthiotis (7.173.1), also probably indicates that a considerable fleet had already been assembled. The troops were probably carried in triremes, and to transport 10,000 hoplites would have required at least about 250. Moreover, although the fleet was apparently left at Halos, and was evidently not intended to play any part in the defence of Tempe itself, it is not inconceivable that it had a role to play apart from just transporting the army. Even if the Greeks had really been unaware that the pass could be turned by land, they would surely have realised that it could be turned by sea. They may have assumed that there was nowhere on the coast of Magnesia which was suitable for a landing, but their own arrival at Tempe *via* Halos should have suggested the possibility of a Persian landing in the Gulf of Pagasai. Thus the fleet may have been intended to guard against such a possibility. If so, it will not have been entirely denuded of marines, and one would have to suppose that there were probably more than 250 triremes present, to allow for 10,000 hoplites going to Tempe, and some being left behind to fight the triremes.[24]

In short, the fleet committed to the Tempe operations may well have been almost, if not quite, as large as the one later committed to Artemision, and everything we know about the composition of the later fleet would suggest that half or more of the ships which went to Halos were contributed by Athens. In other words, the Athenians were already nobly standing by their decision (7.144.3) 'to await the barbarian coming into Greece with all their forces, along with those Greeks who wished,' even if, at this juncture, conformity to joint decisions taken with the allies they had now acquired, meant that they were serving on land as well as at sea.

This raises the question whether the Athenians had also already decided to evacuate Attica. Herodotos, as is well known, says nothing about this until after the Thermopylai-Artemision campaign, when he has the Athenians issue a 'proclamation' (κήρυγμα: 8.41.1) that 'each man should get his children and members of his household to safety where he could'. But a careful analysis of his own account of the movements of the Greek and Persian fleets after the final engagement at Artemision (8.19-5, 66.1),

24 Robertson, *op.cit.*, 116, dismisses any notion that the fleet had a role to play in the Tempe operations, because of the unapproachability of the coast of Magnesia. But this would not have prevented a landing in the Gulf of Pagasai. He also tends to exaggerate the significance of the operations: surely it was *not* 'the greatest effort of the war' (117), even allowing for the fact that Plataia was much closer to home for most participants. If Herodotos is right that 324 triremes eventually took part at Artemision, this involved at least 64,800 men, and probably something like 74,500, to say nothing of the 7000 or so at Thermopylai. Nor do I think that Robertson is right to say '... the subsequent operations of 480 were inadequate or irresolute; the allies had been demoralised.' Leonidas' army may have been 'inadequate', but there was nothing 'irresolute' or 'demoralised' about either its stand or that of the navy.

reveals that only some six or seven days elapsed between the return of the Greek fleet from Artemision, and the arrival of the Persians. It is hardly conceivable that the entire population of Attica can have been evacuated in the time. Thus, if the credibility of Herodotos' narrative is to be saved here, we must interpret it as meaning that the 'proclamation' was only the final warning that those who had not yet left should now do so, and must assume either that he did not realise that the evacuation had already been decided upon and largely carried out, or that he chose to ignore the fact for dramatic purposes.

The evacuation, then, was at least largely carried out at latest before the fleet was sent to Artemision. But there is another point to be borne in mind. Evidently the Athenians then experienced considerable difficulties in manning their fleet: in the event, twenty of their ships were handed over to the 'Chalkidians', whoever precisely these were (8.1.2),[25] and some of the remainder were even manned by volunteer Plataians, 'though they had no experience of naval service' (8.1.1). It is almost certain that every available able-bodied Athenian, and, possibly, resident-alien, would have been drafted aboard, before resorting to these emergency measures, and it would, surely, have been asking too much of Athenian men-folk to require them to go north, leaving their families defenceless behind them. Even if there were some benighted souls who still believed that Athens' salvation lay in her hoplites, once the fleet was mobilized, they would have realised that there would be precious few, if any, hoplites left. As Herodotos says those who interpreted 'the wooden wall' to mean ships argued, making the ships ready meant ignoring everything else (7.142.2). But if all this was true before Artemision, was it not also true before Tempe? The former is, of course, nearer than the latter, but when the Tempe expedition was sent, there was, presumably, every expectation that it would lead to serious fighting: if the enemy broke through, it might take them longer to reach Attica, but what if a large proportion of the Athenian forces had been destroyed?

The evacuation of Attica before the opening of the campaign in 480 would certainly not imply that even Tempe, let alone Artemision and Thermopylai were not 'all-out' efforts, as has been claimed for the latter.[26] It would simply have been a a sensible precaution. Perhaps it is going too far to assume that the whole thing was carried out before even the fleet left for Halos, but once the Athenians realised that mobilizing their fleet meant that no one would be left behind except women, children, old people and slaves, they would surely have begun to think of evacuation. Certainly once the fleet returned from Thessaly, and it was realised that the next feasible line of defence was the Thermopylai-Artemision one, the Athenians would surely have realised that if that failed, the Persians could be in Attica within the week, as events proved. Nor could the

---

25 It is usually assumed that these 'Chalkidians' were drawn from the Athenian cleruchs settled on Chalkidian land (cf., e.g., HW ii 235 *ad loc.*, Munro, *CAH*[1] iv, 284; Hammond, 1972, 261 n.3, and 1982, 86). Hammond argues that the cleruchs 'are always called Χαλκιδῆς', but so are the people of Chalkis (5.74.2, 77, 91.2, 99.1; 9.28.5, 31.4), and when at 8.46.2 Herodotos describes the Chalkidian crews of these twenty ships as ''Ιωνες', he surely implies that they were *not* Athenians, since he has just given an elaborate explanation of how the Athenians came to be called ''Ιωνες', too (8.44.2). It would, moreover, surely be odd if no Chalkidians fought at Artemision and Salamis, when men from Eretria and Styra did.

26 M.H.Jameson, *Greece and Rome* 8 (1961), 11.

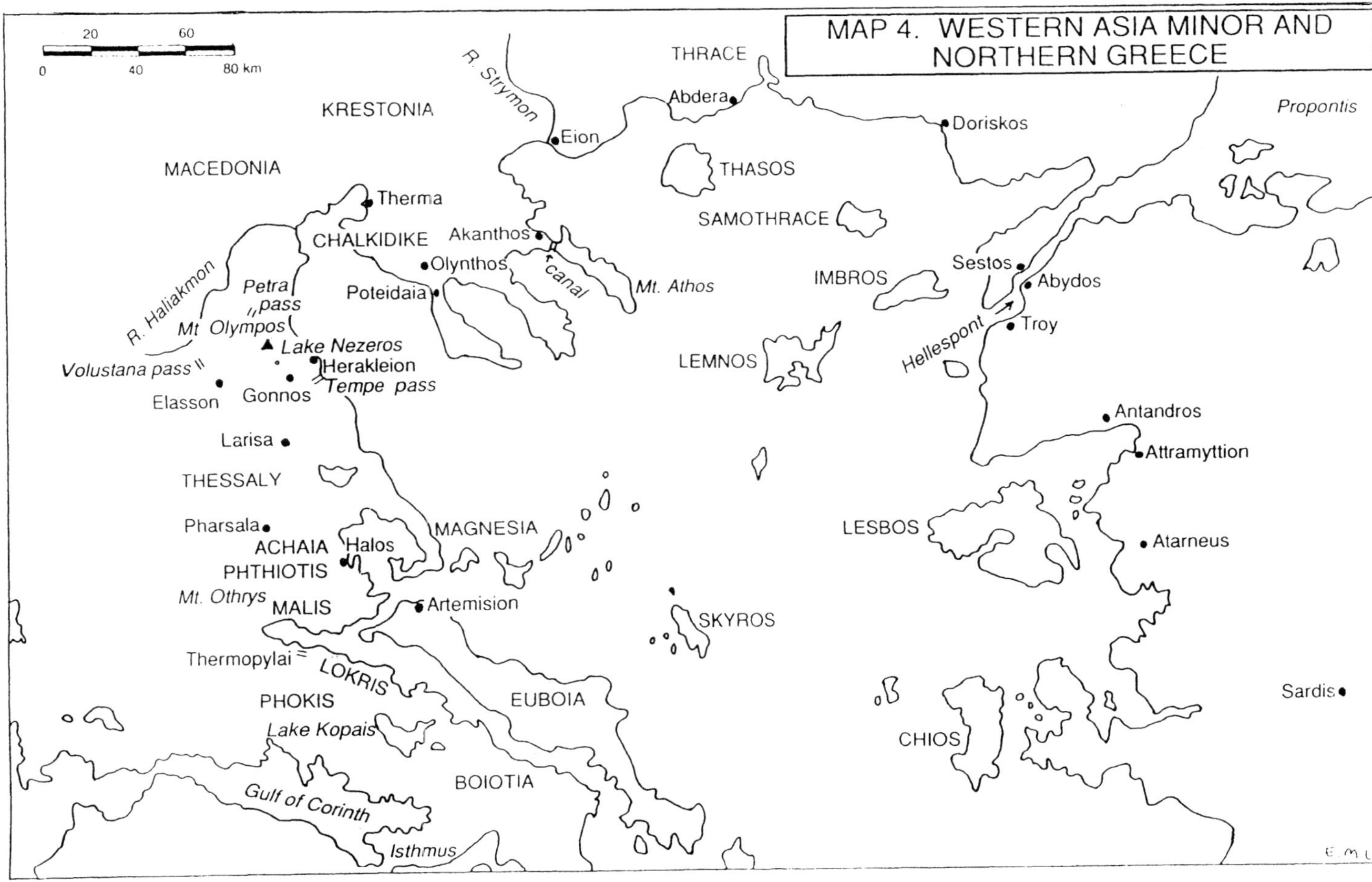

MAP 4. WESTERN ASIA MINOR AND NORTHERN GREECE
0
20
40
60
80 km
KRESTONIA
MACEDONIA
R. Strymon
THRACE
Abdera
Doriskos
Proportis
Eion
THASOS
Therma
SAMOTHRACE
CHALKIDIKE
Akanthos
Olynthos
canal
Mt. Athos
IMBROS
Sestos
Abydos
Poteidaia
R. Haliakmon
Petra pass
Mt Olympos
Lake Nezeros
Herakleion
Tempe pass
Volustana pass
Elasson
Gonnos
LEMNOS
Hellespont
Troy
Antandros
Attramyttion
Larisa
THESSALY
MAGNESIA
Pharsala
ACHAIA
Halos
PHTHIOTIS
Mt. Othrys
MALIS
Artemision
LESBOS
Atarneus
SKYROS
Thermopylai
LOKRIS
PHOKIS
Lake Kopais
EUBOIA
BOIOTIA
Gulf of Corinth
Isthmus
CHIOS
Sardis

men of Athens be expected to carry on the fight, assuming that any of them managed to withdraw from Artemision, if their families had fallen into enemy hands. If the Persians managed to overrun Attica while the non-combatant population was still there, the war, as far as Athens was concerned, was over.

As it turned out, of course, events did not in any case move as fast as some Greeks may have feared. The Greek expedition to Tempe came and went before ever Xerxes even crossed the Hellespont (7.174), and it was probably only about mid-August that he entered Thessaly.[27] The Persian host had set out from Sardis in the spring of 480, the splendour of the occasion somewhat marred, if the story is true, by the dismembering of a young man whose only 'crime' was that his father had begged Xerxes to allow him to remain at home: the army is supposed to have marched out through the two halves of the body.[28] Herodotos says that there was an eclipse of the sun as the army was leaving Sardis (7.37.2), but, as we have seen (above, 97), he has here probably confused the departure from Sardis with the earlier one from Sousa, since the only appropriate eclipse is that of 18 April, 481. Nevertheless, assuming that the battle of Thermopylai took place towards the end of August (see below, 119), it does seem likely that the departure from Sardis took place about mid-April. The route from Sardis to the Hellespont was *via* Atarneus, Karene, Thebe, Atramyttion and Antandros to Troy, to which Xerxes, like many another conqueror after him, paid a visit, and thence to Abydos, where a review of the army and navy was held (7.42-5). The distance from Sardis is about 400 kilometres, and would probably have taken some three to four weeks.

The crossing of the Hellespont took seven days and nights, according to one passage in Herodotos (7.56.1), and although he subsequently says (8.51.1) that the Persians spent a month at the Hellespont, there is no real discrepancy here. The other three weeks might have been taken up with the review and other final preparations, including measures for the governing of the empire in the king's absence – Herodotos says the task was entrusted to Artabanos (7.52.2).[29] The march from Sestos, on the European side of the Hellespont, to Doriskos – a distance of about 170 kilometres – would have taken some eleven or twelve days. Here the fleet, having re-established contact with the army, was ordered to beach the ships a little distance to the west, and dry them out, and it was now that there took place the great review of the army and fleet, which Herodotos describes (7.59.3ff.). After this, the army proceeded to march through Thrace in three columns, according to Herodotos (7.121.2-3), one keeping contact with the fleet along the coast, a second some distance inland, and the third, which Xerxes himself accompanied, between the two.

It is not easy to determine exactly the routes followed by the three columns,[30] but presumably the reasons for the division were partly logistical – to avoid imposing an

---

27 For the chronology of the campaign see 118ff. below and Hignett, 448-57, Appendix XIV. *Contra*: K.S.Sacks, *CQ* (NS) 26 (1976), 232ff.

28 HW ii 145 *ad* 7.39.3, though they doubt the story, quote Gobineau, *Histoire des Perses* ii 195, as saying that it was a Persian custom to make those one wished to preserve from harm pass between two parts of a sacrificial animal.

29 This seems better than the suggestion that the delay at Abydos was due to the fact that the second bridge was not yet finished (HW ii 144 *ad* 7.37.1).

30 See HW ii 171-2; Hammond, 1988, 537-9.

impossible burden on the communities through whose territories the army was marching – partly strategic. As it was, Herodotos claims (7.118-20), the cost of feeding the king's host was ruinous, as the anecdote about Megakreon of Abdera indicates (7.121.1: see above, 97). As for strategic considerations, Herodotos says (7.108.1) that the whole area had already been brought under Persian control by the campaigns of Megabazos and Mardonios. But since it would now form a vital link in the communications of the royal forces, it may have seemed wise to 'show the flag' over as wide an area as possible.

At Therma, near where the modern city of Thessaloniki now stands, fleet and army were reunited, and whilst a third of the army cleared a route through 'the mountains of Macedonia' (7.131), Xerxes himself is alleged to have gone on a sight-seeing trip to the mouth of the Tempe gorge (7.128-30). This episode is often dismissed as fiction, designed simply to allow Herodotos to speculate on the geology of Thessaly, and it certainly seems unnecessary for the whole fleet to have been involved in the operation, as Herodotos implies. However, Xerxes, having spent several weeks with the army since leaving Doriskos, may have had his reasons for showing himself to the fleet, and even if there were no sound military reasons for such a reconnaissance, can we not allow even the king of Persia some natural, human curiosity?[31]

The route followed by the army from Therma to Thessaly has again been the subject of considerable controversy.[32] Herodotos makes it clear that it did not follow the coastal route *via* Tempe (7.128.1, 173.4), but unfortunately does not enable us to see which of the alternatives was used. He seems to have thought that there was only one (7.173.4), but in fact there are, basically, at least two – to the west of Olympos *via* either the Petra or the Volustana pass (these routes unite at Elasson, and then follow the valley of the Titaresios), or a more difficult route over the southern part of the Olympos range from Herakleion *via* Lake Nezeros (ancient Askuris) and Gonnos.

Herodotos' repeated statement that the route lay 'past Gonnos' (παρὰ τὸν Γόννον: 7.128.1 & 173.4), and his claim that a third of the army was engaged on clearing the way (7.131), point to the second alternative. But his description of the route as the upper road through the Macedonians dwelling in the highlands' (τὴν ἄνω ὁδὸν ... διὰ Μακεδόνων τῶν κατύπερθε οἰκημένων: 7.128.1) and 'by way of upper Macedonia' κατὰ τὴν ἄνω Μακεδονίην: 7.173.4), point, if anything, to the route up the Haliakmon and then *via* the Volustana pass to Elasson, though even this hardly passes through 'upper Macedonia' proper; the characterization of the route as 'the safest' (ἀσφαλέστατον: 7.128.1), is also hard to reconcile with the one *via* Lake Nezeros. On

---

31 See, e.g., Macan (1908) i 1 163 ; Jacoby, 'Herodot Nr.7', *R-E Suppl. 2* (1913), col. 446; Fehling, 31-3 and 184. Robertson, *op.cit.* n.13 above, 120, suggests that Xerxes' inspection of Tempe revealed how dangerous the route might be, and decided him to use the alternative one *via* the Petra pass.

32 For a discussion of these routes see Robertson, *op.cit.*, 111ff., and references there. *Pace* Pritchett, *AJA* 65 (1961), 369ff., Herodotos was probably wrong to imply that the whole Persian army used the track that debouches at Gonnos (7.174), cf. Robertson, *op.cit.*, 113 – he plausibly explains Herodotos' mistake as arising from his obsession with the Tempe position (*op.cit.* 115-6). But, following the same fragment of Damastes, he suggests Alexander may have warned the Greeks that the Aleuadai might betray this route to the Persians. For the question which route the Persians actually used see above.

the whole it seems likely that the bulk of the army marched by one of the routes to the west of Olympos, probably the one *via* the Petra pass, though a detachment may have taken the one *via* Lake Nezeros, and if Herodotos' reference (above) to a third of the army means that it was again divided into three columns, part of it may have gone by the Volustana route.

Of the march of the Persian army through Thessaly, Herodotos says very little. When the southern Greeks abandoned their attempt to hold the Tempe pass, they left the Thessalians with little option but to throw in their lot with the Persians, as they had warned they would do (7.2-3), and the leading family of Larisa, the Aleuadai, had long been Persian sympathizers, in any case, if Herodotos is to be believed (7.6.2, 172.1). From now on, he says, the Thessalians gave the king good service (7.174).

It was perhaps to impress them with the superiority of his cavalry, as much as anything else, that Xerxes held races between his horses and those of Thessaly, in which Herodotos says (7.196), those of Thessaly were soundly beaten. The tradition that his guides told the king a local story at Halos in Achaia Phthiotis (7.197) shows that he followed the route round the coast of the Gulf of Pagasai, now followed by the National Highway, rather than crossing Othrys directly from Pharsala to Lamia. He may also have been wanting to link up with his fleet as soon as possible, though, as it turned out, the fleet was delayed by bad weather on the coast of Magnesia, and did not re-establish communications until about a week later. However, the reference to the near-failure of the river Apidanos to supply the army's needs (7.196) may indicate that part of it did follow the route across Othrys.

So far, the Persian invasion of Greece had been a triumphant parade, the only problems logistical rather than military. But despite the alleged attacks by lions on the camels of the baggage-train in Thrace (7.125), even the logistical problems had apparently been overcome, by a combination of an efficient supply-column and living off the land. Also, be it noted, the army had had no contact with the fleet since leaving Therma, and was not to re-establish contact for over a week – so much for the modern notion that it depended upon the fleet for its supplies.

If the Greek expedition to Tempe is historical, the king and his commanders presumably learned from the natives that a Greek army had briefly been and gone, without daring to face them, and it would thus have been with supreme confidence that Xerxes learned, whilst still in Thessaly, that 'a small force' had gathered at Thermopylai (7.208.1).

CHAPTER 6

First Blood

According to Herodotos (7.175.1), when the Greeks left Tempe, they returned to the Isthmus and considered where next to make a stand. 'The idea which prevailed,' he says (*ibid.*), 'was to defend the pass at Thermopylai, for it appeared to be narrower than the one leading to Thessaly, the only one[1] and nearer their own territory'. He adds (7.175.2) that they knew nothing as yet of the track by which Thermopylai was eventually turned, and only learned of it later from the people of Trachis. The intention was, Herodotos continues (*ibid.*), 'by guarding the pass, not to allow the barbarian to pass into Greece, and that the fleet should sail to Artemision in the territory of Histiaia.' There is no hint here, or elsewhere in Herodotos – or in any of the secondary sources for that matter – that the Greeks were not determined to try to stop the Persians from proceeding any further.

The positions at Thermopylai and Artemision were clearly chosen because they were thought to give the best chance of a successful defence against what the Greeks now probably believed – from rumours, their spies' reports, or from Alexander of Macedon – to be numerically greatly superior forces. Thermopylai was obviously such a place (see below, 130ff.), and although there may have been other reasons for choosing Artemision (see below, 125), Herodotos clearly implies that this, too, was partly chosen because it commanded the strait between the island of Skiathos and the mainland (7.176.1). The two positions were thought of as interlinked, as is shown by the arrangements for conveying by ship the news of any disaster suffered by one to the other (8.21.1). Although, as it turned out, the fleet was already contemplating withdrawal before the triakonter attached to Leonidas' army arrived with the news of what was happening at Thermopylai (cf. 8.18), Herodotos certainly gives the impression that the decisive thing was its arrival (8.21.2). Presumably, if the fleet had decided to withdraw, and no such news had arrived, the despatch-boat attached to the fleet would have been sent off to inform Leonidas.

There is no hint here that either position was particularly thought of as the primary one, but the size of Leonidas' army, even compared with the one sent to Tempe, let alone the one that fought at Plataia, has suggested that it had a subordinate role.[2] There are other explanations, however, and everything that we know about Greek warfare in general, down to this time, and Spartan attitudes in particular, would rather suggest that

---

1 Accepting the reading 'μία' ('one'). This, the more difficult reading, is to be preferred to 'ἅμα' ('at the same time'), and is then followed naturally by the remark about the alternative path. E.W.Kase and G.J.Szemler, *Klio* 64 (1982), 353ff., accept the reading 'ἅμα', and argue that Herodotos means the pass was 'nearer to the "Pass through Trachis into Hellas"' of Herodotos 7.176.2. But, as HW ii 207 *ad loc.* comment, this is impossible: how could Herodotos expect his readers to understand that he was contrasting the pass at Thermopylai with one he has not yet mentioned, and in what sense could the 'pass through Trachis' be described as 'their own' (τῆς ἑωυτῶν) from the point of view of the Greeks meeting at the Isthmus? In any case, the 'pass through Trachis' surely means Thermopylai – see below, n.20.

2 The idea was originally put forward by J.B.Bury, *BSA* 2 (1895/6), 83ff.; cf. also HW ii 371.

it was the army that was thought of as primary. Thus it is the army, not the navy, which is commanded by a king, and in Herodotos' account of how it came to be decided to send army and fleet to the new locations, it is the decision to send the army to Thermopylai which comes first. Only after the historian has explained about the path by which the position was eventually taken, does he mention the decision to send the fleet to Artemision (7.175).

The phrase 'the idea which prevailed' (ἡ νικῶσα δὲ γνώμη: 7.175.1), which Herodotos uses in reporting the decision, may indicate that other ideas were put forward, and it is possible that some of the Peloponnesians already advocated defending the Isthmus.[3] However, this would have meant abandoning the whole of central Greece, including Attica and, indeed, the Megarid, to say nothing of Euboia. Even though the delegates from Peloponnesian states were no doubt in the majority, they would probably have been very wary of antagonizing at least the Athenians, with their enormous fleet. It surely did not really require an Arcadian to warn the Spartans, for example, as Herodotos claims was later the case (9.9.2), that Athenian adherence to the Persian cause would open 'huge gates into the Peloponnese'.

The historian gives us a fairly detailed 'Diary' of the operations at Artemision and Thermopylai, and although there are problems with both the 'Diary' itself and with relating it to our calendar, it seems likely that the Greek fleet sailed north in the first half of August.[4] Unfortunately the only fixed point in the chronology of 480 is the eclipse of the sun which was seen when Kleombrotos of Sparta was sacrificing 'against the Persian', shortly after Salamis (9.10.2-3), and which can be equated with the eclipse of 2 October. But this strongly suggests that the battle of Salamis took place towards the end of September, and this is confirmed by Herodotos' story of the vision seen by the Athenian exile, Dikaios, in the plain of Eleusis, shortly before the battle (8.65). This clearly has something to do with the procession in honour of Iakchos, which we know took place about the 19th day of the Athenian month Boedromion (i.e. about 23

3 Cf., e.g., J.A.S.Evans, *Historia* 18 (1969), 393-4.

4 See Hignett, 448ff., for a clear discussion. K.S.Sacks, *CQ* (NS) 26 (1976), 232ff., argues for an Olympic festival culminating in the full moon of 18 September, largely on the grounds that Herodotos (8.67f.) implies that the battle of Salamis took place on the day after the arrival of the Persian fleet at Phaleron. But this seems to me to produce an impossibly tight schedule of events – though it is accepted by, e.g., Hammond, 1988, 570 – and to assume that the Persian fleet would have blithely sailed into the straits without any hesitation. Sacks follows Busolt (ii 702 n.2) in arguing that 'Aeschylus ... describes the night preceding the battle as very dark,' citing *Persai* 357, 364 and 428, and thus plumps for 27/8 September, when the moon rose at 1.55 a.m. as 'the darkest night by far' (232); later he suggests 29 or even 30 September for the battle. But *Persai* 357 & 364 simply refer to the fall of night, not to any particular darkness of the night in question, and line 428 refers to the night *after* the battle! There really is no need to put the battle later than Boedromion 20, i.e. 24 September, and if the Persian army and navy reached Attica about 7 September, the delay is only some 16 days: as argued below (162ff.), the Persians had plenty to do, and, in any case, may well have hesitated to enter the straits. Plutarch twice elsewhere (*Lysander* 15.1; *Mor*. 349f.), gives the date of the battle as 16 Mounychion, but this is impossibly early – Mounychion roughly corresponds to April/May. Possibly the battle was commemorated then, at the festival of Artemis Mounychia.

September in our terms), in normal times (*IG*^{2} 1078). Plutarch actually says, in one passage (*Camillus*, 19.6) that the victory occurred about 20 Boedromion, but this tradition may, of course, derive from Herodotos' story about Dikaios.

We know, too, that the Thermopylai-Artemision campaign roughly coincided with the Karneian and Olympic festivals. It was these which allegedly prevented the sending of the full forces to Thermopylai (7.206); after its fall, Arcadian deserters questioned by Xerxes said that the Greeks were celebrating the Olympic festival (8.26); and when the Peloponnesians heard of Leonidas' death, they hurried to defend the Isthmus, because the festivals were by then over (8.72). Thus if Salamis was fought sometime towards the end of September, the Olympic and Karneian festivals in question almost certainly took place in August, and probably the last day of the Olympic Festival coincided with the full moon of 19 August: if the full moon was that of 21 July, the gap between the Thermopylai-Artemision campaign and Salamis would have been something like two months and this is very difficult to believe. On the other hand, if the last day of the Olympic festival had coincided with the full moon of 18 September, the gap would have been too short. These indications do not enable us to fix the date of the fall of Thermopylai precisely, but it probably took place in the last week of August, and this would mean that Xerxes left Therma on the last stage of his march to Thermopylai in the second week of August.

As was said above, Herodotos' narrative allows us to reconstruct a parallel diary of the movements of the Persian fleet and army during the three weeks following Xerxes' departure from Therma, counting the day of his departure as Day 1,

Diary

Day 1:	Persian army leaves Therma (7.183.2)	Encounter between scouts off Skiathos; Greek fleet retires to Chalkis (7.179–83).
Day 12:	Xerxes reaches Malis	Persian fleet leaves Therma (7.183.2).
Day 13:	Xerxes waits (7.210.1)	Storm off Magnesia (7.188ff.).
Day 14:	Xerxes waits	Storm: Greeks leave Chalkis (7.192).
Day 15:	Xerxes waits	Storm: Greeks return to Artemision.
Day 16:	Xerxes assaults Thermopylai (7.210.1)	Persians reach Aphetai 'early in the afternoon' (8.6.1); 200 despatched; 1st battle 'late afternoon' (8.9); 200 wrecked off 'Hollows' (8.13–4).
Day 17:	2nd day at Thermopylai; Ephialtes betrays path; Hydarnes sets off at nightfall (7.212)	53 Athenian ships arrive; Greeks hear of wreck of 200; destruction of the Cilician ships (8.14).
Day 18:	Leonidas' last stand (7.219ff.)	3rd sea-fight (8.15–16): NB battles on land and sea on same days (8.15.1).

There are, however, three problems. The first arises from Herodotos' own statements. The natural interpretation of his words is that the Persian fleet reached Aphetai 'in the early afternoon' of the same day as the one on which it fought the first battle, 'waiting for the late afternoon of the day'. But elsewhere (8.15.1) he says that the battles off Artemision coincided with the battles at Thermopylai, and Xerxes had waited four days before launching his first assault there (7.210.1). This should mean he had reached Thermopylai four days before the fleet reached Aphetai, but Herodotos earlier appears to say that he had only been there *two* days (7.196).

The second problem is that Herodotos implies that the 200 ships the Persians sent off from Aphetai to round Euboia (8.7), were wrecked at a place called 'the hollows' (τὰ κοῖλα) the night before the second battle (8.12-14). But if they left on the afternoon the fleet reached Aphetai, and if the 'the hollows' were somewhere on the coast of southern Euboia, as later sources allege, the 200 would not have had time to reach them that night.[5]

Thirdly, Herodotos says that the news of the wreck of the 200 reached the Greeks at Artemision in time to encourage them before the second battle, which took place in the late afternoon, like the first (8.14.2). But if the 200 were wrecked off the southern half of Euboia during the night (cf. 8.13), how could the news have reached the Greeks on the north coast of the island before the late afternoon? The distance even from Chalkis to Artemision by the modern road is about 120 kilometres, and one doubts whether communications were as good in the early fifth century.

These problems have led to some desperate remedies.[6] The simplest solution to the first two is to insert a day between the arrival of the Persian fleet at Aphetai and the first battles off Artemision and at Thermopylai, i.e. to place the latter on Day 18 of the 'Diary' instead of Day 16. This would mean that Xerxes arrived before Thermopylai on Day 14, two days before his fleet reached Aphetai, as Herodotos seems to say (7.196), and then waited four days, counting his day of arrival as the first, in the normal Greek way. It would also mean that whenever precisely the 200 were sent off, they would have had plenty of time to reach 'the hollows' in time to be wrecked on the night between the first two sea fights, again as Herodotos says.

However, the similarity of the words the historian uses to describe the 'early afternoon' of the day the Persians arrived at Aphetai, and the 'late afternoon' of the day on which the first battle took place (περὶ δείλην πρωίην: 8.6.1/δείλην ὀψίην γινομένην τῆς ἡμέρης φυλάξαντες: 8.9), strongly suggests that he is talking about the same day, and to insert a day between them does not solve the third problem – how the news of the wreck of the 200 managed to travel from southern Euboia to the north coast in about twelve hours or less.

An alternative possibility, which would solve the last two problems, is that 'the hollows' were not on the southern coast of Euboia at all, but somewhere further north. It must be admitted that this flies in the face of what ancient evidence there is for their location, but Herodotos himself never says where they were, and there is some slight modern evidence to suggest that they were near Kyme, about half way down the east

5 For the location of 'the hollows' according to later sources see H.J.Mason & M.B.Wallace, *Hesperia* 41 (1972), 128ff. I am very grateful to the authors for sending me an offprint of their article, many years ago, but I am still unrepentant!

6 For a detailed refutation of some of them see my article in *Hermes* 92 (1964), 264-84.

Pl. 13 (top): Artemision – possible site of the temple of Artemis. (Photo: N. Fields).
Pl. 14 (bottom): Artemision – Pevki Bay, the probable site of the Greek fleet-base. (Photo: N. Fields).

MAP 5. ARTEMISION
Therma
THASOS
canal
Mt. Athos
Tempe pass
Cape Dermatas
Meliboia (?)
Khorefto
MAGNESIA
Cape Sepias (?)
ACHAIA
PHTHIOTIS
Gulf of
Pagasai
SKIATHOS
Aphetai
Trikeri channel
MALIS
Oreoi channel
Artemision
Histiaia
SKYROS
Thermopylai
LOKRIS
EUBOIA
Kyme
Delphi
PHOKIS
Chalkis
Euripos
Gulf of Corinth
BOIOTIA
Isthmus
Athens
SALAMIS
ANDROS
AIGINA
Cape
Sounion
KEOS
10 30 50
0 20 40 60 km
E.M.L

coast of the island. There is to-day a small island off the site of Kyme called 'Hollow' (Κοίλη), and some islets in the vicinity with the same name Κοιλίαι).[7]

This leaves the first problem – Herodotos' apparent statement that the day on which the Persian fleet reached Aphetai was the third day on which Xerxes had been in Malis (ἐσβεβληκὼς ἦν καὶ δὴ τριταῖος ἐς τὰς Μηλιέας: 7.196), whereas, according to the 'Diary', he should have said that it was the fifth day. However, when elsewhere he uses this kind of phrase, he usually talks of a person or a group of people reaching a destination 'on the nth day *after*' leaving somewhere, not 'on the nth day *before*' something else. Thus Philippides, for example, 'on the second day from the city of the Athenians was in Sparta' (δευτεραῖος ἐκ τοῦ 'Αθηναίων ἄστεο'ς ἦν ἐν Σπάρτῃ: 6.106.1), and subsequently the Spartans 'on the third day from Sparta were in Attica' (τριταῖοι ἐκ Σπάρτης ἐγένοντο ἐν τῇ 'Αττικῇ: 6.120). In the case of Xerxes' arrival at Thermopylai there is no obvious point of departure, but the whole sentence could mean 'Xerxes and the army, having marched through Thessaly and Achaia, had reached Malis on the third day,' and mean no more than that the king and his forces took two days to march from Halos in Achaia to Malis. Herodotos goes on to describe the last incident that took place in Achaia, namely the reporting to the king at Halos of a local legend (7.197), and immediately afterwards says (7.198.1), 'these were the events [which took place] some in Thessaly, some in Achaia, and from these places [the king] proceeded to Malis along the gulf of the sea'. In other words, the passage tells us nothing about how long the king had been at Thermopylai before his fleet reached Aphetai.[8]

The temple of Artemis which gave Artemision its name almost certainly lay on a hill just east of the modern village of Potoki, and the Greek fleet's anchorage was probably in what is now called Pevki bay (Pls 13 & 14).[9] Herodotos implies that the fleet, 271 triremes strong (8.1.1ff.), reached its station during the eleven days between Xerxes' departure from Therma (Day 1) and the departure of his fleet (Day 12). According to the historian, it was during this period that ten Sidonian scout-ships of the Persian navy encountered three Greek scouts off Skiathos, and that, when the main Greek fleet learned of the incident from fire-signals on Skiathos, it withdrew to Chalkis in panic (7.179ff.). Discussion of this incident, too, has led to a number of solutions which depart radically from Herodotos' text, and it must be admitted that it does seem most improbable that the whole Greek fleet withdrew in a panic simply because it learnt of the loss of three scouts. But to reject what Herodotos says about motivation here is one thing, to reject his narrative of events quite another. In other words, what we have to look for is another explanation of the Greek withdrawal, and it is not difficult to find one.[10]

---

7 Cf. *Stielers Hand-Atlas* (Gotha, 1933-5), taf.3, and J.Labarbe, *BCH* 76 (1952), 401 n.4.

8 Cf. Macan (1908) ii 274.

9 H.G.Lolling, *AM* 8 (1883), 7-23.

10 On all this see my article (n.6 above), 75ff. Evans, *op.cit.* n.3 above, 398, says 'Eurybiades withdrew to Chalcis because he hoped to lure the Persian fleet after him', but as Evans himself stresses (*op.cit.*, 390), the Greek navy was 'untried and in part, untrained', and this would have applied to the Spartan contingent as much as anyone: one doubts whether a Spartan admiral would have dreamt up such sophisticated tactics. For even more elaborate ideas about the Greek tactics see S.Sidebotham, *CW* 75 (1982), 177ff.

It usually seems to be assumed that the point of basing scouting-vessels on Skiathos, and arranging for fire-signals from the island, was simply to give warning of the enemy's approach. But if that had been all the Greeks wanted to know, why did they not simply send out patrols from Artemision itself? If these were properly maintained, there was no chance of the fleet's being surprised. But there was another vital piece of information the Greeks needed, and this scouts based on Skiathos were ideally placed to supply. The great danger of the Artemision position, or indeed any position intended to defend the channel between Euboia and the mainland, was that it could be turned by an enemy's choosing to sail down the east coast of the island. But the chances were that if he chose to do that, he would sail to the *east* of Skiathos, whereas if he intended to sail west-about round Euboia, he would keep west of Skiathos.

If, then, this was the reason why the Greeks placed an advanced post on Skiathos, a plausible explanation for their withdrawal would be that they interpreted the fire-signals as meaning something like 'enemy ships proceeding east of island'. A hint that this was the case is provided by Herodotos' statement (7.183.1) that when they departed, they left 'daywatchers on the heights of Euboia'. Eventually, Herodotos says (7.192.1), these reported the wreck of the Persian fleet on the coast of Magnesia to the Greeks at Chalkis, but this is impossible: nobody on any hill in Euboia could have seen anything happening on the coast of Magnesia beyond Cape Sepias. But what the 'daywatchers' could have reported, and what they had presumably been left to report, was whether in fact there were any Persian ships off the east coast of Euboia.

If, then, the Greeks at Artemision believed that the Persian fleet was sailing down the east coast of Euboia, there was little or no point in their remaining at Artemision. It has been argued that their Spartan commander-in-chief, Eurybiadas, cannot have contemplated abandoning the position because this would have meant uncovering Leonidas' seaward flank. But if he really believed that the Persian fleet was proceeding round Euboia to the east, he would have realised that his continued presence at Artemision would be of no use to Leonidas whatsoever. In any case, a glance at the 'Diary' will show that there is no need to suppose that Leonidas was even at Thermopylai at this time: he was presumably there when Xerxes arrived on Day 14, but the incident involving the scouts took place before Day 12!

If Eurybiadas mistakenly believed the Persians had been spotted sailing east of Skiathos, we should perhaps look no further for an explanation than the primitive nature of the signalling-system being used. Any message sent could only be an extremely simple one, and one pre-arranged between senders and receivers – for example, one fire for 'enemy proceeding west of island', two for 'enemy proceeding east of island' – and it may be that the wrong message was accidentally sent. However, there are two hints in Herodotos' narrative that the signallers may have had what seemed to them good reasons for believing that the Persians had by-passed Skiathos. The first is the fact that the Athenian scouting-ship was apparently pursued *north* to the mouth of the Peneios (7.182). Admittedly, ancient sea-fights, particularly between small squadrons where there was plenty of sea-room, probably resembled nothing so much as the 'dog-fights' between fighter-aircraft in World War I, as triremes tried to out-turn each other and strike vulnerable sides or sterns. Thus we can well understand how a Greek ship could end by being pursued north even by an enemy squadron coming from the north. But there is just a faint suggestion here that the enemy approached from the *south*.

The other hint comes in Herodotos' statement (7.183.3) that the man who showed the Persian scouts the Myrmex reef between Skiathos and the mainland was Pammon of Skyros. Skyros, of course, lay well to the south-east of Skiathos, and although again one can think of explanations for Pammon's being on board before the campaign opened, there is a possibility that the Sidonian ships had been south to Skyros and picked him up just before the encounter with the Greek scouts. The signallers on Skiathos, then, may have seen enemy ships approaching from the south, assumed that the main Persian fleet had by-passed them, perhaps during the night, and hastened to get this information off to Artemision.

It is even possible that the Greeks had chosen Artemision in the first place because of doubts about their position's being turned, and that the signals from Skiathos thus merely confirmed their worst fears. Herodotos implies that the position was chosen because it was near Thermopylai (7.175.2), and because it commanded the strait between Skiathos and the mainland (7.176.1). But if proximity to Thermopylai had been the main criterion, one much closer to Thermopylai could surely have been found – for example at Histiaia (the modern Oreoi) – and if command of narrow waters was what was wanted, what is now called the Oreoi channel, west of the mouth of the Gulf of Pagasai, is narrower than the Trikeri channel, to the east, opposite Artemision. Any fleet stationed at Histiaia or anywhere west of there, however, would effectively have been committed to the defence of the channels north and west of Euboia, and cut off from anything that might be happening off Euboia's east coast. The Artemision position, on the other hand, while still guarding the channel west-about round Euboia, also gave the Greeks the chance of learning in time of any Persian move to by-pass their position, particularly if they established an advance-base on Skiathos. There is thus no need to doubt Herodotos' narrative at this point, and if the Greeks really did believe that their position at Artemision had already been turned, there may even have been an element of panic in their withdrawal, as Herodotos says.

The Persians, whether or not their scouts had in fact been down to Skyros, had good reason to be satisfied with the whole episode, and it says much for the efficiency of their navy. Admittedly one of the scout-ships, an Athenian, got away, but at least it was chased northwards and thus prevented from carrying its news to the main fleet. A second ship, from Trozen, was captured almost immediately, and the handsomest of its marines sacrificed on the prow of his ship, probably as 'first fruits' in earnest of victory to come. The third ship, from Aigina, put up more of a fight, and one of its marines, Pytheas, son of Ischenoos, fought so bravely that even the Persians were impressed. They patched him up, and he lived to tell the tale, though his comrades were enslaved (7.181) – one wonders whether Greeks would have behaved as generously or had the requisite medical supplies on board.

Three of the Sidonians proceeded to mark the Myrmex reef,[11] after being shown the way by Pammon, and presumably the whole squadron then returned to Therma with the news that the way south was apparently clear. Accordingly, eleven days after Xerxes' departure, his fleet set out from Therma (7.183.2). Herodotos implies that it took a day (πανημερὸν πλέοντες: 7.183.3) to reach an anchorage which he defines as 'the beach

---

11 Reading 'ἐστάλησαν' ('were despatched') for 'ἐπήλασαν' ('were dashed against') at Herodotos 7.183.2, cf. J.N.O'Sullivan, *CQ* (NS) 27 (1977), 92ff.

between the town of Kasthanaia and Cape Sepias' (loc.cit.). Later (7.188.3), when describing the storm that hit the Persians here, he says that some of the ships were driven onto the so-called 'Ovens' ('Ιπνοί) below Pelion, some onto the beach (i.e. the one off which they were anchored), others to Cape Sepias, others to Meliboia and Kasthanaia.

Unfortunately none of these places can be certainly identified.[12] Cape Sepias, for example, has been identified either with the headland now called 'Kato Georgi' or with the one called 'Pori', Kasthanaia either with Zagora or its harbour, Khorefto, or with Keramidhi. However, wherever precisely the shipwreck occurred, it seems unlikely that the whole Persian fleet could have reached the spot in a single day's sail from Therma, over 100 kilometres to the north, and the widespread places where ships are said to have blown ashore, suggests that not all the fleet is to be thought of as reaching the 'beach' wherever that was. Herodotos himself seems to have thought the wind was from the east (cf. ἀπηλιώτης: 7.188.2). But what he says was its local name – 'Hellespontias' – implies that it was from the north-east, and his story that the Athenians' prayed to Boreas (7.189), even that it was from the north. If so, the ships should have been north of the places where they were blown ashore, and this would mean that some of them were north of the modern Cape Dermatas, only about 90 kilometres from Therma, for Meliboia is probably to be located either at Kato Polydendri or at Thanatou. In other words, only the leading ships may have reached the beach between Kasthanaia and Cape Sepias, and in a 14-hour day, with a favourable wind, this does not seem completely impossible. Alternatively, but less plausibly, Herodotos may not have meant us to understand a single day's voyage by his phrase 'sailing all day' (πανημερὸν πλέοντες), but rather that the ships took several days, 'sailing all day' and putting in each night.

Considerable doubts have also been expressed about whether there is any suitable beach between Khorefto, the probable Kasthanaia, and Kato Georgi, the probable Cape Sepias, and about Herodotos' story of the ships anchoring off the beach in eight rows. If, however, not all the ships were there, such scepticism is not justified, and the method of anchoring has recently been shown to be quite plausible.[13] Nor is there any reason to doubt that the storm took a fearsome toll of the Persian ships – 400 warships and an uncountable number of other vessels is Herodotos' estimate (7.190-1).

These figures only become dubious if one is convinced that the Persian fleet was smaller than the 1207 or 1327 triremes that Herodotos gives it. In any case, it is really absurd to argue that Herodotos was even subconsciously trying to reduce the Persian fleet to a reasonable size, and that he betrays this by his remark, *à propos* of the later wreck of the 200, that 'everything was being done by the god that the Persian fleet might be made equal to the Greek and not much bigger' (8.13). He himself believed that it was brought up to its original strength again before Salamis (8.66.1), though he was probably wrong to do so (see below, 174). He was, however, sensible enough to

12 For Cape Sepias Tarn (1908, 202ff.) proposes Katô Georgi, Wace (*JHS* 26, 1906, 145ff.) Pori; for Kasthania Tarn (*op.cit.*) proposes Zagora/Khorefto, Tozer (*Highlands of Turkey*, ii 104) Keramidhi; for Meliboia see R.Hope Simpson & J.F.Lazenby, *The Catalogue of the Ships in Homer's Iliad* (Oxford, 1970), 138-9; for the 'Ovens' Pritchett, *AJA* 67 (1963), 1ff.

13 Cf. I.M.Whitehead, *The Mariner's Mirror*, 74 (1988), 283ff.

discount some of the taller stories about the wreck, such as that the diver, Skyllias, and still worse, his daughter, Hydne, lifted some of the mooring-ropes of the Persian ships (Pausanias 10.19.1).[14] He does later mention Skyllias' rescue of some of the treasures (8.8.1: see below), but all he says here is that a Magnesian called Ameinokles, son of Kretineus, who owned land in the vicinity, became a rich man because of the precious objects he found after the wreck, and that the Persians were so afraid that they surrounded their remaining ships with a palisade made from the wrecks (7.190).

On the second day of the storm, according to Herodotos (7.191.1), the 'daywatchers' the Greeks had left on the hills of Euboia, when they left Artemision, came running down to Chalkis and reported 'all that was happening in the shipwreck', whereupon, having prayed to Poseidon the Saviour, the Greeks hurried to return to Artemision. As we have seen (above, 124), it is impossible to believe that the 'daywatchers' in fact reported the shipwreck, because they could not have seen it, but they could certainly have seen that there were no Persian ships off the east coast of Euboia, and that a considerable storm was raging. By now the Greek naval commanders will have been getting increasingly anxious, since Leonidas will have reached Thermopylai at about this time – indeed, if the 'Diary' is right, he will have had to have reached it, at latest, precisely by the second day of the storm – and they may have begun to put two and two together. Some movement of the Persian fleet, they probably calculated, might have given rise to the signals from Skiathos, but the daywatchers' report indicated that no substantial Persian force had in fact gone down the east coast of Euboia. Now a storm was raging which would prevent any such move for the time being. Later on these calculations will have been telescoped into the story Herodotos tells, that the 'daywatchers' actually reported the effects of the storm on the Persian fleet off Magnesia.

At all events, there is no reason to doubt that the Greek fleet now returned to Artemision. While it was still in the Euripos it would have been sheltered from the worst effects of the storm by the hills of Euboia, and when it rounded the island's north-west tip, perhaps on the storm's third day, the wind may have been dying away; in any case, Pelion would still have provided a measure of protection. Thus the Greeks could easily have been back at Artemision before the storm finally blew itself out, as Herodotos clearly implies they were (7.192.2, 194-5, 8.6.1).[15]

---

14 F.J.Frost, *Greece and Rome* (2nd series) 15 (1968), 180 n.2, believes that Hauvette, (*Revue de Philologie*, 10, 1886, 132ff.) 'argues convincingly' for Pausanias' story about Skyllias and his daughter, but I am very dubious. W.Klein, *JÖAI* 10 (1907), 141ff., suggests that the so-called Esquiline Venus may be a marble copy of the statue of Hydne mentioned by Pausanias (10.19.1). F.Meijer, *A History of Seafaring in the Classical World* (London & Sydney, 1986), 50, apparently even believes in Skyllias' underwater swim (see below, 129), using a primitive 'snorkel', for which he refers to Aristotle, *Historia Animalium* 659b 8-12. But although he correctly gives the distance from Aphetai to Artemision as '80 stadia' (cf. 8.8.2), he translates this as 'c.1500m', whereas it is actually nearer 16km, and this is, surely, too far to swim even with a snorkel.

15 *pace* Kromayer *Schlachtenatlas* iv, col.5, and Green, 128, 'οὗτοι οἱ καὶ ἐπ' 'Αρτεμίσιον Ἑλλήνων ἀπικόμενοι ὡς εἶδον νέας τε πολλὰς καταχθεισας ἐς τὰς 'Αφέτας' (8.4.1) does not mean that the Persians had reached Aphetai before the Greeks returned from Chalkis. What it means (cf. Hignett, 180) is 'When those of the Greeks who had again arrived

It was probably the next day – the fourth after the beginning of the storm, as Herodotos says (7.191.2) – that the Persians finally rounded Cape Sepias, and even then their troubles were not over. Herodotos says (7.194-5) that fifteen stragglers mistook the Greek fleet for their own and thus fell into enemy hands. This, too, has aroused suspicion, because, it is claimed, it is difficult to see how fifteen stragglers rounding Cape Sepias could have thought the Greek fleet, some 10-15 kilometres away across the straits to the south-west, was their own.[16] But almost anything is believable in such circumstances. These were admittedly stragglers, and had evidently taken a fearful battering in the storm – one of the ships captured, for example, was the sole survivor of the twelve ships from Paphos on Cyprus (7.195) – and sailing in unknown waters, after having been out of touch, perhaps, for several days, they could easily have been totally bewildered by the situation.

The place for which the fifteen stragglers should have been making, and which the main Persian fleet had reached, was called 'Aphetai', allegedly because it was from here that Jason and the Argonauts had intended to 'loose' (ἀφήσειν: 7.193.2). Herodotos seems to imply that it was in the Gulf of Pagasai, but this, though accepted by some, is impossible. Firstly, Aphetai was evidently in sight of Artemision (8.4.1, 6.1), which is not true of anywhere inside the Gulf of Pagasai. Secondly, the Skyllias story (8.8.2: see below) shows that it was only about sixteen kilometres from Artemision. This is admittedly about the distance from Artemision to the mouth of the Gulf of Pagasai, but if the Persian fleet had already got as far as that, it had by-passed the Greeks, so why did it not just continue? In any case, Herodotos may not have meant that Aphetai was in the Gulf of Pagasai. What he says is that the Persians, 'having rounded the point of Magnesia (i.e. Cape Sepias), sailed straight into the gulf *leading to Pagasai* (ἐς τὸν κόλπον *τὸν ἔπι Παγασέων φέροντα* : 7.193.1),' and that 'there is a place *in this gulf of Magnesia* (ἔστι δε χῶρος *ἐν τῷ κόλπῳ τούτῳ τῆς Μαγνησίης*: 7.193.2) ... the name of which was Aphetai'. In other words he may have thought of the Trikeri channel as forming part of the gulf, in which case we should look for Aphetai on its north shore, opposite Artemision. The most plausible location is the bay now called Platania, almost exactly sixteen kilometres north-east of Artemision.[17]

According to Herodotos (8.4.1), the sight of the vast Persian armada at Aphetai was too much for the Greeks, who, he of course believed, thought that large numbers of enemy ships had been destroyed in the storm. Even though he was probably wrong to think this, as we have seen, we can nevertheless still believe that the Greeks were dismayed when they finally came face to face with the enemy. There may even have been some talk of withdrawal, as Herodotos says there was, and it is not inconceivable that the Euboians, having failed to persuade Eurybiadas to stay at least until they could

---

at Aphetai, saw ...', and this does not contradict the clear implications of 7.192.2, 194-5 & 8.6.1 that the Greeks were there first.

16 Hignett, 177-8.

17 For the assumption that Aphetai must be in or near the Gulf of Pagasai see, e.g. Grundy, 326, though he at least places it at the entrance to the gulf, as does Burn, 391 (cf.394), and now Wallace, *GRBS* Suppl.10 (1984), 305ff.; Podlecki, 17, and Hammond, 1988, 552, are more vague. For the location at Platania see A.J.B.Wace, *JHS* 26 (1906), 145-6; Fabricius, *Gnomon* 2 (1926), 13ff.

convey their families to safety, did offer Themistokles a bribe, part of which he then passed on to Eurybiades, and to the Corinthian, Adeimantos, commander of the next largest contingent after that of Athens (8.4.2-5.3). The story has been discounted because it looks typical of the stories told about Themistokles, but there is nothing inherently impossible in it. Even the Spartan commander-in-chief, if he genuinely believed that there was no hope of holding their own against the Persian fleet, may have seen no point in remaining, and may simply have forgotten that part of his job was to protect Leonidas' seaward flank.[18] But if there was some momentary panic, it came to nothing, and whatever the reason, the Greeks decided to stay where they were.

But then they received even more alarming news. According to Herodotos (8.8.1), it was now that Skyllias came across with information not only of the shipwreck – another indication that this had not been previously reported by the 'daywatchers' – but of the despatch of 200 Persian ships round Euboia. The historian alleges that Skyllias had long had it in mind to desert, though he had not so far had the opportunity, and it is here that he mentions his services after the storm. But there were evidently a number of other stories about him, which Herodotos did not believe, including the one that he had swum the whole way from Aphetai under water (8.8.2), and perhaps the ones about him and his daughter which Pausanias told some six hundred years later (10.19.1). Herodotos himself says he believed he came over by boat, but it is difficult to see how he could then have avoided detection. Perhaps he swam part of the way, and was then picked up by a Greek patrol, or alternatively managed to find a boat in one of the isolated coves near Aphetai, and slip away while the Persians were concentrating on regrouping their battered fleet.

The news he brought again raised the spectre that seems to have haunted the Greeks since the beginning of the campaign, and which had already, as we have seen, probably caused their withdrawal to Chalkis. Now, too, their deliberations were complicated by Leonidas' presence at Thermopylai. But there is again no reason to doubt Herodotos when he says that they decided to wait for midnight and then sail to meet the 200 (8.9). The whole story has inevitably been suspected, on the usual, inadequate grounds. It has been argued, for example, that it is nonsense for Herodotos to say that the 200 were sent round Skiathos in order to escape the notice of the Greeks (8.7.1), since they would have been in full view when they set off from Aphetai. But all the Greeks would have been able to see would have been 200 ships heading east and then north up the channel between Skiathos and the mainland: they might have suspected where they were going, but they would not have *known*.[19]

---

18 Hammond, 1988, 552, makes too much of 'strategic considerations', arguing that Eurybiadas' job was not merely to safeguard Leonidas' flank, but 'to go into the attack'. In the anxiety of the moment, he may have simply forgotten what he was there to do. A modern parallel, quoted in n.6, p.276, of my *Hermes* article (cf. n.6 above), might be Admiral Halsey's decision to leave the San Bernadino strait unguarded during the battle for Leyte Gulf (cf. S.E.Morrison, *History of United States Naval Operations in the 2nd. World War*, XII 193-6).

19 On all this see my article (n.6 above), 281f., and refs. there. Hignett, 390, argues that even if a route round Skiathos would have concealed the intentions of the 200 from the Greeks at Artemision, they could have been spotted by the 'day-watchers' on the heights of Euboia. But these were probably set to observe possible movements of the Persian fleet when the Greeks

Similarly, the usual argument that Eurybiadas cannot have contemplated withdrawal because this would leave Leonidas in the lurch, should never have carried any weight. In the first place, if the 200 rounded Euboia and came up the Euripos, a Greek fleet at Artemision could not have protected Leonidas, and the fleet itself would have been in mortal danger. In the second place, all Herodotos says is that the Greeks decided to 'go to meet' (πορεύεσθαι καὶ ἀπαντᾶν: 8.9) the 200; he says nothing about *where*. If they had intended to meet the enemy somewhere off the north west tip of Euboia, for example, they would still have been between the 200 and Leonidas, and also in a position to intervene if the main Persian fleet came west down the Trikeri and Oreoi channels.

The argument that if the Greeks had been contemplating withdrawal from Artemision, they would never have challenged the Persians to battle first, is also worthless: on the contrary, if they were contemplating withdrawal, the last thing they wanted was for the Persians to realise this, and the best way of convincing the enemy that withdrawal was the last thing on their minds was to make a display of belligerence. Herodotos makes it clear that they deliberately waited until late in the day, so that there was no possibility of their getting into any serious danger before night intervened, and if his account of their tactics is correct (see below, 139–40), they were also careful to act on the defensive.

Finally, it is true that Herodotos never tells us why, in the event, the withdrawal never took place, but he leaves little doubt that it was because of the second storm (8.12). Even this storm has sometimes been thought to be a 'doublet' of the first, but in fact Herodotos is careful to distinguish the two: the first was brought on by the Hellespontias (probably a *north-east* wind, as we saw), the second was a violent thunder-storm, perhaps accompanied by a *south-west* wind, since the wreckage from the sea fight is said to have drifted across to Aphetai (8.12.1).

Before this first sea fight took place, the epic struggle at Thermopylai had already begun. Xerxes had probably reached the vicinity of the pass four days before his fleet finally reached Aphetai, as we have seen (above, 119ff.), i.e. on Day 12 of the 'Diary'. He already knew that a Greek force, led by the Spartans under Leonidas, was occupying the pass and he now sent a mounted scout to reconnoitre their position (7.208.1). Herodotos evidently took some care over his descriptions of the terrain (7.176.2ff. & 198.2ff.), and although it is impossible to locate precisely all the features he mentions, there is not much doubt that the Greek position was at the so-called 'Middle Gate', where traces of the Phokian wall which Leonidas and his men reconstructed (7.176.3-5), can still be seen, and where the hillock on which they made their last stand (7.225.2),

---

withdrew to Chalkis, and may have been withdrawn once they had delivered their message during the storm (7.192.1, see above, 127).

Pl. 15: Thermopylai – possible remains of the Phokian wall. (Photo: the Author)

Pl. 16: Thermopylai – the hillock on which the Greeks made their last stand. (Photo: the Author).

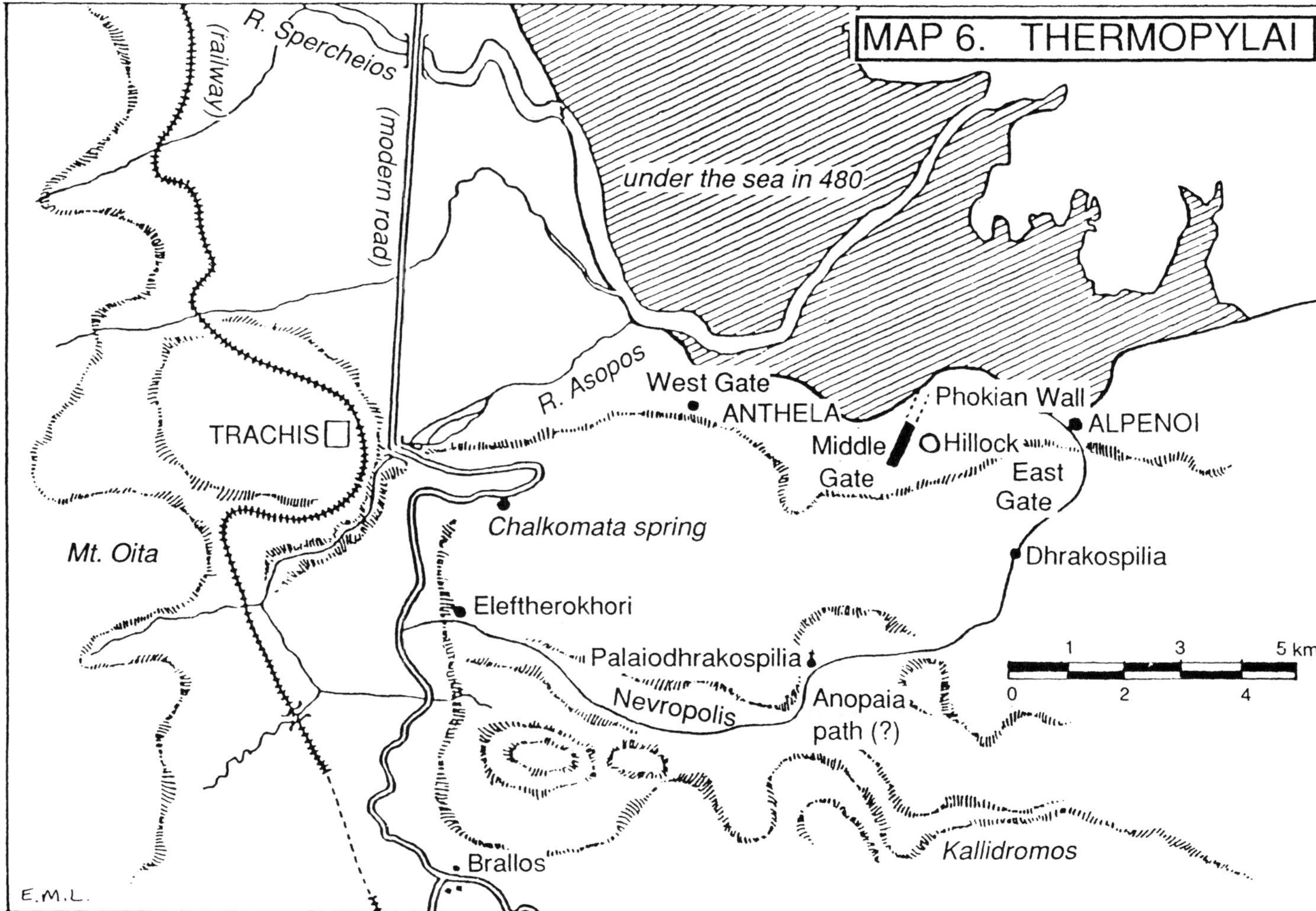
MAP 6. THERMOPYLAI
R. Spercheios
(railway)
(modern road)
under the sea in 480
R. Asopos
West Gate
ANTHELA
Phokian Wall
ALPENOI
Middle
Gate
Hillock
East
Gate
TRACHIS
Chalkomata spring
Dhrakospilia
Mt. Oita
Eleftherokhori
Palaiodhrakospilia
Nevropolis
Anopaia
path (?)
0
1
2
3
4
5 km
Kallidromos
Brallos
E.M.L.

has been excavated (Pls 15 & 16).[20] This, as Herodotos says (7.176.2), was not the narrowest part of the pass, but the existence of the Phokian wall indicates that this was regarded as the pass proper. The narrower gap to the west could have been turned by crossing one of the spurs of Mt. Oita. The so-called 'East Gate' provided a good 'fall-back' position, but beyond it there is no such position as the smaller Greek army required if it was to stand a chance.

The great puzzle about Thermopylai is the size of Leonidas' army. Even allowing for the presence of perhaps large numbers of hoplites serving as marines on board the Greek ships, comparison with the numbers Herodotos gives for Plataia suggests that Leonidas could have had well over 25,000 men. Even if we assume that all the Greek ships had as many as 40 marines, and that the additional ships which either joined the fleet on the second day at Artemision (53 Athenian: 8.14.1), or later at Salamis (27, excluding those from the west and deserters: 8.43-8), were already manned, they would only have required some 14,000 men. Yet at Plataia there were 38,700 hoplites, if Herodotos is to be believed (9.29.1), and, on the same calculation as above, perhaps 4400 serving on board the 110 ships still in commission (8.131.1).

Leonidas, however, only had about 8000 men at most. Herodotos gives him only 5200, with the Opountian Lokrians 'in full force' (πανστρατιῃ: 7.202-203.1), but there may be something wrong with his figures. His 5200 include only 3100 from the Peloponnese, but the epitaph which he quotes (7.228.1) says that 4000 men from the Peloponnese had taken part. Attempts to account for the discrepancy are not very satisfactory. On the basis of Diodoros' statement (11.4.5) that 'there were 1000 of the Lakedaimonians and with them 300 Spartiates,' it has been suggested that Herodotos omitted 1000 *perioikoi*, and it would be somewhat surprising if there were no *perioikoi* there. But if *perioikoi* were present, what happened to them on the final day? Did they stay with Leonidas, or did they depart with most of his allies? Moreover, one might have expected the *perioikoi* only to field the same number of troops as the Spartans, as they did at Plataia. Another, more unfortunate, suggestion is that the extra men from the Peloponnese were helots. Apart from the fact that the story of the blind Eurytos

---

20 Cf. S.Marinatos, *JHS* 59 (1939), 199f.; *AJA* 43 (1939), 699-700. E.W. Kase and G.J.Szemler, *op.cit.* n.1 above, may be right about the route eventually taken by Xerxes' army to Phokis (see below, 151), but are surely wrong to consider that it was 'the key to resist the Persian invasion' (364). If it had been, that is where the battle would have taken place, whereas in fact it clearly played no part in the Greek plans. Kase and Szemler are also wrong to think that this is what Herodotos meant by 'the pass through Trachis' (ἡ διὰ Τρηχῖνος 'έσοδος: 7.176.2), for that is clearly Thermopylai itself – see HW ii 207 *ad* 7.176.2. They seem to think that here and at 7.201 and 203.2 Herodotos must mean the *town* of Trachis. But at 8.21.1 and 8.66.1 'Τρηχίς' clearly means the *district* – in the latter case it is the scene of the 'Lakonian disaster' (τὸ τρῶμα τὸ Λακωνικόν) – and it is arguable that it always means the district, except at 7.199 where the *polis* is specifically mentioned. Kase and Szemler claim that the Middle Gate at Thermopylai was under water in 480, citing geological evidence (364, n.15), but this cannot be right: Herodotos implies that there was a wagon-road through it (7.176.2), and Marinatos' excavations and the existence of the Phokian wall surely indicate that it was this that was 'the key to resist the Persian invasion'.

(7.229.1) implies that each Spartan only had a single helot to attend him, it seems very unlikely that an epitaph would have deigned to mention helots.[21]

If Herodotos must be corrected here, it would perhaps be best to suppose that he has omitted a contingent or contingents from some of Sparta's other Peloponnesian allies, for example Sikyon or Epidauros. But another possibility is that it is not Herodotos that is wrong, but the epitaph: did its composer include the 1100 hoplites from Boiotia Herodotos says were present (7.202), saying '4000' for 4200? Obviously Boiotians were not Peloponnesians, but at least they were not from the locality as the Opountian Lokrians and even the Phokians can have been thought of as being.

But whatever the exact numbers, and even if we add 1000 Lokrians and 1000 Malians, with Diodoros (11.4.7), it is clear that the force was much smaller than it should have been. The explanation given by Herodotos is that these troops were only an advance-guard (cf. 'πρόδρομοι', literally, 'fore-runners'), and that it was intended to send the main forces when the Karneian and Olympic festivals were over (7.206, cf. 203.1). It has been suggested that this was just propaganda, designed to attract support from central Greece,[22] but the religious scruples should not be dismissed out of hand. Obviously the Spartan attitude was crucial, since the other Peloponnesians were hardly likely to commit larger forces to the enterprise if the Spartans were reluctant, and it is clear both from what Herodotos says about Marathon (6.106, 120) and what Thucydides (e.g. 5.54) and Xenophon (e.g. *Hellenika* 4.7.2) have to say about later incidents, that the taboos connected with the Karneia were taken very seriously.

The trouble is that if the Karneia imposed a taboo upon Spartans' fighting, there should not have been any of them at Thermopylai, least of all, one would have thought, a king, to say nothing of those serving at sea, and the same goes for any taboo imposed by the Olympic Games. It is possible, however, that the Spartans and their allies, recognizing the absolute necessity of sending some troops to defend the pass, if the invaders were not to be allowed a free hand north of the Isthmus, got round the taboos in some way, for example by choosing soldiers by lot and thus putting the onus on the Gods to decide who was to go.[23] This might, for example, be the explanation for the number of Spartan soldiers present. It is often assumed that they were the 'Hippeis' ('Knights': cf. 8.124.3), and Herodotos' description of them as 'the usual three hundred' (τοὺς κατεστεῶτας τριηκοσίους: 7.205.2) may seem to bear this out.[24] Later,

21 *Perioikoi*: Munro, 1902, 307, followed by HW ii 222 – Ktesias (*Persika* 25), for what it is worth, gives Pausanias 300 Spartiates and 1000 *perioikoi at Plataia* (!), and Isokrates (*Panegyrikos*, 90, *Archidamos*, 99), 1000 Lakedaimonians in all. Helots: Green, 111 & 140; Hammond, 1988, 549. Burn, 378–9, suggests emancipated helots, serving as hoplites, but Thucydides 4.80 surely indicates that the first such were those sent north with Brasidas in 424. Hignett, 116, suggests Eleians, but would not they have been particularly bound by the Olympic truce?

22 Cf., e.g., Evans, *op.cit.* n.3 above, 395.

23 For these suggestions see my book *The Spartan Army* (Warminster, 1985), 54-5.

24 E.g. Hignett, 125; J.T.Hooker, *The Ancient Spartans* (London, 1980), 164; M.Detienne, 'La Phalange: problèmes et controverses' in *Problèmes de la Guerre en Grèce Ancienne*, ed. J.-P.Vernant (Paris, 1968), 134. I do not know what Green, 111, means by saying that the 300 were drawn from Sparta's *corps d'élite*, nor Hammond 1988, 549 that they were Leonidas' 'personal guard'.

however, the *Hippeis* were chosen by officials known as '*Hippagretai*' (cf. Xenophon, *LP* 4.3), whereas Leonidas himself is said to have chosen his 300, and whereas the *Hippeis* appear to have been young men, probably in their twenties, Leonidas' men are said to have all been fathers of sons. This may smack of the legend that they knew they were going to their deaths, but it is possible that in reality it indicates that the younger men were passed over as being particularly bound by the taboos surrounding the Karneian festival, and that the 300 were selected by the king, perhaps by lot, from those over thirty. Herodotos' description of the force as 'the usual three hundred' may just reflect the fact that this was the number chosen for difficult and dangerous enterprises (cf. 1.82.3-4, 9.64.2). Finally, the king himself may have been held to be exempt from the taboo because he was beyond military age, and possibly those serving with the fleet were also held to be exempt because naval service was unknown when the taboos came into being.

We may feel that the Greeks were naive to think that a token force would be enough to hold the pass until the main body could be sent, but they may have hoped for a greater measure of support from Boiotia and the other Greeks nearer the pass. In the end, the forces sent were adequate to maintain the position for at least a week, though admittedly only under attack for the last three days, and were only defeated, in Herodotos' view, because of lack of vital local knowledge (7.175.2). If the intention really had been to reinforce the position after the festivals, it would possibly only have had to be held for another week to ten days, and this may have seemed by no means an impossible task when the force was originally sent.

But however much one may feel that one should respect the religious scruples of the Greeks, one cannot help but suspect that behind the small size of Leonidas' force lurks the perfectly natural reluctance of the Peloponnesians to commit their forces so far to the north.[25] Another possibility, though less likely, is that the Spartans themselves were divided on the issue.[26] If these suspicions are justified, we have here a good example of the dangers of compromise in war – compromise between the necessity to send some troops to defend the pass, and unwillingness to send as many as were needed. In any case, whatever the true explanation for the size of Leonidas' force, there is no hint in Herodotos or anywhere else that the intention was not to hold the pass. Herodotos repeatedly says that this *was* the intention (7.175.2, 176.5; 8.15.2), and it is difficult to see what else it can have been – suggestions that Thermopylai was some kind of 'delaying action' or 'reconnaissance in force' really do not make any sense.[27]

Herodotos implies that when Leonidas and his army reached their position, they simply camped in the pass, rebuilt the delapidated wall (7.208.2) and waited for the enemy (cf. 7.201). However, a much later writer, Polyainos, writing in the second

25 Cf. Evans, *op.cit.*, 393-4.

26 Cf. J.R.Grant, *Phoenix* 15 (1961), 14ff.

27 Cf. Jameson, *Hesperia* 29 (1960), 205, and *Greece & Rome* 8 (1961), 11, for the notion that Thermopylai and Artemision were some kind of 'delaying actions'. Even Evans' refinement (*op.cit.*, 401-2) that the Greeks hoped to delay the Persians until the campaigning-season ran out perhaps misrepresents what the Greeks really intended, which was just to stop the Persians.

century AD, has a story about a 'Leonidas' sending out troops at night to cut down trees and set fire to farm-buildings (1.32.3), and this has been accepted by some scholars.[28]

But it is very improbable that a Spartan would have thought of risking his hoplites, at night and in unknown country, in this kind of way, and some of the details of the story do not make much sense – what, for example, is 'the city' from which the inhabitants are said to have been afraid to sally out because they thought the enemy numbers too great? This story may have something to do with the even more improbable story Diodoros tells of the night-raid on Xerxes' camp before the final battle at Thermopylai (see below, 142), and both should almost certainly be rejected.

Some scholars have also rejected Herodotos' statement that when Xerxes' army drew near the pass, the Greeks, in yet another of their 'panics', considered withdrawal, and that it was only the pleadings of the Phokians and Lokrians, who of course had most to lose if the defence was abandoned, which prevailed on Leonidas to remain (7.207).[29] The absurdity of the story is shown, it is argued, by Herodotos' further statement that Leonidas sent messengers 'to the cities' bidding them send reinforcements, since he could hardly have expected the reinforcements to reach him in time. However, it is not at all impossible that the Greeks at Thermopylai, like those at Artemision, were dismayed when they finally realised just how large the Persian forces were, and if Leonidas was genuinely expecting reinforcements, as Herodotos believed, it is equally not impossible that he did send off pleas for them to be as quick as possible.

But if there was some momentary panic, the Spartans at least soon recovered their nerve. According to Herodotos, when a Persian mounted scout approached the Greek position, it was the Spartans who happened to be stationed in sight, outside the wall, some of them stripped for exercise, others combing their hair, and all paying him not the slightest attention (7.208.2-3). Questioned about this, the exiled Spartan king, Damaratos, is said to have told Xerxes that combing the hair was a sign that the Spartans were preparing to risk their lives (7.209.3), but Xerxes, refusing to believe him, scornfully waited for four days for the Greeks to run away (7.210.1).

All this may look like legend, and obviously the story eventually lost nothing in the telling, but there was no point in the Persians' assaulting the pass unless and until they had to, and after the tame withdrawal of the Greeks from Tempe, Xerxes may well have believed that the same thing would happen here. No doubt, too, he utilised the wait to try to discover some way to turn the enemy position. It was presumably also during this period of waiting that the Spartan Dienekes made his well-known reply to the gloomy remark of a local Trachinian that when the Persian archers loosed their bows, the arrows were so many that they blotted out the sun's light: 'Good news! The battle will be in the shade' (7.226.1-2).

On the fifth day, perhaps because his patience was exhausted, as Herodotos implies, or because enquiries about alternative routes were proving unsuccessful, Xerxes finally ordered an assault. One should remember that even if the Persian army was much smaller than Herodotos believed, and however good its commissariat may have been, delay in any one part of Greece would have rapidly exhausted local stocks of food, even

28 E.g. Burn, 381; Green, 114.

29 Hignett, 119. Evans, *op.cit.*, 394, suggests one of Leonidas' pleas for reinforcements may have gone to Thessaly – hence the mysterious mission of Pantites (7.232).

if Leonidas had not carried out 'scorched-earth' raids into the surrounding countryside. Thus, finally, the Kissians and Medes first, and when they failed to break through, the 'Immortals' themselves, were launched at the Greeks. But all to no avail.

Although in one passage Herodotos implies that the Persian troops were lacking in morale – 'they made it clear in every way,' he says (7.210.2), 'and not least to the king himself that he had many human beings, but few men' – he praises the courage of the Medes in the immediately preceding sentence, and later makes the point that since the fighting took place in a narrow space, the Persians could not make use of their superior numbers, and that their spears were shorter than those of the Greeks. This raises the question why the Persians allowed themselves to become involved in hand-to-hand fighting with spears in any case, when they were all armed with bows and should have been able to hold off and try to wear the Greeks down with arrow-fire.

Perhaps they were simply over-confident, but Herodotos hints that the Spartans may have used tactics designed to bring about the *mêlée* in which they excelled: 'they would turn their backs,' he says (7.211.3), 'and flee in a body, whereupon the barbarians, seeing them in flight, would come on with a roar and a clatter, only for the Spartans, when caught, to wheel and face them'. Such tactics would have had the effect of bringing about a series of hand-to-hand encounters in which the Spartans would have had the edge, and although one might have thought that the Persians would soon have learned their lesson, it perhaps required more control than their officers had over them to prevent their falling for the trap again and again – each time the men may have felt that the Spartans really were at last in flight. Alternatively, Herodotos' account may have arisen from a misunderstanding of the technique the Spartans certainly used later to drive off missile-armed troops. This was to order the front ranks to charge out from the phalanx (cf. e.g., Xenophon, *Hellenika* 4.5.15-16), and if it was the manoeuvre employed at Thermopylai, the Persians may have been confused into pursuing every time the front ranks closed upon the phalanx.

Meanwhile, off Artemision, the Greeks had also had the better of the first day's fighting. As we saw, at some point after the arrival of the Persian fleet at Aphetai, the Greeks had received information from Skyllias about the shipwreck and the despatch of the 200, and had resolved to sail to meet the 200 that night. As already suggested, the decision to bring about an engagement before they sailed was probably intended to convince the Persians that withdrawal was the last thing on their minds, though Herodotos merely says that it was 'to make trial of them, both their way of fighting and their use of the *diekplous*' (8.9).

It was obviously important, in either case, to avoid being drawn into an engagement which might end in disaster, or even cause serious losses. It is often forgotten that the decision to sail to meet the 200 was not necessarily entirely or even mainly defensive: if Skyllias had been able to bring accurate information about the number of ships in the detached squadron, the Greeks will have realised that they would have a splendid opportunity of achieving numerical superiority over it, if they could catch it on its own, without interference from the main Persian fleet. It thus makes perfect sense for them to have waited until late in the day before rowing across to challenge for battle, as Herodotos says they did (*ibid.*).

The historian claims that the Persians, for their part, had hitherto deliberately avoided a direct confrontation, hoping, by the despatch of the 200, to cut off the Greeks' escape route, and catch them in a trap (8.6-8). Now, however, seeing the enemy rowing forward, the Persians thought they were utterly mad and put out themselves, hoping that they would easily take them. 'Their hope was very reasonable,' Herodotos adds, 'seeing, as they could, the few Greek ships and their own many times more numerous and better sailing' (ἄμεινον πλεούσας: 8.10.1). Almost certainly it was mainly the better training of their crews that made the Persian ships 'better sailing' (see above, 36), rather than any differences in design or construction, though the Greek ships may have been more heavily built (cf. 8.60a – below, 160). But one would like to know whether Herodotos had good reason to believe that the Greeks wanted to try out the Persian 'way of fighting' and 'use of the *diekplous*,' and what he intended us to understand by this. Did he mean that the Persians used different tactics from those of the Greeks, and, in particular, did he mean that the Greeks knew the Persians employed the '*diekplous*', whereas they did not, or merely that the Greeks wanted to see how good they were at it?

What he says about the 'better sailing' qualities of the Persian ships might suggest that the Greeks assumed the enemy would be better at the *diekplous* than themselves, and certainly, if we are to believe Herodotos, they themselves adopted a defensive formation: 'when a signal was given to the Greeks,' he says (8.11.1), 'first, coming bows on to the barbarians, they drew their sterns together into the middle, and, at a second signal, they commenced action, caught as they were in a narrow space and bow to bow'.

Here it usually assumed that 'they drew their sterns together into the middle' (ἐς τὸ μέσον τὰς πρύμνας συνήγαγον) means that they formed a circle,[30] and this was later the formation adopted at least twice by Peloponnesian fleets during the Peloponnesian War (cf. Thucydides 2.83.5 and 3.78.1). However, the latter fleets were much smaller than that of the Greeks at Artemision – on the first occasion 44 ships, on the second 33 – and one wonders whether it was really feasible to form a circle with over 250 triremes. In the two Thucydidean episodes, moreover, it was the larger, Peloponnesian fleet which formed circle, while smaller, though faster and more manoeuvrable, Athenian squadrons rowed round them in line ahead, hoping that they would back away and fall foul of each other. At Artemision, however, the 'better sailing' Persian ships were also numerically far superior, and were apparently 'bows on' to the Greeks (cf. 'κατὰ στόμα' in 8.11.1).

It is also perhaps significant that Herodotos uses a vague phrase of the formation adopted by the Greeks at Artemision, whereas Thucydides actually uses the word 'circle' (κύκλος) to describe the formation adopted by the Peloponnesians, on both occasions. This perhaps implies that instead of forming a complete circle, the Greeks at Artemision in effect 'refused' their wings so as to prevent their opponents from getting round behind them, and crowded together towards the centre so as to leave no gaps for them to

30 Cf., e.g., HW ii 238 ad loc.; Green 134; Morrison & Coates, 53-4. Macan (1908 i 2 372f) and Tarn (*JHS* 28, 1908, 217) suggest the Greeks were retreating in a crescent formation, having gone out to attack an isolated Persian squadron at one of the scattered anchorages to which Diodoros refers (11.12.5-6: see below, 141), but, as Hignett points out (185-6), it is hardly what Herodotos says; Burn, 397-8, ignores the difficulties. Hammond's elaborate account of what happened in this action (1988, 553-5), seems to me to be vitiated by his view that it was the Greeks who relied on ramming, the Persians on boarding. Apart from anything else, Herodotos does say the Greeks *captured* 30 Persian warships (below, 140).

employ the *diekplous*. Thus they compelled the enemy to ram prow to prow, and, in the end, brought about a *mêlée* in which the speed and manoeuvrability of the enemy ships were of no advantage.

Even so, however, if Herodotos' account is at all accurate, it is clear that the Greeks had given some thought to how to deal with a numerically superior and 'better sailing' fleet, and the historian's references to the two signals suggest that they had even practised the manoeuvre, whatever precisely it was. Their boldness and forethought was rewarded, according to Herodotos, by the capture of 30 enemy ships, the first to take one being the Athenian, Lykomedes, son of Aischraios (8.11.2). Herodotos also adds that Antidoros of Lemnos deserted to the Greeks in this first encounter, and was rewarded by the Athenians with a piece of land on Salamis: since Lemnos had once been Athenian (cf. 6.137ff.; *IG* xii Suppl. 337), one suspects that Antidoros may have been of Athenian descent. When night put an end to the fighting, we can well believe that the Persians returned to Aphetai in some surprise, as Herodotos says (8.11.3), and the storm which burst upon them during the night did nothing to raise their spirits (cf. Herodotos 8.12). It was also this second storm, we have suggested, which put an end to all thought among the Greeks of sailing to meet the 200, though Herodotos does not say so, and which, in any case, though the Greeks did not know it until next day, led to the destruction of the 200 at 'the hollows' of Euboia (8.12-13).

Next day – Day 17 of the Diary – saw the renewal of Xerxes' assault on Thermopylai, which fared no better than the first. Herodotos says that the Persians, having seen how few the Greeks were, assumed that many of them would have been wounded, and that they would no longer be able to raise a hand against them (7.212.1). But, he adds (7.212.2), the Greeks fought contingent by contingent, nation by nation, thus allowing those not engaged to rest – the only contingent not involved was that of the Phokians, guarding the upper path. However, the day ended with better news for the Persians, when the traitor Ephialtes, son of Eurydemos, came to Xerxes with information about the upper path. As has been pointed out, what Ephialtes did was probably not so much divulge the *existence* of the path, as offer to guide the Persians along it: anyone who has done any extensive walking in Greece knows how easy it is to get lost, even after receiving apparently clear directions, unless one has a guide.[31]

Meanwhile, at Artemision, the Greeks had been encouraged, first, by the arrival of 53 additional Athenian ships, and, secondly, by news of the destruction of the 200. Herodotos does not say why the Athenian ships arrived at this particular juncture, but the casual way in which he introduces them implies that they were, simply, late arrivals, perhaps due to the evident difficulties the Athenians had experienced in manning their fleet. Modern speculation has, of course, been rife – there has even been a suggestion that it was these ships and these ships alone which had been sent south to Chalkis on receipt of the fire-signals from Skiathos, before the campaign opened.[32] Nor does Herodotos say that it was they who brought the news of the wreck of the 200, and, if anything, his language implies that it was not. In any case, if the 53 arrived in time to encourage the Greeks in the second sea fight, which took place at the same time as the

31 Cf. Burn, 299.

32 Bury, *BSA* 2 (1895/6), 83-97; Munro, 1902, 307-12, and *CAH*[1] iv 286; Tarn, 1908, 218; Miltner, *RE* suppl. v 868.

first (8.14.2), i.e. in the late afternoon (cf. 8.9), they had presumably spent the previous night somewhere near the north west cape of Euboia, perhaps sheltering from the second storm. If so, they could hardly have known anything about what had happened at 'the hollows'.

Herodotos says almost nothing about the second day's fighting off Artemision, merely that 'having waited until the same hour, they sailed out and fell upon some Cilician ships; having destroyed them, when night came, they sailed back to Artemision' (8.14.2). It has been plausibly suggested that these 'Cilician ships' were remnants of the 200, crawling back to Aphetai.[33] Of course, if 'the hollows' were on the southern half of Euboia, none of the 200 could have got back to the vicinity of Artemision in time, and Herodotos implies that all the 200 were destroyed. But if 'the hollows' were near Kyme, and if any ships survived, there may have seemed little point in going on, and they could have been caught by the Greeks as they rounded the north-east corner of Euboia on their way back to Aphetai. But all we really know is that somehow the Greeks contrived to catch part of the Persian fleet isolated from the rest, and here, for once, Diodoros may be of some help. He tells us (11.12.5-6) that the Persians were scattered about in a number of harbours, and there is every reason to believe that he was right: Platania, if it was Aphetai, would not have been large enough to accomodate the whole Persian fleet, even if it had been reduced by now to some 5-700 vessels.

Meanwhile, at Thermopylai, 'at about the time the lamps were lit', in Herodotos' evocative phrase (7.215), Hydarnes and the Immortals set off, guided by the traitor, Ephialtes, along the track of which he had informed Xerxes. Herodotos has left us a fairly clear and detailed account of its route (7.215-217.1), and although there has inevitably been much controversy about it, and its beginnings are still in dispute, it is now fairly clear that at least the latter part of it ran from somewhere near the Chalkomata spring *via* Eleftherochori and the Nevropolis valley to Palaiodhrakospilia, Dhrakospilia, and then down to the 'East Gate' of Thermopylai, near Alpenoi.[34] The implication in Herodotos that Hydarnes was accompanied by *all* the Immortals, i.e. 10,000 men, has been disputed, but there is really no need to do so: the route outlined above is comparatively easy and Xerxes would have wanted to make quite sure not only that when his turning-force reached the rear of the Greek position, they could prevent the Greeks' escape, but that they could brush aside any opposition they might encounter on the way.

As it was, they almost surprised the Phokians, who were guarding the track, somewhere along the upland valley of Nevropolis – it was only the swishing sound the Persians made as they tramped through the fallen leaves, that betrayed their presence as dawn was breaking (7.217.2-218.1). It may seem extraordinary that the Phokians had not posted pickets, and Leonidas has been criticized for not stiffening the Phokians with

---

33 Munro, 1902, 311.

34 See P.Wallace, *AJA* 84 (1980), 15ff., for a splendidly clear analysis of the problems, including an account, with recorded times, of his own 'march', leaving his starting point at 21.05 and reaching the Middle Gate next day at 11.00: my only quarrel with Wallace is where he says (19) 'the Persian Immortals must have been similar to a modern commando battalion'; see also, e.g., Hignett, Appendix III, 361-70; Burn, 407–10; Green, 115–7. For doubts as to whether all the Immortals accompanied Ephialtes see Hignett, 377.

some Spartan troops, or putting them under a Spartan officer.[35] But this sort of thing will only occur to those who imagine that ancient Greek troops were like trained, modern, professional soldiers. In fact it would have been even more extraordinary if the Phokians had placed pickets, and even Spartans could be surprised in their beds (cf., e.g., Thucydides 4.32.1, and Xenophon, *Hellenika* 7.1.16). It was also typical of the lack of professionalism among Greek hoplites, though indicative also of their courage, that when the Phokians found themselves under attack from the Persian archers, they should have assumed that they were themselves the primary objective, and retired to the nearest hill to sell their lives as dearly as they could (7.218.3).[36]

The Persians, for their part, had been momentarily disconcerted by the appearance of armed men blocking their way, and Hydarnes had allegedly been dismayed at the thought they might be Spartans. When, however, he learned the truth from Ephialtes, Persian professionalism took over: a few volleys of arrows drove the enemy from the track, and the Immortals took no more notice of them, but hurried on as fast as possible – a lesson in adhering to the main objective. But one would like to know how Ephialtes could tell that the Phokians were not Spartans: were the shields of the latter already marked with a *lambda*, one wonders?

So began one of the most famous days in the history of warfare – the last day at Thermopylai. Unfortunately, Herodotos' account of it is fraught with problems. According to him (7.219.1), the first warning to the Greeks of 'the death about to be upon them with the dawn' came from the seer, Megistias, when he examined the sacrificial victims – presumably at the sacrifice which was still performed, while it was still dark, in the fourth century (Xenophon, *LP* 13.3). Then deserters confirmed that the Persians were carrying out a turning-movement. Diodoros (11.8.5) names one of these deserters as Tyrrhastiadas of Kyme, and since one of his main sources, the fourth century historian, Ephoros, was also from Kyme, it has been claimed that he preserves here a precious piece of local knowledge. However, the story is just as likely to be a local invention,[37] and one certainly cannot accept Diodoros' story of the night-raid by Leonidas and his men on Xerxes' camp, even if Plutarch accepted it (*Moralia* 866a-b). Apart from the fact that Herodotos obviously knew nothing about the story, Greek hoplites were not commandos, and such an attack would be quite unparalleled.[38] Megistias' warning and that of the deserters were given, Herodotos says (loc. cit.), while it was still night, but finally, 'as day was already breaking' (ἤδη διαφαινούσης ἡμέρης), 'daywatchers' came running down from the hills to confirm the news.

It has been argued that if 'day was already breaking' when the 'daywatchers' reached Leonidas, they cannot have reported that the pass had been turned, since the Persians only reached the Phokian position when 'dawn was breaking' (cf. ἠώς τε δὴ διέφαινε: 7.217.1), and the 'daywatchers' would probably have had between ten and

35 E.g. Burn, 418; Hignett, 141; Green, 116; but see R.Hope Simpson, *Phoenix* 26 (1972), 4 n.23.

36 For the Phokian position see Pritchett, *AJA* 62 (1958), 210.

37 Cf. Hignett, 16 n.7. The story is accepted by Burn, 416, and Green, n. on p.139.

38 *Pace* Green, 139, who cites the Long Range Desert Group's raid on Rommel's H.Q. in November, 1941 – not 1942, as he says: cf. David Irving , *The Trail of the Fox* (London, 1977), 107-8.

fifteen kilometres to run from there to the Middle Gate.[39] But dawn does not 'break' instantaneously – a 'stand-to at dawn' in the modern British Army can still last for anything up to an hour or more – and Herodotos here seems to have been at some pains to distinguish between the time at which the Persians reached the summit of the pass, 'when dawn (ἠώς) was breaking (7.217.1),' and the time at which the 'daywatchers' reached Leonidas, 'when *day* (ἡμέρα) was breaking (7.219.1).'

Presumably the 'daywatchers' had been stationed at or near the Phokian position, though Herodotos does not actually say this, but they did not necessarily wait to see whether the Phokians would be successful in holding the path. It was absolutely vital that Leonidas be informed of what was happening as soon as possible, and they were probably sent off the moment it became clear that a Persian force was approaching the Phokian position. If so, they would, probably, have had time to reach Leonidas before full daylight.

The great problem is what the Greeks decided to do, when Megistias' prophecy and the deserters' information was finally confirmed by the 'daywatchers'' report. According to Herodotos (7.219.2), opinions were divided, some being for holding their position, others against, and in the end some simply decamped, whilst the rest prepared to remain with Leonidas. But then he goes on to give another story, according to which Leonidas himself dismissed those who went away, because he did not want them to be destroyed, but thought it was not fitting for him and the Spartans with him to desert their post (7.220.1). Herodotos says he rather agreed with this view (7.220.2), but adds that by staying where he was Leonidas not only won great fame, but also preserved Sparta, since it had been prophesied that either Sparta itself would be destroyed, or would have a king of the race of Herakles to mourn (7.220.2-4). 'Not the least piece of evidence for this,' according to the historian (7.221), was that Leonidas dismissed the seer, Megistias, though in the event he refused to go, sending his son instead. It is not clear how Herodotos knew this, let alone why he regarded it as good evidence for his view, but perhaps he based his opinion on the epitaph Simonides wrote for Megistias, in which the seer was said 'not to have had the heart to abandon the leaders of Sparta' (οὐκ ἔτλη Σπάρτης ἡγεμόνας προλιπεῖν: 7.228.3). Finally, the historian says that all the allies went off in obedience to Leonidas' orders, except the Thespiaians and Thebans, the latter under compulsion because Leonidas wanted to keep them as hostages, the former because they simply refused to go (7.222).

In the end we can never know the truth. Of those who stayed with Leonidas, all the Spartans and Thespiaians were killed and it is unlikely that any of the Thebans ever told Herodotos, at least, their version of the story. Of the two Spartans who are said to have survived the disaster, neither was actually present on the fateful morning: one, Pantites, is said to have been sent on a mission to Thessaly – even so, he hanged himself on his return to Sparta, as though disgraced (7.232); the other, Aristodemos, was at Alpenoi, suffering from ophthalmia (7.229-31). As for the Greeks who went away before the final battle, they are unlikely to have admitted that they had simply deserted, if that had been the case. Nevertheless, it may be significant that despite the recriminations and *post mortem* wranglings to which the disaster will have given rise, Herodotos was

39 Beloch, ii 2.91-105.

evidently inclined to give them the benefit of the doubt, and perhaps we should do the same.

It is also probably significant that there was no hint in the tradition that those who got away had been sent by Leonidas to try to hold Hydarnes off, or anything of that sort.[40] Although it might be argued that whatever they claimed might have seemed less creditable than that Leonidas dismissed them, it could hardly have seemed less creditable than one of the traditions that *did* emerge, namely that they simply departed. In any case, it seems on the whole unlikely that Leonidas would have thought of trying to hold the Persians off, if they were coming from two directions at once. He could hardly have hoped to succeed, and if he was going to fail, what was the point of wasting good men? Suggestions that he hoped to give the fleet one more day to win a victory, or to prevent the Persians' cutting its escape route, really make no sense.[41]

But what of those who stayed? There are really four questions to be answered here: did Leonidas and his Spartans simply refuse to contemplate retreat? Was there really a prophecy that either Sparta would be destroyed or would lose a king? Were the Thebans kept back as hostages? Did the Thespiaians volunteer to stay? Of these questions we can probably answer the second and third with some certainty. On the whole it is unlikely that Leonidas' decision to stay was really influenced by a prophecy. It is far more likely that the prophecy was invented or bandied about, *after* the disaster, to re-embolden spirits dejected by the death of the Spartan king: he had not died in vain, was essentially its intended message.[42] As for the Thebans, as was pointed out long ago by Plutarch (*Moralia* 865d), if Leonidas had really wanted to keep them as hostages, he would have sent them off under guard with the Greeks he dismissed. Almost certainly these Thebans represented those in Thebes who were inclined to resist the Persians, and had reason to fear either Persian vengeance, or that they would be sacrificed by their fellow-countrymen on the altar of appeasement. As Diodoros, indeed, says (11.4.7) they were 'from the other party'.

The question why the Thespiaians remained with Leonidas also admits of a fairly certain answer. It has been argued that the Spartan king would never have chosen or allowed all the hoplites of a single state to stay and die with him,[43] but this is not what Herodotos says: he says (7.222) that they refused to go, and if this is so, the king may have had little or no choice in the matter. The Thespiaians do seem to have been a stubborn lot: later they are said to have fought to the death on at least two occasions – at Delion (Thucydides 4.96.3) and again at the Nemea (Xenophon, *Hellenika* 4.2.20). Nor can the answer be that Leonidas thought there was no point in their going home since their country was bound to be overrun. Even if it had not already been evacuated, as it certainly eventually was (8.50.2), if the Thespiaians had accompanied the contingents who withdrew from Thermopylai, they could probably have managed both to escape themselves, and to get their families to safety. Herodotos says that the Plataians who had helped row Athenian warships at Artemision, were put ashore in

---

40 Bury, *BSA* 2 (1895/6), 98ff.; Grundy, 305-10.

41 Munro, 1902, 318; Miltner, *Klio* 28 (1935), 228ff.; criticized by Hignett, 377-8.

42 Cf. Munro, *op.cit.*, 316. Green 67-8, seems inclined to accept the prophecy as genuine.

43 Delbrück, 97 n.3; Hignett, 376.

Boiotia on the fleet's return, and apparently they managed to evacuate their families (8.44.1).

It is really the first question that is the most intractable: did the Spartans stay simply because their code precluded retreat, or was there some other reason? Here the problem is compounded by the myth of Thermopylai itself – it is this episode which gave rise to the idea that Spartans never retreated. But in fact there is no particular reason to believe that the Spartan military code would have prevented Leonidas from retreating, if he could have done, and if the military situation warranted it: it was running away, surrendering or even being defeated, which were frowned upon, not retreating under orders.

If, then, there was some other reason for the failure of the Spartans, Thespiaians and Thebans to get away, what was it? One suggestion is that Leonidas did not receive the news of the turning-movement until it was too late,[44] and that while most of the Greeks got away by simply fleeing the moment Hydarnes and the Immortals came into sight near Dhrakospilia, the Spartans and Thespiaians reacted too slowly, indeed in too disciplined a fashion, for their own good; a variation on this is that the Thespiaians and Thebans were caught in trying to retreat, and whereas the former then fought to the death, the latter surrendered.[45] The main objection to all this is that it is not what Herodotos says, but it is also difficult to see how the Immortals can have been seen in time for some of the Greeks to get away, while the rest were caught: the track the Immortals were following may have been visible from the East Gate, but it was almost certainly not visible from the Middle Gate. In other words, if Leonidas and his army had had to depend on *seeing* the Immortals for their first knowledge that they were about to be taken in the rear, the Immortals would probably have had to have descended to the coast road, and none of the Greeks would have been able to escape.

It is true that it is difficult to see how Herodotos can have got his information about what happened after the departure of the contingents that escaped, but it is not totally impossible that some knowledge of what occurred filtered through to contemporary Greeks either from the Thebans, or from the Greeks in Xerxes' entourage (e.g. the Spartan king, Damaratos), or from the Persians themselves. In any case, Herodotos is all we have, and it is better to adhere to what he says, rather than try to 'reconstruct' what happened *ab initio*, though, as usual, we do not necessarily have to accept the reasons he gives for what happened.

Here, if we are right to think that Leonidas' decision not to retreat was neither taken because retreat was against the Spartan code nor because of the prophecy, the most plausible reason for it would seem to be that he wanted to provide time for as much of his army to retreat as possible. But if he wanted a rear-guard, it is obvious that he would have had to retain his Spartans, since no one is likely to have been willing to stay if the Spartans departed. He may have called for volunteers,[46] as is suggested by Herodotos' statement that he 'rather adhered to the view that Leonidas, when he realised that the allies were not eager and unwilling to share the danger with him, bade them

44 Beloch, *loc.cit.* n.39 above, criticized by Hignett, 373-4.
45 Delbrück, 97 n.3.
46 This is one of Green's happier suggestions (140).

go',[47] and why should we not believe that the Thespiaians thereupon volunteered? Why, for that matter, should we not also believe this to be true of the Thebans, since Herodotos' explanation of why they stayed is so implausible? They may have felt there was no point in going home, and the same may have been true of the smallest of all the contingents which fought at Thermopylai, the eighty hoplites from Mykenai. Herodotos does not mention them here, but Pausanias (10.20.2) says that they stayed with the Spartans and Thespiaians, and they too may have feared to go home: in the event of a Persian triumph, Argos would almost certainly recover control of Mykenai, and then woe betide any Mykenaian who had fought against Persia![48]

Herodotos' account of what happened after the Greek army had divided is entirely consistent with the hypothesis that Leonidas had stayed with part of it to act as a rear-guard. According to him (7.223.1), when the sun rose, Xerxes poured libations, and waited 'for the time when the market-place is just about full' (i.e., presumably, about nine or ten o'clock), before launching his assault. If this is the case, the Greeks will have had several hours to make their dispositions after the 'daywatchers' brought their news 'as day was already breaking' (7.219.1). Herodotos adds that Xerxes had been told to do this by Ephialtes, and since he goes on to remark that the descent from the summit of the pass was quicker than the ascent, he presumably wishes us to understand that Xerxes' attack was intended to coincide with Hydarnes' blocking the escape. In the event it appears that Hydarnes was late, but this is understandable in view of the difficulty of synchronizing a military operation like this,[49] though it is possible that Xerxes deliberately attacked early in order to pin the Greeks down until Hydarnes could move into position.

But the Greeks did not wait passively for the assault. Instead, according to Herodotos (7.223.2), they moved out much farther into the broader part of the pass than they had previously done. Herodotos says that this was 'as though they were marching out to their deaths,' but it is not impossible that they still hoped to beat a fighting retreat: a bold front might disconcert Xerxes' army enough to prevent it from pressing too closely, and give even the rear-guard a chance to escape. Unfortunately we do not know how many men Leonidas had left, for Herodotos does not say, and although Diodoros says 500 (11.9.2), this seems too few, and he appears to have forgotten the Thebans. Probably the number was something like twice as many, and it was perhaps because they now all deployed together, on a wider front, instead of fighting in relays, that the enemy losses were even heavier than in the previous fighting, as Herodotos says (7.223.3). The enemy, too, may have been making an even greater effort: Herodotos says that officers armed with whips urged their men forward, and there is no reason to doubt him – at the Somme, for example, each British battalion had its 'battle police' to compel its men into battle, and some stragglers were shot.[50] Some Persians perhaps tried to work their way round the seaward flank of the Greeks, because Herodotos says

---

47 The Greek for 'unwilling to share the danger' is 'οὐκ ἐθέλοντας συνδιακινδυνεύειν,' and although 'ἐθέλοντας' is, of course, here a participle, as a *noun* it means 'volunteers'.

48 Hignett, 146 n.5, argues that Pausanias 2.16.5 does not mean that the Mycenaeans stayed to the end, but 10.20.2 certainly does.

49 Cf. R.Hope Simpson, op.cit. n.35 above, 10.

50 John Keegan, *The Face of Battle* (London, 1976), 277.

(loc.cit.) that 'many fell into the sea and were drowned.' Others were trampled under foot by their own comrades – something that could easily happen in these close-fought *mêlées*.

Perhaps the very success of the Greeks was their undoing. Herodotos says they knew they were doomed, because of the turning-force, and even if this may not be strictly true, they may still have fought with the reckless abandon of desperate men, as he implies (7.223.3). The fury of the fighting is suggested by his statement that when most of their spears were broken, they began to use their swords (7.224.1), for the spear was the main weapon of the hoplite, and swords were not usually necessary unless the fighting was prolonged. Once their spears were broken, the Greeks will have lost the advantage their longer ones had given them in the earlier fighting (cf. 7.211.2). Worse still, it was now that Leonidas fell, and this will not only have left the Greeks temporarily leaderless, but probably have made the surviving Spartans refuse even to contemplate retreat until they had recovered their king's body. Herodotos says there was 'much shoving' (ὠθισμὸς ἐγίνετο πολλός: 7.225.1), until the Greeks recovered it, flinging the enemy back four times.

At last the moment came when the Greeks learned that Hydarnes was approaching to their rear. Falling back, they crossed the Phokian wall, and took their stand, all but the Thebans, on the hillock, 'where the stone lion now stands in honour of Leonidas' (7.225.2). The lion has long gone, but the hillock has been securely identified, and is now marked by a slab of pink marble bearing the famous epitaph for the Spartans (see below). Here the remnants of the Spartans and Thespiaians fought on with swords and even teeth, until, surrounded now on all sides, they were finally overwhelmed by a storm of missiles (cf. 'κατέχωσαν οἱ βάρβαροι *βάλλοντες*':7.225.3).

The only survivors were the Thebans, who, if Herodotos is to be believed (7.233.2), broke away from the rest when they were pressed back to the hillock, holding out their hands in token of surrender, and claiming that they had been compelled to fight. Herodotos adds the surely authentic detail that some of them were killed, before the Persians grasped what was happening. He also says that the survivors were branded with the 'royal marks', and although this may be true,[51] it is suspicious that he here reminds his readers that among those so branded was the Theban commander, Leontiades, and that it was his son, Eurymachos, who later commanded the Theban attack on Plataia. The incident to which this refers took place in March, 431, and led directly to the commencement of the Peloponnesian War, and although Thucydides says the attack was actually commanded by others, he does say that the plot had been arranged with Eurymachos, son of Leontiades, by Plataian traitors (2.2). Clearly, then, there would have been considerable hostility towards Eurymachos and his family in Athens, from where Herodotos clearly derived so much of his information, and the story of Leontiades' behaviour at Thermopylai may well have been tainted by the later behaviour of his son.

Herodotos gives us some of the names of those who had allegedly been conspicuous for their bravery, including the Spartans, Dienekes, Alpheos and Maron, the latter two brothers; of the Thespiaians he mentions only one, Dithyrhambos, son of Harmatides (7.226-7), though he earlier gives the name of their commander, Demophilos, son of

---

51 Cf. HW *ad loc.*, and C.P.Jones, *JRS* 77 (1987), 149-70.

Diadromeus (7.222). He goes on to quote three epitaphs, one for all those who fell with Leonidas, including those who died before the army was divided, the second for the Spartans themselves, and the third for the seer, Megistias.

As it stands, the first of the epitaphs seems to be incomplete, for it simply says that four thousands from the Peloponnese once *fought* (ἐμάχοντο: 7.228.1) here against 3,000,000(!), whereas epitaphs are usually for the dead. It is true that Herodotos later says that the Greek dead numbered 4000, but the dead certainly included the Thespiaians, and, one would have thought, some of the Lokrians who fought on the first two days (cf. 7.203.1), and these were not from the Peloponnese. Herodotos may, however, himself have misunderstood the epitaph,[52] for his total for the dead seems too high. Taking his own figures, and including at least one helot for each of the 298 Spartans who perished (cf. 7.229 & 232), something like 2700 would have had to have been killed on the first two days, and among the Thebans on the final day, to make the total 4000.

Herodotos says that the Amphiktyones, the body who administered the nearby shrine of Demeter at Anthela (cf. 7.200) were responsible for the first two epitaphs, and Simonides for the third (7.228.4), but it is usually assumed that Simonides also wrote the famous epitaph for the Spartans – 'Passer-by, tell the Lakedaimonians that here we lie, obeying their words' – and all Herodotos may mean is that the Amphiktyones paid for the other inscriptions, whereas Simonides personally put up the third for his friend.

Later (7.238) Herodotos says that Xerxes searched out Leonidas' body, cut off the head and stuck it on a pike, and although it was most unusual for Persians to so dishonour a brave man, there are parallels – Kambyses, for example, is supposed to have desecrated the tomb of Amasis of Egypt (3.16), and Artaxerxes maltreated the body of his brother, Cyrus, after Kounaxa (Xenophon, *Anabasis* 1.10.1, 3.1.17). The other Greek dead were collected and left lying in heaps until the sailors of the fleet had had a chance to view them. Herodotos says (8.25.1) that the sailors thought they were all Spartans and Thespiaians, though they were also looking at helots, but that Xerxes' attempt to conceal his own losses – he had buried all but 1000 of the 20,000 killed (8.24.1) – did not succeed. One suspects that the Persian losses were not as high as 20,000, though it is not impossible – it is certainly most unlikely that they were as low as 1000.

Meanwhile, some sixty kilometres away to the east, the Greek fleet had also been taking a battering. As we have seen, Herodotos says that an Athenian triakonter, commanded by one, Abronichos, had been attached to Leonidas' force to warn those at Artemision should anything happen to the army, just as a ship commanded by Polyas of Antikyra had been attached to the fleet in case the latter got into trouble (8.21.1). Probably one of Leonidas' last acts had been to order Abronichos to go and warn the fleet of his desperate situation, for it was vital that the fleet should know that the Persians might soon be able to block the Euripos. Herodotos says (8.21.2) that Abronichos told the fleet 'what had happened to Leonidas and his army' (τὰ γεγονότα περὶ Λεωνίδην καὶ τὸν στρατὸν αὐτοῦ: 8.21.2), and this would naturally mean that he brought the news of the fall of Thermopylai. This may, however, be another example of 'telescoping' by the tradition, for one would have thought that Abronichos

52 As HW ii 230 *ad loc.* suggest.

would actually have got away before the end, even if Leonidas did not send him before the fighting began. Perhaps the message actually spoke of Leonidas' dire straits and later became one that he had been overwhelmed.

At all events, when Abronichos reached Artemision, according to Herodotos, he found the fleet already preparing to abandon its position (8.18-21.1). Hitherto, for two days, it had been the Greeks who had taken the initiative, choosing to fight late in the day in each case, so that there was little prospect of any decisive result; in the case of the second day's clash with the Cilician ships, they had also apparently somehow been able to take advantage of the isolation of the Cilician squadron from the rest of the Persian fleet (see above, 141). On the third day, however, Herodotos says (8.15.1), the Persian commanders, 'disgusted that few ships should do them such harm, and fearing Xerxes' reaction, did not wait for the Greeks to begin operations, but made their preparations and put to sea about midday.' This does not necessarily mean that Xerxes had actually ordered his naval commanders to concert their actions with his own – even though the timing of his assault as 'when the market-place was just about full' (7.223.1), is vague, it almost certainly means two or more hours before midday. But it is possible that the King had informed his admirals that he hoped finally to overcome resistance at Thermopylai that day, and that they should make every effort to destroy the Greek navy at the same time.

On this day, then, the Greeks did not row out into the Trikeri channel, but 'remained motionless near Artemision,' while the Persians, 'forming their fleet into a crescent, made to encircle them, in order to capture them' (8.16.2). Presumably, if the Greeks on the first day had really formed a complete circle in mid-channel, as some believe (see above, 139), now they held their wings back, close in shore, and the Persian crescent-formation was an attempt to work their way round both Greek flanks. When combat was joined, Herodotos says (8.16.2), 'they were evenly matched,' and though the sheer size of the Persian fleet caused their vessels to fall foul of each other, and they still suffered the heavier losses, 'many of the Greek ships were destroyed' (8.16.3). An interesting detail is that the Egyptians particularly distinguished themselves on this occasion, capturing five Greek ships with their crews, for the Egyptian marines, with their big shields, long boarding-spears and pole-axes (cf. 7.89.3), were rather better armed for fighting across the decks than most of the Persian fleet. After Salamis, Mardonios allegedly even picked them out to remain with him and his army (9.32), though immediately after the battle he is supposed to have spoken scathingly of them (8.100.4).

When the action was broken off, Herodotos says (8.18), both sides gladly made for their moorings, and although the Greeks were left masters of the field, they had been roughly handled, 'and not least the Athenians, half of whose ships had been damaged.' Immediately they began to consider retreat, and at Themistokles' suggestion slaughtered as many as they wanted of the animals the Euboians had driven to their camp, and lit fires – though Herodotos does not say so, this was a common device for convincing an enemy that one intended to stay where one was. But Themistokles is alleged to have said that the hour of departure would be his concern, and there is no doubt that Herodotos believed that the decision to retreat had been taken before, at this point, Abronichos arrived with his news from Thermopylai (8.19-21.1).

The fact of the matter is that the Greeks had done very well to maintain their position as long as they had. Assuming Herodotos' figures for the two fleets are correct, even after the losses in the two storms and by enemy action, the Persians will have had between 500 and 700 ships left to face at most 324 Greek ships, on the final day, and whatever tactical precautions the Greeks may have taken to offset their numerical inferiority, they could not offset the facts of geography. The Trikeri channel is some eight kilometres wide at its narrowest point, i.e., to all intents and purposes, is the open sea, and, in the end, the Persians were really bound to win. It may have been now that Themistokles finally learned the vital lesson – that if the Greeks were to stand a chance of victory at sea, they had to find narrower waters.

So away they sailed from Artemision, in the order they had been drawn up – Corinthians first, Athenians last. But Themistokles had one last trick up his sleeve. He had told his fellow-commanders that he had a plan which might succeed in persuading the Ionian and Carian contingents in the Persian fleet to desert the enemy (8.19.1). Now taking the 'best sailing' Athenian ships, he called in at all the places where there was drinking water, and had messages carved on the rocks calling upon the Ionians and Carians either to join the Greeks, or at least to remain neutral. Herodotos says that he had two alternatives in mind: either Xerxes would not get to know of this, and the Ionians really would desert, or, if the king heard of it, he would begin to distrust his Greek subjects (8.22). Even if the story is untrue, at least the psychology is right!

Wars are not won by defeats, nor by withdrawals, as Churchill reminded the British after Dunkirk. But like Dunkirk, Thermopylai soon began to act as an inspiration to the Greeks, and as for the war at sea, the poet Pindar was surely right to see a chink of light amidst the gloom – Artemision, he said (*ap.* Plutarch, *Themistokles* 8.2), was 'where the sons of the Athenians laid the shining foundation-stone of freedom.'

CHAPTER 7

Divine Salamis

For the Greeks the Thermopylai-Artemision campaign was a disaster. The fleet might have held its own, though not without some losses and considerable damage to its ships, but the army had lost over half its men, if there really had been 4000 killed, and its commander-in-chief, the King of Sparta, was dead. Above all, the whole of central Greece, and particularly Attica, was now exposed to the invader, letting the Persians loose on some of the areas of Greece which had refused to submit.

Herodotos implies that the Persian army proceeded to ignore the route through Thermopylai which it had fought for three days to secure, and to advance instead up into Doris (8.31). But although there is no reason to doubt that part of the army went that way, it seems more likely that most of it went through Thermopylai into Lokris and then turned inland *via* Atalanta and Hyampolis to join the rest in the Kephisos valley. Admittedly, we hear of no reprisals taken against the Lokrians, despite their presence at Thermopylai, but perhaps their withdrawal before the final fight, and swift submission thereafter, helped to save them.[1]

Doris, too, was left untouched, presumably because no troops from there had joined Leonidas, but Phokis was ravaged from end to end, from Drymos and Amphikaia (Amphiklea) in the north-west to Hyampolis and Abai in the south-east (8.33). Most of the Phokians had taken refuge on Parnassos or at Amphissa (8.32.1), but some were caught in the foothills (8.33). Presumably the flight of the inhabitants was enough to convince the Persians that they were not prepared to submit, though there may also be some truth in Herodotos' story that the Thessalians encouraged the ravaging of Phokis out of enmity towards its inhabitants, who had rejected their demand for fifty talents as payment in return for mediation.

At Panopeus, on the borders of Boiotia, the army divided again, according to Herodotos (8.34-5), the main body accompanying Xerxes into Boiotia, a detachment proceeding to Delphi, by way of Daulis and Aiolidai. The people of Delphi, the historian says (8.36), when they had enquired of the oracle whether they should remove or bury the temple treasures, had been told that the god was capable of protecting his own. Nevertheless, they had taken the precaution of sending their women and children across to Achaia, though the majority of the men had taken refuge in the cave of Korykos, some at Amphissa, leaving sixty men and the priest at Delphi. However, when the Persians drew near, the Delphians still left in the town were encouraged by the priest's report that sacred weapons kept in the temple had miraculously appeared outside it. Then a thunderstorm sent two pinnacles of rock crashing down on the raiders and a battle-cry was heard from the temple itself. A large number of Persians were killed and

1 E.W.Kase and G.J.Szemler, *Klio* 64 (1982), 353ff., may well be right about the route taken by Persian troops through Doris to Phokis, but are probably wrong to insist that this was the only route the Persians took, even that there was no route through Thermopylai at this date. Their explanation of why, if so, there was a battle at Thermopylai at all, is very weak. If the Persians did use their route, or any other that bypassed Thermopylai, they presumably only learned of them later – perhaps from Ephialtes?

the rest fled in panic, pursued by the triumphant Delphians and the gigantic phantom shapes of the heroes, Phylakos and Autonoös (8.37-9).

Obviously legend has been at work here, no doubt partly in a later attempt to exonerate Delphi for its defeatist attitude.[2] Diodoros even quotes an inscription set up to commemorate the miracle (11.14.4), which has been found this century. But it is one thing to doubt the supernatural elements in the story, another to doubt the story altogether. The Persians were well aware of the importance of such international shrines in influencing Greek opinion, even if they were not simply out for plunder. They had, for example, plundered and burnt the shrine at Didyma, after the Ionian revolt (6.19.3), but had scrupulously respected Delos on their way to Marathon (6.97). Thus it is more than likely that they would have taken steps to win control of so important a centre as Delphi, particularly in view of its hitherto equivocal stance.[3]

Perhaps, then, the legend ultimately derived from a Persian raid on western Phokis, which turned back before reaching Delphi, or perhaps a Persian force sent either to plunder the shrine, or to protect it, actually was defeated by a combination of natural forces and heroic Delphian resistance. After all, the gigantic rocks said to have fallen from Parnassos can still be seen, lying on the ruins of a sixth century shrine or 'treasury', near the remains of the temple of Athena Pronaia, as Herodotos said (8.39.2), though they may, of course, have had nothing to do with the alleged Persian attack.[4]

Meanwhile, Xerxes and his main force advanced into Boiotia, where most of the towns were left unharmed, thanks to the good offices of Macedonians sent by King Alexander, according to Herodotos (8.34), and those of the exiled king of Sparta, Damaratos, according to Plutarch (*Moralia* 864f). However, the Plataians who had served at Artemision, had made sure that they were set ashore at Chalkis by the returning Greek fleet, so that they could get their households to safety (8.44.1), and the remaining inhabitants of Thespiai had also escaped to the Peloponnese. Both their towns were duly burned by the enemy. Herodotos says (8.50.2) that this was because the Thebans told the Persians they had not 'medized', though one would have thought Thespiaian intransigence, at least, would have been obvious from the heroic part they had played at Thermopylai. Since the time for all this would have been very short – the Persian army probably reached Attica within a week of the fall of Thermopylai (see

---

2 N.Robertson, *CPh* 82 (1987), 6-7, argues that Delphi was not defeatist.

3 For the inscription see B.Merritt, *Hesperia* 16 (1947), 58ff.; for doubts about the attack on Delphi see, e.g., Meyer, 383, and Hignett, 447. Fehling, of course, even thinks that Herodotos made up his two sources – Persian survivors and Delphians – because to believe they existed involves the assumption that 'there really was such an event and that it was independently observed by the two sides' (13-6). But why is such an assumption 'impossible', as he claims? On the rocks see Parke & Wormall, *The Delphic Oracle* (Oxford, 1956), 187ff.

4 For the suggestion that a raiding-force turned back before reaching Delphi see Burn, 426. Herodotos says the force was sent to plunder the shrine (8.35.2), but it has been argued that Xerxes would not have wanted so gratuitously to offend Greek religious susceptibilities, particularly since so many states represented on the Amphictyonic Council had now 'medized' (Meyer, 384; HW ii 246; Hignett, 447). Hence Munro, 1902, 320, suggested the force was sent to protect the shrine, and Casson (*CR* 28, 1914, 145ff.) that its task was to take an inventory of temple treasures! Pomtow (*Jahrb. kl. Philol.* 129, 227ff.) takes the view that the Persians were just a band of plunderers acting without orders.

below) – it is likely that the majority of the inhabitants of both Plataia and Thespiai had in any case already been evacuated, and that all that was left to do now was to get the more stubborn or dilatory away to safety.

Thus it was that three months after they had left the Hellespont, probably about the end of the first week in September, the triumphant Persians entered Attica. They found a deserted land, apart from some people who had got left behind for some unspecified reason, and were taken prisoner (9.99.2), and a few priests and poor persons on the acropolis (8.51.2). Herodotos says that apart from their inability to leave with the rest because of their poverty, the last had believed, all along, that the oracle about the 'wooden wall' referred to an ancient palisade guarding access to the acropolis (cf. 7.142.1), and this they had proceeded to replace or reinforce 'with planks and beams' (8.51.2). The so-called 'Themistokles Decree' says that the priests had been ordered to remain on the acropolis, and modern scholars have suggested that the rock was in fact regularly garrisoned, though this seems doubtful.[5]

According to Herodotos (8.41), it was only after the return of the Greek fleet from Artemision that the Athenians 'made a proclamation that each of the Athenians should get his children and household to safety where he could,' but, as we have seen (above, 111–2), it is very unlikely that this can be true. If the historian's detailed time-table of the movements of the Greek and Persian forces after Artemision is at all accurate, the last sea-battle off Artemision took place in the early afternoon (8.15.1), and presumably the Greek fleet left that night. During the night a man from Histiaia made his way over to the Persians in a boat, and reported the Greek withdrawal, whereupon, after sending swift ships to reconnoitre, next day, as the sun was rising (8.23.1), the whole Persian fleet sailed across to Artemision. There they waited until mid-day (8.23.2), and then sailed for Histiaia, overrunning the coastal villages on the way. At Histiaia they were met by a herald from Xerxes, inviting them to view the scene of his triumph at Thermopylai.

At this point there is some variability in the account, for although Herodotos implies that the sailors of the fleet – presumably, in fact, only some higher-ranking officers – then spent the rest of the day sightseeing at Thermopylai, it is much more likely that it was the next day.[6] Thus it would have been on the third day after the final battle off Artemision that the naval sightseers returned to the fleet, and the army began its march on Athens (8.25.3). The fleet then waited another three days (8.66.1: i.e., presumably, the day the sightseers returned and the following two), before setting out for Phaleron, which they reached 'in another three days' (loc.cit.). In other words, the fleet set out on the sixth day after the final battle off Artemision, and reached Phaleron on the ninth. Presumably the Greek fleet had taken approximately the same time to get from Artemision to Salamis, and, if so, it would have arrived six days before the Persian fleet.

The time available for evacuation would have been even less, if, as Herodotos implies (8.67.1), the Persian army reached Athens before the fleet. It is true that this will have given the army only five or six days to march from Thermopylai to Athens, and that this seems too short a time for a march of between 150 and 250 kilometres,

---

5 For the date of Xerxes' arrival in Athens see Hignett, 453; for the view that the acropolis was properly defended see, e.g. Burn, 431; Green, 160-1; N.Robertson, *CPh* 82 (1987, 10 n.16.

6 Cf. Macan (1908) i 2 390, on 8.25.3.

depending on which route it took.[7] However, it is possible that the army, or at least an advance-guard, made a series of forced marches precisely in order to try to anticipate an evacuation of Athens, or, of course, Herodotos may be wrong in implying that it reached Athens before the fleet. In either case, it seems extremely unlikely that the evacuation really took place now, especially if, as Herodotos says (8.41.1), most of the evacuees were taken to Trozen – a day's sail from Phaleron. In fact there is one indication in Herodotos' own narrative that the evacuation had taken place quite early in the year. He later has Spartan envoys refer to the loss of *two* harvests by the Athenians (8.142.3), and this would most naturally mean those of 480 and 479. But the former should have been reaped by the end of May, even if threshing would normally have gone on into August.[8]

For those who believe in the 'Themistokles Decree', which provides for the evacuation of Attica before the departure of the fleet to Artemision, there is no problem. But even if the decree is not authentic, it seems probable, as we have seen (above, 112), that the Athenians would have taken steps to evacuate as many non-combatants as possible, before the fleet sailed. Manning the fleet would have required every free, adult male, and it would, surely, have been realised that if the attempt to hold Thermopylai and Artemision failed, the enemy could be in Attica within a week. If this is right, Herodotos' 'proclamation' will be a last-minute warning to any who had stayed that they now had to get to safety, or risk falling into enemy hands. Perhaps some had stayed on in the expectation that the defence of Thermopylai and Artemision would be successful, or even that the main Greek army would bring the enemy to battle in Boiotia (cf. 8.40.2). Perhaps it was also now that word got round that the priestess of Athena had declared that the honey-cakes put out each month to feed the goddess' sacred snake on the acropolis, had not been touched, and thus, presumably, that the snake, too, had left (8.41.2-3).

Later sources (Plutarch, *Themistokles* 10; Aristeides 46, p257 Dindorf) add dramatic and pathetic tales of old people and household animals who had to be left behind, and of the tearful separation of families, as most of the women and children went off to Aigina and Trozen, and the men to Salamis. Some of the stories, one suspects, come from family traditions, for example that of Xanthippos' dog, which swam across to Salamis beside its master's trireme, and, dying, gave its name to the place called 'The Dog's-tomb' ('Kynossema': Plutarch, *Themistokles* 10.6), or of Kimon's leading a procession of his fellow *hippeis* ('Knights') up to the Acropolis to dedicate their horses' bridles, which they would not be needing, and taking instead some of the shields hung up as trophies around the temple (Plutarch, *Kimon* 5.2-3). The author of the Aristotelian *Athenian Constitution* (23.1) even has a tale of how the members of the aristocratic 'Council of the Areiopagos' raised enough to pay 8 *drachmai* to each of the sailors of the fleet, and a very improbable variant (Kleidemos, *ap.* Plutarch, *Themistokles* 10) has Themistokles

---

7 Cf. Hignett, 195-6.

8 Cf. Beloch, ii 2.51, and *pace* Gianelli, *La spedizione di Serse da Terme a Salamina* (Milan, 1924), 43f., and Hignett, 198-9. See also my article in *Hermes* 92 (1964), 265–7. For the 'two crops' see Hammond, *JHS* 102 (1982), 84-5; *contra*: Robertson, *op.cit.* n.5 above, 15 n.28.

searching the baggage of evacuees, on the pretext of looking for a missing ornament from Athene's cult statue, and impounding any money he found for the public use.

These stories are more appropriate to the last-minute evacuation of legend than an earlier, more carefully planned operation. But whether or not they are true, no praise is too high for the collective moral courage shown by the Athenians at this hour. When the people of Phokaia in Asia Minor, two generations earlier, had decided to emigrate rather than submit to Persian rule, they had tried to bolster their courage by flinging a lump of iron into the sea and swearing not to return before it appeared again, but even then half of them had been overcome by homesickness and broken their oath (1.165). The Phokaians were making a permanent break with home, but at least they had somewhere to go, their colony on Corsica. The Athenians faced a more uncertain future, dependent, for the time being, on the charity of Trozenians (cf. Plutarch, *Themistokles* 10.3) and other Peloponnesians (cf. 8.142.4). There was no guarantee that they would ever be able to go back home, and the sneers of the Corinthian, Adeimantos, that Themistokles was a man with no 'fatherland' (πατρίς), a 'city-less man' (ἄπολις ἀνήρ: 8.61.1), even if unhistorical (see below), vividly illustrate what it must have meant to a people, who proudly claimed to be autochthonous, to abandon their city.

Meanwhile the Persians set about reducing the acropolis. They occupied the Areiopagos, and shot fire-arrows at the wooden barricade, though they were still unable to take the rock until a party of soldiers managed to scramble up an unguarded section of the precipitous cliffs.[9] Realising that it was all over, some of the defenders leaped to their death, others took refuge in the temple, where they were slaughtered to a man. The Persians then stripped the temple of its treasures and burnt everything on the site (8.52-3).

For Xerxes the capture of Athens had probably always been the first main objective, and we can well believe Herodotos when he says that the king sent a rider off to Sousa to announce his success. But while the Greek fleet was still more or less intact and the Peloponnese remained free, his triumph could not be complete. One would like to believe that when, feeling some misgiving at the desecration of even enemy shrines, he sent the Athenian exiles in his entourage up to the acropolis to placate their gods with traditional rites, Athena's sacred olive-tree, which had been burned like everything else, was found to have put out a new shoot (8.54-5). If the story were true, it would be a fitting symbol of the possibility of Athenian rejuvenation at even this darkest of dark hours.

The strategic situation at this point must, as always, be looked at from both points of view, and this is precisely what Herodotos does, in his own way. According to him, the Greek fleet had only put into Salamis at the request of the Athenians, in order to help with the evacuation of Attica (8.40.1), and even if most of the population had already been evacuated, there is no reason to doubt that some still remained. But presumably the historian would have us understand that if the Athenians had not made their request, the fleet would have gone elsewhere, and although he does not say where, its obvious destination would have been the Isthmus.

---

9 For the route used by the Persians to scale the acropolis see G.Dontas, *Hesperia* 52 (1983), 48ff.

As soon as the news of the death of Leonidas and his gallant band had reached the Peloponnese, he says (8.71.1ff.), the full forces of Sparta and her Peloponnesian allies had begun to assemble at the Isthmus, now that the Karneia and Olympic festivals were over. They had blocked one of the routes from Attica, the ancient 'Skeironian way', and had begun to construct a wall across the Isthmus. No certain remains of this wall have yet been found, and by as early as the next century it appears to have vanished, since Diodoros does not mention it in his account of the campaign of 369 when Epameinondas was trying to force his way across the Isthmus (15.68). But there is no reason to doubt that it existed, and it probably ran along the line of later walls, traces of some of which can still be seen south of the modern canal and particularly near the Isthmia sanctuary.[10] Although the wall does not appear to have been finished until the following summer (9.7), and could hardly even have been begun much before the arrival of the fleet at Salamis, the idea of defending the Isthmus, if all else failed, had probably long been in the minds of at least the Peloponnesians, however much the Athenians may have hoped for a stand in Boiotia (cf. 8.40.2). We can readily believe Herodotos, then, when he says that when the Greek commanders conferred at Salamis, and Eurybiadas posed the question where they should make their stand, 'since Attica was already lost, ... the majority of the views expressed came to the same conclusion, namely to sail to the Isthmus and fight for the Peloponnese' (8.49).

While this discussion was going on, the historian continues, reports reached the fleet of the overrunning of Attica (8.50.1), and when, in particular, news of the capture of the acropolis arrived, it caused consternation. Some of the commanders did not wait for any decision, but rushed to their ships and began to hoist sails for flight, whilst even those who stayed hurriedly adopted the proposal to withdraw (8.56). The implication is that this was at the same conference, but it was probably a later one, since one would have expected news of the capture of the acropolis to reach the fleet several days after that of the arrival of the Persians in Attica – Herodotos says the siege of the acropolis went on 'for some time' (8.52.2). In any case, according to him, when Themistokles returned to his ship and told his friend, Mnesiphilos, what had been decided, the latter urged him to re-open the question with Eurybiadas (8.57). This Themistokles proceeded to do, and, after much argument (8.59-62), the Spartan was persuaded to change his mind and adopt the plan of remaining and fighting where they were (8.63).

Herodotos then interrupts his account of these discussions among the Greeks to tell two stories. First, he says (8.64), there was an earthquake, which led the Greeks to pray to the gods, call upon the heroes of Salamis, Aias and his father, Telamon, and to send a ship to Aigina to fetch the images of Aiakos, Telamon's father, and his other descendants. Secondly, he tells the story of how the Athenian exile, Dikaios, in the company of ex-king Damaratos of Sparta, saw a cloud of dust in the Thriasian plain, from which proceeded a sound like the 'Iakchos' hymn sung at the time of the annual procession from Athens to Eleusis. This, Dikaios declared, portended disaster for Xerxes' forces – for his army, if it blew down upon the Peloponnese, for his fleet if it

10 For possible traces of the wall see J.R.Wiseman, *Hesperia* 32 (1963), 255f. and 270f., and *The Land of the Ancient Corinthians* (Göteborg, 1978), 59ff.; see also A.W.Lawrence, *Greek Aims in Fortification* (Oxford, 1979), 169 and 377; O.Broneer, *The Princeton Encyclopedia of Classical Sites* (Princeton, 1976), 418, is sceptical.

drifted towards Salamis. Damaratos urged Dikaios to keep quiet about it, and, of course, the cloud was duly borne towards the Greek base on Salamis (8.65).

Herodotos next (8.66ff.) turns to the Persian fleet, and gives an account of a conference of commanders, attended by Xerxes, at which it is decided to bring about a battle. The fleet duly puts to sea, but finding that it is too late for battle that day, begins to prepare for the next (8.70.1). Herodotos then reverts to the Greeks (8.70.2ff.), whom he describes as gripped by panic. This eventually leads to a further meeting of the war-council from which Themistokles, realising that the previous decision to stay and fight at Salamis is about to be reversed, slips out and sends a message to the Persians. As a result, the Persians put to sea at midnight, and at dawn next day, attack the Greeks (8.76-83).

This narrative is obviously not without its difficulties, but much of it can be accepted as it stands, and sense can be made of the rest. It provides a coherent framework for understanding what happened, and should not be treated nearly as cavalierly as it often is.[11] Thus there is no reason at all not to accept that it was originally decided to withdraw to the Isthmus, once the evacuation of Attica was complete. As suggested above, this was probably what the majority of the commanders had assumed they would do, from the moment they left Artemision, and there was much to be said for their reasons, as reported by Herodotos. If they were defeated off Salamis, they would be blockaded on the island, with no way of escape, whereas if they fought at the Isthmus, they could at least run ashore and escape by land (8.49.2). We may, if we like, take with a pinch of salt, the story of the panic that ensued when news of the fall of the acropolis was received, as a product of Athenian bias, but we are possibly too prone to believe that all the Greeks were equally courageous. In war, panics do occur, and when one side consists of a loose alliance of independent states, subject to considerable mutual suspicion and hatred, we might expect such things to happen with some frequency.

Nor is there any compelling reason to doubt the story of Mnesiphilos. This has often been called in question on the assumption that it derives from attempts by Themistokles' enemies to deprive him of the credit for Salamis, and Mnesiphilos himself has even been regarded as a fiction.[12] In fact, however, we now know from surviving *ostraka* that he did exist and that he came from the same deme as Themistokles. Thus it is not at all inconceivable that he played a part in helping Themistokles to get his strategy adopted. This in no way detracts from any credit due to Themistokles, and it is noticeable that not only does Herodotos give the latter different arguments from the

11 I am astonished, for example, that a historian as sensible as J.A.S.Evans usually is, can say that 'we may dismiss Herodotos' account of the quarrels in the Greek camp before Salamis' (*Historia* 18, 1969, 389).

12 Cf., already, Plutarch, *Mor*. 869d-f; and, e.g., Busolt, 641n; Meyer, 223n; Grundy, 363f.; Hignett, 204 n.1; Green, 293 n.4; G.L.Cawkwell, 'The Fall of Themistocles' in *Auckland Classical Essays Presented to E.M.Blaiklock* (Auckland & London, 1970), 41-2. For Mnesiphilos as fiction see Macan (1908) i 2 444. Burn, 446, thinks the story may have come from personal reminiscences, and for other defences see K.Goldscheider, *Die Darstellung des Themistokles bei Herodot* (Diss. Freiburg in Breisgau, 1965), 56-64; C.W.Fornara, *Herodotus: an interpretative essay* (Oxford, 1971), 72 n.19. For the 14 Mnesiphilos *ostraka* see F.J.Frost, *CSCA* 1 (1968), 124, and G.Daux, *BCH* 92 (1968), 732.

ones used by Mnesiphilos, but that he clearly did regard Themistokles as the chief architect of the victory.

Far more important is the question whether Herodotos' account of the wrangling among the Greek leaders approximates to the truth, and if so, what lay behind it. It is, of course, very unlikely that he had access to accurate information about what actually went on in the conferences, though probably not because tight security would have been exercised, as has been alleged[13] – at this date, such precautions would probably not have entered anyone's mind. But it is very unlikely that anyone took notes at the conferences, and presumably those who took part were already men of mature age and thus likely to have died before Herodotos began to write his story. Themistokles himself, for example, was almost certainly at least forty-three, if the archon of 493/2 is the same man, and even if we did not have evidence that he was dead by about by about 459,[14] we would probably have assumed that he died before 450 at the latest. Aristeides, if he is to be identified with the archon of 489/8, was probably a slightly younger man, but the way Herodotos talks about him (8.79.1), strongly suggests that he had never met him. Adeimantos, if it is true that he sired three daughters and a son after the war (Plutarch, *Moralia* 871a), was possibly, though not necessarily, even younger, but even he is unlikely to have lived much beyond, say, 440. In any case, Herodotos never claims here to have got his information from anyone who took part in the discussions, and so, presumably, at best relied on second-hand information, and on the general traditions of his own day, at worst on his own imagination.

Even in the last case, however, at least what he says represents what an intelligent and more or less contemporary Greek thought might have been said, and there is, surely, likely to have been considerable discussion. Nor is there any reason to doubt that – broadly speaking – there would have been two points of view, as Herodotos suggests, the Peloponnesians favouring falling back to the Isthmus, the Athenians, certainly supported by the Megarians, and probably also by the Aiginetans (cf. 8.74.2), favouring a stand at Salamis. It may also be true that the principal advocate of the latter course was Themistokles, and that Adeimantos of Corinth argued for the former. After all, there was nothing cowardly or silly about the former point of view, and Herodotos does not here suggest any such thing. It is different with his tales of Adeimantos' desire to leave Artemision (8.5), and of his flight before Salamis (8.94). The latter was certainly an Athenian slander, which Herodotos himself says was rejected by the rest of Greece (8.94.4).[15]

Modern commentators, indeed, have perhaps too readily accepted that Themistokles was right and Adeimantos wrong. Thus the Peloponnesians were right to argue that if they remained at Salamis and were defeated there, they might be trapped on the island,

---

13 Burn, 441.

14 For the chronology of Themistokles' life see Podlecki, Appendix A, 195-9.

15 It is worth stressing, in view of criticisms such as Burn's, 444-7, that the Peloponnesians in Herodotos, led by Adeimantos, merely argue that it would be better to fight at the Isthmus, not that it would be better not to fight at all, and if Persian moves just before the battle seemed even more of a threat to the Peloponnese, we would have expected their fears to have become more pronounced. It is no argument that they fought bravely in the battle: they had every intention of fighting bravely for their homeland, and, when compelled to fight at Salamis, fought bravely there.

MAP 7. SALAMIS AND ENVIRONS

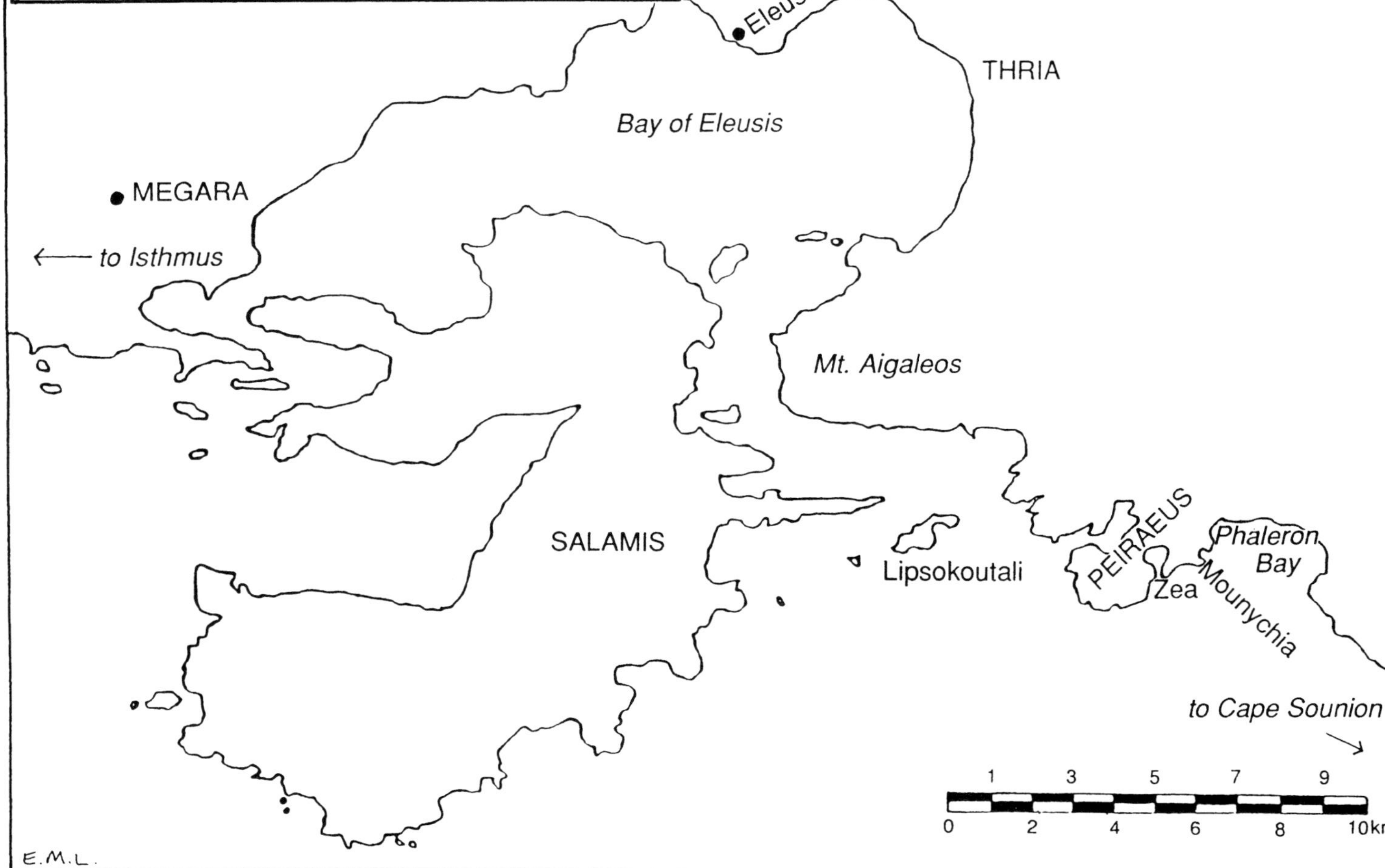

whereas at least there was some possibility of escape by land if they fought at the Isthmus (8.49.2, cf. 70.2). Nor is it as certain as sometimes claimed that defeat would have been inevitable if the Greeks had chosen to give battle at the Isthmus, guarding the Saronic Gulf end of their wall. Both the vicinity of Isthmia, and that of Kenchreai, Corinth's seaport on the Saronic Gulf, could have provided suitable bays for the Greeks to protect their flanks by promontories, as they may have done at Artemision (see above, 149), and as the Corinthians were to do, albeit on a smaller scale, at Erineus during the Peloponnesian War (Thucydides 7.34). The Greeks had, after all, come off best at Artemision, against probably greater odds, for it is difficult to believe that the Persian fleet was now as numerous as it had been in the previous campaign, as Herodotos claims (8.66.1), and the Greek fleet may now have been larger than it had been (see below, 172–3).

On the other hand, Themistokles' arguments, as set out by Herodotos (8.60), are by no means cast-iron. He begins by claiming that if Eurybiadas chose to give battle at the Isthmus, this would mean fighting in the open sea, but this, as we have seen, was not necessarily the case. He then goes on to claim that fighting in the open sea was 'least advantageous' to the Greeks, with their 'heavier' (βαρυτέρας) and less numerous ships. Here, although it was obviously true that a battle in the open sea would not favour the smaller fleet, it is not clear what 'heavier' ships means. One ingenious modern suggestion is that whereas the Persian ships had been hauled ashore and dried out at Doriskos (7.59.2), the Greek ships had become waterlogged through being continuously in the water for perhaps as long as a year.[16] But although Herodotos does not mention any attempt to dry out the Greek ships, this does not prove that it had not been done, for he tends to be much more interested in the Persian side of operations than the Greek. There is no reason why the Greeks should not have dried their ships out before the Artemision campaign, if not in the interlude before Salamis, if it had been really necessary, and in either case this would have probably meant that they were in a better state than the Persian.

Another possibility is that the Greek ships were 'heavier' in the sense that they were more 'heavily', i.e. stoutly, constructed. This is, admittedly, contrary to what Plutarch claims (*Kimon* 12.2), but, as we have seen (above, 83), what Plutarch says is dubious. Thucydides (1.14.3) implies that the Athenian triremes which fought at Salamis, though the most recent built in Greece, were nevertheless old-fashioned in not having complete decks, and it may well be that they were, in other respects, not built as well as the best in the Persian navy. But ships built for speed and manoeuvrability were actually at a

16 The idea was first propounded by Morrison and Williams in their book *Greek Oared Ships 900–322 BC* (Cambridge, 1968), 134f., and is repeated in Morrison & Coates, 153f., and by Morrison in *JHS* 111 (1991), 197. In the last, Morrison states that I attribute the greater heaviness of the Greek ships at Salamis 'not to thicker planking but to the greater number of armed men they carried,' but I do not know where he gets this idea: I make no such assertion in the review (*JHS* 108, 1988, 250) to which he is replying. Morrison's view that the Greek ships had been in the water since the previous autumn depends on assuming that the 'Themistokles Decree' is authentic, and that Hammond's date for it – *JHS* 102 (1982), 75ff. – is right. But even if both these assumptions are correct, which is by no means certain, it is very difficult to believe that the Athenian fleet would not at least have been laid up for the winter.

disadvantage in confined waters, and it is possible that Themistokles had realised this as a result of Athenian experiences off Artemision: it may be significant that whereas Herodotos records that half the Athenian ships were 'damaged' (τετρωμέναι 8.18) on the final day, he does not say that any were 'destroyed' or 'sunk'. Whatever the meaning of 'heavier', however, clearly such ships would have been less at a disadvantage in confined waters.

It was also, of course, true, as Themistokles allegedly argued (8.60α), that by withdrawing to the Isthmus, the Greeks risked losing Salamis, but it is difficult to see how their continued presence at Salamis could really have prevented the Persians' invading the Megarid, as he also implies (*loc.cit*), or provided any protection for Aigina. As for Themistokles' positive arguments, even he did not claim that if the Greeks fought at Salamis, the outcome was certain. All he claimed was that they would win, 'if what usually happens in war turns out' (8.60β), and 'if what I hope happens' (8.60γ).

It is hard, too, to see in what sense the Greeks at Salamis could properly be said to be defending the Peloponnese as much as if they withdrew to the Isthmus (8.60 end). Despite their presence at Salamis, the Persian army could, at any time, have advanced on the Isthmus, and the Persian fleet could also have gone to its support, thus rendering the Isthmus lines useless. What could the Greeks have done? If they came out the Persians would have the battle in the open sea which they wanted. It was only if the Persians opted to fight them in their chosen position that they could be said to be fighting for the Peloponnese there, and the fatal flaw in Themistokles' whole argument is the assumption that if the Greeks remained where they were, the Persians were bound to attack them.[17]

It has, of course, been maintained that the assumption was correct, on the grounds that the Persian army could not turn the Isthmus without the aid of the fleet, nor long maintain a position at the Isthmus without sea-borne supplies, while the Persian fleet could not leave the Greek fleet in its rear, and was no longer strong enough both to cover it and to give aid to the army.[18] But although it may be true that the Persian army could not have forced the Isthmus-lines without the aid of the fleet, the rest of the argument is full of holes. It is almost certainly not the case that the Persian army depended on sea-borne supplies, as we have seen (above, 96–7), and, in any case, the only way in which the Greek fleet could have interfered with the carrying of supplies would have been to come out and attack the convoys, which again was probably what the Persian admirals wanted. It is not even certain that the Persian fleet was now too small both to cover the Greek fleet and support the army (see below, 173–4).

But although, when analysed, Themistokles' arguments seem dubious, this is not to say he did not use them, or something like them. He may well have genuinely felt that the Salamis channel offered a better chance of victory to the Greeks than the waters off the Isthmus, and his arguments may not have seemed unconvincing to many who heard them. After all, it was true that a confined space suited heavier and less numerous ships, and the Megarians and Aiginetans may have been seduced into lending him their

17 E.g. Green, 169ff. Evans, *op.cit.* n.11 above, 392, rightly argues that the Persians did not have to enter the Salamis channel

18 Most forcibly argued by R.Custance, *War at Sea: Modern Theory and Ancient Practice* (Edinburgh & London, 1919), 26ff., quoted with approval by Hignett, 208.

support, since at least the Greek fleet's continued presence at Salamis gave them some slight measure of protection, which is more than withdrawal to the Isthmus would have done.

There were, however, probably other considerations, which Themistokles dared not use, but which weighed far more heavily with him than abstract 'principles of naval warfare' he probably did not understand.[19] The first was the one Herodotos says Mnesiphilos had originally put to him, namely that withdrawal to the Isthmus would lead to the dispersal of the Greek fleet (8.57). Herodotos implies that Themistokles repeated this argument to Eurybiadas, in private, and this makes sense, since it is likely to have carried weight with the man whose job it was to hold the alliance together. But he rightly remarks that Themistokles could not hint at the possibility of such conduct with the allies present (8.60).

But there was possibly another argument, fundamental to Themistokles' way of thinking, which he could use even less. The withdrawal of the fleet to the Isthmus would have meant abandoning the last piece of Athenian territory, with no guarantee that the other Greeks would ever again assemble to fight for it. Themistokles could use the argument that there were Athenian women and children on Salamis (8.60β), but these could be evacuated: territory could not, and remarks about last pieces of Athenian territory would have cut no ice with men who were already disgruntled at the thought of fighting for land already 'taken by the spear' (8.74.2, cf. 8.49.1 & 70.2). Herodotos even has Queen Artemisia of Halikarnassos make the point to Xerxes (8.68β.2).

Thus Themistokles might well have lost his temper if Adeimantos really challenged his right to speak at all since he had no 'fatherland' and was 'a man without a city', as Herodotos says (8.61.1). 'He had a greater city and land than they,' he is supposed to have declared (8.61.2), 'whilst he and his countrymen had two hundred ships manned, since none of the Greeks could repulse them if they came against them'. It is even more plausible that he threatened that the Athenians would collect their families and sail off to Siris in Italy, if Eurybiadas rejected his plan (8.62.2). In short, even if Herodotos' version of what went on in these discussions is largely fiction, at best based on the traditions of his day, it makes sense and is likely to come fairly close to the kind of thing that was actually said, given the strategic situation.

As for the Persians, Herodotos implies that as soon as their fleet reached Phaleron, Xerxes went down to confer with its commanders, that the decision to fight was taken there and then, and that the fleet immediately put out, though by then night was drawing on and the battle itself took place next day (cf. 8.67.1ff.). But this can hardly be true.[20] As we have seen (above, 153–4), the Persian army cannot have reached Attica much, if at all, before the fleet, and the overrunning of Attica, and the capture of the acropolis

---

19 Hignett declares (*loc.cit.*) that 'there is no difficulty in the supposition that the principle of naval warfare enunciated by Custance was understood and acted upon by Themistokles,' but there is *every* difficulty! Even Custance's 'principle' is dubious: the two more recent parallels he cites – the Armada campaign and the battle of Tsushima – are somewhat unfortunate for his purposes, since the English fleet failed to prevent the Armada sailing up the channel, and Admiral Tojo was hardly just trying to 'limit the movements of a hostile fleet by taking up a position flanking its advance'!

20 Though accepted by Macan (1908) ii 293, and, more recently, by Sachs, *CQ* (NS) 26 (1976), 241ff., and Hammond, 1988, 570.

would have taken some time, though probably not as long as has sometimes been argued.[21] One would have thought, too, that the Persian fleet would have needed some time to regroup and refit after the Artemision campaign, even if Herodotos has exaggerated its losses and is wrong about the number of reinforcements which would have had to be integrated into it. Moreover, his own account of what went on among the Greeks, after they received the news of the fall of the acropolis, seems to imply the passing of at least several days.

Another task which may have occupied the Persians during the time between their arrival in Attica and the battle, was an attempt to build a mole across to Salamis. Herodotos only mentions this *after* his account of the battle, and says that Xerxes was merely trying to conceal his intended departure from both the Greeks and his own forces (8.97.1), which may seem implausible. Strabo, on the other hand, implies that the attempt to build the mole came before the battle (9.1.13), and although he is wrong that the distance to Salamis was 'about two stades' (c. 400 metres) – this is less than half the distance even at the narrowest point – he is supported by Ktesias (*Persika* 26) and Aristodemos (*FGH* 104F1). The former, however, does not help by saying that the Athenians, on the advice of Themistokles and Aristeides, hired Cretan archers to hinder the work, for there obviously would not have been time for recruiting officers to go to Crete, hire the men and then return.

In the end, indeed, although the view that construction of the mole began before the battle is supported by some modern commentators,[22] it is probably wrong. It is contrary to what Herodotos says, and there is also one detail in his account, which, although probably untrue as it stands, possibly supports his view. According to him (8.97.1), 'Phoenician merchant-ships' were used in the construction of the mole, and although it is very improbable that such ships could have been got up the channel even before the battle, let alone after it, it is possible that the hulks of Phoenician *warships* may have been available. Diodoros implies that some of them were run ashore during the battle (11.19.2), and Herodotos says (8.90.1) that some Phoenicians whose ships had been 'destroyed', complained to Xerxes about the behaviour of the Ionians (8.90.1). This suggests that their ships had come ashore near where Xerxes' 'throne' was situated, and that was probably near where the mole started. It presumably began from the south east corner of the Aigaleos peninsula, where there is now a reef, which would probably have been a small island in antiquity (seed Pls 17 & 18).[23] It is possible, then, that it was not Phoenician *merchantmen* which were used in the construction of the mole, but stranded Phoenician warships, and this would mean that Herodotos was right to place the attempt to construct it after the battle. Nor is the idea that it was begun then as daft as it may seem (see below, 198).

But even if the Persians were not busy with the construction of a mole before the battle, they probably had plenty to occupy them after they reached Attica, as we have

---

21 Originally argued by Bury, *CR* 10 (1896), 414-8; followed by Busolt, 693; Munro, 1902, 321, and *CAH*[1] iv 300, 303-4; Grundy, 357-9; and, more recently, by Sealey, *Hermes* 91 (1963), 376-7, and *CSCA* 5 (1972), 183-94.

22 E.g. Burn, 436-40, though with reservations; Green, 172 (also with reservations, cf. 293 n.6); Hammond, 1956, 42-3, and 1988, 569-70.

23 See W.K.Pritchett, *AJA* 63 (1959), 257; Burn, 439.

Pl. 17 (top): Salamis – one of the possible locations for Xerxes' throne (centre) from the Paloukia-Perama ferry, Ayios Georgios on the left. (Photo: N. Fields). Pl. 18 (bottom): Salamis – view from west of Perama across to the Kamatero (ancient Salamis-town?), with the south-eastern tip of the island of Ayios Georgios just showing on the right. The pylons probably mark the approximate line of Xerxes' proposed mole. (Photo: the Author).

seen, and the likely chronology of 480 as a whole makes it fairly certain that there was a delay of some two to three weeks between the arrival of their fleet at Phaleron and the battle (see above, 118–9). What, then, finally caused the battle to take place?

Herodotos' account of the immediately preceding day or two is difficult to understand, but sense can be made of it. According to him (8.67.1ff.), as we have seen, it was as soon as Xerxes' fleet reached Phaleron that the King went down to confer with his admirals, and this may well be true. But, given the lapse of time between the fleet's arrival and the battle, there was probably more than one such conference, and Herodotos may well have telescoped them together – in particular, the first and the last. His account of his own, single conference itself suggests this, for he reports disagreement among the Persian commanders. The majority were for fighting, but Queen Artemisia of Halikarnassos argued that it would be better to wait for lack of supplies and worries about the Peloponnese to lead the Greeks to disperse (8.68). In the end, Xerxes, though 'very pleased' with her view (8.69.2), decided to accept that of the majority.

Obviously Herodotos is even less likely to have had hard information about Persian naval conferences than Greek, though it is not inconceivable that he picked up some tales about Artemisia in his and her native city. However, it is again quite probable that there was disagreement among the Persian leaders along the lines he suggests, as there was among the Greek. If so, Xerxes might well have initially decided to give some such plan as Artemisia's a chance to work, and only finally accepted the alternative when it appeared that the Greeks were not going to disperse. This would have fitted in very well with his evident predilection for psychological warfare – with his release of the Greek spies, for example, after they had been shown how vast his preparations really were (7.145.2-148.1), and his four-day wait before the assault on Thermopylai (7.210.1). It would also provide an additional explanation for the delay before the battle.

Herodotos' account of what the Persian navy did when finally ordered to sea, is also very perplexing. 'They put out their ships (ἀνῆγον τὰς νέας) towards Salamis,' he says (8.70.1), 'and formed for battle, taking station at leisure. But by then there was not enough of the day left to fight a battle, for night was drawing on, so they began to prepare for the next day'. He does not make it clear here whether they remained at sea or returned to their anchorages, but although he says later that the Greeks thought they had remained in the position in which they had seen them during the day (8.78), what he says about their movements the night before the battle (8.76.1-2), particularly his repeated use of the semi-technical term for putting to sea (ἀνῆγον), implies that they had returned to base. Aischylos also clearly has them set out from shore the night before the battle (*Persai* 377-9).

This is all very odd. By the time the fleet was ready, it should have been obvious that there was not going to be enough time for a full-scale battle that day, so why did it not simply wait for the morrow, in the first place? Assuming that what Herodotos says is true, a number of possible explanations suggest themselves. Firstly, the Persian admirals, remembering Artemision, where the Greeks had shown a tendency to fight late in the day (8.9. & 14.2), may have hoped to tempt them out to fight. Even if there was not enough time for a decisive result, they might still be able to inflict significant losses, and this would be better than nothing, particularly if, at the conference, Xerxes had made his displeasure apparent, as Herodotos hints (8.69.2). But this does not really explain what Herodotos means by saying that 'they began to prepare for the next day' (8.70.1).

A second possibility is that the fleet's abortive movement was concerted with moves made by the army, and was designed to prevent any possible interference with the latter by the Greek fleet. Herodotos implies (8.71.1) that the Persian infantry was marching towards the Peloponnese during the night which followed the fleet's move, and it is possible that the 'miracle' experienced by Dikaios and Damaratos also had something to do with movements of the Persian army.[24] 'A cloud of dust as of 30,000 men on the move' (8.65.1) could well have been kicked up by thousands of marching feet, to say nothing of the hooves of thousands of horses. Even the 'Iakchos song' might be explained by the presence of Athenian exiles with the Persian army, perhaps sent specifically by Xerxes to placate Demeter and her daughter, as they had been sent to placate the gods of the acropolis (8.54), and only too well aware that this was the day of the procession to Eleusis, in normal times. Dikaios was, after all, one such exile, and Damaratos could also have gone along as an observer. They ought to have realised that there was a perfectly rational explanation for the 'miracle', but perhaps, in the tension of the moment, Dikaios was overcome by the emotion of seeing and hearing something the like of which he had seen many times before, in happier days.

The object of these moves by the army may have been to panic the Greek fleet into withdrawal. The Persians may well have believed that it had been the fall of Thermopylai which had caused the Greek fleet to withdraw from Artemision, even if this was not the case (see above, 149), and hoped to repeat the process by threatening the Isthmus. They may have calculated, as Artemisia suggests in Herodotos' account of the war-council, that any threat to the Peloponnese would cause alarm among the Peloponnesians, in particular. If so, the plan succeeded, if Herodotos is to be believed. The Greeks *were* seized with alarm, especially the Peloponnesians, who were worried by the prospect of 'sitting on Salamis to fight a sea battle for the land of the Athenians, and feared that if defeated, they would be cut off and besieged on the island, leaving their own land unguarded, while the barbarian foot was that very night marching on the Peloponnese' (8.70.2-71.1). Despite all that was being done to fortify the Isthmus (8.71-3), those on Salamis 'were afraid not so much for themselves as for the Peloponnese. For a time, individuals had words in secret, expressing amazement at Eurybiadas' folly, but in the end it came out into the open. A gathering was held and much was said on the old matters, some maintaining that they should sail away to the Peloponnese and risk all for that, not stay and fight for a land conquered by the spear, the Athenians, Aiginetans and Megarians that they should stay there and fight' (8.74).

But if the moves of the Persian fleet and army were designed to bring all this about, why did the Persian fleet still risk entering the Salamis channel, and, again, what does Herodotos mean by saying that after their abortive demonstration outside, 'they began to prepare for the next day'? This surely implies that they began to prepare for battle, and raises the possibility that their puzzling behaviour in apparently challenging for battle when it was too late for a battle to take place, was just a cover, designed to lull the Greeks into a false sense of security. The latter would see the enemy assembling in the open waters outside the straits, and then retiring tamely to their anchorages, and would

---

24 Cf. Munro, *CAH*[1] iv 306; J.L.Myres, *Herodotus: Father of History* (Oxford, 1953), 265.

assume that they were baffled by the Greek refusal to come out and fight. But possibly the Persians had *already* decided to infiltrate the straits and try to take the Greek fleet by surprise.

This was obviously risky, but, with winter coming on, it might have seemed preferable to gamble on trying to finish the naval war, than to have it all to do the following year, particularly, again, if Xerxes had made known his displeasure at the fleet's earlier showing. The alternatives, after all, were either to lay the fleet up in Attica for the winter, which would have meant having to feed perhaps between 140,000 and 160,000 men, in a hostile and devastated land already crawling with Persian troops, or to withdraw it across the Aegean to bases in Asia Minor, with the prospect of having to re-assemble it and bring it back the following spring. There is, however, a further possibility – that the Persians had already received a message from Themistokles which had led them to believe that infiltrating the straits would not be as risky as they had hitherto assumed. At first sight, of course, this is the exact opposite of what Herodotos seems to imply, which is that it was the movements of the Persian fleet and army we have been discussing which led to the sending of the message, not that it was the message which led to the movements. The latter caused such alarm on Salamis, he implies (8.70.2ff.), that the Peloponnesian leaders, who were in the majority, were all for abandoning the position and withdrawing to the Isthmus, and it was then that Themistokles, realising that his view was about to be voted down, secretly slipped out of the meeting, and sent his slave, Sikinnos, to the Persians with the message (8.74-5).

Obviously the first question to be considered is whether a message was sent in the first place, for it is just the kind of tale which Herodotos loved, and modern commentators distrust.[25] But there are good reasons for believing it. Firstly, it is referred to by Aischylos in his play 'The Persians' (*Persai*, 355ff.), which was produced in 472, within eight years of the battle. The play will have been performed before an audience which included thousands of men who had taken part, and this is powerful confirmation that at least the story was by then widely believed.

There is no significance in the fact that Aischylos' version of the story differs, or appears to differ, from Herodotos' in some details. Thus, in Aischylos the messenger is an anonymous Greek (*Persai* 355), whereas in Herodotos he is given a name – 'Sikinnos' – the form of which, and the description of him as 'a slave and pedagogue of Themistokles' children' (8.75.1) has suggested that he was not Greek: Plutarch (*Themistokles* 12.3) says he was a Persian. But Herodotos does not actually say that he was not a Greek, and his statement that Themistokles got him made a citizen of Thespiai after the war, 'when the people of Thespiai were admitting new citizens,' – presumably because of their heavy losses at Thermopylai – suggests that he was. It would have been most unusual at this date for a non-Greek to have been made a citizen of a Greek city.

Aischylos also differs from Herodotos in having the message sent to Xerxes himself instead of to his commanders, but this is probably for dramatic effect, since the message is referred to in a speech delivered to Xerxes' mother. In reality, if there ever

25 Cf., e.g., Hignett, Appendix IX, 403-8. On the following discussion see my article in *Hermes* 116 (1988), 168ff. Köster (*Klio* beiheft 32, 1934, 110), suggests Sikinnos might have been a Phrygian.

was such a message, it would, surely, have been passed on up the chain of command to the king, and thus both Aischylos and Herodotos would be right. In such a matter, the Persian naval commanders are hardly likely to have acted on their own initiative.

More importantly, in Aischylos the message is merely to the effect that the Greeks are going to try to escape, whereas in Herodotos it is far more elaborate (8.76). In the historian's version, Sikinnos specifically says that he has been sent by the Athenian commander, without the knowledge of the other Greeks, because his master favours the king's cause and wishes it to triumph, and he goes on to suggest that the Persians could achieve a spectacular success if they did not allow the Greeks to escape. The latter were not of one mind and would no longer resist – rather, the Persians would find them fighting each other, with those favouring the Persians against those still opposed. But again the simplicity of Aischylos' version may be due to a playwright's feeling for effect, or he may not have wanted even to hint at the possibility that some Greeks were willing to change sides, least of all his own fellow-countrymen, in what amounts to a hymn of praise for the Greek victory.

In addition to the evidence of Aischylos, and the circumstantial details provided by Herodotos, it is also worth noting that Thucydides evidently believed the story. He has an Athenian envoy at Sparta claim that Themistokles was mainly responsible for the battle's taking place in the straits (1.74.1), and in quoting from what purports to be a letter from Themistokles to Xerxes' son and successor, Artaxerxes, has Themistokles refer to his 'forewarning from Salamis of the [Greeks] retreat' (1.137.4). The letter itself may not be authentic, but Thucydides would presumably not have quoted from it unless he believed the details to be genuine.

Nevertheless, there are difficulties about the story of the message. Firstly, why was Sikinnos allowed to depart after delivering it (8.75.3)? Herodotos says the Histiaian who brought the news of the Greek departure from Artemision was put under guard because the Persians did not believe him (8.23.1), and one would have thought that they would have been even more suspicious of Sikinnos. Even more difficult to believe is that after being instrumental in leading the Persians to disaster at Salamis, Sikinnos was later one of a number of messengers sent to Xerxes by Themistokles to claim credit for preventing pursuit of his fleet and the destruction of the Hellespont bridges. Yet this is what Herodotos says (8.110.3), and again his story is confirmed by Thucydides evident belief in the details of Themistokles' alleged letter to Artaxerxes, in which the Athenian claims credit for both messages (see below, 199ff.).[26]

All this might, however, be true. In the first place, the Persians had good reasons for believing in the fragility of Greek unity, and that treachery was always a possibility. That was, after all, how Lade had been won, and the mere arrival of any message would have seemed to confirm their assumptions. Thus, even if Herodotos' expanded version of the first message is not authentic, and it simply said the Greeks were going to flee, as Aischylos says and Thucydides implies, it might still have seemed sensible to send the messenger back, perhaps with some assurances that those who did not resist, would be leniently treated, and, if they fought for the king, rewarded. If Herodotos' version is

---

26 For a detailed discussion of this second episode involving Sikinnos see M.Milton, *Proceedings of the African Classical Association* 17 (1983), 22ff.

closer to the truth, of course, it would have seemed even more sensible to return the messenger.

As for Sikinnos' second mission, and Themistokles' later boasting of his messages to Artaxerxes, again, if Aischylos' version of the first is correct, Themistokles might well have claimed that the Persians had spoiled everything by trying to prevent the escape of those Greeks who wanted to go, and by entering the channel: if they had just allowed the Greeks who wanted to go, to escape, he (Themistokles) would have been able to hold the Athenians, and perhaps the Aiginetans, Megarians and Euboians as well, and bring them over to the king's side. In the event, once the Persian fleet had entered the channel, there was nothing he could have done to prevent his fellow-countrymen and the others from fighting. If Herodotos' version of the message is correct, Themistokles would have found it more difficult to explain away what had happened, but he might still have claimed that his advice had not been to enter the channel, but simply, again, to prevent any escape: if the Persians had done just that, he could have argued, the Greeks would in the end have come to blows amongst themselves, as he had said they would; again it had been the Persian intervention which had finally united the Greeks in resistance.

It is even possible that Themistokles had really not intended the message as a trick, for there are considerable difficulties in the way of believing that it was. Firstly, as has been pointed out, none of the versions of the message contains any suggestion that Xerxes should send his fleet into the straits, though if it was a trick, this was presumably the whole point.[27] Secondly, if Themistokles kept his fellow-commanders in ignorance, as Herodotos implies (8.75.1), how was he supposed to get them to make ready to counter the infiltration of the straits he hoped would result from the trick? If he left it until the infiltration was detected, it might be too late, and he had no means of knowing that information about the Persian moves would be brought by Aristeides and Panaitios.

Admittedly the message is described as a 'trick' in Aischylos' play (*Persai* 361), and Herodotos almost certainly intended us to understand that it was a trick, though the nearest he actually comes to saying so is when he has Themistokles tell Aristeides that he was responsible for what the Persians had done (8.80.1). But Aischylos may have been trying to exonerate Themistokles at a time when he was under attack, and by the time Herodotos came on the scene, although Themistokles had been ostracised and had fled to Persia rather than face trial for 'medism' (Thucydides 1.135.2ff.), his reputation had been restored by the triumph of Ephialtes, Perikles and their associates over his enemies. Thus by the time Herodotos came to write his account, the canonical view would have been that the message was a trick. Originally, however, it may have been used by Themistokles' enemies to prove that his 'medism' extended back to the time of Xerxes' invasion, and it is worth considering the possibility that they were right.[28]

We should remember that a Greek was first and foremost a citizen of his own city: it was probably only in this very war that the notion of Greece as a common 'fatherland' for all Greeks began to appear. Thus the Spartans bade any 'stranger' who saw their

27 Hignett, 404-5.

28 On the attacks on Themistokles see, e.g., Podlecki 34ff.; Lenardon, 98ff. Themistokles may have got in quickly with his version of events, if, as is likely, Simonides' poem on Salamis made much of his friend's cleverness: see Podlecki, *Historia* 17 (1968), 267 & 271-2.

grave at Thermopylai, carry the message home to the *Lakedaimonians* that there they lay 'obedient to *their* words' (7.228.2), and if, after the war was over, the Corinthians claimed they had fought and died for 'holy Hellas' (Plutarch, *Moralia* 870e-f), nevertheless, if Herodotos is to be believed, the Corinthian admiral, Adeimantos, had called Themistokles himself a man without a fatherland (8.61.1), once Athens had been captured.

It is true that Herodotos later has the Athenians make a ringing declaration to Spartan envoys of their refusal to contemplate 'enslaving Greece' at any price (8.144.2). But the envoys were there in the first place precisely because the Spartans were afraid the Athenians might succumb to the blandishments of Alexander of Macedonia (cf. 8.142). In any case, this was after Salamis, when the Athenians had returned to Attica, and the sentiments are not said to have been those of Themistokles. When Mardonios moved south again in the late spring of 479, and Attica once more became 'a land taken by the spear' (9.4.2), a member of the Athenian council actually proposed that the renewed terms offered by Mardonios be laid before the people, and although both he and his family were lynched as a result, the Athenians still sent envoys to Sparta to inform their allies of Mardonios' offer, and to express their displeasure at Spartan procrastination (9.4.2ff.). In short, the Athenians were within an ace of taking the line Herodotos says the Thessalians had taken before Tempe, when the latter had told the Greeks assembled at the Isthmus that if they did not help defend Thessaly, they, the Thessalians, would have to 'try to work out some form of salvation for themselves' (7.172).

If, before Salamis, as was suggested above, Themistokles' underlying motive for arguing so passionately for remaining where they were, was the desperate fear that if they left, the last piece of Athenian territory would be gone, when he realised that he had finally lost the argument, he might well have felt that his first duty now was to Athens, and the message he sent with Sikinnos may, in effect, have been a request for terms. This would explain even better why the Persians sent Sikinnos back; how, after Salamis, Themistokles was able to send him to Xerxes with a second message, and how, finally, he was able to claim credit for *both* messages with Xerxes' son, as Thucydides says (1.137.4).

Certainty, of course, is not possible, since, in the end, perhaps only Themistokles himself ever knew what he had originally intended, and very few people would even have known what the message had said. But that a message of some sort was sent, there is no good reason to doubt. The fact that the story was current so soon after the battle, the circumstantial details supplied by Herodotos and the fact that Thucydides accepted it, are good reasons for believing that it is true. It explains what happened, and although we could probably just about understand the course of events, even if we had never heard of the message, this is no argument for believing that it is false. The onus is on those who do believe this, to prove it.

The problem of timing, however, remains. Herodotos certainly implies that the night which put an end to any Persian hopes of battle after the war-council, was the same night which saw the Persian army moving on the Isthmus (8.70.1 & 71.1); that it was the alarm which this caused which led the Peloponnesians to reopen the question of withdrawal, and that it was this in turn which led to the sending the message. But we have already seen that there is something wrong with the historian's timing hereabouts, since he has clearly telescoped events between the arrival of the Persian fleet at Phaleron and the decision to challenge for battle, and there is an odd air about the whole passage from the first move of the Persian fleet (8.70.1) to the sending of the message (8.75).

Firstly, as we have seen, when the Persian fleet makes its first, abortive move, Herodotos just seems to abandon it, with the remark that 'they began to prepare for the next day' (8.70.1), and turns to the alarm among the Greeks. When he returns to the Persian fleet six chapters later, it is apparently back at its anchorage. Secondly, it is noticeable that in the section (8.70.2) which immediately follows the account of the Persian fleet's abortive move, the verbs used to describe the anxieties among the Greeks are in the imperfect, as though to indicate that they had been growing for some time: 'fear and alarm *were* gripping the Greeks (τοὺς δὲ Ἕλληνας εἶχε δέος καὶ ἀρρωδίη) ... they *were* alarmed that ...' (ἀρρώδεον δέ). Thirdly, the two references to 'the night' (8.70.1 & 8.71.1) are separated from the account of the meeting during which the message was sent (8.74.2), by three chapters (8.71-73) which have nothing to do with the night before the battle, but are about the building of the Isthmus wall and the races which inhabited the Peloponnese.

To believe, moreover, that everything that happened between the return of the Persian fleet to its anchorages at the approach of nightfall and the moves it made 'when it was midnight' (8.76.1), happened *on the same night*, produces a very crowded timetable. Individual Greek murmurings at Eurybiadas' folly in not withdrawing have to lead to a meeting (8.74.2); Themistokles has to realise that his views are not going to carry the day; Sikinnos has to get to the Persian admirals and they, presumably, have to get Xerxes' approval and make their preparations, all in the four or five hours between nightfall and midnight.

Finally, whereas Herodotos seems to imply that the message was sent after night had fallen, Aischylos clearly implies that Xerxes received it before nightfall, since the king orders his admirals to carry out a series of moves *when night falls* (*Persai* 361ff.). This may be another example of Aischylos' altering the story for dramatic effect – it certainly leads to some striking imagery for the fall of night – but in view of the difficulties in Herodotos' implied timing, the poet may be right.

If, however, we suppose that the message was actually received before Xerxes and his admirals held their final conference, everything begins to fall into place. It would then be the movement of the Persian *army*, perhaps two or three days before the battle, which caused such consternation among the Greeks on Salamis, not the apparently farcical behaviour of the Persian fleet on the preceding day: why should the Peloponnesians be particularly worried by a demonstration outside the straits which led to nothing? A move by the Persian army, on the other hand, directly threatening the Peloponnese, might well have alarmed them, as, indeed, Herodotos implies (8.71.1). Hence the growing mutterings which led to the final Greek war-council and so to Themistokles' despairing message. This could have been sent at any time during the two or three days before the battle, but was possibly sent during the penultimate night.

Receipt of such a message is very likely to have led Xerxes and his admirals to decide to try to break the deadlock by sending their fleet into the straits. But the last thing they would have wanted would have been the enemy to have any inkling of what was afoot. Hence the demonstration outside the straits, which appeared to indicate that they were still baffled by the Greek refusal to come out and fight, and hence Herodotos' statement that when the onset of night put paid to prospects of battle, 'they began to prepare for the next day' (8.70.1). Aischylos naturally omitted this first move, for dramatic purposes, but was essentially right to have Xerxes issue orders that preparations for the serious operations should begin at nightfall, to conceal them from the Greeks. Nor is there any real discrepancy between the playwright and the historian. Aischylos describes the preparations as beginning at nightfall, but they are likely to have taken several hours, and Herodotos may well be right that the various squadrons did not actually move until midnight.

The differences between Aischylos' and Herodotos' versions of the message-story are thus more apparent than real, but they certainly do differ on the size of the Greek fleet. Aischylos is equivocal, but whether he means that the Greeks had 300 or 310 ships (*Persai* 338-40) – almost certainly the latter – his total is smaller than the historian's. Herodotos says that a number of extra ships had gathered at Pogon, during the Artemision campaign, and that as a result there were now 'many more ships' than had fought at Artemision (8.42.1). He then proceeds to give a list, contingent by contingent, and concludes by saying that 'the overall total of the ships, apart from the pentekonters, was 378' (8.43-48). Later (8.82.2) he says that with the addition of two deserters from the Persians – the Tenian ship which came over before Salamis, and the Lemnian which had come over at Artemision – the total came to 380. In fact, if one adds up the numbers in each contingent, the total comes to 366, or 368 with the deserters, but the discrepancy is usually explained by assuming that the totals include twelve Aiginetan ships which were guarding Aigina. Herodotos says (8.46.1) that the Aiginetans had other ships engaged in this task, but sent their 'best sailing' thirty to the main fleet.[29]

Here there seems no reason why Aischylos should have tampered with the figures, and as a contemporary who almost certainly took part in the battle (cf. Ion, *FGH* 397F7), he should perhaps be believed.[30] The main difficulty with Herodotos' figures

---

29 For the view that the extra 12 ships were guarding Aigina see Hignett, 210. Some scholars have even gone so far as to insert 'δυοκαίδεκα' or 'δέκα' in the text of Herodotos 8.46.1, the latter on the supposition that the historian mistakenly included the two deserters twice: see Hignett, *loc.cit.* n.4. Plutarch (*Moralia* 869a) criticizes Herodotos for saying that the Naxians sent 'three' ships to join the Persians, which eventually joined the Greeks, but Herodotos actually says *four* ships (8.46.3). Plutarch then quotes Hellanikos as giving the number as six, and Ephoros five. These figures may have been derived from the Simonides epigram on the Naxian commander, Demokritos, which Plutarch also quotes, Ephoros assuming that if he took five enemy ships, he must have had five himself, Hellanikos that if he took five enemy ships, and recaptured a 'Dorian', he must have had six. There is really no reason to doubt Herodotos here.

30 Grundy (n. on 354) dismisses Aischylos' testimony for the Greek numbers, and see also Hauvette, 349f. Labarbe's hypothesis that Aischylos did not include the Corinthians and others in the total (*BCH* 76, 1952, 432ff.), is based on the erroneous view that they were detached from the fleet before the battle – see below, 189–90. 300 seems to have become the conventional number for the Greek fleet – cf. Demosthenes 18.238; Cornelius Nepos, *Themistocles* 3, though the latter combines this with Herodotos' 200 for the Athenians. An Athenian speaker in Thucydides 1.74.1 claims that 'of the 400 ships, we provided nearly two-

are that he seems to make no allowance for losses at Artemision. Unfortunately he only gives one actual figure for these losses – the five 'Greek' ships said to have been captured by the Egyptians on the final day (8.17) – but he says that half the Athenian ships were damaged on the same day (8.18), and one would have thought that some at least of these would have been 'write-offs'. It also seems unlikely that there had been no other losses. Yet the Athenians still furnish 180 ships at Salamis (8.44.1), the Corinthians and Megarians the same totals (8.43 & 45), and the Chalkidians, Eretrians, Keians and Styrians the same ships (8.46.2 & 4). Other states – Sparta, Sikyon, Epidauros and Aigina – actually have more ships at Salamis than at Artemision.

Of course, we can well believe that the Athenians and the other naval powers were able to make good some of their losses, and it is not inconceivable that there were some extra ships from states which had either been slow to mobilize, or were at a considerable distance. This would certainly account for the seven ships from Ambrakia, three from Leukas (8.45), and, above all perhaps, the one from Kroton in southern Italy (8.47), unless Pausanias is right in saying (10.9.1) that this was manned by Krotoniates – presumably exiles – living in Greece. Others – for example, the Aiginetans – may previously have deliberately held ships back to guard the Saronic Gulf, and the four from Naxos which fought at Salamis had actually been sent to join Xerxes (8.46.3). But unless the Athenians had borne the brunt of the fighting on the final day at Artemision, and no other Persians, apart from the Egyptians had been successful in taking Greek ships, it is not at all impossible that the overall Greek strength had been reduced to Aischylos' total of 310 ships, i.e. some fourteen fewer than had fought on the final day at Artemision.

As for the Persians, Aischylos almost certainly meant that they had 1207 ships at Salamis, though, again, it is just possible that he meant that there were 1000 in all, of which 207 were particularly fast.[31] However, the grammar of the passage (*Persai*, 341-3) is in favour of the former, and it can hardly be a coincidence that Herodotos says that there were 1207 ships from Asia, at the outset of the invasion (7.89.1). The historian may have got his figure from Aischylos, but it seems more likely that both authors derived the number from a tradition that the Persian fleet had once been that size, Aischylos using it in his messenger-speech describing Salamis, for dramatic effect, Herodotos correctly assigning it to the beginning of the campaign. There is, in any case,

---

Athenian speaker in Thucydides 1.74.1 claims that 'of the 400 ships, we provided nearly two-thirds,' and this might be held either to confirm Herodotos' figure of 380 for the total, or the figures of Nepos above. But one cannot really have it both ways: if the total was c.400, the Athenians provided half, if the total was c.300, one would guess the Athenians provided less than 200. K.R.Walters (*RhM* 124, 1981, 199ff.) plausibly suggests that Thucydides made his Athenian boast in the fashion of the funeral oration. Ktesias' total of 110 ships for the Athenians (*Persika*, 26), might explain the discrepancy between Aischylos and Herodotos, but it would be odd if only Athens had lost ships off Artemision, and Ktesias has the absurdly inflated figure of 700 ships for the whole Greek fleet.

31 For the meaning of Aischylos' remarks about Persian numbers see Hignett, 345. Ktesias (*Persika*, 23) has 1000 ships, and is followed, among ancient writers, by Plato (*Laws* 699b), Demosthenes (*On the Symmories*, 29) and the Scholiast on *Persai* 342; among modern scholars by Tarn, *JHS* 28 (1908), 203. On the implication of Achaimenes' alleged remarks to Xerxes for the size of the Persian fleet see above 93–4.

(see below), that any losses suffered earlier in the year had been made up before Salamis (8.66.1), though, strictly speaking, that should have meant the Persian fleet had 1327 ships (cf. 7.185.1).

It is, of course, possible that the Persian fleet had never been anything like so large, but there is no compelling reason to believe this (see above, 92–4). On the other hand, it does seem very unlikely that the losses suffered in the Artemision-campaign can really have been made up by ships from central Greece and the islands, as Herodotos claims (8.66.1). At most one might have expected, perhaps, about 50 ships from such places. Thus, assuming that the Persians had once had 1327 ships, their fleet had probably been reduced to some 600 serviceable vessels by the end of the fighting off Artemision. According to Herodotos they had lost 600 in the two storms (7.190; 8.7.1 & 14.1), 15 stragglers which mistook the Greek fleet for their own on rounding Cape Sepias (7.194.1), 30 in the first sea-fight (8.11.1), an indeterminate number of Cilician vessels on the second day (8.14.2), and an equally indeterminate, but presumably substantial, number of other ships on the final day (cf. 8.16.3 & 18). Thus if they received about 50 more ships from states which came over to their side after Artemision, and possibly some reinforcements from elsewhere, they would perhaps have had between 600 and 700 ships at Salamis. If so, though greatly reduced in strength, their fleet would still have outnumbered the Greek by two to one, and this may explain the boldness with which they embarked on the hazardous operation of infiltrating the Salamis channel.

On receipt of the message, Aischylos says, Xerxes ordered his captains, when night fell, 'to range the main body of ships in three lines to guard the exits and the straits of the roaring sea, and others in a circle round Aias' isle' (τάξαι νεῶν στῖφος μὲν ἐν στοίχοις τρισίν/ἔκπλους φυλάσσειν καὶ πόρους ἁλιρρόθους,/ἄλλας δὲ κύκλῳ νῆσον Αἴαντος πέριξ: *Persai* 366-8).[32] Clearly the poet envisages the Persian fleet as divided into two broad divisions, a 'main body' (στῖφος) and 'others' (ἄλλας). Some scholars believe that he also means us to understand that the 'main body' was further divided into three squadrons, and then proceed to look for three 'exits'.[33] But this is not necessary. The relevant words properly mean 'in three lines', and the 'exits' are then naturally the channels on either side of the island now called Lipsokoutali.

But what does Aischylos mean by 'others in a circle round Aias' isle'? 'Aias' isle' is certainly Salamis, and the most natural interpretation is that the 'others' were to form a cordon round the island, to prevent escape from any part of the coastline. But although this is accepted by some scholars,[34] it does not make sense: Aischylos imagines Xerxes as envisaging a Greek flight *in their ships* (lines 358-60), not in small boats from coves and beaches round the island.

Another view is that Aischylos is here referring to the Egyptian squadron which Diodoros (11.17.2) says was sent round the island to block the channel between it and

---

32 Some editors transpose lines 367 and 368 – e.g. Murray in the Oxford Text, following Koechly, and cf. Wallinga, *Mnemosyne* 43 (1990), 148, n.34 – but this is not necessary.

33 E.g. Hignett, 223; Munro, 1902, 327.

34 E.g. C.Conradt, *Persae* (Berlin, 1888), *ad loc.*; Hauvette, 416 and n.1; Munro, 1902, 327; Beloch, ii 2. 221; Broadhead, *The Persae of Aeschylus* (Cambridge, 1960), 329.

the Megarid.[35] But the poet earlier refers to the deaths of Egyptians in his list of the losses the Persians suffered (*Persai*, 311-3), and this implies that he believed that the Egyptians took part in the battle. More seriously, it is doubtful whether the Egyptians were sent on any such mission. Herodotos certainly says nothing about it, and although the absence of any reference to the Egyptians in his account of the battle has been used to confirm Diodoros,[36] it really does nothing of the sort: he does not mention any contingents on the Persian side, except the Phoenicians, Ionians and a single ship from Samothrace. That he, too, believed that the Egyptians had taken part is indicated by the remark he later gives Mardonios (8.100.4) – that the Egyptians, along with the Phoenicians, Cypriots and Cilicians, had played the coward.

A third possibility is that Aischylos is here referring to the ships, almost certainly Phoenician, which Herodotos describes as 'circling towards Salamis', indeed, that Herodotos' phrase echoes that of the playwright.[37] 'When it was midnight,' he says, 'they put out on the western wing circling towards Salamis, and those assigned to Keos and Kynosoura also put out, and they held all the strait as far as Mounychia with the ships' (ἀνῆγον μὲν τὸ ἀπ' ἑσπέρης κέρας κυκλούμενοι πρὸς τὴν Σαλαμῖνα, ἀνῆγον δὲ οἱ ἀμφὶ τὴν Κέον τε καὶ τὴν Κυνόσουραν τεταγμένοι, κατεῖχον τε μέχρι Μουνιχίης πάντα τὸν πορθμὸν τῇσι νηυσί: 8.76.1).

The first thing to notice about this is that Herodotos, like Aischylos, seems to conceive of the Persian fleet as in two broad divisions, a 'western wing' and 'those assigned to Keos and Kynosoura'. There can be little doubt that the former are the Phoenicians, for these are later described as holding 'the wing towards Eleusis and the west' (8.85.1: τὸ πρὸς Ἐλευσῖνος τε καὶ ἑσπέρης κέρας), as opposed to the Ionians, who hold 'the wing towards the east and the Peiraeus (*ibid.*: τὸ πρὸς τὴν ἠῶ τε καὶ τὸν Πειραιέα). If so, there can equally be little doubt that when Herodotos describes the former as 'circling towards Salamis', he means that this wing moved along the shore of Attica, 'circling towards Salamis', possibly, though not necessarily, in the sense of the *town*.[38] The alternative – that Herodotos also here refers to the Egyptian squadron – will not do, not only because he obviously knew nothing of any such squadron, but also because his words do not mean 'circling *round* Salamis'.

It is also not certain what Herodotos means by his reference to those 'assigned to Keos and Kynosoura' (8.76.1). The most natural interpretation of the Greek is that Keos

---

35 E.g. Goodwin, *Papers of the American School of Classical Studies at Athens*, 1 (1882-3), 237ff.; Grundy, 377 & 381; Macan (1908) ii 306 n.1.

36 E.g. Burn, 453, though he also mentions the possibility that Diodoros or his source may have inferred the absence of the Egyptians from Herodotos' silence. Grundy, 382, and HW ii 383, claim that Diodoros is supported by Plutarch, *Themistokles* 12.5 and *Aristeides* 8.2, but neither passage mentions the Egyptians, and Plutarch appears rather to be talking of the blocking of the channels near Peiraeus.

37 Cf. *Hermes* 116 (1988), 174-5.

38 Hignett, 219. But if the emphasis falls on 'κυκλούμενοι' ('circling'), the island might still be meant: these were 'circling towards Salamis', not going directly across from Phaleron. That Herodotos envisaged this western wing as moving along the shore of Attica towards Salamis was seen long ago by Leake, *Topography of Athens and the Demi* ii, Appendix (1841). For the alternative see, e.g., Goodwin, op.cit. n.35 above, and *HSCPh* 17 (1906), 75ff.; HW ii 383.

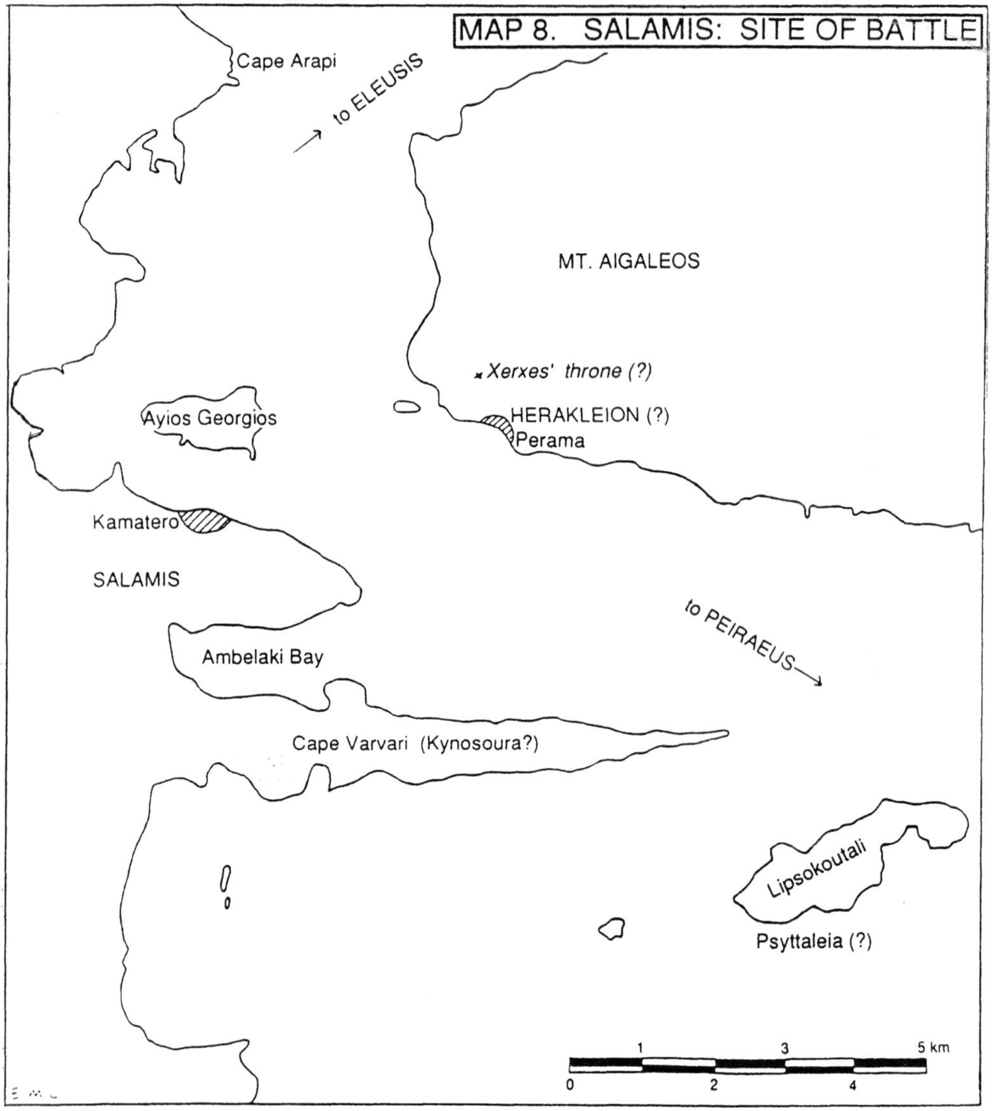
MAP 8. SALAMIS: SITE OF BATTLE
Cape Arapi
to ELEUSIS
MT. AIGALEOS
Xerxes' throne (?)
HERAKLEION (?)
Perama
Ayios Georgios
Kamatero
SALAMIS
to PEIRAEUS
Ambelaki Bay
Cape Varvari (Kynosoura?)
Lipsokoutali
Psyttaleia (?)
0
1
2
3
4
5 km

and Kynosoura were the places where the ships were stationed before they put out, but the only known 'Keos' is the island east of Sounion, and the only known 'Kynosoura' the promontory at the northeast end of the bay of Marathon: neither of these can be what Herodotos means here.[39] The best suggestion is that 'Keos' is the later Athenian naval harbour of Zea (now Pasalimani) on the Peiraeus peninsula. The change of name is readily explicable – in modern Greek the island of Keos/Kea is sometimes called 'Zea' or 'Dzia'.[40]

As for 'Kynosoura', although attempts have been made to locate it, too, on the coast of Attica,[41] it is almost certainly to be identified with the modern Cape Varvari, the long, tapering promontory jutting out eastwards from Salamis. 'Kynosoura' ('Dog's-tail') would be an appropriate name, and Plutarch's story of the burial of Xanthippos' dog at a place called 'Kynossema' ('Dog's-tomb), on Salamis, provides some confirmation. That 'Keos' was on the Peiraeus peninsula and 'Kynosoura' on Salamis may also be borne out by the oracle of Bakis which Herodotos quotes, and which refers to a time 'when they bridge with ships the holy cape of Artemis of the golden sword and Kynosoura in the sea' (8.77: ὅταν Ἀρτέμιδος χρυσαόρου ἱερὸν ἀκτὴν/νηυσὶ γεφυρώσωσι καὶ εἰναλίην Κυνόσουραν). 'The holy cape of Artemis of the golden sword' could well be another way of referring to the Peiraeus peninsula, for there was a temple of Artemis at Mounychia (Pausanias 1.1.4), and the phrase 'bridge with ships' presumably means 'place a bridge of ships between' the holy cape and Kynosoura.

If, however, 'Keos' is Zea and 'Kynosoura' Cape Varvari, these can hardly be where the Persians in question were stationed before they put out, but must mean the places to which they were sent.[42] If so, they surely correspond to Aischylos' 'main body of ships in three lines' which Xerxes orders his admirals to 'assign' – Aischylos uses part of the same verb as Herodotos (τάξαι/τεταγμένοι) – to 'guard the exits and the straits of the roaring sea' (*Persai* 366-7).

But what precisely was to be their station? The oracle seems to envisage them as being strung out between the Peiraeus peninsula and Cape Varvari, and this is, perhaps, confirmed by the most natural interpretation of Aischylos statement that they were to 'guard the exits' (see above). But after mentioning those 'assigned to Keos and Kynosoura', Herodotos remarks (8.76.1end) that 'they held all the channel as far as Mounychia with the ships,' and this seems to be picked up later by his reference to the eastern wing 'towards Peiraeus' (8.85.1). If so, he may have meant that the whole Persian fleet was strung along the coast of Attica, with the 'eastern wing' stretching from off Zea to opposite Cape Varvari.[43]

Ships deployed like this would not literally have blocked the exits from the channel, but they could be said to 'guard' them (cf. Aischylos' word 'φυλάσσειν': *Persai* 367), for

39 Despite J.W.Blakesley in his edition of Herodotos (London, 1854). Munro, 1902, 327, suggests that Herodotos got the name 'Kynosoura' from the Bakis-oracle which he quotes (8.77), but that the oracle actually referred to the Artemision campaign!

40 Burn, 372. Hammond, 1956, tries to identify Keos with the island now called 'Talantonisi', but that must surely be the ancient Atalante, as Burn, 472-4, argues.

41 A.Wilhelm, *Wiener S.B.* 211, 1929, 29-32.

42 Wilhelm, *op.cit.*, 35ff.; Hignett, 219.

43 This seems to be the way Hignett, 218, takes it.

Pl. 19 (top): Salamis – Lipsokoutali (Psyttaleia?) from Cape Varvari (Kynosoura?), with the Peiraeus beyond. (Photo: N. Fields). Pl. 20 (Bottom): the reconstructed trireme 'Olympias' with only the oars of the top bank fully extended, those of the lower banks 'shipped'; it is difficult to believe this could have been done in battle conditions. (Photo: courtesy of Times Newspapers Ltd.).

any ships trying to escape through the exits, and particularly the wider one east of Lipsokoutali, would have been exposed to a flank attack. Some confirmation that the exits were not literally blocked is provided by the story of how Aristeides got through to the Greek fleet the night before the battle, and the possibly more dubious story of the arrival of the ship carrying the images of the Aiakidai on the very morning of the battle (see below, 182–4).

It could also be argued that the placing of Persian troops on the island of Psyttaleia suggests that the eastern wing of the Persian fleet was disposed across the channel between Cape Varvari and Zea, for Psyttaleia was almost certainly what is now called Lipsokoutali (Pl 19). This has sometimes been denied,[44] but Lipsokoutali perfectly fits Aischylos' description of Psyttaleia as 'an ill anchorage for ships' (δύσορμος ναυσίν: *Persai* 448), and it is difficult to see how the Persians could have put troops ashore on Ayios Georgios, which is the alternative suggestion. Herodotos says (8.76.2) that the thinking behind the action was that 'when the battle took place, this was the most likely place for men and wrecks to come ashore, since the island lay in the path of the coming battle; thus they could rescue their own men and kill those of the enemy'. This would make good sense if, in effect, the island formed part of the 'bridge' between the Peiraeus and Cape Varvari. But it could also have formed a vital part in the Persian strategy if their fleet was flanking the exits, particularly if they envisaged the Greeks' attempting to break out past the island on either side.

To imagine the Persian fleet strung out along the coast of Attica not only fits Herodotos' description of the alignment of the two fleets at the outset of the battle (8.85.1), but makes more sense. If, instead, the left wing curled round to block the exits past Lipsokoutali, it would be difficult to imagine what happened on that side of the battle. Persian ships stationed between Lipsokoutali and Salamis would have been in a position to take the Greek right in the rear, unless it kept very close to the tip of Cape Varvari, and even if it did, the whole of this end of the Persian line would have been facing other Persian ships across the channel, near the shore of Attica. As for the oracle of Bakis, it is, perhaps, a mistake to assume precision in such a source, and, in any case, the prophecy – which was presumably *post eventum* – may have referred to the chaotic scenes in the dying stages of the battle as the Persian fleet tried desperately to get away, using both channels past Lipsokoutali.

But wherever precisely the 'eastern wing' took station, if it is Aischylos' 'main body' guarding the exits, it seems probable that Herodotos' western wing 'circling towards Salamis' is to be identified with Aischylos' 'other ships'. It is true that Aischylos' description of their assignment does not naturally mean the same thing as Herodotos', but they use very much the same words, bearing in mind that Aischylos' 'isle of Aias' *is* Salamis ('κύκλῳ νῆσον Αἴαντος πέριξ/κυκλούμενοι πρὸς τὴν Σαλαμῖνα'), and, as we have seen, the natural interpretation of the poet's words does not make sense.[45]

---

44 E.g. Beloch, *Klio* 8 (1915), 447, followed by Hammond, 1956, 32-54. Pritchett, *AJA* 63 (1959), 251ff., and *Studies in Ancient Greek Iconography* i (1965) 94ff.; Burn, 454 & 473-4, and Hignett, 397ff., all rightly argue that Psyttaleia is Lipsokoutali.

45 See the reference in n.37 above. It is also interesting that Herodotos twice talks of the Greeks' being 'encircled' before Salamis: 'σφέας περιεκυκλεύντο τῇσι νηυσὶ οἱ βάρβαροι' (8.78), and 'περιεχόμεθα γὰρ ὑπὸ τῶν πολεμίων κύκλῳ' (8.79.4). It has been suggested that the

Unless, then, Aischylos had no very clear idea what he meant, we must look for some other interpretation of his words, and 'in a circle off Aias' isle', could refer to the position of these ships just before the battle commenced, *curving* round the shore of Attica opposite Salamis.

If this is accepted, Aischylos and Herodotos are in complete agreement about what the Persians did on receipt of the message, and they are almost certainly also agreed that they did it during the night. Aischylos says that Xerxes ordered his captains to commence operations at nightfall (*Persai*, 363ff.), that they did so (377ff.), and that the operation went on 'all night long' (cf. 'πάννυχοι': 382). Some commentators suggest that this refers to ships 'rowing across' (cf. 'διάπλοον' in the same line) from Phaleron to Cape Varvari. But this would not have gone on 'all night long', and in any case Aischylos says the captains kept 'all the naval force' (πάντα ναυτικὸν λεών: 383) at it 'all night long', whereas it was only part of the fleet which was assigned to block the exits. Better is the suggestion that he means something like 'kept them at the oar' all night, but it is possible that he was thinking particularly of the ships rowing up the channel, and that this is the force of the word 'διάπλοον', i.e. it means not 'rowing across', but 'rowing *through*'.[46] The leading ships could well have taken all night to row along the shore of Attica, feeling their way in the dark, to somewhere off Aigaleos.

Herodotos, too, obviously believed that the Persians commenced operations at night – at midnight, to be precise (8.76.1) – and sums up his account of what they did by saying that 'they made these preparations at night, without getting any sleep' (8.76.3), perhaps again echoing the poet. The historian, moreover, clearly believed that the Persians were in a position to attack the Greeks shortly after dawn *as they were putting out* (cf. 8.83.2end: ἀναγομένοισι δέ σφι αὐτίκα ἐπεκέατο οἱ βάρβαροι), and wherever precisely the Greek base was, it was certainly west of Cape Varvari and, most likely, centred on what is now called Kamatero, the site of the ancient town of Salamis.[47]

It seems probable, indeed, that the objective of the western wing of the Persian fleet was to prevent the escape of the Greeks northwards into the Bay of Eleusis, and that this was achieved – in other words, that this wing of the Persian fleet reached a position somewhere off Aigaleos, from which it could attack any Greek ships which attempted to

---

Phoenician ships were the 207 'ὑπέρκοποι τάχει' ('of exceptional speed') singled out by Aischylos (*Persai* 342) – cf., e.g., Munro, *CAH* iv[1] 273ff. However, although I accepted the possibility in *Hermes* 116 (1988), 183–4, now I am much more dubious. As we have seen, Aischylos' 207 are not to be included in his 1000 (line 341), they are additional to them, i.e. Aischylos is here making use of the tradition that at one time there were 1207 ships in the Persian fleet, and according to Herodotos the Phoenicians numbered 300 in that fleet (7.89.1).

46 For the view that Aischylos was referring to the Persian fleet rowing across from Phaleron to Cape Varvari see HW ii 384; for the view that he meant simply that the Persians were 'kept at the oar' see, e.g Liddel & Scott[9] *s.v* διάπλοος I; Broadhead, *op.cit.* n.34 above, 329; Hignett, 224-5. Keil (*AS* iv 83) suggested he meant 'rowing through'. It is no argument to ask, as Hignett does, 224, why Aischylos should have said this movement went on all night, because it probably did.

47 Hammond, 1956, 42; Burn, 455–6; Pritchett, 1965, 95, and Morrison & Coates, 55, locate the Greek base at Paloúkia, but Wallinga, *op.cit.* n.32 above, 147, objects that this was 'probably very difficult to reach and leave for triremes en masse because of the shoals'.

use this escape route.[48] Herodotos says (8.78) that as the wrangling continued amongst the Greek commanders, 'they did not yet known that the barbarians were encircling them with their ships,' and that when Aristeides arrived, he first told Themistokles that 'we are blockaded by the enemy in a circle' (8.79.4), and then the Greek commanders that 'the whole Greek fleet was blockaded by the ships of Xerxes' (8.81). For those who believe that the Egyptian squadron had been sent to block the channel near Megara, these remarks by Herodotos may seem the best evidence for their view. But since the historian clearly knew nothing of any such mission, this cannot be what he means. The only moves by the Persian fleet he has described are that of the western wing 'circling towards Salamis', and that of the eastern to take station 'off Keos and Kynosoura' (8.76.1). Thus when he says that by the time Aristeides arrived, escape for the Greeks was impossible, he can only mean that these moves by the Persian fleet had prevented it, and since, presumably, the eastern wing prevented escape southwards past Lipsokoutali, the western wing prevented escape northwards.

It has been objected, firstly, that the Persians cannot have infiltrated the channel at night without the Greeks' being aware of it, despite Herodotos' statement (8.76.3) that they carried out their moves in silence so that the enemy would not hear them; secondly, that if the Persians had managed to get so near the Greeks during the night, they would never have let slip the opportunity of attacking them before they could man and deploy their fleet – in other words, Salamis ought to have been like Aigospotamoi; thirdly, that both Aischylos (450-3) and Herodotos (8.76.2) say that the reason for putting troops on Psyttaleia was that the Persians thought it would play a crucial part in the battle.[49]

But none of these arguments is convincing. It is probably true that in rowing up the channel the Persians could not have escaped the Greeks' notice, however little noise they made. At sea sounds notoriously travel a long way at night, and even if spotting ships moving along the shore at night is sometimes quite difficult (cf. Thucydides 8.102.1-2), one would not have thought that as large a fleet as the Persian could have escaped detection. But what are the Greeks supposed to have done about it? To try to attack the Persians while it was still dark would have been extremely hazardous.[50] It was much better to wait for daylight and in the meantime stay on the alert and prepare for any eventuality. Indeed, if the message sent to the Persians had been a trick, at least those in the know would quickly have guessed what was happening, though they probably had not expected the enemy to move so soon.

This is also the answer to the second objection: if some of the Greeks were hoping and expecting the Persians to enter the channel, they would clearly have made sure that they were prepared to fight at any time, and even if the Persian move came as a complete surprise, they would have begun to make ready as soon as they became aware that something was going on across the channel. In any case, according to Herodotos (8.79-82.1), they were warned of what was happening, first by Aristeides, coming from Aigina, and then by Panaitios of Tenos, deserting from the Persian fleet.

---

48 See Keil *loc.cit.* n.46 above; Hignett, 223.

49 On all this see e.g. Blakesley in his edition of the *Persai*, ii 400-19; Löschcke, *Neue Jahrbücher* 115 (1877), 25ff.; Goodwin, *op.cit.* n.35 above, 237ff.; Grundy, 392–3; HW ii 382 & 384; Burn, 455–7.

50 Hignett, 226.

The story of Aristeides' warning has been doubted, partly because Herodotos implies (8.79.1) that only now did he return from ostracism, in which case, it is argued, he would hardly have commanded Athenian troops on Psyttaleia after the battle (cf. 8.95), partly because it is difficult to see how he could have got through the channel between Salamis and the mainland if the Persians were now blocking its entrances. On the other hand, if he landed elsewhere on the island, he could not have known that the Greeks were now in some sense 'surrounded', as Herodotos says he did (8.79.4, 80.2, 81). In any case, stories which contrast Themistokles and Aristeides are always open to suspicion.[51]

It is possible, however, that Herodotos did not mean that Aristeides was only now returning from ostracism, or he may have been wrong. The Aristotelian *Constitution of the Athenians* says that those who had been ostracized were recalled 'in the archonship of Hypsichides' (22.8), i.e. before July 480, and, for what it is worth, the 'Themistokles Decree' provides for their return before Artemision. If Aristeides had already been recalled from ostracism, he might, for example, have been sent to Aigina to ask for the images of the Aiakidai (8.64.2), and have now been returning to say they were on their way. But even if he was only now returning from ostracism, we should remember that this form of exile was no disgrace: though the circumstances were different, Kimon, son of Miltiades, for example, was sent to Cyprus in command of Athenian and allied forces, later in the fifth century, soon after returning from ostracism.

As for the argument that either Aristeides could not have avoided capture by the Persians, or that he could not have known that the Greeks were surrounded, it is possible that he was able to slip through by hugging the shore of Salamis, particularly if the Persians were not literally blocking the channel west of Lipsokoutali. If so, he could well have been aware that the Persian fleet was at sea on the other side of Lipsokoutali, and moving up the channel north and west of the island. Putting two and two together, he might thus have described the Greeks as 'surrounded'. We should remember that the Persians did not need literally to block the exits to make it impossible for the Greeks to escape: merely getting their fleet into a position to attack any Greek ships trying to escape, was enough.

The alternative is to suppose that Aristeides had been landed elsewhere on Salamis, and that his report that the Greeks were 'surrounded' referred to the sending of the Egyptian squadron to block the channel between Salamis and the Megarid. But, again, Herodotos' evident unawareness of any such mission, means that this cannot be what he thought Aristeides meant. He can only have intended us to understand that Aristeides' tidings referred to the actions of the Persian fleet he has previously reported, and assuming that Aristeides arrived fairly late in the night, and that the leading ships of the

---

51 Cf. Grundy, 388ff.; Burn, 454-5; Green, 183-4. Bury (*CR* 10, 1896, 414-8) suggested that Aristeides had been sent to fetch the Aiakidai from Aigina, and returned on the Aiginetan ship which brought the images, but Herodotos has him arrive during the night, and before Panaitios (8.79-81), not just before the battle, which is when he says the Aiginetan ship arrived (8.83.2). Grundy suggested (n. on 390) that Herodotos mistook the time of his arrival, and Burn (454) that the Aiginetan ship first put him ashore in the western bay of Salamis, and then went on to rejoin the fleet. But it is simpler to suppose that he returned on a different ship, perhaps with a message that the Aiakidai were on their way.

Persian western wing were by then far up the channel, any attempt by the Greeks to escape would by then have been, if not quite impossible, at least extremely hazardous.

In any case, even if there are doubts about the Aristeides story – after all Herodotos himself says that the Greeks did not believe what he said (8.82.1)! – no such doubts attach to the story of Panaitios of Tenos. As Herodotos says (8.82.1), 'the Tenians *were* inscribed among those who defeated the barbarian, at Delphi', though on one of the coils of the serpent-column, with the other names, not actually 'on the tripod', and the apparently late addition of their name may even be said to confirm Herodotos' story.[52] Panaitios' ship would probably have belonged to Aischylos' 'main body', i.e. to those 'assigned to Keos and Kynosoura', in Herodotos' words, and could thus have found it easy to slip away, in the darkness, and row up the channel to the Greek base, keeping to the Salamis side. He would probably also have known about the 'other' squadron, 'circling towards Salamis', and would thus have been able to tell the Greeks 'the whole truth', as Herodotos says (*loc.cit.*). This would also have enabled them to make preparations for the coming fight before dawn, as the historian implies (8.83.1).

As for the third objection to believing that the Persians infiltrated the channel during the night – that they had put troops on Psyttaleia because it was important to their plans – they may have hoped to drive any Greeks who did try to fight, down channel, where they could be taken in flank by those off Kynosoura and Keos, and in that case the island could well have figured in their plans.

It seems likely, then, that just before dawn the leading Persian ships would have been somewhere off the western end of Aigaleos, thus forming the western wing 'towards Eleusis', as Herodotos describes it (8.85.1). These were the Phoenicians, and strung out behind them was the rest of the Persian fleet. Opposite them, across the channel, perhaps from what is now Ambelaki Bay round the cape to the north and all along the shore to Kamatero (the site of the ancient town of Salamis) and beyond, lay the Greek fleet, ships already in the water, crews probably already embarked, but perhaps marines still ashore.

It was after dawn had broken, Herodotos says (8.83.1), that the assembled marines were addressed by Themistokles, though presumably these can only have been those of Athens. If Themistokles' message had been intended to trick the Persians into the channel, one might have expected him to make some exultant reference to it in his speech, as he had done, according to Herodotos (8.80.1), albeit somewhat vaguely, when he spoke to Aristeides. Instead, however, Herodotos summarises the speech to the marines by saying that 'its words were all about the contrast between the better and the worse things in man's nature and condition, and urged them to choose the better' (8.83.2). Hardly the stuff to inspire the troops, one would have thought! But if the message had not been a trick, and had even been treasonable, Themistokles may well have been somewhat abashed by what had happened, and his usual eloquence have deserted him. He had got what he wanted after all – his battle in the straits – but only hours before he had thought he had finally lost the argument. Perhaps, too, this was why he found nothing to say when, later in the battle, Polykritos of Aigina taunted him with remarks about *Aiginetan* medism (8.92.2).

52 See ML 27, critical note on 59.

It was soon after the marines had embarked, according to Herodotos (8.83.2), that a trireme arrived from Aigina, bringing the images of the Aiakidai for which the Greeks had sent after the earthquake. This may seem too much of a coincidence, and it is difficult to believe that a ship could still have evaded the Persians. But if it is true, and the ship had arrived by way of the southern channel, hugging the shore of Salamis, this is another indication that this channel had not literally been blocked; if it had come *via* the northern channel, yet another reason to believe that no Egyptian squadron was blocking that channel. Immediately afterwards, according to Herodotos, the Greeks began to row out from the shore and 'at the very moment they were putting out, the barbarians attacked them (ἀναγομένοισι δέ σφι αὐτίκα ἐπεκέατο οἱ βάρβαροι: 8.83.2end).'

Some modern scholars, however, believe that Herodotos was mistaken here, and taking their cue from Aischylos, think that the Greeks were somewhere out of sight of the Persians at this point. Indeed, as we have seen (above, 181), some have even been led to argue that despite all the evidence to the contrary, the Persians had not yet entered the channel. But although Aischylos appears to imply that the Persians could *hear* the Greeks' singing before they came in sight (*Persai* 388ff.), in this, the most dramatic and stirring passage in the whole great messenger-speech, it is absurd to insist that the dramatist must be putting events in precise order. He is far more interested in the psychological effect on the Persians of hearing singing when they had thought the Greeks were going to flee, and all he is really saying is that it was the singing which was the first thing that impinged upon them. In any case, if one must be pedantic, is it certain that the Greeks would have been immediately visible? They were putting out in the dawn, possibly with early autumnal mist clinging to the shore, some of them, perhaps, from the deep bay of Ambelaki, some from behind the island of Ayios Georgios. Anyone who has sailed around the Aegean will agree that one's eyes can play peculiar tricks at such a time.

Others have devised elaborate schemes to explain what they claim Aischylos proves. For example, it has been suggested that the Greeks rowed north past Aigaleos into the Bay of Eleusis, where they assembled, and then returned to envelop the head of the Persian line.[53] But any such hypothesis flies in the face of Herodotos' plain statement that the Persians attacked the Greeks '*as they were putting out*', on the basis of a pedantic and highly dubious interpretation of Aischylos.

Even more methodologically unsound is the belief of some commentators that Diodoros somehow got it all right, where Herodotos got it wrong.[54] According to the later historian (11.17.1ff.), it was from a man persuaded by Themistokles to desert that Xerxes learned that the Greeks were about to withdraw to the Isthmus, and he first sent the Egyptian squadron to block the channel separating Salamis from the Megarid. We have already seen that this is unlikely to be true, and it is possible that it derives from a mistaken interpretation of the line in Aischylos (*Persai* 368) about the 'other' ships 'in a

53 Burn, 457-60; Green, 186ff.

54 E.g., Grundy, 392; Hammond, 1956, map on 33, and 1988, maps on 572 & 577.; Burn, 460ff.; Green, 187ff. Burn, 459, followed by Green, 189 & 191-2. Burn tries to reconcile Diodoros with Herodotos on the position of the Spartans by suggesting that they were on the right of the main body, but this is not what Diodoros implies.

circle about Aias' isle'. Diodoros goes on to say that Xerxes then sent the main body of his fleet towards Salamis to engage the enemy, with the Phoenicians on the right and the Greeks serving the Persians on the left, in this at least agreeing with Herodotos.

Next Diodoros has a faintly ridiculous story of how a Samian swam across to the Greeks to tell them of the Persian plans, and that 'they' (the Samians? all the Greeks with the Persians?) were going to desert in the battle. Diodoros appears to know nothing of any report by Aristeides, let alone one by Panaitios, though the latter, as we have seen, seems to be confirmed by the inscription on the serpent-column. As for the Greeks, Diodoros has the Athenians *and* Spartans on their left opposite the Phoenicians (11.18.1), whereas Herodotos, surely rightly, has the Spartans on the right, where the commander-in-chief normally took station, both on land and at sea. In Diodoros the Aiginetans and Megarians form the Greek right wing.

But it is in his alignment of the two fleets that Diodoros differs most seriously from Herodotos. He says (11.18.2) that the Greeks 'held the strait between Salamis and the Herakleion', and this means that he envisaged a roughly north-south alignment, with the Greek left near the shore of Attica – the Herakleion was on that shore (Phanodemos *ap.* Plutarch, *Themistokles* 13.1), probably somewhere near modern Perama.[55] But if the Greeks were aligned roughly north-south, so presumably were the Persians, and that this is what Diodoros supposed is confirmed by his further statement (11.18.4) that at first the Persians were able to maintain their formation, since they had plenty of room, but that when they came to the narrow part (τὸ στενόν) they had to withdraw some ships from line, and thus caused great confusion. Herodotos, however, clearly has the two fleets in an east-west alignment (8.85.1), and this makes more sense, for it is hardly likely that either the Greek or the Persian left would have rested on a shore held by the enemy. Diodoros' statement also seems to imply that the Persian fleet only moved into the straits in the morning, which contradicts both Herodotos and Aischylos.

Diodoros' main source was probably the fourth century historian, Ephoros, of Kyme in Asia Minor, but although we have Polybios' word for it (12.25f) that Ephoros 'had some idea of naval tactics', as opposed to his apparent ignorance of land-warfare, it is difficult to believe that he had access to good evidence of which the earlier Herodotos knew nothing. It has been plausibly suggested that Ephoros' version was merely a critical reconstruction of Herodotos, based partly on deductions from Aischylos which were probably false.[56]

Plutarch also has an account of the battle in his life of Themistokles, which contains details not in Herodotos, but many of which are dubious or absurd. It was at daylight, he says (13.1) that Xerxes took his place, high up, to view the battle. He quotes the Athenian historian, Phanodemos, for the location of the king's throne above the Herakleion, but also refers to a ridiculous statement by one Akestodoros that it was on the border of the Megarid, above the so-called 'horns', i.e. the southeast end of the

---

55 See, e.g., Macan (1908) i 2 500; Hammond, 1956, 38.

56 Tarn, e.g., imaginatively suggested that Ephoros had access to a Phoenician version of what had happened (1908, 232f.). Conversely, Morrison & Coates, 58, unaccountably declare that 'Herodotos' information must have been second-hand, and gathered from Persian sources'! For the view that Ephoros' account is a critical reconstruction of Herodotos based on inferences from Aischylos see Munro, 1902, 329f.; Hignett, 221.

Pateras ridge, still called 'Trikerato' ('Three-horns'). Herodotos (8.90.4) describes Xerxes' position as 'under the mountain opposite Salamis called Aigaleos', which fits Phanodemos' statement.

Plutarch goes on to tell, on the authority of Phanias of Lesbos, who, he claims, was 'a philosopher and not unacquainted with historical literature,' the equally absurd story that Themistokles was compelled by the mob (presumably of sailors or marines) to sacrifice three of Xerxes' nephews just before the battle. More sensibly, Plutarch quotes Aischylos as to the numbers of ships in each fleet, but then goes on to state (14.1) that each of the Athenian vessels had eighteen marines on board, of whom four were archers, the rest hoplites. This not only seems to rest on a misunderstanding of the later standard complement of fighting-men on Athenian warships – four archers and *ten* hoplites – but also seems too few for this early date (see above, 35–6).

The only interesting thing which Plutarch says about the preliminaries to the battle is that Themistokles waited for 'the usual hour of the day to come, which always brings a fresh breeze from the open sea and a swell through the straits' (14.2). Here there is some evidence that some such phenomenon occurs, but although Plutarch's testimony has often been accepted, it should probably be rejected.[57] As has been pointed out, even if we assume that he or his source was thinking primarily of the Athenian fleet, since Themistokles was not in a position to give orders to the rest, it is more likely that it was the Persians who chose the moment to attack. Nor do the details of Plutarch's account of the effects of the phenomenon carry conviction. He says 'it did no harm to the Greek ships which were low in the water and rather squat, but as for the barbarian ships, with their towering poops, lofty decks and heavy movement, it was fatal: as it hit them, it slewed them broadside to the Greeks.' In part, this seems to put things the wrong way round, because according to Herodotos (8.60-), it was the Greeks who had the 'heavier' ships. Possibly, as a modern scholar has put it, Plutarch succumbed to the romantic notion that 'the just cause must have the smaller ships'.[58]

Returning to the earlier accounts, we find that Aischylos says (*Persai*, 399-400) that the right wing led the Greeks into battle, and this, too, has led to some extraordinary hypotheses.[59] But the explanation is probably very simple. The easiest and quickest way for the Greeks to have deployed into line-of-battle would have been for the ships which were to form the right wing to row down channel in line-ahead, or several lines ahead, until they reached their appointed station, followed by the rest in order, and then turn to port into line, or lines, abeam.[60]

If it is objected that the Persians would not have allowed this to happen, one may answer that the Greek order of battle was presumably the same as the order in which contingents were moored, so that the ships which eventually formed the right wing,

---

57 Cf., e.g., Grundy, 398n.; Hammond, 1956, 46f.; Burn, 461; J.S. Morrison & R.T.Williams, *Greek Oared Ships* (Cambridge, 1968), 161-3; Green, 190. Rejected by Munro, 1902, 330; Tarn, 1908, 208 n.28; Hignett, 233.

58 Tarn, *loc. cit.* It is similarly a myth that the ships of the Spanish Armada were larger than their English opponents – the biggest ship in either fleet was probably Frobisher's *Triumph* – though it is true that the Spanish galleons tended to have higher 'castles' at bow and stern: Michael Lewis, *The Spanish Armada* (London, 1966), 75-6.

59 Cf., e.g., Grundy, 397; Burn, 457ff.; Green, 191; Morrison & Coates, 59.

60 See Thucydides 2.83ff. and cf. Keil, *AS* iv 96; Hignett, 234-5.

would have been nearest that station. There is also no reason to believe that most ships could not have rowed to their station before dawn, for although Herodotos implies that it was only when dawn had broken that Themistokles addressed the marines (8.83.1), he could hardly have addressed them all, even if the other commanders had let him – would Spartans, Corinthians or Aiginetans have been happy to be addressed by an *Athenian*? – and the Athenians would have had the least distance to go. We do not, of course, know for certain where the Greek right wing was at the commencement of the battle, but it was probably somewhere near the tip of Cape Varvari, and in that case even the Spartan contingent, which probably formed the extreme right wing, as we have seen, would only have had at most some three kilometres to row, which should only have taken about a quarter of an hour.[61] In any case, if Persian morale was at a low ebb because of the sudden realisation that they had a fight on their hands after all, they may well have hesitated until it was too late.

Soon after dawn, then, we should imagine the Greek fleet strung out in line-of-battle, perhaps from somewhere off the modern Kamatero to somewhere near the tip of Cape Varvari. Their front would thus have been about four kilometres long, not enough to accomodate 310 triremes in single line-abeam, let alone 368, but easily enough for two such lines.[62] This would have enabled the ships in the second line to cover the gaps between those of the first, and so prevent the *diekplous*, as the Athenians did at Arginousai (cf. Xenophon, *Hellenika* 1.6.29-31). On the left, and forming at least a third, if not half, of the whole fleet, were the Athenians. On the right were the Spartans, with probably next to them the other larger contingents, Corinthians, Aiginetans and Megarians, together numbering perhaps as many as the Athenians, in the centre the smaller contingents (cf. 8.85.1; Diodoros 11.18.2).

As for the Persians, we can be fairly certain that the Phoenicians were on what was eventually their right wing, the Ionians and presumably the other Greeks serving in the Persian navy, on the left (cf. 8.85.1; Diodoros 11.17.3). Diodoros (11.19.1) has the Cypriots next in line to the Phoenicians, followed by the Cilicians, Pamphylians and Lycians, but this is suspicious because it is the order in which Herodotos lists the contingents at Doriskos (7.89-92), with the Egyptians naturally missing because Diodoros believed them to have been sent round Salamis: in Herodotos' list they come after the Phoenicians. However, it may be more or less correct.

As we have seen, there is also considerable doubt about how many ships the Persians had, and even if we could be certain of the total, we would still have no means of knowing whether the various contingents had suffered proportionate losses. Herodotos, for example, suggests that the Cypriots and Cilicians had lost heavily in the Artemision campaign (7.195 & 8.14.2), and although he says that the Egyptians had fought particularly well on the final day (8.17), they, too, might have suffered heavy

---

61 Trials with the reconstructed trireme *Olympias* (see 178, Pl 20) have shown that such a ship could be rowed at 6 or 7 knots for some time, perhaps faster for short bursts: at even 5 knots, a trireme could then have covered 3km. in under 20 minutes.

62 The maximum width of a trireme, as given by the surviving ship-sheds at Zea, is 6 metres, the maximum length 37 metres: see D.J.Blackman *ap.* Morrison & Williams, *op.cit.* n.57 above, 181-92; I.X.Dragatzes, *PAE* 1885, 63-8. Allowing for the outstretched oars and gaps between vessels, something like 50 triremes would have taken up a kilometre in line-abeam.

losses in the process. The Phoenicians, if, as is quite likely, they had led the fleet down to the coast of Magnesia, possibly did not suffer too badly in the first storm, since the first comers are said to have been able to moor along the shore (7.188.1). But it is quite likely that at least some Phoenician ships had been sent with the 200 round Euboia and had perished at 'the hollows', and the rest are also likely to have played a full part in the fighting. We also do not know how many additional ships had been added from central Greece and the islands. If, however, we assume that the Persian fleet had been approximately halved, and that the various contingents had suffered proportionate losses, the Phoenicians would have had approximately 150 left, the Egyptians 100, Cypriots 75, Cilicians, Pamphylians and Lycians 90, Carians and Greeks from Asia Minor 170, and Greeks from Thrace and its off-shore islands 60; in addition, perhaps some 50 had joined fom central Greece and some of the southern islands.

The whole fleet, in single line abeam, would have had a front of some fourteen kilometres, allowing twenty metres per ship, including intervals. But, if we are to believe Aischylos, the 'main body' was in three lines, and if we assume it consisted of approximately two-thirds of the whole fleet (c.450 ships?), its front would have been about 3000 metres, stretching along the shore of Attica from near Zea to somewhere off Cape Varvari, as Herodotos appears to say (8.76.1, see above, 175–7). The Phoenicians certainly formed part of the other division of the fleet, 'circling towards Salamis', and in view of their prowess at Artemision, the Egyptians may have accompanied them. It would have been easiest for these ships to row up the channel in a single line ahead, but they would have turned into line-abeam to fight, and since the Phoenicians furnished the 'best sailing' ships in the Persian fleet (7.96.1), they would probably have been deployed in a single line, just as the Spartan fleet was at Arginousai (Xenophon, *Hellenika* 1.6.31). If the Egyptians were next in line, they may also have adopted the same formation, and, if so, the front of this wing would have been about 5000 metres, stretching from about the end of Aigaleos to off Cape Varvari, where it joined the 'main body'.

If the two fleets were disposed like this, it is true that the Athenians would not literally have been opposite the Phoenicians nor the Spartans opposite the Ionians, as Herodotos says they were (8.85.1). Rather, the Athenians would have been opposite the right of the Phoenician line and the Spartans opposite the Egyptians. However, the point need not necessarily be pressed, for Herodotos may simply have assumed that the Greek left would have been opposite the Persian right and *vice versa*, which could not have been true unless either the two fleets were approximately the same size, or the Persians were ranged in a deeper formation. In fact, the whole of the Greek fleet may originally have confronted just the Phoenicians and Egyptians, if the latter were next in line, and this may go a long way towards explaining the Greek victory, for though outnumbered – perhaps two to one – in total number of ships, the Greeks would have had more ships than the enemy squadrons they actually confronted at the outset.

It is important to remember, too, that if the story of the message is true, whatever its precise contents, the Persians would have thought they were going to fight a very different battle from the one they eventually had to fight. Thus the duty of Aischylos' 'main body' and of Herodotos' 'those stationed off Keos and Kynosoura', was to 'guard the exits' from the channel, while only 'others' – i.e., presumably, fewer – had been sent 'circling towards Salamis'. Whether the job of these 'others' was to cut off the Greeks' escape route *via* the northern channel, or to engage any Greeks who showed fight, or both, theirs was, in one way, the lesser task. On the other hand, it was the most dangerous, and might be the one to involve serious fighting. This is probably why the Phoenicians formed at least the majority of this squadron. As it turned out, of course, the Greeks did not attempt to flee, and thus the rôles of the two wings were reversed: the 'others' found themselves fighting for their lives, the 'main body' probably had little or nothing to do in the early stages.

Of the battle itself we can say little that is at all certain. Herodotos says that the Greeks at first backed water (8.84.1), and this has suggested sophisticated tactical manoeuvring to some modern commentators.[63] But even if true – it is connected in Herodotos' story with the appearance of a phantom-woman (8.84.2) – it was surely nothing more than the jockeying for position which presumably always went on as ships took up their fighting formation.

Herodotos also tells us later (8.94) that 'the Athenians say that right at the beginning of the battle, as the ships were about to engage,' the Corinthian commander, Adeimantos, hoisted sails and fled, followed by the rest of the Corinthians. But this is extremely unlikely to be true. Herodotos himself admits (8.94.4) that the rest of Greece bore witness to the Corinthian claim to have taken a prominent part in the battle, and the discovery on the island of Salamis itself of the remains of the Corinthian monument bearing the inscription to which Plutarch refers (ML 24, cf. Plutarch, *Moralia* 870e), proves that not even contemporary Athenians knew anything of the story. The semi-miraculous elements in it also do not carry conviction: a mysterious boat – who sent it no one knew – 'by divine guidance' (8.94.2) met the Corinthians off the temple of Athena Skiras – possibly on Cape Arapi[64] – and shamed them into returning with news of the Greek victory. Even then they were too late to take part and only agreed to return when the crew of the boat offered to go as hostages.[65]

It has been argued that the voyage of the Corinthians is a 'public fact [which] must be accepted',[66] and it has been suggested that either they went off to deal with the Egyptians, or that they were detailed to do this but returned to join in the main battle after being told by the mysterious boat that the Egyptians were nowhere in sight. But if the 'rest of Greece', apart from the Athenians, denied the truth of the story, in what sense can the incident be regarded as a 'public *fact*'? Why should any part of the story be true? Of course, if the Egyptians had not been sent round Salamis, any explanation involving them cannot be right, and unless the Corinthians were embarked on a fairly lengthy voyage, it is unlikely that they would have hoisted sails (8.94.1): the sails triremes carried were invariably stowed away or even left ashore, before battle. It is also difficult to see how the Corinthians can have become separated from the rest of the

63 E.g.Munro, 1902, 328; Burn, 460-1; Green, 187. *Contra*: Hignett, 234.

64 Cf. *RE* 1,2, col.1829, and 3,I col.534.

65 Since Adeimantos' son, Aristeus, played a prominent part in the events leading up to the Peloponnesian War, and was later executed by the Athenians (7.173.3 & Thucydides 2.67), it has been suggested that this and the other slanderous tales Herodotos tells about the father, grew up in Athens as a result of the son's activities – see HW ii 267.

66 Burn, 458. For various explanations of what the Corinthians may 'really' have been doing see, e.g., Delbrück, 108; Grundy, 405; Munro, 1902, 329, and *CAH*[1] iv 306; Myres, *Herodotos, Father of History* (Oxford, 1953), 270.

Greek fleet in the last moments before the battle, unless they were at the extreme left of the line, and this is where Herodotos (8.85.1) says the Athenians were – even Diodoros (11.18.1) has the Athenians and Spartans there. Thus it is better to dismiss the whole story out of hand.

The preliminary jockeying for position was brought to an end, Herodotos says (8.84.1), by Ameinias of Pallene, who rowed out and rammed an enemy ship, the rest of the Greeks coming to his aid when he could not disentangle himself: it is, presumably, just a careless slip on the part of Plutarch or his source that he becomes Ameinias of 'Dekeleia' in the former's life of Themistokles (14.3). But Herodotos again says that this was the Athenian story: the Aiginetans claimed that the fighting was begun by the ship which had been sent to fetch the images of the Aiakidai. This seems too good to be true, but may be based on a perfectly genuine doubt as to who had struck first in a line of ships several kilometres long. Even the story (8.84.2) of the female apparition which shouted, 'wretched men, how long are you going to back water?' – might be based on some such shout from the shore, by one of the women waiting anxiously to see how the battle would go. Aischylos confirms that it was 'a Greek ship' which 'began the ramming' (*Persai* 409-10), and his statement that its victim was a Phoenician (410-1) suggests that it was Athenian. The playwright's further statement that his 'Greek ship' sheared off the Phoenician's 'stern-crest' (κόρυμβα: *Persai* 411), if it is to be pressed, suggests that either the Athenians outflanked the Phoenicians, or that Ameinias had successfully carried out a *diekplous*, rowing between two enemy ships before turning to ram one in the stern.[67]

Thereafter Aischylos says no more than that at first the 'stream' (ῥεῦμα) of Persian ships held firm, but that when more and more crowded into the narrows, they began to ram each other or shear away each other's oars (*Persai* 412-6). This might be thought to confirm Diodoros' view of the battle, with the two fleets aligned north-south, but, as we shall see (193–4 below), the details Diodoros gives only make sense if in fact the fleets were aligned east-west as in Herodotos. If what Aischylos says is to be pressed, he may mean no more than that the Persian fleet, already in confusion at the unexpected resistance, fell into even worse confusion as the 'main body' tried to close up and render assistance to the hard-pressed 'others' on the right. Herodotos also says (8.89.2) that most of the leading ships perished because they collided with others pressing on to perform some action before the king. First to turn three lines to starboard in order to move up channel, and then to turn to port again to face the enemy, might well have led to the kind of confusion Aischylos describes.

Aischylos contrasts the confusion among the Persians with the orderliness of the the Greeks (*Persai* 399-400), and Herodotos, too, talks of the orderliness of the Greeks, fighting in formation, compared with the lack of formation among the enemy (8.86), but claims that the Persians fought much better than off Euboia, largely because – as he vividly puts it (8.86end) – 'each thought the king was watching him'. This, too, may imply that ships to the left of where the fighting had started crowded up the channel to

67 That this *is* what the *diekplous* was I hope to have shown in *Greece & Rome* 34 (1987), 170ff. Morrison continues to believe, against all the evidence, that it was a manoeuvre carried out by squadrons of ships in line-ahead - see, most recently, Morrison & Coates, 43, and *JHS* 111 (1991), 197ff.

join the fray. At some point the Ionians certainly got into action, if the historian is to be believed, for he singles out the Greeks serving in the Persian fleet for special praise (8.85.2-3). He states that few of them 'played the coward', and claims that he could list many captains who captured Greek ships, though he contents himself with naming two Samians, Theomestor and Phylakos.

Apart from this, Herodotos merely presents us with three vignettes from the battle, interspersed with general comments, declaring that he cannot say for certain how each of the various contingents fared, whether Greek or barbarian (8.87.1), and this should make one wary of attempting to 'reconstruct' the battle in detail.

The first vignette (8.87.2-88.3) is the story of how Artemisia, pursued by an Athenian ship, and unable to escape because there were friendly vessels in the way, proceeded to ram one of them, which turned out to be from Kalynda (Kalymnos) and to be carrying its king – if true, the ship was not only 'friendly' but one of those actually under Artemisia's command (cf. 7.99.2)! Herodotos says he did not know whether she knew this and had some quarrel with the man, or whether it was an accident. The result was that the Athenian captain – who later turns out to have been none other than Ameinias of Pallene (8.93.1) – assuming that Artemisia's ship was either friendly, or had deserted, broke off the pursuit and went after other prey: when he learned the truth, he was furious because the Athenians had offered 10,000 *drachmai* to the trierarch who captured the queen! As for the latter, her standing with Xerxes was further enhanced, for when he enquired which ship had done the ramming, he was told that it was Artemisia's, and luckily for her no one from the Kalyndaian vessel survived. It was on this occasion that the king is supposed to have exclaimed that his men had become women and his women men (8.88.3).

This story leads on to the comment (8.89) that Xerxes' brother, Ariabignes, perished in the battle, as well as many other noted Persians, Medes and allies, but few Greeks, since the latter knew how to swim. When their ships were disabled, those who were not killed in hand-to-hand fighting, swam to Salamis, whereas most of the Persians, not knowing how to swim, were drowned. Herodotos here also makes the general point that when the leading Persian ships (i.e. those on the right) turned to flight, most of them were put out of action, since those stationed in the rear (i.e. on the left) were pressing on to perform some creditable action before the king, and so collided with the fugitives (8.89.2).

The second story Herodotos tells (8.90) is the one which suggests that some of the Phoenicians had run their ships ashore below where the king sat (see above, 163), and also, perhaps, implies that there was a period in the battle during which, while the Phoenicians were already fully engaged on the right, the Ionians on the Persian left had yet to come into action.

According to Herodotos, the Phoenicians went to the king and complained that they had been betrayed by the Ionians, but while they were speaking, a Samothracian ship rammed an Athenian. The Athenian ship began to settle in the water, but, at that moment, an Aiginetan came up and rammed the Samothracian, whereupon the javelineers aboard the latter swept the Aiginetan's decks clear of its marines and captured it. Seeing a Greek ship, albeit not an Ionian, performing so well, Xerxes' response to the Phoenician complaint was to have them beheaded.

This in turn leads to the comment (8.91) that as the barbarians turned to flight and rowed out towards Phaleron, the Aiginetans did wonders, 'withstanding them in the channel'. The Athenians in the *mêlée* smashed those that stood up to them and those that fled, and the Aiginetans the fugitives, those escaping the former falling to the latter. This seems to imply that at one point the Aiginetans managed to cut right through the Persian line, since, with thirty ships, they can hardly have stemmed the flight of the entire Persian fleet.

Herodotos follows his remarks about the Aiginetans' exploits, with the best story he tells about the battle (8.92). In these dying stages, two Greek ships encountered each other, one carrying Themistokles, the other the Aiginetan, Polykritos, the latter engaged in ramming a Sidonian, the very ship which had captured the gallant Pytheas in the Aiginetan scout-ship, off Skiathos, before the Artemision campaign. Seeing the Athenian ship, and recognizing the commander's 'sign' (a flag or crest of some kind?), Polykritos 'taunted Themistokles, chiding him with the medism of the Aiginetans' (8.92.2).

Shorn of the detail about Pytheas, which is, perhaps, too much of a good thing, the rest of the story is so typical of everything we know about the Greeks that we can surely believe it. The point is that Polykritos' father, Krios, had been amongst those leading Aiginetans arrested for 'medism' by Kleomenes, King of Sparta, at the instigation of the Athenians, before Marathon, and handed over to the Athenians (6.49-50). But the fact that Polykritos could remember this at such a time, while it tells us much about the bitter antagonisms lurking just below the surface of Greek co-operation, also tells us something of the passionate spirit of resistance which animated the patriots.

Herodotos' stories seem mostly to belong to the later stages of the battle, when the Persians were trying to escape, and even more chaos reigned than was normal in ancient naval battles – this would explain how an Aiginetan ship, possibly originally towards the right of the Greek line, could meet an Athenian from the left. The historian tells us nothing of how the battle was won, though his story of the Phoenician complaint to Xerxes hints that the Phoenicians may have been driven ashore, and his account of the Aiginetan exploits perhaps suggests that at one stage the whole right wing of the Persian fleet was cut off from the rest. This may be confirmed by something in Aischylos' messenger-speech. When the Persians fell into confusion, the messenger says, 'the Greek ships not unskilfully in a circle roundabout struck at them' (Ἑλληνικαί τε νῆες οὐκ ἀφρασμόνως/κύκλῳ πέριξ ἔθεινον: *Persai* 417-8). It can hardly be true that at any point the Persians were literally surrounded,[68] but the Phoenicians and those next to them could have been separated from the rest and backed up against the shore of Attica, and, if so, the simile of men killing tunny (lines 424-6) would be particularly appropriate.

---

68 Morrison, *ap*. Morrison & Coates, 59, seems to accept that the Persians were literally surrounded, and repeats the view in a reply – *JHS* 111 (1991), 199f. – to my review of *The Athenian Trireme* in *JHS* 108 (1988), 250. In particular, Morrison takes exception to my comment that I would like to know where Aischylos says that 'after a clash they (*sc*. the Greeks) moved behind the Greeks and surrounded them,' and proceeds to explain what he, Morrison, meant. But the point is that the words of which I complained were included by him in inverted commas, as though they were Aischylos' own words, which they are not!

Diodoros' account of the battle (11.18.4-19.3) is superficially more detailed, but hardly makes sense. As we have seen (above, 185), he seems to envisage the two fleets as ranged north and south, and we have already noted the improbability of either fleet's having one flank resting on a hostile shore. He further says that when the Persians came to 'the narrow part' (τὸ στενόν), they fell into confusion because they were forced to try to withdraw some ships from the line, but it is difficult to see how ships could even have attempted to withdraw in this kind of way. If, as Diodoros appears to believe, the whole Persian fleet was heading west up channel, with its right nearest Attica and its left nearest Salamis, there would not have been room for more than 50 to 60 ships side by side at the narrowest point of the channel. This would have meant there were something like eleven lines of ships behind those in front, if there were about 700 in all, five even if the Persian fleet was now only about as strong as the Greek, as some modern scholars believe. Apart from the fact that Aischylos talks of *three* lines, would it have been possible to contract the frontage with such a press of ships behind? Certainly, it would have ended in colossal confusion, as Diodoros says.

The Persian admiral, Diodoros goes on (11.18.5-6), was the first to engage, and was killed after putting up a magnificent fight: when his ship sank, confusion seized the whole fleet, there being many commanders, each giving contrary orders. Thereupon, seeing the confusion among the enemy, the Athenians advanced and rammed some, shearing away the oars of others. This seems to suggest that the enemy flagship had rowed out in front of the line, which seems very unlikely and looks like mere rhetoric – neither Aischylos nor Herodotos says anything about so crucial a blow – and although the idea that a trireme could shear of the oars of an enemy vessel as it rowed past seems to be accepted by many scholars,[69] it is difficult to see how it could be done. The oars of the attacking vessel would have had to be got out of the way before the moment of impact, or risk equal damage, and this would have meant shipping those of the lower banks, even if those of the top bank could be raised. But all oars were strapped to the thole-pins, as Aischylos describes in his account of the Persian preparations (*Persai*, 375-6), and those of the lowest bank also projected through a tight-fitting sleeve to prevent the sea coming in through the hole. It is noticeable that no classical writer ever describes ships shearing away the oars of enemy vessels: in Aischylos' messenger-speech, for example, it is oars belonging to ships in their *own* fleet that the Persians shear away (*Persai*, 415-6).

But it is in his next passage (11.19.1-2) that Diodoros seems most confused. What he says is that 'while the Phoenician and Cypriot ships were being worsted by the Athenians, the ships of the Cilicians and Pamphylians, and also of the Lykians, which were next in line to them, at first stoutly held out. But when they saw their best ships turning to flight, they too abandoned the fight. On the other wing, a tough sea-fight developed, and up to a point, the battle was evenly poised. But when the Athenians, having pursued the Phoenicians and Cypriots to land, turned back, the barbarians were forced out of line by them, and were put to flight, losing many ships.'

---

69 Cf., e.g., Grundy, 399; A.Köster, *Das Antike Seewesen* (Berlin, 1923), 207ff.; W.W.Tarn, *Hellenistic Military and Naval Developments* (Cambridge, 1930), 146; W.L.Rogers, *Greek and Roman Naval Warfare* (Annapolis, 1937), 10; Green, 193.

This can only mean that the Athenians somehow contrived to break through between the Cypriots and the Cilicians and drive the Cypriots and Phoenicians north onto the Attic shore. But if the Persian right was near that shore and their left near Salamis, this means, as we have seen, that the whole Persian fleet was ranged on a narrow front of perhaps 50 to 60 vessels, in at least five, and probably many more, lines abeam, depending on how many warships it now contained. But it is impossible to believe that triremes could have broken through even five or six lines of enemy ships, let alone eleven or twelve.[70]

The only way one can make sense of Diodoros here is to assume that he has forgotten his north-south alignment. If the opposing fleets were really aligned east-west, as Herodotos says (8.85.1), it is possible to understand how the Greeks could have driven the Phoenicians and those next to them ashore – indeed, as we have seen, Herodotos implies that this is what happened (8.90.1: see above, 191). Of course, if the dispositions of the two fleets outlined above is anything like correct, it would not have been just the Athenians who were involved, but virtually the whole Greek fleet. But this is no problem. Herodotos clearly had information about the Athenians, and about the Aiginetans, but none about other contingents on the Greek side, and one doubts whether Ephoros or his source(s) had better information. Thus it was natural for them to talk as though it was the Athenians who did all the good work on the left wing, the Aiginetans elsewhere.

Diodoros' account can thus be reconciled with Aischylos and Herodotos, though not without difficulty, but Plutarch's is quite absurd. After mentioning the dawn wind, he goes on (*Themistokles* 14.3) to describe how Xerxes' admiral, Ariamenes, 'a good man and by far the best and justest of the king's brothers', confronted Themistokles 'having a great ship', and shot arrows and javelins 'as though from a wall', until Ameinias of Dekeleia and Sokles of Paiania, having rammed his ship, struck him with their spears and hurled him into the sea, whereupon Queen Artemisia recognized the body as it drifted past and had it conveyed to the king.

This looks as though it is derived from the same source as Diodoros' story of the Persian admiral's demise, but with extra embroidery, and is rhetorical 'history' at its very worst.[71] For a start 'Ariamenes' is probably a mistake for Xerxes' brother Ariabignes, who was killed in the battle according to Herodotos (8.89.1), possibly confusing him with Ariaramnes, who, Herodotos says (8.90.4), was present when the unfortunate Phoenicians were executed, and who, since he bore the same name as the great-grandfather of Darius (cf. 7.11.2), was presumably also a member of the royal family. Secondly, it is extremely unlikely, to put it mildly, that Artemisia, whose station was almost certainly somewhere on the left of the Persian line, would have ever been

70 Morrison & Coates say, 59, 'a breakthrough of a line six deep was a notable achievement,' but this is an understatement: if it occurred, it was a miracle!

71 Though swallowed by, e.g., Grundy, 404. Burn, 474, and Green, 192, also accept the story, identifying 'Ariamenes' with Ariabignes. But, as Hignett says, 233, 'confidence in Plutarch's accuracy is not enhanced' by this kind of slip – cf. Ameinias 'of Dekeleia' instead of 'Pallene' (*Themistokles* 14.3, cf. Herodotos 8.84.1), and the transference of Lykomedes' exploit in being the first Greek to take an enemy ship from Artemision (8.11.2) to Salamis (*op.cit.* 15.2). Hignett suggests 'Ariamenes' is a conflation of Achaimenes and Ariabignes.

anywhere near 'Ariamenes" body, since he had been killed by Athenians somewhere on the right. Thirdly, as we have seen, Ameinias almost certainly came from Pallene, not Dekeleia.

Plutarch then goes on (15.1) to tell the story of the miracle in the Thriasian plain, which Herodotos implies occurred before the battle (8.65), and says that others thought they saw the phantom shapes of armed men, believed to be the Aiakidai, stretching out their arms from Aigina to protect the Greek triremes, which looks like a garbled version of Herodotos' story of the bringing of the Aiakidai to the Greeks just before the battle. Returning to the battle, Plutarch claims (15.2) that the first man to capture an enemy ship was the Athenian, Lykomedes, though Herodotos (8.11.2) says Lykomedes performed this exploit at Artemision. In any case, as we shall see, there is some reason to believe that the Greeks did not go in for boarding at Salamis.

The only thing of interest Plutarch says about the actual battle in his life of Themistokles is that the Greeks were put on terms of numerical equality, because the enemy had to attack them in detachments in the narrow strait (*loc.cit.*). But even this looks like the tradition we have already met in Diodoros, which pictures the Persians as crowded in a north-south alignment between the shore of Attica and Salamis, and which we have seen is almost certainly wrong. If the Greeks were put on equal terms, numerically, at any point, it can only be because they initially encountered just the leading squadrons of the Persian fleet, Aischylos' 'others', 'circling towards Salamis' in Herodotos' words. Elsewhere (*Moralia* 869c) Plutarch quotes an epigram by Simonides, which credited Demokritos of Naxos with the capture of five ships, and the rescue of a Dorian, which was about to be taken by the enemy.

The final episode of the battle was the assault on the Persian force on Psyttaleia by Athenian troops under Aristeides. Herodotos implies that this took place while the naval battle was still raging, and that the Athenian troops had been stationed 'along the promonotory of Salamis' (παρὰ τὴν ἀκτὴν τῆς Σαλαμινίης: 8.95), which is presumably Cape Varvari (see 178, Pl 19). However, it seems more likely that it happened after the battle was over, or during its dying stages. Aischylos gives a very exaggerated account of the exploit in the *Persai* (447-71), and his claim (465ff.) that it was witnessed by Xerxes from his throne can hardly be true if the throne was above Perama and Psyttaleia was Lipsokoutali.[72]

Aischylos seems to imply that the fighting went on until nightfall (*Persai*, 428), and it is possible that the killing of Persians who came ashore, which he so vividly describes (424ff.), and isolated struggles with trapped or fleeing Persian ships, went on a long time. When the battle was over, the Greeks dragged ashore on Salamis such of the wrecks as were near (8.96.1); others, he says, were carried by a west wind to 'the shore called Kolias' (8.96.2), which Strabo (9.1.21) locates near Anaphlystos (modern Anavissos), but which Pausanias more realistically, perhaps, places only twenty stades (c.4km) from Phaleron: it may be the modern Cape Ayios Kosmas.[73] Herodotos gives no figures for the losses on either side, but Diodoros (11.19.3) says 40 Greek ships were

72 Hammond, 1956, 38 and n.4, makes use of this to support the view that Psyttaleia was Ayios Georgios. C.W.Fornara, *JHS* 86 (1966), 51ff., suggests that the 'hoplite' achievement on Psyttaleia was exaggerated by conservative elements in Athens.

73 HW ii 268 *ad loc.*

disabled (διεφθάρησαν), and more than 200 Persian 'apart from those captured with their crews'. This seems an exaggeration, though it is possible that the Persians lost very heavily once the rout began. It is true that Herodotos says that the Greeks prepared to fight again, assuming that the king would make use of his surviving ships (8.96.1). But, in the end, within a few days and possibly even on the next night but one (cf. 8.107-108.1), the Persian fleet slipped away from Phaleron.

In the ultimate resort, Salamis appears to have been a sailor's battle, won not by tactical brilliance, whatever some modern commentators may think,[74] but by hard fighting. To the extent, then, that they represented their men, the Greek commanders were perhaps justified in each claiming the prize for himself (8.123.2). It is true that each is supposed to have put Themistokles second to himself, and that as early as Simonides' time, the victory was ascribed to Themistokles' 'judgement and cleverness' (Plutarch, *Themistokles* 15.2). But this need refer to no more than Themistokles' insistence that the Greeks' best chance was to fight at Salamis, and, possibly, to the trick by which he had induced the Persians to attack them there. Similarly, an Athenian speaker in Thucydides (1.74) claims that it was largely because of Themistokles that the battle was fought in the straits. In other words, credit was given to Themistokles' strategic sense, but not to any tactical planning; indeed, it is difficult to believe that the other commanders would have accepted any tactical plan worked out by one of their number, even if it had had the backing of Eurybiadas.

The fact of the matter is that there was no room for fleet-tactics in most ancient sea-battles, though, of course, individual trierarchs and their steersmen could use their skill. Phormio's first victory in the Gulf of Corinth is an exception, but that was on a much smaller scale. Since the only means a trireme had of eliminating an opponent were ramming and boarding, and both these literally involved contact with the enemy vessel, there was an inevitable tendency for battles to degenerate into a series of one-to-one encounters. It was probably very unusual for any trireme to manage to ram or board more than one or two enemy ships in the course of a single action. Ameinias of Pallene's ship, for example, is said to have become so entangled with his first opponent's, that he could not get away (8.84.1), and he was lucky to be able to free himself in time to chase Artemisia. All our sources also stress that one reason why the Greeks won was because the battle was fought in a confined space, and there was even less chance of tactical manoeuvring in such conditions. Salamis was almost certainly a battle much more like those fought in the Grand Harbour of Syracuse, in 413 (cf. Thucydides 7.36-41, 60-71), than, for example, Arginousai.

We might also have expected the Greeks to rely on boarding more than ramming, for the trireme was probably invented in the east, and the mainland Greeks may well have lagged behind in tactics, even if their Ionian cousins had practised the *diekplous* at Lade.[75] Thus one might have thought the fighting would have been 'old-fashioned', as Thucydides describes Sybota (1.49). In the event, however, the Greeks seem to have

---

74 Cf., e.g., Burn, 449, 458ff. & 467, and, above all, Green, 162: '... the actual conduct of the battle itself ... reveals meticulous staff-planning at every stage'; and 182: 'the battle of Salamis was *planned* [his italics], down to the last detail.' Grundy, 396, sees better.

75 Cf. H.T.Wallinga, 'The Ancient Persian Navy and Its Predecessors', in *Achaemenid History* I, ed. H.Sancisi-Weerdenburg (Leiden, 1987), 47ff.

grasped, perhaps as a result of their experiences against the Egyptians on the final day at Artemision (cf. 8.17), that a boarding-fight could easily turn into a battle of attrition, which they were bound to lose. More positively, they may have realised, perhaps this time as a result of Themistokles' urging (cf. 8.60α), that with their 'heavier' ships, they stood a better chance in a ramming-fight, if the confined space was going to preclude fancy manoeuvring.

It may be significant that neither of our two principal sources for the battle, Aischylos and Herodotos, refers to the capture of an enemy ship at Salamis. The only exception, perhaps, is Herodotos' story of Polykritos' rescue of Pytheas from the Sidonian vessel he had just rammed (8.92.1), for this implies that the Sidonian was boarded. However, this was, in any case, in the closing stages. Elsewhere, it is only some of the Ionians and the Samothracians, fighting on the Persian side, who are said to have *captured* ships (8.85.2-3 & 90.2). Instead, there are frequent references to ramming (*Persai* 408-9, 410-1, 418, and cf. 278-9 & 561-2; 8.84.1, 86, 87.2-4, 90.1-2, 91, 92), and the greatest loss of life amongst the Persians is said to have been by drowning (8.89.2), not in fighting across the decks. The only early reference to the *capture* of Persian ships is the epigram by Simonides in praise of Demokritos of Naxos, quoted by Plutarch (*Moralia* 869c).

But however the Greeks managed to win, Salamis was a magnificent achievement. Hitherto they had been on the defensive and had simply reacted to the enemy's moves. Now they had removed one prong of the Persian strategy. Victory was by no means yet assured, for Mardonios' operations prove, if proof is necessary, that the Persian army could operate quite independently of the fleet. But at least the Greeks no longer had to worry about the possibility of defensive positions being turned by sea. Thus the Peloponnese was safe, so long as the Isthmus lines were held, and although this was to have unfortunate repercussions in 479, it meant that so long as the Greek alliance stood firm, Greece could no longer be conquered. In this sense, Salamis was the turning-point of the war.

CHAPTER 8

With Friends Like These?

When darkness at last put an end to the fighting around Salamis, neither side probably fully appreciated what had happened. Herodotos twice states that the Greeks thought they would have to fight again (8.96.1, 108.1), and although he says that Xerxes planned flight as soon as he realised what had happened (8.97.1), this is probably just part of Greek legend. As we shall see (below, 202–3), there is some reason to believe that the king and his army did not leave Attica until several weeks later. There is just a hint, too (*loc.cit.*), that Xerxes ordered his fleet to prepare to renew the conflict, and if it is true that it was only now that his engineers began the attempt to construct a mole over to Salamis (*loc.cit.*), this also shows that he had not given up. Herodotos represents both these moves as merely a cover for flight, but this is unlikely. It is true that the Greek fleet could have sailed to the Hellespont and destroyed the bridges, as the historian says the king feared, but even this probably could not have prevented his eventual return to Asia, and there was certainly little the Greeks could have done to prevent his retreat by land as far as the Hellespont.

As usual, however, although we may discount Herodotos' motivation, there is no particular reason to doubt his facts. The Greek victory at sea had not made it any harder to attempt to construct a mole across to Salamis, since even before the victory, the Greeks would have been in complete control of the straits, except, perhaps, within arrow-range of the Attic shore. To construct a mole might now have appeared well worth the effort, though previously, with the Persian fleet still probably outnumbering the Greek, victory at sea might have seemed the easier option.

It may be true that the mole was only abandoned when the Greeks brought up archers of their own to deter the engineers, as Ktesias alleges (*Persika*, 26), but it is impossible to believe that the archers were only now hired from Crete. If they were Cretan, they had been hired long before – perhaps at the time of the Greek embassy to the island, in the autumn of 481 (7. 169-171). But the Athenians probably already had archers of their own, judging by their presence at Plataia the following year (9.22.1 & 60.3). In any case, it seems unlikely that in an archery duel, the Persians would have come off worst, and the mole was probably abandoned because it was decided to withdraw from Attica for other reasons.

As for Herodotos' statement (8.97.1) that Xerxes also made ready to fight another battle at sea, this, too, may be true. If Diodoros' figures for losses at Salamis are correct (11.19.3), the Persians could probably still muster something like 400 to 450 warships, and the Greeks probably only had some 270 left. But morale is the crucial factor in a battle of attrition, and it seems likely that the Persian navy's morale had cracked. Even if we discount Herodotos' story (8.107.2) that off Cape Zoster (now Lombarda), when heading for the Hellespont, the Persians mistook the headlands[1] for enemy ships and

1 Strictly speaking, Zoster is the modern Lombarda, the central prong of the three-pronged peninsula where the now fashionable resort of Vouliagmeni lies. It is sometimes said that it was rocks off the headland that the Persians mistook for Greek ships – e.g. Grundy, 412;

gave them a wide berth, their reluctance to fight the Greeks off Mykale the following year (9.96) suggests their nerve had gone.

It is possible, then, that the Persian fleet did make a show of regrouping and refitting as though to fight again, if only to deter the Greeks from interfering with its eventual withdrawal. But soon, one night, it quietly slipped from Phaleron and made for the Hellespont.[2] As soon as the Greeks learned that it had gone, Herodotos says (8.108.1), they set off in pursuit, but having got as far as Andros without catching sight of the enemy, gave up the chase and conferred about what to do next. Themistokles proposed that they 'turn aside through the islands and having continued the pursuit of the [enemy] ships, make straight for the Hellespont and destroy the bridges' (8.108.2). Eurybiadas, however, argued that this would only trap Xerxes in Europe, where he might still do untold harm – better to let him return to Asia, as he was likely to do after his defeat at sea (8.108.2-4). Finding himself outvoted, since the other Peloponnesians supported Eurybiadas, Themistokles is then supposed (8.109.1-4) to have used more or less the same arguments to persuade the Athenians to accept Eurybiadas' view, and to have sent messengers to Xerxes, once again including Sikinnos, to claim credit with the king for having persuaded the Greeks do adopt the course they did.

Needless to say, this whole episode, and particularly the alleged second message to Xerxes, has been viewed with the gravest suspicion.[3] Commentators have tended to regard it as another product of a tradition hostile to Themistokles, and have preferred, instead, the alternative tradition in Plutarch (*Themistokles* 16.1-5, *Aristeides* 9.3-4) and Diodoros (11.19.5-6). According to this tradition, the message to Xerxes in fact informed him that the Greeks were going to destroy the bridges, and was part of a plan devised by Themistokles at Salamis, to persuade the king to leave Greece as quickly as possible, Themistokles himself pretending that he would try to delay the Greeks as long as he could. It is also claimed that this is the story that lies behind Thucydides' version of the letter which Themistokles subsequently sent to Xerxes' successor, Artaxerxes, claiming credit for the fact that the Greeks had not destroyed the bridges (1.137.4). Diodoros and Plutarch appear to know nothing of any voyage to Andros, but their story is brought into harmony with Herodotos' by supposing that the voyage to Andros was partly at least intended to convince the king that the Greeks did intend to sail to the Hellespont. Themistokles' speech to the Athenians at Andros, on this hypothesis, represented his own genuine views, and was intended to do what it did – heal Athenian disappointment at not going on to the Hellespont.

It must be admitted that Herodotos' story looks dubious as it stands. After the disastrous sequel to Sikinnos' first message, it seems hardly likely that he could have got

---

Burn, 468; *Blue Guide to Greece*[4] (1981), 180 – but Herodotos refers to the 'ἄκραι λεπταί', i.e 'narrow headlands'. As Green says, 201, 'as anyone who has swum off Vouliagmeni by moonlight can testify, this [the Persian mistake] represents a remarkable feat of the imagination.'

2 Herodotos' narrative has been held to imply that the Persian fleet left the night after the battle – cf. Busolt, 708 n.2 and HW ii 271 – or the next night but one – Burn, 467; Hignett, 240. But in reality several days probably intervened, as Burn, *ibid.*, says.

3 Cf., e.g., Grundy, 413-7; Hignett, 241-3; Burn, 468-70; Green, 205-8; Podlecki, 25-7; Lenardon, 83-4. For a thorough treatment see M.Milton, *Proceedings of the African Classical Association* 17 (1983), 22-52.

away with it a second time, and even if we accept Plutarch's version, in which the messenger is a prisoner-of-war, the eunuch, Arnakes, why should Xerxes now have trusted any messenger from Themistokles? It is also suspicious that Herodotos has Themistokles' messengers proceed to Xerxes while he is still in Attica (8.110.2), whereas one would have expected the king to have left there before any such message could reach him.

One wonders, however, whether the versions of Diodoros and Plutarch really do represent a genuine, alternative tradition, and not just an attempt to 'rationalize' Herodotos, in particular by representing Themistokles as not only wily, but still 'patriotic'. Diodoros, for example, follows Herodotos in having the second message carried by the '*paidagôgos*' of Themistokles' sons, though he does not name him, but avoids the difficulty of having Sikinnos twice venture into the lion's den, by ascribing the first message to an unnamed 'deserter', as we saw. Plutarch gives the first message to Sikinnos, but the second to Arnakes, and suspiciously puts Themistokles' second stratagem into the context of yet another confrontation between him and Aristeides. He even gives the latter the arguments Herodotos gives to Eurybiadas, after Themistokles has suggested the destruction of the bridges to test him. As for Thucydides, there is really nothing in what he says which suggests that the tradition he followed differed from that of Herodotos. In particular, the claim that he supports the implication of Diodoros and Plutarch that the second message was sent from Salamis is curious.[4] What Thucydides in fact *says* (1.137.4) is that the warning of the Greek *retreat*, i.e. the *first* message, was sent from Salamis, not that *both* messages were.

The various modern 'reconstructions' also presuppose too sophisticated a level of strategic thinking even for Themistokles, and Herodotos' version of events is, as usual, more in keeping with what one would imagine the Greek actions to have been. It is, thus, quite likely that news of the flight of the Persian fleet prompted an immediate and almost unthinking pursuit,[5] and that this was only called off when it was realised that there was no hope of catching the enemy. There is no necessity to suppose that a conference had to be held at Salamis before the fleet took such a course of action, since it was so obviously necessary to determine whether and where the Persian fleet had gone.

But once it was realised that it had apparently left mainland waters, it did become necessary to decide what to do next, and it is, again, likely that there were, broadly speaking, two points of view – to go on with the pursuit and then proceed to the Hellespont, or call a halt to naval operations for the winter. If so, it is not impossible to

4 Hignett, 242; Milton, *op.cit.*, 23 & 26-7; see also Gomme, *HCT* i 441. Gomme translates the passage in question – 'τήν τε ἐκ Σαλαμῖνος προάγγελσιν τῆς ἀναχωρήσεως' – as 'the announcement of the impending retreat of the Greeks from Salamis', whereas, surely, what it means is 'the announcement from Salamis of the [impending] retreat of the Greeks.' But Thucydides certainly did not mean that the message about the bridges was from Salamis.

5 It has been objected – e.g. by Macan (1908) i 2 524 & 533, ii 324-5 & 329-30; Meyer, 372 n.1 – that the Greeks cannot have thought of going in pursuit of the Persian fleet while Xerxes was still in Attica. But only a few ships would have been needed to ensure the safety of Salamis: see Grundy, 413; HW ii 271; Hignett, 240-1; Burn, 469 n.52. I also do not think that any conference was necessary at this point, as some have asserted, e.g. Macan (1908) i 2 525.

believe that Themistokles, who had been a strong advocate of a naval policy since at least 483, and who had just won such a reputation as the architect of the naval victory at Salamis, should now have argued for the former course, nor that the Peloponnesians should have been reluctant to adopt so aggressive a strategy. It is, finally, not inconceivable that Themistokles did adopt Eurybiadas' arguments – adding, noticeably, some of his own – in order to pacify his fellow-countrymen and so avoid another potentially damaging split in the alliance. This time, after all, it was not absolutely vital to Athens' interests that his views should prevail, as it had been in the arguments whether to abandon Salamis.

What *is* dubious in Herodotos' story is, as is so often the case, the motive he attributes to Themistokles for his speech to the Athenians, namely 'to lay the basis for a future claim upon the Persian, so that if he should ever suffer any disgrace at the hands of the Athenians, he would have somewhere to go' (8.109.5). This was obviously written with the knowledge of what was later to happen to Themistokles – ostracism and then flight to Persia – and it is very difficult to believe that in 480, at the height of his fame, he should already have been thinking in terms of having to take refuge in Persia.[6]

The dubious motive Herodotos ascribes to Themistokles is closely linked with the story of the second message, and this alone may be enough to discredit the latter. On the other hand, Thucydides evidently believed there was a second message[7] – it is Themistokles' claim to have prevented the destruction of the bridges which he describes as a lie – and if his version of the letter Themistokles allegedly sent to Artaxerxes is a more or less correct copy of a genuine original, then one has to accept that such a message was sent, and that Herodotos' version of it is also the right one. If so, it is possible that Themistokles was, perhaps, trying to set the record straight with the King, and thus 'to lay the basis for a future claim' upon him, not for himself, but *for Athens*.

We have seen that his first message may have been a perfectly genuine attempt to see what terms the king might offer, if Athens were to change sides, sent at a moment of the blackest despair, when it looked as though the Peloponnesians were finally going to abandon Salamis. Now it might appear that Peloponnesian reluctance to continue the naval campaign was of a piece with their earlier reluctance to fight for anything more than the Peloponnese, a reluctance which, as we shall see, they were to evince more and more strongly in the coming months. So perhaps Themistokles felt it desirable to reopen the Persian option, if he could.

It may be significant, then, that in the speech Herodotos says he delivered to the Athenians (8.109.2-4), Themistokles puts a brave face on things, stressing the dangers of pursuing defeated men and compelling them to fight, urging his fellow-countrymen to rebuild their homes and concern themselves with sowing, and suggesting that in the spring they could sail for the Hellespont and Ionia. All this presupposed that the threat to Attica would not be renewed, and this was conditional upon the withdrawal of the Persian army and the Greeks' taking the offensive on land, neither of which could be assumed. In other words, Themistokles, in urging his fellow-countrymen to return to Attica was at the same time placing the Peloponnesians under an obligation to protect

6 So Grundy, 415.
7 See Gomme, *HCT* i 440-1.

them. Only if Attica was safe, could they even think of sending the fleet to the Hellespont and Ionia in the spring.

Against this background, Themistokles might well have thought of having a second string to his bow. If the Peloponnesians refused to protect Attica, it might still be necessary to seek an accomodation with the Persians, and before that could be done, it was first necessary to reassure the king as to his own *bona fides*. Thus the second message sought to show that Themistokles was still secretly working in the king's interest, and sending Sikinnos was a sign of confidence that Salamis had changed nothing.[8] It had not been a battle of Themistokles' making, but the king's, and, in the event, it had been impossible to prevent the Athenians from fighting.

It is obvious that at the time of his decline and fall, the rôle of Themistokles in the defeat of Xerxes became the subject of great controversy, and we are unlikely ever to know the truth. His enemies were later to accuse him of medism (cf. Thucydides 1.135.2ff.; Diodoros 11.54.2ff.; Plutarch, *Themistokles* 22.3ff.), and some of his more devious dealings in 480 could easily be taken two ways. On the one hand he could be depicted as the wily manipulator who had twice tricked the king of Persia; on the other, he could be shown up as a traitor, who had played a double game throughout and later merely showed his true colours. Herodotos seems to have stood somewhere between these two extremes, evidently believing that the message to Xerxes before Salamis was a trick, but that the second one, from Andros, was treasonable. Though certainty is not possible, the above reconstruction at least has the merit of making Themistokles consistent, while at the same time adhering as closely as possible to what Herodotos says.

There still, however, remains the problem of timing. It is usually assumed that when Kleombrotos sacrificed 'against the Persian' (9.10.3) and was deterred by the eclipse of the sun, on 2 October, the Persian army must already have left Attica.[9] But, it is argued, if Salamis was fought on 24 September, and still more if it was fought later in September, the Greek fleet could hardly have reached Andros before Xerxes left Attica, and thus Herodotos must be wrong to say (8.110.2) that Xerxes was in Attica when Themistokles sent the second message to him. There is also the point that in the speech Themistokles supposedly delivered to the Athenians at the time, he seems to assume that the Persians have already left Attica. He twice appears to refer to their repulse ('νέφος τοσοῦτον ἀνθρώπων ἀνωσάμενοι' – 109.2; 'παντελέως ἀπελάσας τὸν βάρβαρον' – 1.109.4), and urges the Athenians to see to rebuilding their homes and sowing their crops, suggesting that they can sail to the Hellespont and Ionia in the spring. This does not really make sense if the Persians were still in Attica.[10]

---

8 As Arnold noted in his edition of Thucydides, vol. i (Oxford, 1830), 189.

9 Cf., e.g., Busolt, 703-4 n.3; Meyer, n. on 392; HW ii 256. It may be objected to my hypothesis that Herodotos says (8.113.2) that Xerxes and his army only waited 'a few days' (ὀλίγας ἡμέρας) before making for Boiotia. But, as we have seen, he tends to telescope events here – e.g. in implying that the Persian fleet left Phaleron only some twenty-four hours after the battle. In any case, if the army really left in, say, the second week in October, could not this be described as 'a few days' after a battle fought on 24 September or even later?

10 Stein, *Herodotus*[6] vol. v (Berlin, 1912), 82, followed by Milton, *op.cit.* n.3 above, 36 and n.47, take 'παντελέως ἀπέλασας τὸν βάρβαρον' to mean 'once the barbarian has been driven away', and the latter argues that Themistokles here assumes that a land campaign will

The first objection to what Herodotos says can be be got round fairly easily by supposing that Xerxes and his army were still in Attica when the eclipse of the sun occurred, and that it was really their continued presence, rather than the eclipse, which deterred Kleombrotos from advancing. If so, Xerxes could still have been in Attica when Themistokles sent his second message, and this is in fact what Herodotos implies, for he only begins to describe the king's departure after his account of the naval operations and the sending of the message (8.113.1). But this does not solve the problem of how Themistokles could speak to the Athenians with him in the fleet as though the Persians had left Attica, when he obviously thought that they were still there.

The simplest solution to this problem is that Herodotos just 'nodded' here. We should remember that all the speeches he reports are inventions of his own, even if he did have some information as to what had actually been said, and he, unlike Themistokles at the time, did know that the Persians eventually retreated from Attica. But we are possibly reading too much into what he has Themistokles say, in any case. It would have been reasonable to assume that Salamis would lead to a Persian retreat from Attica at least, and the language Themistokles uses of the 'repulse' of the barbarians is pretty vague, and could refer to the naval victory. After all, a great 'cloud' had been lifted from both the Athenians and the Greeks in general, as Themistokles says (8.109.2), and if the 'barbarian' had not yet 'entirely' been driven away (8.109.4), in a speech designed to placate the Athenians and turn their thoughts to rebuilding their lives, to claim this was a pardonable exaggeration.

According to Herodotos (8.111.1), after the Greeks had decided not to pursue the enemy fleet any further or to proceed to the Hellespont, they laid siege to Andros. The historian implies that Themistokles' greed was responsible. He had demanded money from the islanders, saying that the Athenians had two great gods with them, 'Persuasion' and 'Necessity', but the Andrians had responded by producing two of their own, 'Poverty' and 'Inability'. In reality, the demands on Andros and other island states such as Karystos and Paros (8.112) are more likely to have been made in common by the patriot Greeks, now that they were at last in a position to take measures against the 'medizers', though some of the money may have stuck to Themistokles' fingers. Plutarch quotes a poem by the contemporary Timokreon of Rhodes, vilifying Themistokles for taking his money, but still doing nothing to restore him to his native city of Ialysos, on the island of Rhodes (*Themistokles* 21.2-3).

After the failure of the siege of Andros, Herodotos says (8.121.1ff.), the Greeks attacked Karystos, and then returned to Salamis. Here they busied themselves with dividing the spoils and arranging for various dedications. They then proceeded to the Isthmus where there took place the famous vote on prizes for the most deserving, in which all the leaders voted for themselves first and Themistokles second (8.123.2). It may have been only now, i.e. some time after the eclipse on 2 October, that

---

still be necessary, and that it will be fought before naval operations recommence. But the phrase surely picks up Themistokles' earlier remarks about the Greek victory – e.g. 'νέφος τοσοῦτον ἀνθρώπων ἀνωσάμενοι,' which can only mean '*having* repulsed so great a cloud of men.' Logically and grammatically 'παντελέως ἀπέλασας τὸν βάρβαρον' is connected with the rebuilding of homes and the sowing, not with sailing to the Hellespont and Ionia in the spring.

Kleombrotos led his army home from the Isthmus (9.10.3). Shortly afterwards he died, and was succeeded in the regency for Leonidas' young son by his own son, Pausanias.

Meanwhile, after the departure of the other leaders to their own cities, Themistokles himself proceeded to Sparta, where he received a great welcome. He was honoured with an olive-wreath, like Eurybiadas, but also received the finest chariot in Sparta, and was escorted to the border by the *Hippeis*, the three hundred-strong Spartan élite-unit[11] – an honour, Herodotos says (8.124.3), which Themistokles alone received of all the men he knew.

If this is true, it may mean no more than that the Spartans genuinely felt that Themistokles deserved to be honoured for the part he and the Athenians had played in the victory, and possibly even that he had not been treated properly at the Isthmus, as Herodotos says (8.124.2). On the other hand, it is possible that they went out of their way to flatter Themistokles because they wanted something out of him. By the spring they had committed themselves to a renewal of some kind of naval action, despite Eurybiadas' rejection of this at Andros, and although the size of the fleet which assembled at Aigina – 110 ships (8.131.1) – may have been disappointingly small, at least it now had a king of Sparta to command it, in the person of Leotychidas (8.131.2), which suggests that in Spartan eyes, this was to be a serious effort. By contrast, as we shall see, they seem to have been very reluctant to commit themselves to an offensive on land. But any effort at sea required the co-operation of Athens, and this is where Themistokles came in. At Andros, if we are to believe Herodotos (8.108.2), he had advocated a continuation of the naval campaign, and although he had eventually accepted Eurybiadas' point of view, he had suggested to the Athenians the possibility of sailing to the Hellespont and Ionia in the spring (8.109.4). Now the Spartans hoped that he would be able to persuade his fellow-countrymen once again to commit themselves to a naval offensive.[12]

But as is so often the case when two parties have similar but not indentical interests, the Spartans appear to have forgotten or ignored two things – that the corollary to the proposed naval strategy for 479, was a guarantee of safety for Attica, and that without this guarantee Themistokles would not be able to 'sell' the proposed strategy to his fellow-countrymen. In a not dissimilar way, twenty years later, they were to reject the force Athens had sent to help them in their war with the rebel-helots, forgetting that thereby they would irretrievably undermine the standing of Kimon, the Athenian chiefly responsible for the policy of *détente* which Athens had pursued since Themistokles' downfall (cf. Thucydides 1.102). In 480/79, at least at first, they had the excuse that the Persian army was in retreat, and they may genuinely have believed that it would altogether withdraw from Europe – hence, perhaps, the dedications made to various

---

11 Green, 213-4, describes these men as 'the three hundred horsemen of the Royal Household Cavalry', but, despite their title, the 300 *Hippeis* (i.e 'horsemen') fought on foot: the Spartans had no cavalry until 424 (cf. Thucydides 4.55.2).

12 On all this see K.W.Nitzsch, *RhM* 27 (1872), 258ff.; Grundy, 419ff.; Hignett, 274ff.; Burn, 490ff. Milton, *op.cit.* n.3 above, argues that Themistokles' strategy was the one finally pursued in 479, but this depends on the erroneous interpretation of 'παντελέως απελάσας τὸν βάρβαρον' in Herodotos 8.109.4 – see n.10 above.

shrines, after Salamis (8.121.2-122), and the honours bestowed on Eurybiadas and Themistokles (8.124.2-3).

But, of course, the Persians had no intention of withdrawing from Europe, whatever the Greeks may have believed. Herodotos, it is true, implies that Xerxes himself was so shattered by the naval defeat that he was determined to abandon the whole enterprise. Thus the attempt to build the mole across to Salamis and the preparations by the fleet as though to renew the conflict, were only a disguise, though everybody was fooled except Mardonios (cf. 8.97). But this is on a par with Aischylos' description of Xerxes' immediate and panic-stricken flight after witnessing the massacre on Psyttaleia (*Persai* 465ff.). In reality, it may well be that it was Xerxes who was determined to persist, after Salamis, and his advisers who persuaded him that the safety of the empire required his return to its centre, for however important Greece may loom in our eyes and in those of contemporary Greeks, to the Persians it could only ever have been a relatively unimportant and, no doubt, troublesome province on the empire's fringes.

There is, as usual, much plausibility in the arguments Herodotos gives his protagonists, first Mardonios, and then Artemisia. After establishing his credentials by suggesting the possibility of an immediate attack on the Peloponnese, Mardonios uses arguments which are just the kind of thing one would expect from a Persian grandee: the naval defeat meant nothing – the decisive struggle was not one of planks, but of men and horses; the Persians had not played the coward, but only Phoenicians, Egyptians, Cypriots and Cilicians; give him the men and he would finish the job (8.100.2-5). Artemisia's argument, too, that if Mardonios succeeded, it would still be Xerxes' triumph, whereas if he failed, the defeat would not endanger the royal house (8.102), also makes sense: had not Darius, similarly, entrusted the conquest of Thrace to a subordinate, after the Skythian *débâcle* (4.143)?

Not surprisingly, then, according to Herodotos, Xerxes accepted the advice given him by Mardonios and Artemisia, and having entrusted the latter, together with the eunuch, Hermotimos, with the task of escorting his bastard sons to Ephesos, himself set off with the army. Mardonios, who had decided to winter in Thessaly, accompanied the king thus far, and it was there that he made his pick of the troops who were to remain in Greece (8.113). Herodotos and our other sources (cf. Aischylos, *Persai* 803-4; Thucydides 1.73.5; Diodoros 11.19.5-6; Plutarch, *Themistokles* 16.5), consistently maintain that the forces Mardonios retained were only a part of the whole army, but there are hints in Herodotos that in reality they constituted most of it. Firstly, he says that the 60,000 men under Artabazos' command, who were to form part of Mardonios' army, escorted the king as far as the Hellespont (8.126.1) whereas, if the King was taking most of the army with him, there would seem to have been no need for such an escort.[13] Secondly, Herodotos admits that when the king reached the crossing-place, he had 'hardly any part of his army, so to speak, under command' (ἀπάγων τῆς στρατιῆς οὐδὲν μέρος ὡς εἰπεῖν: 8.115.1).

13 Cf., e.g., Busolt, 712-3 n.4. Some scholars – e.g Grundy, 429, and Hignett, 270, deny that Artabazos did have the job of escorting Xerxes, but think he was sent to safeguard communications, or to deal with the revolt of Poteidaia. But there is no good reason to doubt Herodotos here, even if he does not mention Artabazos in his account of Xerxes' retreat.

The historian attributes this to the horrors of the retreat (8.115.2-4), and this tradition is already in Aischylos (*Persai* 482ff.). But other things Herodotos tells us suggest that the retreat was orderly and relatively unscathed. Firstly, he says it took forty-five days (8.115.1), and although commentators have assumed that this means forty-five days from Athens, and therefore that the return took only half the time of the advance (cf.8.51.1),[14] even this would not indicate excessive haste, since there was no longer any need to prepare the way. But in fact Herodotos probably meant the forty-five days to be the time taken for the march from *Thessaly* to the Hellespont. Secondly, he says that the sick were left in various towns on the way, with strict instructions for their care (8.115.3), and, thirdly, we know from subsequent events that some of the places on the route were garrisoned, for example Doriskos (cf. 7.106) and Eïon (cf. 7.107 & 113.1). Thus there is no reason to believe that Xerxes' army suffered heavily in the retreat, and if he had only a small force with him when he reached the Hellespont, this was because that was all he took.

According to Herodotos (8.117.1, 130.1), he and his entourage were ferried across to Abydos by the remaining ships of the fleet, which had made their way thither from Salamis, because the bridges had already been destroyed in a storm.[15]

The losses suffered on the retreat, if historical, may in fact have fallen on Artabazos' troops, for though they are said to have numbered 60,000 when escorting Xerxes, later, at Plataia, they number 40,000 (9.66.2), and although they had had some tough fighting at Olynthos and, particularly, Poteidaia, on the way back to rejoin Mardonios (8.126.2-129), one would not have thought their losses would have amounted to a third of their total.

The fighting resulted from the rebellion of the people of Poteidaia 'as soon as the King had passed by and the Persian fleet had fled from Salamis' (8.126.3), and the Poteidaians were joined by the rest of the inhabitants of the Pallene peninsula. Artabazos laid siege to Poteidaia, and at the same time attacked Olynthos, suspecting that it too had rebelled. Having taken the latter, he massacred its inhabitants and handed the town over to one Kritoboulos of Torone, repopulating it with loyal Greeks descended from the Chalkidian colonists of the region (8.127). The siege of Poteidaia was, however, less successful. Artabazos first tried treachery, but his method of communicating with his agent in the town broke down, when the arrow carrying the latest message hit a Poteidaian in the shoulder and the message was discovered (8.128). Then, after three months had passed (i.e. in February or March, 479), an exceptionally

---

14 Cf., e.g., HW ii 273 *ad loc.*, where the reference to Herodotos 8.57.1 is a mistake; Burn, 471. Hignett, 268, rightly takes the starting-point as Thessaly.

15 Herodotos reports another tradition about Xerxes' return to Asia, according to which he took ship at Eïon at the mouth of the Strymon, and left Hydarnes to take the army on to the Hellespont (8.118-120). He says he doubted the story on two grounds, firstly because, when a storm arose, Xerxes was said to have ordered the Persian nobles on deck to jump overboard to lighten the ship: Herodotos says it is much more likely that he would have ordered them to go below and an equivalent number of the Phoenician oarsmen to go overboard. But it seems hardly likely that Persian nobleman could have been got to take a hand at the oars – better death by drowning in the king's service! More cogent is Herodotos' second argument, namely that there was evidence that Xerxes passed by Abdera on his retreat, for, as he says, that was nearer the Hellespont than Eïon.

low tide apparently exposed the seaward end of the wall spanning the isthmus on which Poteidaia stood. Troops were sent to exploit the opportunity, but after getting two-fifths of the way round, were overtaken by the returning tide, and those of them who were not drowned, massacred when the Poteidaians put out in boats. Thereupon, Artabazos gave up the siege, and marched to join Mardonios. Poteidaia remained free, and was actually able later to send three hundred hoplites to join the Greeks at Plataia (9.28.3).

According to Herodotos (8.113), the troops Mardonios had selected to remain with him included the Immortals, apart from their commander, Hydarnes, who said he would not leave the king, the other Persian 'corslet-wearers' and 'the 1000 cavalry', the Medes, Sakai, Baktrians and Indians, both horse and foot, and picked men from other contingents. Subsequently we learn that the latter included Egyptian marines from the fleet (9.32).

Apart from the question of numbers, there are some difficulties about this list. Firstly, although the Immortals were the crack division in the Persian army and had played a prominent part at Thermopylai, they are never mentioned in connection with the campaign of 479, and since their commander is said to have returned with Xerxes, it is possible that Herodotos is mistaken and that they accompanied the king to Asia.[16] On the other hand, if so, it is odd that Herodotos should be so insistent that the corps remained despite the absence of its commander. Moreover, the argument that one might have expected the Immortals to accompany the king, is even stronger in the case of the '1000 cavalry'. This unit was presumably one of the two which formed part of the king's personal escort both at the march-out from Sardis (7.40.2, 41.1) and at the crossing of the Hellespont (7.55.2-3), and yet these men *are* mentioned in the account of Plataia (9.63.1).

The Persian 'corslet-wearers' are, presumably, the ordinary Persian troops mentioned in the description of the review at Doriskos, where – although there is evidently a *lacuna* in the text (7.61.1) – their corslets are apparently described as 'of iron scales, like those of a fish'. The '1000 cavalry' are, however, a puzzle, since, as we have just seen, Herodotos previously mentions two such units. Perhaps we are meant to understand that one accompanied the king, as presumably did the two infantry units 1000 strong associated with them. Of the other units, only the Indians seem an odd choice, since one would not have thought that with their cotton garments and cane bows (cf. 7.65), they would have been particularly formidable, nor their cavalry, which allegedly included war-chariots, some drawn by horses, some by wild asses (cf. 7.86.1) – certainly no chariots appear in the account of Plataia.

Whatever the truth about the size and composition of Mardonios' army, however (see below, 228), the Greeks may have had early intelligence of its continued presence. According to Herodotos (8.114), while Xerxes himself was still in Thessaly, an oracle came to the Spartans from Delphi telling them to demand satisfaction from Xerxes for Leonidas' death, and to accept whatever he offered them. When the Spartan herald delivered his message, the king laughed, and, after a pause, pointed at Mardonios and said, 'Mardonios here will give them all the satisfaction they deserve.' Even if the details are legendary, it is not inconceivable that the Spartans did send a herald to Thessaly to find out what the king's intentions were, and their action may well have been prompted

16 Macan (1908) i 2 539, though he believes they returned to Greece in 479; Hignett, 267.

by Delphi, which had close connections with Thessaly. It has been suggested that the Spartans may have been trying to salve their consciences for not having advanced from the Isthmus, and hoped for some kind of 'acknowledgement of defeat' from the King which would be enough to satisfy their honour,[17] but this is far-fetched.

Even if the story of the herald is untrue, the Greeks presumably learned soon enough that a large Persian army had remained in northern Greece, since its presence could hardly have been long concealed, and serious splits began to develop in the alliance as a result. The Spartans and other Peloponnesians, on the one hand, seem to have decided that since their lines across the Isthmus were now nearing completion, and there was no longer any possibility of the Persians' turning them by sea, there was no pressing need for further action on land. Thus it was probably not until July, 479, that their army finally crossed the Isthmus, and then it was only after the Athenians had threatened to change sides (see below, 214ff.).

Attempts to explain this by reference to the necessity of first getting in the harvest, or opposition from Argos, Mantineia and Elis,[18] are unconvincing. The Spartans, with their helot labour-force, are the least likely of all Greeks to have worried about the harvest, even if this was a cause for concern to some of their allies. It is true that Herodotos believed that no fewer than 35,000 helots were eventually mustered for the Plataia campaign, but it is is very unlikely that so many were really taken (see below, 227–8).

Still more dubious is the notion that the Spartans were worried about the situation in the Peloponnese. It was only some fifteen years since the Argive army had been crippled at Sepeia, with the loss of 6000 hoplites (7.148.2), and it is most unlikely that the Spartans had any fears in that direction. As for Elis and Mantineia, it is true that their contingents arrived late for Plataia (9.77), but this proves no more than that they were reluctant to honour their obligations, not that they were actively hostile. Nor is it any argument that within ten years of Plataia, Argos was involved in war with Sparta alongside a coalition of Arcadian states, including Tegea and Mantineia, and possibly Elis (9.35.2), for by then the situation in Greece had been completely changed by the growth of Athenian power. As for the helots, they too may have been in rebellion within ten years of Plataia, but this tells us little or nothing about their attitude in 479. Nevertheless, although the possibility of active opposition in the Peloponnese may not have been a serious factor in Spartan thinking, we should not forget that they had to carry their allies with them. They could not just assume that the Peloponnesian states would all meekly go along with their strategy.

However, the most likely explanation for Spartan behaviour in the first six months of 479 is that they had now adopted the strategy allegedly adumbrated by Themistokles at Andros, namely a naval campaign to the Hellespont and Ionia (8.109.4). They thereby hoped to secure the withdrawal of Mardonios' army, without the risks of a land offensive, by threatening his communications and raising the possibility of revolt in

---

17 Burn, 488, cf. Green, 211. Both assume that Sparta approached Delphi first, but this is not what Herodotos actually says.

18 Beloch, ii 1.32; Meyer, 404f.; Munro, 1904, 147f.; Nitzsch, *op.cit.* n.12 above; Busolt, 719; HW ii 289-90.

western Asia Minor.[19] Even if this was not why they did such honour to Themistokles, and appointed a king to command the fleet instead of the commoner, Eurybiadas, it explains why, whereas they were apparently so slow to mobilize their army, it was in the spring that their king took command of the fleet at Aigina (8.131.1).

For the time being the fleet may not have proceeded further than Delos, but this was almost certainly because of its comparatively small size. Unfortunately, Herodotos does not tell us how many of its 110 ships were Athenian, and some scholars have suggested that the Athenians, now in favour of a land-offensive, deliberately witheld all but a token force in order to cripple the naval offensive.[20] This may be going too far, since the Athenians played a prominent part at Mykale later in the year (9.102ff. and esp. 105). But the relatively small size of the fleet almost certainly means that the Athenians had not contributed anything like their full capability, and their reluctance is also likely to have affected states like Aigina and Megara – indeed all that did not think themselves safe behind the Isthmus lines.

If, then, Themistokles had proposed that Athens once more pursue a naval strategy, this had evidently not commended itself to his fellow-countrymen, and, despite the scepticism of some scholars,[21] there can really be little doubt that this is ultimately why he appears to have played no part in the events of 479. Herodotos offers no explanation, though he hints that the favour shown to him by the Spartans may have been unpopular. He says that when he returned to Athens, a certain Timodemos of Aphidna scornfully declared that he owed his honours not to his own efforts, but to his city – Themistokles is supposed to have replied that he would not have been so honoured if he had been from Belbina (an insignificant island), but that Timodemos would not have been, even though he was an Athenian (8.125). Diodoros (11.27.3) actually says the people of Athens removed him from office and replaced him with Xanthippos. This may be no more than an attempt to explain his absence from the scene in 479, and, even if true, may mean no more than that he was not re-elected to the *stratêgia*. But Herodotos says that Xanthippos was in command of the Athenian contingent in Leotychidas' fleet, in the spring (8.131.3), and this, if true, means before the new *stratêgoi* took office, so possibly Xanthippos had replaced Themistokles.[22]

If it is true that Themistokles was deposed from office before the Greek fleet assembled at Aigina, his fall from favour was not a reaction to Mardonios' second

---

19 See the references in n.12 above.

20 Busolt, 717f.; Meyer, 402f.

21 E.g. Beloch, ii 1.52, 2.142ff.; Munro, 1902, 301; Milton, *op.cit.* n.3 above, 38-9.

22 It has been argued that the fact that Xanthippos was already in command of the Athenian contingent in the fleet, in the spring, means that he was *stratêgos* for 480/79 (Beloch, *locc.cit.*, n.21), and that, therefore, he had been recalled from ostracism before the elections in spring, 480. But this is not necessary: in the later 5th century it was certainly possible for the people to depose a *stratêgos* and replace him with another, though there is the difficulty that Themistokles and Xanthippos belonged to different *phylai*, Themistokles to *Leontis*, Xanthippos to *Akamantis*. The argument that because Aristeides commanded the Athenian troops on Psyttaleia, he must also have been *stratêgos* in 480/79, is even weaker: such a command did not necessarily warrant a *stratêgos*. Barron, 594, drawing attention to the *ostrakon* describing Aristeides as 'Datis' brother', suggests he and Xanthippos were elected *stratêgoi* to negotiate with the Persians, but this is very far-fetched.

occupation of Athens, for that was probably not until June (see below, 213). Presumably, however, the mere knowledge that a Persian army remained in northern Greece was enough to shake Athenian confidence in Themistokles' strategy. Talk of the 'repulse' of the barbarians would have started to ring increasingly hollow when they were still only a matter of two or three weeks march from Attica, and men began to realise that manning the fleet would once more drain Attica of its manhood. Presumably Themistokles argued that the Spartans would see to it that Attica was safe, but the Peloponnesians had failed to stop its being overrun the previous year, and the more Themistokles tried to maintain that this time the Spartans would not let them down, the more the Athenians probably remembered what had happened the previous year. Instead, perhaps, they began to listen to those who tried to revive memories of Marathon, and talked of laying up the fleet in favour of a great land-offensive to drive the barbarians completely out of Greece. Thus though some ships were sent to join Leotychidas at Aigina, they were nothing like as numerous as the ones sent the year before to Artemision.

If, then, the Spartans had been hoping for a full-scale naval offensive, they would have been grievously disappointed, for even if they had no accurate intelligence of the number of Persian ships still in Aegean waters, they can hardly have believed that a fleet of 110 would be sufficient. In fact, Herodotos says (8.130), the Persian fleet, having ferried Xerxes and his army across the Hellespont, had wintered mainly at Kyme, some at Samos, where the whole fleet reassembled in the spring. He gives the total number of ships, including the Ionian contingents, as 300 (8.130.2), and, if anything, this seems too few, unless the Phoenician contingent, which he says departed later (9.96.1), had already gone home. For what it is worth, Diodoros (11.27.1) says over 400 ships mustered at Samos. The Persian intention, according to both historians, was mainly to guard Ionia, though they did not expect the Greeks to take the offensive, in the light of their failure to press the pursuit after Salamis.

In the event, at the urging of Ionian exiles who had previously been to Sparta with pleas for the liberation of their homeland, the Greek fleet did venture as far as Delos. Diodoros (11.34.2) says it numbered 250 ships, and it has been suggested that it had by now more than doubled in size.[23] But a fleet of 250 triremes could not have been got together without a substantial Athenian contribution, and this would have meant a considerable number of hoplites as marines. We do not know how many hoplites Athens could muster in 479, but, according to Herodotos (9.28.6) there were 8000 at Plataia, and it is difficult to believe that they had more than about 10,000 in all – enough, perhaps, to supply marines for about 50 triremes, but certainly not 100 or more.

A fleet of as many as 250 warships also seems inconsistent with the pusillanimity shown by Leotychidas and his fellow-commanders in the initial stages of the campaign. Herodotos says (8.132) that they did not dare to go beyond Delos, 'because they had no experience of the area, and everywhere seemed to be full of enemy forces. As for Samos, they took the view that it was as far away as the Pillars of Herakles.' This is obvious exaggeration, since the Greeks had been sailing the eastern Aegean for

23 Munro, 1904, 146f.; *contra*: Hignett, 250. Green, 229 & n., tries to save Munro's hypothesis by supposing that 'all hoplite marines were drafted out of the fleet and replaced by thetes, metics or slaves,' but this is absurd.

centuries, but it may well be true that with only 110 ships, they were very reluctant to venture beyond Delos in the face of a Persian fleet possibly two or three times as strong. Nevertheless, any forward movement by the fleet was in contrast to the complete lack of movement on land, and is a further indication that the Spartans were still in favour of a naval strategy.

Neither they nor the Athenians, however, can have been happy at the prospects for the coming year, and this was a situation Mardonios knew well how to exploit. If the story of Themistokles' second message is true, the Persians will have been aware of the possibilities of a split in the Greek alliance, and even if it is not, their whole experience of fighting Greeks, from Lade onwards, would have suggested that any 'unity' they might temporarily achieve, was likely to prove extremely precarious. Herodotos implies that it was when the Greek fleet sailed to Delos that Mardonios made his first move (8.133), sending one Mys, from Europos in Caria,[24] to sound out all the oracles in Greece he was able to contact. But Mys' mission may well have been earlier, since the temporal implications of the passage in question can hardly be pressed.

Herodotos states that he himself could not say what Mardonios hoped to discover (*ibid.*), so speculation is, perhaps, pointless. It has been suggested that his purpose was 'to satisfy the Greek states still loyal to Persia', that the consultations were 'a measure of his anxiety', or that he was sounding out his principal Greek allies, the Boiotians, on their attitude to a possible *rapprochement* with Athens, for all the oracles Herodotos actually names were in Boiotia, with the exception of the one at Abai in Phokis. Possibly, more simply, he was trying to show the Greeks now under Persian rule that life would go on as it always had done. The omission of Delphi has also been remarked upon, but is understandable enough if Phokian partisans controlled Parnassos (cf. 8.31.1). After giving an account of Mys' consultation of the oracles, Herodotos guesses that their advice may have been to try to win the alliance of Athens (8.136.3), and this was certainly the next move Mardonios tried. The man he chose to head the embassy was Alexander of Macedonia, since he was the Athenian *proxenos* ('consul') and a benefactor of the city (8.136.1).

Herodotos' account of this mission is so shrewd that even if one is not prepared to believe that he had good evidence for it, and largely made it up from his own imagination, it is difficult not to concede that he has almost certainly got the calculations and attitudes of the various parties exactly right. He begins by giving the reasons for Mardonios' wanting to win Athens to his side (8.136.2-3). He had heard that the Athenians were a numerous and powerful people, and that they had been principally responsible for the disasters the Persians had suffered at sea: 'if they came over to him, he had every hope that he would easily win control of the sea, as indeed was the case,

---

24 The MSS of Herodotos both at 8.135.1 and 8.135.2 describe Mys as 'a European' (i.e. from Europos - 'Εὐρωπέα'). This has been emended to 'Euromean' ('Εὐρωμέα' – i.e. from Euromos), since Mys evidently understood Karian (8.135.3), and there was a town of that name in Karia (Strabo 14.1.8; Stephanos of Byzantion *s.v.*). The only known towns called 'Europos', at this date, were in Macedonia (Thucydides 2.100.3), and, possibly, Syria (Stephanos of Byzantion *s.v.*); the one in Media (Strabo 11.13.6) was a later foundation by Seleukos Nikator. However, Pausanias (9.23.6) also says Mys was from Europos, and Stephanos of Byzantion (*s.v.*) says this was another name for Idrias in Karia. For the various suggestions as to the purpose of Mys' mission see Hignett,, 272; Burn, 499; Green, 221-2.

and as he thought that he was far superior on land, he calculated that the conquest of Greece would be assured.'

Turning, then, to Alexander's embassy, after a very typical excursus on the Macedonian's ancestry (8.137-9), Herodotos goes on to describe how he first passed on a message Mardonios claimed to have received from Xerxes. The king declared his willingness to forget all the injuries the Athenians had done him, ordered Mardonios to restore their territory, with the addition of any more they might claim, promised them autonomy, and offered to restore the shrines he had burned, if they came to terms. Mardonios himself, Alexander said, urged them to to prefer freedom in alliance with Persia to the uncertainties of a continued war which they could never hope to win, and the Macedonian added his own arguments, emphasising in particular how Athenian territory lay right in the path of any hostilities, like a kind of 'no man's land' (μεταίχμιον: 8.140β3).

How shrewdly Mardonios had calculated was demonstrated by the hasty despatch of Spartan envoys to Athens, as soon as news of Alexander's mission reached Sparta, and instead of brusquely rejecting the terms offered, the Athenians deliberately dragged things out so that the Spartan envoys could be present to hear their reply (8.141). But first they let the Spartans have their say, and if Herodotos' report is accurate, what they said probably did not go down too well with an Athenian audience. They began with a plea to the Athenians not to change their attitude to Greece by accepting the barbarians' terms – such conduct would not be just or decent for any Greeks, but least of all for the Athenians, who had begun the war. It had at first been a struggle for their territory, but now it involved the whole of Greece, and it would be intolerable if the Athenians, who had so often in the past helped to free others, should now be responsible for the slavery of Greece. But the only concrete help Herodotos says the Spartans offered was a promise to provide for Athenian women and other non-combatants for as long as the war lasted (8.142), though he claims the Athenians later affected to believe they had been promised that the enemy would be met in Boiotia (9.7).

The Athenians, Herodotos implies, had intended to reject the Persian terms in any case, and he puts their rejection in stirring terms (8.143) – Plutarch says the speech was delivered by Aristeides (*Aristeides* 10.6). But what he reports they said to the Spartans is more interesting (8.144). After more or less repeating their determination to resist to the last man, and in effect politely declining the offer of aid for their families, they end (8.144.4-5) by telling the Spartans to send their army out as soon as possible, since they guess that the moment Mardonios hears his terms have been rejected, he will invade their territory – 'the time to meet him was in Boiotia before he appeared in Attica'.

Even if Alexander did not know what the Spartans and Athenians had said to each other, he probably had a reasonably good idea. In any case, he would have been shrewd enough to guess that a serious split had developed between Persia's principal foes, with the Spartans, in effect, refusing to do anything to protect Attica and the Athenians demanding a stand in Boiotia. Mardonios' response to the rejection of his terms was obviously calculated to make the best of this situation. As soon as Alexander returned with the Athenian answer, he marched south as quickly as possible, levying troops from the medizing states as he went. The Thebans allegedly urged him to remain in Boiotia, and to try to split the Greek alliance by bribing its leading men (9.2), but he would have none of it, and pressed on into Attica. Herodotos attributes this to a 'terrible desire' to capture Athens a second time, partly out of arrogance, partly so that he could inform the King in Sardis, by means of a chain of fire-signals through the islands, that he held Athens (9.3.1). But this is part and parcel of the historian's consistent picture of Mardonios as a fire-brand (see below, 218–9). It is more likely that he intended, as Herodotos himself later says (9.4.2), to bring added pressure to bear on the Athenians, 'in the hope that they would give up their folly now that all the land of Attica had been taken by the spear and was under his control.'

Herodotos says he took Athens 'in the tenth month' (δεκάμηνος: 9.3.2) after its previous capture by Xerxes, which, reckoning inclusively in the normal Greek manner, and assuming Xerxes arrived early in September, 480, probably means in June, 479. He found the city again deserted and learned that most of the Athenians were on Salamis, though some were serving with the fleet. Thereupon he sent a Hellespontine Greek, named Mourychides, over to the island, presumably to offer the same terms. Mourychides is said (9.5.1) to have delivered the message to the Athenian *boulê* (council), and one of the councillors argued that it would be better to accept the proposal and lay it before the people – Herodotos says (9.5.2) either because he had been bribed by Mardonios, or because this really was his view. However, the infuriated Athenians, both members of the council and those outside, stoned the wretched councillor to death, and his wife and daughters suffered the same fate at the hands of the Athenian womenfolk, though Mourychides was allowed to depart unharmed.[25]

Herodotos says (9.6) that the Athenians had waited as long as possible before again evacuating their city, in the hope that the Peloponnesian army would come to their aid, but on hearing that the enemy was in Boiotia, had delayed no longer. At the same time, however, they sent envoys to reproach the Spartans for failing to come to their assistance and meet the enemy in Boiotia, reminding them of the offers the Persians had made, and warning them that if they did not act to help them, 'they themselves would find a way out.' The Athenian delegation, he subsequently tells us (9.7.1), was accompanied by envoys from Megara and Plataia.

In his life of Aristeides (10.10), Plutarch quotes an account of this embassy by the late fourth/early third century historian, Idomeneus of Lampsakos, which makes Aristeides himself the principal Athenian envoy. This Plutarch rejects, on the ground that 'in Aristeides' decree, he himself is not named as ambassador, but Kimon, Xanthippos and Myronides.' Plutarch was probably right to reject the testimony of Idomeneus, who does not seem to have been a very trustworthy source, but although it is usually assumed that the decree came from Krateros' collection,[26] this is by no means certain, and even if it did, it may not have been authentic. The names are suspiciously

---

25 Demosthenes also refers to this ugly episode (*On the Crown*, 202 & 204), but calls the victim 'Kyrsilos'. Cicero (*de Officiis* 3.11.48) evidently misunderstood Demosthenes and transferred the incident to 480 – cf. Verrall, *CR* 23 (1909), 36-40. Lykourgos (*Against Leokrates*, 122) cites a decree condemning the unfortunate councillor to death, but Habicht (*Hermes* 89, 1961, 21) argues that this is likely to have been a 4th century forgery. HW ii 288 argue that 'Kyrsilos' is the correct name, and that Herodotos substituted the ill-omened name 'Lykides' ('Wolfling'), but this is far-fetched. Barron, 596, points out that Mourychides was possibly an Athenian – cf. the archon of 440/39 and the proposer of a decree in honour of Sigeion (Meiggs, *JHS* 86, 1966, 95). But names were often shared by citizens of different cities.

26 E.g. Burn, 500 n.34 and 505-6 n.49.

obvious, all three being those of prominent Athenians, though unless the embassy is to be dated earlier than the mobilization of the fleet, the 'Xanthippos' mentioned cannot be the famous one, since he was in command of the Athenian naval contingent (8.131.3). It is possible that the 'Xanthippos' of the embassy was the archon of 479/8, who would not yet have entered office if the embassy went in June (see below),[27] but even this seems unlikely: archons, at this date, were usually comparatively young men, whereas ambassadors, as their Greek title – *presbeutai* – suggests, tended to be more elderly. The same objection holds for Kimon and Myronides. As for the suggestion that there were two embassies, one consisting of Kimon, Xanthippos and Myronides, the second, headed by Aristeides,[28] since Plutarch's evidence is, in any case, so unreliable, it seems best to adhere to Herodotos.

According to Herodotos (9.7.1), the envoys arrived while the Spartans were celebrating the Hyakynthia, which probably means in June,[29] thus confirming his statement about the time-lag between the two captures of Athens. Granted an audience with the ephors, the principal Spartan civic officials, they reminded them of the terms offered by the King, and of the Athenian response, reproached the Spartans for breaking their promise to meet Mardonios in Boiotia, and demanded, instead, that they send their army to the plain of Thria (9.7). The ephors responded by declaring that they would give an answer on the following day, but then kept putting it off. This went on for ten days, until at last, on the eve of the final audience, a certain Chileos of Tegea, hearing from the ephors what the Athenians had said, told them bluntly that if the Athenians made an alliance with the Persians, however strong the wall across the Isthmus, 'huge doors into the Peloponnese would be opened to the Persian' (9.9.2). Thereupon, without informing the ambassadors, the ephors sent off a force of 5000 Spartan hoplites, and next day, when the envoys delivered their ultimatum, bidding the Spartans stay and celebrate the Hyakinthia, and threatening to join the Persians, blandly informed them, on oath, that the army was already on the march and probably in Arcadia. Not surprisingly, the ambassadors were amazed, but having learned the whole story, set off in haste after the Spartan army, accompanied by 5000 hoplites of the *perioikoi*, the free, but non-Spartan inhabitants of Spartan territory (9.10-11).

This story is difficult to believe as it stands, and obviously owes something to the anti-Spartan bias of Herodotos' informants. But it may be true in its basic essentials. Herodotos himself expresses puzzlement at the apparent contradiction between the Spartans' evident anxiety lest Athens medize at the time of Alexander's mission, and what looked like their subsequent indifference (9.8.2). His own explanation was that when Alexander went to Athens, the wall across the Isthmus was not yet finished, but that once it was, the Spartans thought they no longer needed the Athenians. This will not do, however, because Sparta's anxiety lest Athens medize was surely mainly due to fear of the Athenian fleet's falling into enemy hands, in which case the wall was useless, complete or not. But Herodotos himself gives the true explanation when he has the Athenian envoys say that Spartan anxieties about Athenian medism were allayed when

---

27 Busolt, 371 n.5.

28 Green, 230-1, following a suggestion by Hignett, 284. Barron, 597-8, also accepts the suggestion.

29 Busolt, 722 n.2; HW ii 288 *ad loc.*; Hignett, 283-4.

they clearly ascertained the Athenian attitude (9.7β1). We may think they should have realised that the Athenian attitude might change if the Persians again invaded Attica, but the Athenians had, after all, promised to continue the fight 'so long as the sun moves along its present course' (8.143.2), and 'while one Athenian remains alive' (8.144.3), and the Spartans may have believed that nothing would shake their resolve.

We may also feel that the Spartans did not require a man from Tegea, in land-locked Arcadia, to remind them that the Isthmus lines could be turned by sea. But perhaps, if the Chileos story is not just an example of how Herodotos loves to introduce the 'wise counsellor' into his narrative, it did need an outsider to warn the Spartans how near the precipice they were treading.[30] If we can press Herodotos' narrative, it is worth noting that up to the time of Chileos' warning, though there may have been an implied threat in what the Athenian envoys had said (9.7), they had not yet delivered an explicit ultimatum – that was to come next morning (9.11). Thus the Spartans may still have been clinging to the belief the Athenians would not go back on their grandiloquent declarations, and it may have taken an outsider to jolt them out of their complacency. Chileos may also have acted as the representative of some of Sparta's more important allies, and not merely have served to bring the Spartans to their senses, but to assure them that the Peloponnesians would stand by them, if they did take the offensive.

There is certainly no difficulty about the speed with which the Spartans eventually took the field, nor the good security which cloaked their move. Even Herodotos seems to have forgotten that they had intended to defend the Isthmus all along, if it became necessary, and presumably they had mobilized their forces, and sent word to their allies, at least as soon as they heard of Mardonios' advance south. Mobilization was, in any case, much simpler for an ancient Greek state than for a modern one, and even more so for the Spartans who were more or less permanently on a war footing. This may be sufficient to explain how the final mustering and departure of the Spartan army itself escaped the notice of the envoys. If not, we have Herodotos' word for it that it left at night (9.10.1), and Thucydides' that Spartan military affairs were habitually shrouded in secrecy (5.68.2). Even the detail that the *perioikoi* took the field after the Spartans (9.11.3) looks authentic. It frequently happened in the fourth century (cf. Xenophon, *Hellenika* 3.5.7 and 5.1.33). As for the helots, these are really only a problem for those who believe that there were 35,000 of them.[31] If, as is much more likely (see below, 227–8), there was only one helot for every Spartan, they could have left as silently as their masters.

It may even be the case that the actual departure of the army had been decided upon for some time, and that Chileos' warning, if historical, did not so much affect the decision to march as the destination. But, if so, why the charade? Possibly the ephors, assuming that the Athenians still accepted that on land there was to be no more than a static defence of the Isthmus, had become annoyed by the delegates' constant demands

30 Grundy, 442; Burn, 504-5, suggests that Chileos may also have been able to reassure the Spartans of Tegea's attitude and that of the other Arcadians.

31 At Herodotos 9.10.1 many of the MSS omit the words referring to the seven helots accompanying each Spartan, though presumably Herodotos did believe that these helots left with the Spartans at this point, for he certainly mentions their presence at Plataia (9.28.2, 29.1).

to know when their army would march – they may have felt that it was nobody's business but their own. They may thus have taken a malicious delight in the evident discomfort of their tormentors, when their army finally made its exit without any foreigner's being the wiser.

But whatever the tensions of the last ten days, and whatever the reasons behind them, once the Spartans had resolved to march 'against the strangers' (9.11.2), there was no longer any hesitation. 5000 hoplites were probably not the full manpower of Sparta, judging by what Damaratos is alleged to have told Xerxes (7.234.2), but they probably amounted to five-eighths of the total number available, and were possibly the largest force of full Spartan citizens – *homoioi* – ever put into the field. With the 5000 *perioikoi* (9.11.3), who also counted as '*Lakedaimonians*', though not full citizens, they made up the largest contingent in the greatest hoplite army ever assembled. No wonder the Argives, who had undertaken to stop the Spartans from marching, contented themselves with sending a runner to Mardonios in Attica, with the stark message, 'Mardonios, the Argives sent me to tell you that the young men have left Lakedaimon, and that the Argives are not able to stop their going' (9.12.2).

CHAPTER 9

The Dorian Spear

When the Athenian ambassadors at Sparta appeared to deliver their final ultimatum, Herodotos says (9.11.2), the ephors told them that the Spartan army was already at Orestheion. This implies that it had not taken the route due north *via* Sellasia to Tegea, but instead the one up the Eurotas *via* Pellana and Belmina to where Megalopolis was later situated.[1] This was almost certainly not because the other route would have taken it too near Argos – there was little the Argives could have done to hinder it, despite their promises to Mardonios (cf. 9.12) – still less because of the alleged 'medism' of Karyiai.[2] The reason was possibly because this was the easiest route for an army accompanied by wagons, for Herodotos' story of how, later, the Greeks paraded the body of the dead Persian cavalry-commander on a wagon (9.25.1), suggests that they had them at Plataia.[3] The *perioikoi*, presumably, caught the Spartans up at Orestheion, and then the whole army marched to the Isthmus, no doubt being joined by some contingents on the way, and by others there. In command was Pausanias, son of Kleombrotos, regent for Leonidas' young son, Pleistarchos, and associated with him, Herodotos says (9.10.3), Euryanax, son of Dorieus, 'a man of the same house'.[4]

Even if Mardonios had not been informed of the Spartan army's departure by the Argives (9.12), there is no reason to doubt Herodotos' assertion that he knew about it before Pausanias reached the Isthmus (9.13.2). He immediately decided to withdraw from Attica, first destroying everything still left standing (9.13.1-2). His reasons, Herodotos says (9.13.3), were that Attica was not good cavalry country, and that if he were to be defeated, his only way of retreat would be through narrow passes which a few men could hold. Thus he decided to withdraw to Thebes, where he could fight near

---

1 See *HCT* v 91-3; *contra* HW ii 290-1 *ad loc*.

2 Despite Grundy, 444; Burn, 506; cf. Hignett, 285-6; Cartledge, *Sparta and Lakonia* (London, 1979), 208. Karyai is said to have medized by Vegetius (1.1.5), but though this is accepted by G.L.Huxley (*GRBS* 8, 1976, 29ff.), Cartledge (*op.cit*., 205, 216, 297) and by M.Vickers (*RA* 1985, 3ff.), it seems incredible that a perioecic town, only some 25 kilometres from Sparta, can have 'medized' in 480/79, when Argos, the one state which might have given it some measure of protection, was unable even to prevent Mykenai and Tiryns joining the patriotic cause (cf. 7.202 & 9.28.4).

3 In 418, similarly, Agis followed this route on his way to Mantineia (Thuc. 5.64.3); for his wagons see 5.72.3.

4 The obvious explanation is that Euryanax was Pausanias' cousin, the son of his father's oldest brother, Dorieus, who, on the accession of his half-brother, Kleomenes, had emigrated from Sparta and been killed in Sicily (5.39-48). But, if so, when Kleomenes died without male issue, Euryanax should have succeeded to the throne, instead of Leonidas, Dorieus' younger brother. Hence it has been suggested that the Dorieus who was the father of Euryanax was another member of the royal house of the Agiadai, not Anaxandridas' second son, or that Dorieus forfeited his right to the throne when he emigrated – cf. Beloch ii 1.53ff., ii 2.158f.; HW ii 290; Hignett, 286-7. But it seems unlikely that there were two royal princes of the same name at about the same time, and would Dorieus' emigration have affected the rights of his son? Another possibility is that Dorieus was held to be illegitimate – Herodotos says that this was suspected at the time of his birth (5.41).

a friendly city, in good cavalry country. Modern commentators have tended to accept Herodotos' comments,[5] but it may be questioned whether he was right. The plain of Eleusis, or the one between Athens and the coast, are just as suitable for cavalry as Boiotia, and although the passes out of Attica[6] may individually be capable of being held by relatively small forces, there are really too many of them for Mardonios to have been worried that his escape could be prevented. If anything, too, the exits from the plain of Thebes were more difficult in the fifth century, when the Kopais basin was still under water.

Herodotos, like his modern followers, appears to have based his views on Mardonios' strategy on the assumption that he wanted to fight a battle. Apart from the present passage, the historian consistently represents the Persian general as eager to fight (cf. 9.37.1 & 41.4), but it is difficult to see how he could have known this, and all Mardonios' actions, up to the very morning of the final confrontation, are arguably more consistent with a strategy of avoiding battle. Thus, during the winter, as we have seen, he had set himself to divide the Greek alliance by offering Athens terms, which may well have seemed overgenerous to the Greek states which had already sided with the Persians. Now that these diplomatic moves had ended in failure, Mardonios possibly set himself to achieve the break-up of the alliance by more subtle means.

He may have known, and in any case could probably have surmised, that the Spartans and their Peloponnesian allies had been very reluctant to advance beyond the Isthmus, and he may even have been aware, or guessed, that the Athenians had wanted a confrontation with him in the plain of Thria (cf. 9.7.2). Thus the withdrawal from Attica could have been the first step in a plan to weaken Spartan resolve by giving them the impression that they were being drawn further and further away from the Isthmus. That the Greeks wanted a battle is strongly suggested by the size of their army and by their continual willingness to advance. In any case, confrontation in a set-piece battle was their normal way of fighting wars, as Mardonios himself is alleged to have pointed out (7.9β.1), and one doubts whether anything else ever entered Pausanias' head. But it may be questioned, after Marathon and even Thermopylai, whether the Persians were all that willing to engage the Greeks in a hand-to-hand fight, despite Mardonios' alleged vaunting to Xerxes after Salamis (8.100.2-4). Although the withdrawal of one army and the advance of the other does not, of course, prove that the one wishes to avoid battle, and the other to engage, it is at least suggestive.

Apart from his supposedly 'hawkish' temperament and alleged assumption of superiority on land (cf. 8.100.2ff. 8.136.3), there was really no reason for Mardonios to seek a battle. The only one that seems even half-way convincing is that he thought the situation in Asia Minor would become increasingly dangerous once he knew about the disintegration of the Persian fleet, and the advance of the Greek across the Aegean.[7] But this is to assume, firstly, that Mardonios was aware of the naval situation, and, secondly, that he would have felt under compulsion to risk everything on direct confrontation, because of it. But neither assumption is necessarily valid. Sardis is over a thousand kilometres from Boiotia by land, and it is difficult to believe that Mardonios

---

5 Busolt, 274 n.3; Hauvette, 453; Wright, *The Campaign of Plataea* (New Haven, 1904), 51; Grundy, 444-5; Burn, 509-10; Green, 233; Barron, 597.

6 See Grundy, 445-8.

7 Best expressed, perhaps, by Hignett, 319-20.

was in regular contact. In any case, he is quite likely to have thought that the situation in Asia Minor was none of his business. His job was to bring about the subjugation of Greece, and he may well have felt that this could better be done by diplomacy, including bribery, than by force of arms.

The hypothesis that Mardonios was hoping to avoid direct confrontation with the Greek army is not belied by the one aggressive move he made before his withdrawal from Attica. Hearing that 1000 Spartans had reached the Megarid, Herodotos says (9.14), he swung his army round and led it towards Megara in the hope of cutting off this isolated force. In fact, as many commentators have pointed out,[8] it is unlikely that the whole Persian army carried out this operation, though there is no good reason to doubt what Herodotos says was the reason for it. Anything that might cause the Peloponnesians to hesitate to continue their advance would suit Mardonios' strategy of avoiding full-scale confrontation. Alternative suggestions – that the raid into the Megarid was a reconnaissance to discover what the Greeks were up to, a cavalry screen to cover the retreat of the main Persian army, or an attempt to stop the Greeks using the more easterly passes over Kithairon – are not convincing, still less the recent suggestion that the Greeks deliberately sent a small force ahead into the Megarid in the hope of tempting Mardonios to return.[9] In any case, whatever the reason for it, this raid was the furthest the Persians penetrated into Greece, though not literally the furthest west they got in Europe, as Herodotos says (*loc.cit.*).[10]

The Persian force sent to the Megarid may have withdrawn northwards over the Gyphtokastro pass into Boiotia,[11] but the main Persian army took the easternmost route out of Attica, by way of Dekeleia (Tatoi), Sphendaleai (Aulon) and Tanagra, to the vicinity of Skolos in the territory of Thebes (9.15.1). Here they began the construction of a stockade which had sides ten stades (c2000m) long, though the whole position 'beginning from Erythrai, stretched past Hysiai to the territory of Plataia' (9.15.3).

The mention of these three places would most naturally mean that the position was south of the Asopos, where all three were certainly situated, wherever their precise location (see below). However, Skolos was probably north of the river, and at a later stage in the campaign, the Persians were certainly north of it (cf. 9.36). They could, of course, have moved there from an original position south of the river, but the stockade, which Herodotos implies formed part of the position, was also certainly north of the river, since otherwise it would have prevented the Greek advance to it. Thus Herodotos probably just mentioned Erythrai, Hysiai and Plataia to indicate the extent of the Persian

8 Grundy, 448-9; HW ii 291 *ad loc.*; Macan (1908) i 2 615f.; Hignett, 291-2; Burn, 510.

9 Grundy, 448-9, suggests it was a reconnaissance; Macan, *loc.cit.*, and HW ii 291, that it was a cavalry-screen; Munro, 1904, 151f., that it was an attempt to stop the Greeks using the passes; Barron, 598, that the idea was to lure the Greeks into battle.

10 Hammond, 1988, 582, argues that the burning of the temple of Poseidon at Isthmia, for which there is archaeological evidence (Broneer, *Isthmia* I, New Jersey, 1971, 3ff.), was due to the Persians, and that Herodotos 9.14 implies that another Persian force had reached a different limit, but this is far-fetched. As for the rocks peppered by Persian arrows pointed out near Pagai (Pausanias 1.44.4), to which Hammond also draws attention, this is surely of a piece with the marks of Artaphernes' tent-poles in the rocks at Marathon (Pausanias 1.32.6).

11 Macan, *loc.cit.* n.8 above; Hignett, 292.

position, since there were no such places north of the Asopos where that position actually was.[12]

It is at this point in his narrative (9.15.4ff.) that Herodotos tells the story of the banquet given in Thebes by Attaginos, son of Phrynon, for Mardonios, fifty of the most notable Persians and fifty Thebans, claiming to have heard the story from Thersander of Orchomenos, who was also present (9.16.1). At the banquet each Persian was placed beside a Greek, and during it the Persian reclining beside Thersander told him, with tears running down his face, that of all the Persians he could see and those they had left beside the river, in a short while only few would be left alive. Obviously one is bound to be suspicious of such stories, but there is no real reason why a Persian noble, in his cups, could not have said some such thing, and even if Thersander's story grew in the telling, it is quite another thing to accuse Herodotos of inventing his informant in order to lend credence to the story.[13]

Another story Herodotos tells at this point concerns the Phokians. According to him (9.17-18), the Phokians had by now embraced the Persian cause, though under compulsion, and had sent 1000 hoplites to join Mardonios' army. On their arrival, Mardonios ordered them to take up a position in the plain, by themselves, and then sent his entire cavalry, ostensibly to attack them. The Phokians closed ranks and prepared to sell their lives as dearly as possible, but after a few missiles had been sent their way, the cavalry retired. Herodotos states (9.18.2) he could not say whether the cavalry had really been asked by the Thessalians to destroy their hated enemies, and left off when they realised they were liable to suffer losses themselves, or whether Mardonios wanted to test Phokian courage. One modern suggestion[14] is that Mardonios deliberately set out to make a show of intimidating the Phokians because he distrusted his Greek troops, but, if so, the demonstration appears to have backfired. If the story is true, he may rather have wanted to see how Greek troops would react to a cavalry attack.

Meanwhile, the Greek army had moved from the Isthmus to Eleusis, where it was joined by the Athenian hoplites, who had been ferried across from Salamis, under the command of Aristeides. Plutarch (*Aristeides* 11.1) says that Aristeides has been elected 'general with full powers' (στρατηγὸς αὐτοκράτωρ), but this looks like an anachronism. Later (*op.cit.* 20.1) he mentions Myronides and Leokrates as also present as generals, but although there is no particular reason why this should not be true, there was always a tendency, in later tradition, to associate famous men with famous events. It was possibly at Eleusis, in connection with the sacrifices Herodotos records (9.19.2), that the Greeks took the so-called 'Oath of Plataia',[15] though its terms as preserved on a

---

12 See Grote, *A History of Greece* (London, 1862), iii 496; Hauvette, 456; Macan (1908) i 2 619; HW ii 292-3; Burn, 511. Hignett, 296, is more cautious. For the location of Skolos, Erythrai, Hysiai and Plataia see now J.M.Fossey, *Topography and Population of Ancient Boiotia* (Chicago, 1988), 101-126.

13 Cf. Fehling, 117. (In the English translation, 'Thrasybulus of Orchomemos' is clearly a mistake for 'Thersander').

14 Barron, 598-9.

15 For the oath see Lykourgos, *Against Leokrates*, 81; Diodoros 11.29.3; Tod, *GHI* ii no.204; accepted by, e.g., Burn, 512-5; Green, 239-41; rejected by Hignett, 460-1; cf. also F.W.Walbank, *A Historical Commentary on Polybius ii* (Oxford, 1967), 181, and W.K.Pritchett, *GSW* iv, 116-7. Barron, 604, suggests that it was connected with the alleged plot amongst Athenian aristocrats, recorded by Plutarch (*Aristeides* 13), but, as he says, 'what

fourth century inscription from Acharnai do not carry conviction, and since it is not mentioned by Herodotos, its authenticity is very doubtful.

From Eleusis the combined army moved to Erythrai and took up a position along the foothills of Kithairon (9.19). Since Herodotos does not tell us anything about the route followed, it is impossible to determine which pass the Greeks used, and unfortunately, it is still not even certain where the ancient Erythrai lay, despite the confidence which led the modern village of Kriekouki to be given the ancient name. Ancient Erythrai was probably some distance to the east, perhaps just west of the modern village of Dharimari (or Dhaphni, as it is now called).[16] Thus Pausanias could either have used the Phyle-Thebes route and deployed westwards along the foot of Kithairon, or the Gyphtokastro pass and deployed eastwards. In either case the first Greek position probably lay east of Kriekouki.

According to Herodotos (9.20), when Mardonios saw that the Greeks were not going to move further down into the plain, he sent his whole cavalry force, under Masistios, to attack them. This implies that he waited for some time before launching the attack, and, if this is true, the attack had nothing to do with the modern principle that the best way to defend a mountain chain is not to hold the passes, but to attack the enemy when he debouches from them.[17] Mardonios, in any case, is unlikely to have known anything about such principles, and other modern attempts to explain his motives are not much better. He surely knew, for example, that his cavalry probably had little chance of doing serious damage to Greek hoplites in such a position, and would not have wanted to damage one of his own most valuable assets just to prove a point. This also weighs against the idea that he assumed his cavalry would be defeated, but hoped thereby to give the Greeks the confidence to move down into the plain.

These theories again depend on the assumption that Mardonios wanted a battle. If he did not, then it is natural to suppose that he launched his attack to give the Greeks such an experience of what his massed cavalry could do, even under adverse circumstances, that they would withdraw. This would probably have been as good as a victory. Greek confidence would have been shattered, and it is doubtful whether the Peloponnesians, in particular, could ever again have have been prevailed upon to cross the Isthmus. Thus the Megarians and Athenians would have been once more isolated, and open to renewed suggestions about changing sides. If Mardonios had wanted a battle on suitable ground, he would surely not merely have avoided attacking the Greeks under such unfavourable conditions, but have withdrawn from the Asopos. The river

---

is remarkable and abnormal, is that Pausanias thought it necessary to bind his army in this way'. I would regard the mixing up of Athenian and Spartan military terms in the version of the oath on the inscription from Acharnai, which Burn regards as evidence of authenticity, as precisely the opposite.

16 See now, Fossey, *op.cit.* n.12 above, 116-9.

17 As suggested by Delbrück, 93; accepted by Munro, 1904, 157, and Macan (1908) i 2.630. Hignett, 299, toys with the notion that Mardonios wanted to test his cavalry. Green, 245, begins by suggesting this, only to declare, a few lines later, that Mardonios 'knew perfectly well that the chances of a cavalry charge succeeding under such conditions were minimal'; he then suggests that Mardonios hoped to lure the Greeks into the plain. The schemes of Munro, 1904, 156f., and Grundy, 461, are too elaborate to be true.

can never have been much of a barrier, in summer,[18] but the ground beyond it to the north would have been, if anything, even more suitable for an army strong in cavalry and missile-armed troops.

As it was, according to Herodotos (9.20-24), the cavalry attack inflicted some losses on the Greeks, and in particular on the Megarians who were in the most vulnerable position. The latter appealed for help, threatening to abandon their position, and their call was answered by the Athenians, who sent 300 picked men under Olympiodoros,[19] and their archers, to take over the position. After some time, luckily for the Greeks, the Persian commander's horse, hit in the flank by an arrow, reared and threw its master, and he was killed by a thrust through the eye after his enemies had in vain tried to pierce his golden armour – Plutarch (*Aristeides* 14.5) says with the spiked butt of a javelin. After failing to recover the body, the cavalry then returned to camp.

Although there is nothing basically wrong with this story, and some of the details look authentic, one is bound to be suspicious of anything which seems to single the Athenians out like this. It has been suggested that Herodotos got the story from the family of Olympiodoros himself, and, if so, too much should not be made of it, particularly the description of the men as 'picked' (λογάδες).[20] But the suggestion that the Athenians responded because they were next in line to the Megarians is only based on Herodotos' description of the Greek army as it was deployed in its next position (9.28.6), and even there the Plataians are said to have come in between. More likely, if the story is true, the Athenians responded because they alone had a proper force of archers (cf. 9.22.1 & 60.3).

More interesting is what Herodotos tells us about the tactics of the Persian cavalry.[21] He thrice says they attacked 'by squadrons' (κατὰ τέλεα: 9.20, 22.1 & 23.1), until they learned of their commander's death, whereupon they charged *en masse* (9.22.3), and the Athenians, 'seeing them no longer charging by squadrons, but all together' (9.23.1), called for help. The technique seems to have been for squadron after squadron to charge to within missile-range, fire its arrows or hurl its javelins, and then wheel away. Thus, Masistios' fall at first passed unnoticed, 'because they were in the course of withdrawing and wheeling round' (ἀναχωρήσιός τε γινομένης καὶ ὑποστροφῆς:

---

18 Fossey, *op.cit.* n.12 above, 124, n.96, says 'Anyone who does not consider the Asopos a real potential obstacle should remember the words of Thoukydides (ii, 5, 2) – ὁ γὰρ 'Ασωπὸς ποταμὸς ἐρρύη μέγας καὶ οὐ ῥαδίως διαβατὸς ἦν.' But Thucydides is talking about an incident in March, 431, and specifically mentions a recent heavy fall of rain.

19 Diodoros, who inevitably has the attack take place at night (11.30.2), says that the 300 were Aristeides' body-guard, but since we never hear elsewhere of Athenian *stratêgoi* having bodyguards, this is probably confusion with the 300 Spartan *Hippeis*. If Olympiodoros was a *lochagos* – he is described as such by Plutarch (*Aristeides* 14.3), and Herodotos uses the word 'ἐλοχήγεε' of him – he may have commanded half one of the ten *taxeis* into which the Athenian army was probably divided.

20 As Burn, 517, and Green, 246, do. Busolt, 727 n.2, suggests the story came from Olympiodoros' family.

21 G.Shrimpton, *Phoenix* 34 (1980), 32-4, gives an interesting account of Persian cavalry tactics, but if they always attacked 'from left to right in a clock-wise rotating motion across the enemy's front', they would have to have done it in a series of such motions, since otherwise only the right of an enemy line of any length would suffer. Here – 9.21 – it is the Megarians who suffer most, and they are presumably not on the Greek right, while at 9.49.2-3 it is the whole Greek army that suffers.

9.22.3). Clearly the cavalry were not regarded as 'shock-troops', intended to ride the enemy down in one great charge. Rather, the idea was to whittle away enemy resistance and morale by repeated attacks, until they broke and fled.

Although it had probably not been Mardonios' intention, the defeat of his cavalry and the sight of Masistios' dead body borne on a wagon down the ranks, certainly did encourage the Greeks, Herodotos says (9.25.2), to shift their position to Plataian territory, where, in particular, there were better water-supplies (9.25.2).[22] He implies that the move involved moving *down* (cf. ἐπικαταβῆναι: *loc.cit.*), and describes the new position as 'near the Gargaphian spring and the *temenos* of the hero Androkrates, along hills of no great height and level ground' (9.25.3).

Unfortunately, neither the Gargaphian spring nor the *temenos* of Androkrates can be certainly located. The spring is clearly either the one now called Alepotrypi, about 500 metres south-west of the chapel of Ayios Ioannis, or, more probably, the one called Retsi, about a kilometre south-east of the chapel. (see Pl. 21).[23] The *temenos* of Androkrates is also mentioned by Thucydides in his splendid account of the break-out of part of the Plataian garrison during the Peloponnesian War. He appears to locate it on the right of the road from Plataia to Thebes, and not more than 1400 metres from the former (3.24.1-2). The problem is that neither the spring nor the *temenos* seems to have been anywhere near the Asopos, which is where Herodotos repeatedly implies the Greek position to have been (cf. 9.31.1, 36, 40, 49.3). However, as with the Persian position (above, 219–20), it is possible that there were no landmarks nearer the river which could have been used to fix the Greek position, and, in any case, nearly 40,000 hoplites and their soldier-servants would have occupied a large area when encamped. Herodotos later implies that both the Spartans on the Greek right and the Athenians on the left occupied relatively high ground (9.56.2), and it is likely that the former were on what modern scholars have termed the Asopos ridge, and the latter on what is now called Pyrgos hill (see Pl. 22). The centre contingents would then have occupied the low ground astride the Plataia-Thebes road, and the whole position may have stretched

22 I agree with Hignett that we can ignore Plutarch's story of the oracle obtained by Aristeides and interpreted by Arimnestos of Plataia as foretelling victory in Plataian territory, despite its acceptance by scholars like Burn, 515-6; Green, 243-4; and Barron, 601, the latter relying on the explanation of the oracle by H.W.Parke & D.E.W.Wormell, *The Delphic Oracle* (Oxford, 1956), i 174ff. In general, Plutarch's account of the Plataia campaign is so muddled as to be practically worthless: see Hignett, Appendix X, 418-21.

23 Cf. Leake, *Travels in Northern Greece*, ii 332f.; Grundy, n. on 465-6; Munro, 1904, 159; Kirsten, *RE* xx 2, 1950, 2270; Pritchett, *AJA* 61 (1957), 21 n.78; Burn, 522.

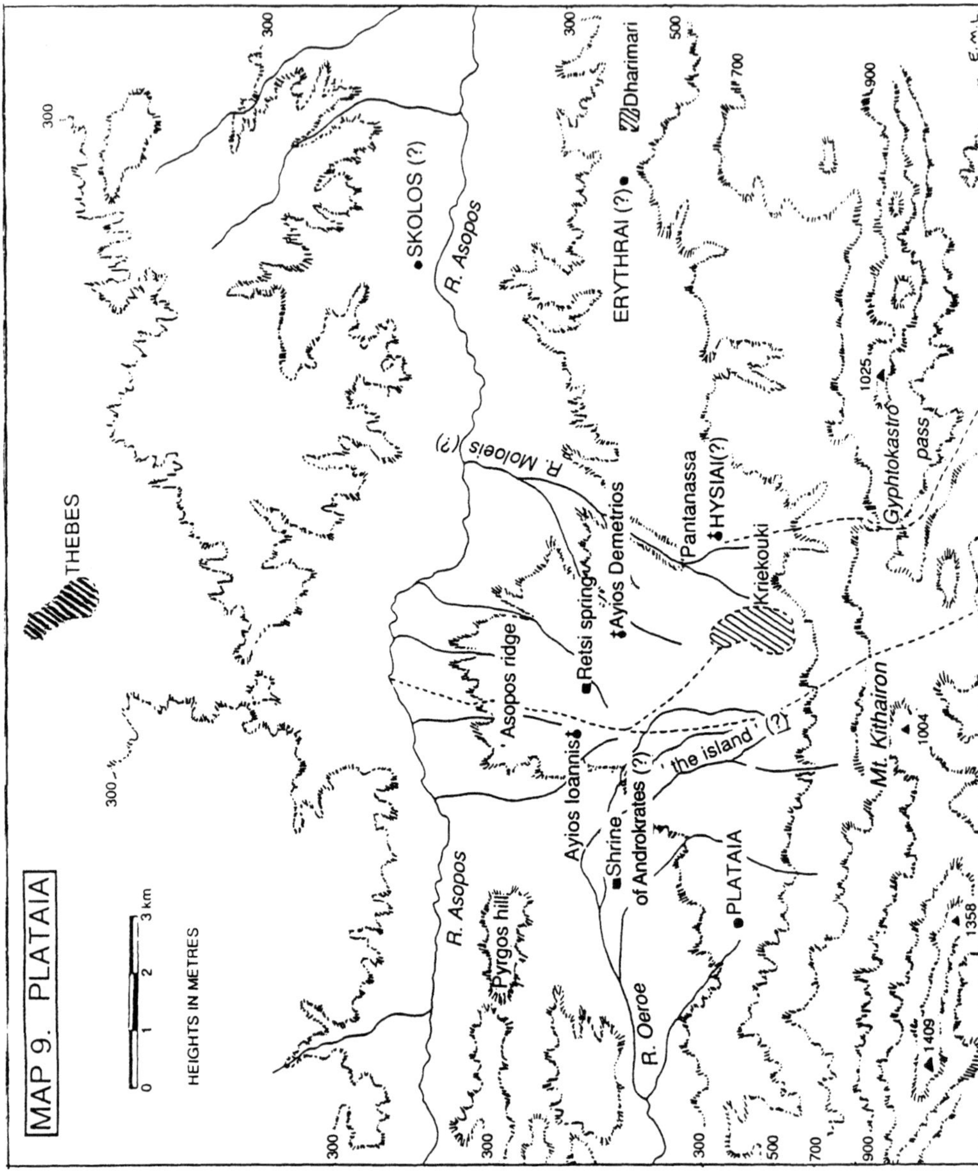

Map 9: Plataia.

Pl. 21: Plataia – the Retsi spring (Gargaphia?) – note how easy it would have been to choke it up. (Photo: N. Fields).

Pl. 22: Plataia – panorama showing the second Greek position from near Plataia, 'Pyrgos hill' on the left, 'Asopos ridge' on the right. (Photo: N. Fields).

back to the *temenos* of Androkrates on the left, and the Gargaphian spring on the right.[24]

Having described the new Greek position, Herodotos launches into a digression about the dispute between the Tegeates and the Athenians on the question which were to occupy the left wing (9.26-28.1) – won by the Athenians – and then (9.28.2ff.) gives a muster-list of the Greek army.

There is no compelling reason to doubt his figures,[25] and if there really were 38,700 hoplites, this was by far the largest number of such troops ever assembled in one place. Such a force was extremely formidable in a set-piece battle, and it would have required generalship of a high order to defeat it. Mere odds, even if the Persian army was two or three times as large (see below, 228), were not enough. This Mardonios may well have realised, since he appears to have avoided battle, at least until the moment when he thought his enemy was hopelessly divided.

Herodotos also thought that the Greeks had 69,500 light troops, made up of 35,000 helots and 34,500 others (9.29). He arrives at these totals by calculating seven helots for each of the 5000 Spartans, and one soldier-servant for each of the other hoplites, though actually, the latter should only have produced a total of 33,700; it has been suggested that the extra 800 were the Athenian archers.[26] These last were useful soldiers, as the fight with Masistios' cavalry showed, and when the Spartans found themselves isolated on the final day, they asked the Athenians at least to send their archers, even if they could not come themselves (9.60.3).

The helots are also all said to have been armed for war (9.29.2), but it seems very doubtful that there really were 35,000 of them. It is true that Thucydides twice appears to talk about a mass mobilization of helots later in the fifth century (5.57.1 & 5.64.2), but that was for campaigns in the Peloponnese, whereas the logistical problem of transporting so many to Boiotia would surely have been prohibitive.[27] It has been suggested that as many as possible were taken because the Spartans were afraid to leave them behind when so many Spartans were taking the field,[28] but one would have thought that it was even more dangerous to gather so many together and then arm them.

---

24 For the topography see Burn, 519-22, and Hignett, 301-11. The latter is rightly critical of the over-elaborate scheme of Grundy, 466ff. & 473f., and there is no need to resort to Ufer's hypothesis (*AS* iv, 127ff.) that Gargaphia should be identified with one of the springs on the north slope of the Asopos ridge. The name 'Apotripi' used by some modern scholars (e.g. Hignett, 302, 304, 428 and map p.290), for one of the springs which might be Gargaphia, is almost certainly a corruption of 'Alepotrypi' (Burn, 522 n.26). Munro, 1904, 159ff., is probably right to put the Athenians on Pyrgos hill, but it is invalid to calculate this on the basis of the probable length of the whole Greek army, for it was never actually drawn up for battle in this position – see N.Whatley, *JHS* 84 (1964), 124, on this kind of problem. Hignett (418-21, cf.430-1) is rightly sceptical about the topographical information about Plataia contained in Plutarch's life of Aristeides.

25 Cf. Hignett, Appendix XII, 435-8. There is still less reason to doubt the story of the dispute between the Tegeates and Athenians.

26 Meyer, 360 and n., 408 and n.

27 Macan's suggestion (1908, i 2 650) that those not in direct attendance upon the Spartans formed an army service corps, may be part of the answer, but a 'service corps' 30,000 strong seems far fetched.

28 Hignett, 280 & 437; Green, 231.

All in all, there really is no place for so large a number of light-armed troops in the complex manoeuvres that took place at Plataia, and the suggestion that the helots were mostly left to guard Kithairon is pure guesswork.[29] Thus it seems more likely that each Spartan was just accompanied by a single helot, as Herodotos implies was the case at Thermopylai (see 7.229.1). There may have been others engaged in commissariat duties (see below, 233), but surely not as many as 30,000. Herodotos does not specifically say that the other soldier-servants were armed, but although they probably were, their military value, as well as that of the helots, was probably negligible, though Herodotos believed that some of the helots, at least, were killed in the battle (9.85.2).

As for Mardonios' army, Herodotos says the Asiatic troops numbered 300,000 foot, and guesses there were 50,000 Greek foot-soldiers in addition (9.32.2) – he gives no numbers for cavalry. These figures are obviously too high, but it is impossible to arrive at lower totals without resorting to the kind of methods discussed above (see 90–1), in connection with the numbers of Xerxes' forces as a whole. A very rough estimate may be provided by the size of the stockade. If it was a square with sides ten stades (c2000m) long, as Herodotos says (9.15.3), comparison with Roman camps suggests it could have held 60-70,000 men, including 10,000 cavalry.[30] Despite Herodotos' guess, one would doubt whether there were more than 20,000 Greek troops, including cavalry, at the outside, of whom about half would probably have been provided by the Boiotians.

When the Greeks took up their new position nearer the Asopos, Mardonios moved his army up the other bank to cover them (9.31.1), but there then followed a period of inaction, due, Herodotos says (9.3-38), to omens which warned both sides not to cross the river. Here it is, perhaps, natural for us to rationalize this into a cynical manipulation of superstition by the two generals,[31] but we must be careful. The Spartans, in particular, quite clearly continued to take such religious observances extremely seriously right down to Herodotos' time and beyond, and it would be very odd if a cosmopolitan like Herodotos evidently believed such practices were genuine, whereas a Spartan of an earlier generation manipulated them. What we are dealing with here is more a case of 'seeing what you want to see': with both generals reluctant to fight, both they and their seers would, perhaps unconsciously, believe the omens they saw were unfavourable to fighting.

Whatever the reason, it is fairly clear that neither side was eager to fight at this point, and this is odd, if, as most scholars appear to believe, both sides ultimately wanted to fight[32] – Herodotos actually describes Mardonios here as 'eager to begin the battle' (9.37.1). The answer in Mardonios' case is possibly quite simple: despite what Herodotos says here and elsewhere (cf. 9.13.3, 41.4), the Persian commander actually

29 Burn (521), Green (244) and Barron (604) all argue that the presence of such Greek forces – Green, inevitably adds 'stiffened by brigades of more reliable troops' – explains why the Persians never attempted to cut the Greek communications in the mountains, as they did on the plain. But the explanation is, surely, that Kithairon really did not lend itself to cavalry operations.

30 Burn, 511. On the same basis, however, Peter Connolly (*Greece and Rome at War*, London, 1981, 29) suggests a total of 120,000, apparently for the whole army, including cavalry.

31 Cf., e.g., Grundy, 474; Hignett, 313ff. Green, 252, is rightly more circumspect. See now M.H.Jameson, 'Sacrifice before Battle', in *Hoplites: the classical Greek battle experience* (ed. V.D.Hanson, London & New York, 1991), 197ff.

32 Cf., esp., Woodhouse, *JHS* 18 (1898), 41f.

did not want a battle, and was prepared to play a waiting game, in the hope that the Greeks would start to melt away. In Pausanias' case, however, the answer cannot be so simple, since his intention was presumably to fight. Perhaps his hesitation was due to nothing more than a reluctance to risk everything on an attack, now that he was, at last, face to face with the enemy – such a delay is not unknown in other ancient battles (for example, Marathon and the Nemea). Perhaps, he was waiting for the last of his expected troops to arrive, for Herodotos appears to have believed that they were continuing to come in all the time (9.38.2), and, indeed, that some did not arrive until the battle was over (9.77).

If Plutarch's story of treachery in the Athenian camp (*Aristeides* 13) is true, it presumably refers to this period of inactivity, though his account of the campaign is a muddle. Here he puts the plot *after* the dispute between the Athenians and Tegeates, but *before* Masistios' cavalry attack, whereas Herodotos has these episodes the other way round. In any case, though accepted by some scholars,[33] the story is really quite incredible. It was one thing for a member of the Athenian council to suggest that Mardonios' terms should be laid before the people, when the Persians were occupying Athens and the Peloponnesians apparently content to let them do so, but quite another thing for Athenian aristocrats, however disgruntled, to engage in plotting when the battle lines were drawn: what could they possibly hope to achieve? It was different the previous autumn, when the Peloponnesians had shown a tendency to abandon Athenian territory without a fight, and in the spring when they had appeared so reluctant to cross the Isthmus. But now the greatest Greek army yet assembled was prepared to fight where the Athenians had long wanted it to fight, in Boiotia.

At all events, after eight days had passed (cf. 9.39.1), Herodotos says Timagenidas of Thebes advised Mardonios to guard the exits from Kithairon in the hope of cutting off the continuous flow of Greek reinforcements (9.38.2). In response, the Persian general sent the whole of his cavalry to 'the exits of Kithairon leading to Plataia, which the Boiotians call the "Three-heads" and the Athenians "Oak's heads"': this was probably what is now known as the Gyphtokastro pass.[34] Here the Persian cavalry caught a wagon-train coming out into the plain and fell upon it, sparing neither man nor beast, until, presumably, some more intelligent officer stopped the slaughter and had the remaining wagons driven to the Persian camp (9.39.2).

Despite this Persian success, however, the inactivity continued for two more days, although Herodotos implies that the Persian cavalry, with the Thebans showing the way, became increasingly bold in harassing the Greeks along the Asopos (9.40). Consistently with his belief that Mardonios was eager for battle, Herodotos represents him as chaffing at the delay (9.41.1), and rejecting outright Artabazos' proposal, supported by the Thebans, that they should fall back on Thebes, and resort to bribery (9.41.2-4). Instead, he declared, they should let the sacrifices go hang and join battle 'in the Persian way' (νόμῳ τῷ Περσέων: 9.41.4).

---

33 E.g. Busolt, 729; Burn, 525-7; Green, 252-4; Barron, 603; dismissed by Hauvette, 148 and 465; Wright, *op.cit.* n.5 above, 107; HW ii 306; and Hignett, 320-1.

34 Cf. Hignett, 422-4.

The problem with this kind of passage in Herodotos is that it is very difficult to imagine how he can have had good evidence for what was actually discussed even at the Greek conferences, let alone the Persian. It seems very unlikely that he could ever have talked to someone who had taken part, and he never claims to have done so. Thus his information, even if it came from Persian sources, would have been at best second-hand. More likely his accounts are a combination of Greek tradition and his own imagination. They are always worth examination, since at least they represent what an intelligent and knowledgeable Greek, far closer to the events than we are, believed to be the truth. Often, as we have seen, they are very likely to approximate closely to the truth. But they should not be treated as though they represented minutes taken at the meetings.

In this case, one of the reasons Artabazos allegedly gave for moving to Thebes, namely that there was an abundance of supplies there, appears to be contradicted four chapters later (9.45.2) by Alexander of Macedonia's statement that the Persians only had supplies for a few more days. There is, perhaps, no formal contradiction, since Alexander could have meant that there were only a few days' supply in the camp itself. But Thebes was less than ten kilometres away,[35] and if there were supplies there, there should have been no problem.

It is not at all impossible, however, that there were divided opinions in the Persian high command, and that the Thebans also had views. If so, and if it is right that Mardonios' strategy all along was to pressurize the Greeks into retreat, but to avoid a direct confrontation, he would certainly not have wanted to withdraw to Thebes. But this does not mean that he had now decided to fight, and Herodotos' statement that he had is belied by his own account of what happened the next day. The historian consistently represents Mardonios as a 'hawk' from the outset of the invasion (cf. 7.5ff.), and various other Persians as the counterbalancing 'doves' – Artabanos in an earlier episode (*loc.cit*), Artabazos here. But if this is the product of anything more than the historian's imagination, it may only go back to Persian attempts to explain away their defeat, for Mardonios would no longer have been there to speak for himself.

Herodotos' account of the Persian conference is followed by even more dubious episodes (9.42-3). First, Mardonios, having asked the Greek commanders in his army whether they knew of any prophecies which foretold the destruction of the Persians in Greece, and got no response, declares that he knows of one which foretold their utter destruction if they plundered the temple at Delphi: knowing this, they would not do so and would thus defeat the Greeks. Herodotos believed that the prophecy in question referred to a quite different invasion, but it is odd that he does not mention here the abortive Persian raid on Delphi he earlier records (8.35-9), though, strictly speaking, since he believed it had failed, it would not have affected the prophecy in any case.[36]

After Mardonios' enquiry about the prophecies, Herodotos says (9.44.1), night fell, and when 'quiet seemed to reign in the armies and the men to be deepest in sleep,' Alexander of Macedonia rode over to the Athenian outposts and demanded speech with their commanders. On their arrival, he told them, interlarded with patriotic declarations, that Mardonios had decided to ignore the omens and join battle next day: if he still

---

35 Cf. Hignett, 318f.

36 HW ii 306-7 say 'Mardonius' knowledge of this oracle seems inconsistent with the expedition to Delphi in the previous year,' but there is no formal inconsistency in Herodotos' narrative.

postponed confrontation, Alexander advised, they should hang on where they were, because the Persians only had a few days' supplies left (9.45).

We have already noticed the apparent discrepancy between this and Artabazos' claim that there were abundant supplies in Thebes, and the message as a whole is very odd. It looks as though Herodotos had picked up a tradition that Alexander had warned the Greeks of an impending attack, but because he believed that no such attack had in fact taken place, had to improvise the advice to hang on if no attack materialized. The whole idea of kings of Macedonia riding about the Plataian landscape in the darkness is ludicrous, and notions that he was engaged in some kind of deception plan on Mardonios' behalf even worse.[37] The episode smacks of later attempts to exonerate the king of Macedonia from charges that he had collaborated.

According to Herodotos (9.46.1), Alexander's information was relayed to Pausanias by the Athenian generals, and he, 'in fear of the Persians,' suggested that the Athenian and Spartan contingents should change places to meet the expected attack at dawn. Even Plutarch (*Moralia* 872b) regarded this story as ridiculous, and it may simply be untrue.[38] It is possible that Pausanias genuinely felt that the Athenians, after their experiences at Marathon, were the best troops to deal with the Persians,[39] but it seems unlikely that any Spartan would want to give the impression that he and his men could not deal with any situation. Pausanias' reported reasons for suggesting the exchange, moreover – that the Athenians had had experience of the Persians and the Spartans had not, whereas the latter had had experience of the Boiotians and Thessalians – are difficult to accept as they stand. It is true that the Spartans had never fought and beaten Persians as the Athenians had, but, as far as is known, they had also never fought Boiotians, and their one experience of fighting Thessalians, when they had faced the cavalry of Hippias' Thessalian allies, had not been a happy one (5.63.2ff.). The Athenians, on the other hand, *had* fought and decisively beaten Boiotians (5.77), and at least knew something about Thessalian cavalry. Thus, on the whole, the story of the proposed exchange looks like an Athenian *canard*.

---

37 Cf. Woodhouse, *op.cit.* n.32 above, 43; Ph.-E.Legrand, *Hérodote, Histoires* (Paris, 1951), ix 42 n.2; HW ii 307-8 *ad loc.*; Hignett, 316-7. Grundy, 476-7, appears to accept the story, as does Barron, 605, who says that Alexander's mission was 'almost certainly' with Mardonios' knowledge. This is also the view of Green, 258-60. But it really does not make sense to have Mardonios warn the Greeks of an impending attack, if what he wanted was for them to stay, even if his emissary advised them to do so if the attack did not materialize. Barron, *loc.cit.*, finds it even harder to understand why Mardonios did not interpose his whole army between the Greeks and the hills, but the answer is simple – he wanted to give them free passage back to the hills.

38 Cf. Boucher, *RA* 1915, 294; Hauvette, 469; Hignett, 317; Woodhouse, *op.cit.*, 47.

39 Shrimpton, *op.cit.* n.21 above, 28-9, makes out perhaps the best case for believing the story more or less as it stands, but puts too much emphasis on Pausanias' fear of Persian *cavalry*. In n.29 on 32 he states that the the Persian cavalry 'comes in its entirety against the Greek right on the day of the final battle', but the reference to '9.47.3' is wrong: if '9.49.3' is meant, this refers to the day *before* the final battle, and Herodotos in fact says in 9.49.2 that the Persian cavalry attacked 'the whole Greek army' (πᾶσαν τὴν στρατιὴν τὴν Ἑλληνικήν); if 9.57.3 is meant, the 'the whole cavalry force of the barbarians' (ἡ ἵππος ἡ τῶν βαρβάρων ... πᾶσα) presumably attacked the Spartans because they alone were in sight (cf. 9.59.1).

The alternative is that Herodotos misunderstood some manoeuvre, but it is difficult to see what this could have been. Some suggest that it had actually occurred earlier, when the Greeks moved up to the Asopos,[40] but this does too much violence to Herodotos' narrative. Another suggestion is that the story arose from the sending of Athenian archers to help the Spartans,[41] but it seems unlikely that the transfer of so small a force could have given rise to the story. The hypotheses that keep closest to Herodotos are either that Pausanias hoped to surprise Mardonios by defeating his Greek allies on his left and then rolling up his line, or that he hoped to mislead him into thinking that Spartan morale had cracked.[42] But, if so, Pausanias was a general far in advance of his time.

In any case, Mardonios is supposed to have realised what was happening, and switched his Persian troops to his right, whereupon everyone reverted to their original positions (9.47), so the manoeuvre, whatever it was, and if it ever took place, was a failure. Mardonios is then alleged to have used the whole episode to taunt the Spartans, and to have ended by challenging them to fight an equal number of Persians, to decide the issue on behalf of all. This is not entirely unbelievable, in view of previous episodes in Spartan history, such as the so-called 'Battle of the Champions' against the Argives (5.82.3ff.). But if such a challenge was ever delivered, the Spartans ignored it. Perhaps, by now, they already regarded such things as 'folly', like those of a later generation (cf. Thucydides 5.41.3).

More important is the question why, if Mardonios had decided on battle the previous day, as Herodotos believed, he now merely sent out his cavalry to continue harrying the Greek lines. Perhaps the historian meant us to understand that the exchange of positions, and Mardonios' challenge, had taken up so much of the day that there was no time left to fight a full-scale battle. But he later implies (9.52.1) that the Greeks had to endure the harassing from the cavalry for a considerable time, during the rest of the day, and it is more likely that the story about Mardonios' decision to fight is untrue. In this case the harassing by his cavalry was simply a continuation of his previous tactics. Such tactics can hardly have been designed to do anything but force the Greeks to retreat, and, if so, it is very difficult to believe that Mardonios had ever actually wanted to fight a pitched battle. To achieve that he would have been better advised, as we have seen (above, 221–2), to retreat from the Asopos line in the hope that the Greeks would pursue him into flatter, more open terrain.

As it was, the cavalry attacks were apparently pressed even more closely than on previous days, and again Herodotos' narrative provides us with a precious glimpse of how Persian cavalry operated. 'They caused damage to the whole Greek army,' he says, 'flinging their javelins and firing arrows, being horse-archers and difficult to come at' (ἐσακοντίζοντές τε καὶ ἐστοξεύοντες ὥστε ἱπποτοξόται τε ἐόντες καὶ προσφέρεσθαι ἄποροι: 9.49.2). In particular, they somehow contrived to collapse and choke the Gargaphian spring, from which the whole Greek army now drew its water, since they no longer dared approach the Asopos (9.49.3). Herodotos does not say how

40 Meyer, 40; Munro, 1904, 159-60.

41 Wright, *op.cit.* n.5 above, 90.

42 Burn, 528-9; Barron, 605-6.

this was done, but presumably some of the cavalry contrived to ride round the open Greek right flank, and thus come up on the spring from the rear.[43]

As a result, the commanders of the various Greek contingents gathered on the right wing to discuss the situation with Pausanias. In addition to the loss of the water-supply, they were also running out of food, since the 'servants' (ὀπέωνες: helots?) who had been sent to the Peloponnese to fetch it, were unable to reach the camp because of the Persian cavalry (9.50). After some discussion, it was decided that if the Persians did not bring about a general engagement that day, they would withdraw to a place called 'the island', located 'ten stades (c2000m) from the Asopos and the Gargaphian spring ... in front of the city of Plataia' (9.51.1). Herodotos describes the place as a stretch of land formed by the river Oeroe, which, 'separated high up, runs down from Kithairon into the plain, keeping its streams about three stades (c600 metres) apart, and then mingles into one' (9.51.2). Here the Greeks hoped to find limitless water and better protection from the attacks of the cavalry. The intention was to move 'at the second watch of the night' (9.51.3: i.e. probably about 10.30 p.m.),[44] to avoid harassment from the Persian horse. When they reached 'the island', finally, half the army was to proceed 'towards Kithairon' and rescue the 'servants' sent after supplies (9.51.4).

The first problem, obviously, is to identify 'the island'. One view is that Herodotos' description means that it lay in the plain,[45] but no such locality exists there today, and it is difficult to believe that if it had been in the plain, it would have provided a good water-supply or protection from cavalry attacks. In any case, a more natural interpretation of Herodotos' words is that he meant the river flowed down from Kithairon in two branches, three stades apart, and then united in the plain. This has led to the identification of 'the island' with one or more of the ridges between the upper courses of the streams which unite to form the Oeroe, and this is probably right, though even then one would not have thought there would have been much water in such streams in August (see Pl. 23).[46]

There are, however, two difficulties with this. The first is that such a location for 'the island' would put it about twice as far from the Asopos as Herodotos' 'ten stades'. One solution is that by 'Asopos' here, Herodotos meant a different river from the one usually so-called,[47] but this is far fetched. Even more drastic is to resort to emendation of Herodotos' text and insert 'κ'' (i.e. '20') after the words 'from the Asopos', so that he would be saying 'the island' was twenty stades (c4000m) from the Asopos and

43 Cf. Grundy, 479; Boucher, *loc.cit.* n.38 above; Green, 261, has the cavalry 'cutting its way through south of Pyrgos hill and the ridge.' He also wonders how the Persians managed to 'block and foul' the spring, but Herodotos says nothing of 'fouling', and although it would have been difficult to stop the flow of water completely, it could have been made very difficult for more than a handful of men to draw water by smashing or removing the stone surrounds, if there were any (see Pl. 21).

44 See Hignett, 330.

45 Kirsten, *RE* xvii 2.2031ff. and xx 2.2294, reviving the view of Leake.

46 Grundy, 480ff., accepted by Munro, 1904, 160; HW ii 309; Pritchett, *op.cit.* n.23 above, 26; Hignett, 325.

47 Grundy n. on 470-1.

Pl. 23 (top): Plataia – one of the possible locations for the 'island' (Kithairon behind): note the relatively lush vegetation suggesting the proximity of good water-supplies. (Photo: N. Fields). Pl. 24 (bottom): Plataia – Kreikouki from the north-west (Kithairon behind). It would have been somwhere here that the Greeks of the centre were caught by the Theban cavalry. (Photo: N. Fields).

ten from the spring'.[48] This is not necessary. As we have seen (above, 223–7), Herodotos seems not to have realised that the spring was some distance from the river, and may loosely have given the distance from the spring to 'the island' – which would, in fact, be about 2000 metres, if 'the island' was formed by tributaries of the Oeroe – as though it was also the distance from the river.

The second difficulty is even more illusory. It has been objected that if 'the island' lay between the upper courses of streams which united to form the Oeroe, there would not have been room for the whole Greek army.[49] This is true if we imagine the army trying to form a phalanx across 'the island', since, assuming such a phalanx was eight deep, and allowing a metre per man, it would have had a front of nearly 5000 metres, whereas Herodotos implies 'the island' was at the most only some 600 metres wide. But, in the first place, the Greeks probably did not actually envisage deploying for battle on 'the island' – Herodotos implies that it was to be more in the nature of a temporary refuge. In the second place, he says that the intention was to send half the army 'towards Kithairon' to rescue the supplies, and it is mere pedantry to argue that he implies that the whole army was first to assemble on 'the island'. Those who were to be detached on the rescue-mission were to go off 'that same night' (9.51.4), and it would have made sense if the intention was that the first arrivals should move off when the rest of the army reached 'the island'.

In any case, Herodotos believed that no part of the Greek army ever actually reached 'the island'. Instead, he says (9.52), when the time came for the move, most of it went off in disorder, not to the agreed new position, but towards Plataia, only finally grounding arms at the temple of Hera outside the city, some twenty stades (c 4000m) from the Gargaphian spring. Subsequently it transpires that these troops were all those except the Athenians, Tegeates and Lakedaimonians. It has been suggested that Herodotos was misled by the bias of his informants here, and that these troops were only carrying out orders.[50] But most of the suggestions as to what these orders may have been are too complicated to be believed, and even the simplest – that these troops formed the half of the army which was to proceed towards Kithairon to rescue the supplies[51] – would mean that they had been intended to cross the Athenian line of retreat. This may be what they did, but it can hardly have been what was intended. Here, as so often, there is no compelling reason to doubt Herodotos' acount. He may have exaggerated the element of panic in what occurred, but even this is not all that improbable, in the light of what had recently been happening. Panic aside, it is more than likely that part-time soldiers, from twenty-four different states, ordered to retreat at night over ground new to most of them, would have gone astray.[52]

---

48 Woodhouse, *op.cit.* n.32 above, 57, accepted by Hignett, 429.

49 Ufer, *AS* iv 156; Woodhouse, *op.cit.*, 52ff.; Grundy, n. on 492ff.; Munro, 1904, 161f.; Hauvette, 471; Hignett, 325-6.

50 Woodhouse, *op.cit.*, 50-1; Munro, 1904, 161-2; Macan (1908) i 2 706; Burn, 531-4. Hignett, 327, rightly castigates the notion that Pausanias would have tried to get his left and centre to change places while withdrawing at night.

51 Burn, 531.

52 Ufer, *op.cit.*, 157; Hignett, 327; Green, 262. Both Hignett and Green say these troops were from twenty different states, but although Herodotos couples the Mycenaeans and Tirynthians, Eretrians and Styrians, and Leukadians and Anaktorians, twenty-two states were represented.

Much more difficult to understand is the behaviour of the remaining contingents. According to Herodotos (9.53-5), when Pausanias ordered the Lakedaimonians to move off, Amompharetos, '*lochagos* (i.e. commander) of the Pitanate *lochos*' (λοχηγέων τοῦ Πιτανήτεω λόχου: 9.53.2), refused to budge, despite all that Pausanias and Euryanax could do. Meanwhile the Athenians sent a horseman across to find out what was happening, and he was witness to the dramatic moment when Amompharetos, picking up a boulder in both arms, and laying it at Pausanias' feet, declared that with this 'pebble' (ψήφῳ – meaning in Greek either 'pebble' or 'vote'), he voted against running away from the 'strangers', which is what Herodotos says the Spartans called barbarians (9.54-5, cf. 11.2). When the Athenian trooper asked for orders, the exasperated Pausanias could only request that the Athenians close up on his troops and conform to their movements (9.55.2). By now day had dawned, and assuming that Amompharetos would not in fact want to be left behind if the others moved off, Pausanias led the rest away 'along the hills', with the Tegeates following, and the Athenians, too, moved off, presumably after receiving the horseman's report (9.56).

Here one can at least detect an element of Athenian bias in Herodotos' comment that the reason they sent a horsemen to find out what the Spartans were doing was that 'they knew the Spartans' thoughts – the way they thought one thing and did another' (9.54.1).[53] One is, indeed, tempted to believe that it was the Athenians who had not moved, prevented by the withdrawal of the centre across their line of retreat,[54] and that the horseman was sent to ask Pausanias what they should do.[55] If so, Pausanias may also have decided not to move until the situation to his left had clarified. But this fails to explain why he was not already on the move when the Athenian horseman arrived, since it had presumably originally been planned to synchronize the movement of all the contingents.

In the end, Pausanias may have delayed for some simple reason,[56] unknown to us, but we should not, perhaps, be too hasty in dismissing Herodotos' story.[57] It was certainly not unknown later for Spartan senior officers to disobey orders, even those of a king, and even in the very face of the enemy, as is shown by the conduct of Aristokles and Hipponoïdas at Mantineia in 418 (Thucydides 5.72.1), and Pausanias perhaps did not have the same authority as a king.[58] Unfortunately, Amompharetos' actual position must remain in doubt, in view of Herodotos' later implication that he was an '*eirên*' (9.85.1), i.e., probably, a young man in his twenties, and Thucydides' denial that there ever was a 'Pitanate *lochos*' (1.20). But if Amompharetos commanded one of the five *lochoi* into which the Spartan army was supposedly divided at this time, or was a

53 HW ii 311-2 *ad loc.* have an excellent note, and cf. additional n.3 on 397.

54 Ufer, *loc.cit.*; cf. Munro, 1904, 164, and CAH[1] iv 335.

55 Hignett, 328 & 331.

56 Cf., e.g., Ufer, *loc.cit.*; Woodhouse, *op.cit.* n.32 above, 53; Boucher, *op.cit.*, n.38 above, 299f.

57 As, e.g., HW ii 311 *ad loc.*, and, even more, Green, are.

58 Green, *loc.cit.*, seems to think he *was* a king!

polemarch in command of one of the six *morai*, his views would have carried very considerable weight.[59]

However, the story is still dubious. In connection with Thermopylai we saw that there is no good reason to believe that the Spartan code frowned on retreat as such (above, 145), and in this case it was ordered by Amompharetos' superiors. The story about the boulder is also odd since the Spartans, as far as we know, did not vote with 'pebbles', but usually by acclamation (cf. Thucydides 1.87.1). There is, moreover, one compelling reason to doubt that Amompharetos was really guilty of refusal to obey orders. Herodotos says that he was one of the three Spartans who 'behaved best' (ἠρίστευσαν: 9.71.2) in the battle, after the unfortunate Aristodemos, and this was, presumably, a detail he learned in Sparta. But however bravely Amompharetos fought in the end, would this have been enough for the Spartans to forget his earlier disobedience? Aristodemos was not so highly thought of, Herodotos believed, for all his heroism (*loc.cit.*), and after Mantineia, Hipponoïdas and Aristokles were exiled (Thucydides 5.72.1).

On the other hand, there is no particular reason to doubt that Amompharetos and his command *were* left behind. Possibly, then, the dispute was not about whether to withdraw or not, but about who was to form the rear-guard.[60] It has been objected that there should not have been any need for one,[61] but if the planned withdrawal had gone wrong, whether because of the ill-discipline of the centre, or for some other reason, it is possible that Pausanias found he had waited too long to get away under cover of darkness, and thus felt he had to cover his retreat. If Amompharetos really was an *eirên*, it is even possible that the whole story of his insubordination again arose from a misunderstanding of Spartan tactics when faced with missile-troops, as was suggested in the case of the alleged feigned retreats of the Spartans at Thermopylai. Later – the earliest example belongs to the 420s (Thucydides 4.125.3) – it was customary for the younger men, forming the front ranks of the phalanx, to be ordered to charge out and drive the enemy away, and it is possible that Amompharetos was appointed to take charge of this dangerous manoeuvre, or rather, in this case, series of manoeuvres. He may even have volunteered for it, using some such dramatic gesture as Herodotos records.

At all events, there is no reason to doubt that the position at dawn, on the Greek side, was as follows. We do not know how many casualties there had been in the previous days' fighting, but taking Herodotos' original totals, the centre, consisting of some 19,200 hoplites, was drawn up near the temple of Hera outside Plataia, the left, consisting of the 8000 Athenians, was on Pyrgos hill, and the right – 11,500 Spartans, *perioikoi* and Tegeates – on the Asopos ridge. Herodotos clearly believed that this

---

59 On all this see Lazenby, *The Spartan Army* (Warminster, 1985), 48-52. D.H.Kelly, *GRBS* 22 (1981), 31ff., puts forward the interesting idea that Amompharetos may have been one of the *Hippagretai*, and his men the *Hippeis*, but this, perhaps, departs too radically from Herodotos. R.F.Willetts, *Mnemosyne* 33 (1980), 272ff., suggests Herodotos' text should be emended to <σφα>ιρέας/<σφα>ιρέες, but there is no evidence that there was a group of Spartans called '*Sphaireis*' before the Roman period.

60 Suggested by Woodhouse, *op.cit.* n.32 above, 52ff.

61 Hignett, 329.

situation had come about by a combination of cowardice, ill-discipline and mutual suspicion, and this is only what one would expect. Apart from the Spartans, the Greek troops were part-time soldiers, drawn from over twenty states, many of them mutually hostile in normal times. Even Spartan training, judging by later accounts,[62] consisted largely of what we would call 'square-bashing'. Pausanias, in particular, is very unlikely to have received any kind of training in command, and, as far as we know, had never before held any command, let alone command of so huge – by Greek standards – and so heterogeneous an army. The Greeks were simply not accustomed to warfare of this scale or complexity. Even the most highly-trained troops can go astray at night, and Herodotos' explanation of what went wrong here is much more likely than most of the modern theories. In particular, the notion that the Greek position at dawn was somehow *planned* makes little sense, and those who take this view do not help their case by comparing the alleged feigned retreat of Pausanias with 11,500 men, to the feigned retreats practised by Leonidas' 300 at Thermopylai.[63]

The truth of the matter is that Mardonios had, so far, won hands down. He had achieved the break-up of the Greek army without being drawn into a set-piece confrontation, which he had probably been scheming for all along. All he needed to do now was to continue with the harassing that had been so successful in the last few days, and the chances were that the Greek retreat would continue, entailing a collapse of morale and, probably, the opening up of all the old cracks in the alliance.

It is possible that this *is* how Mardonios at first intended to play the game. According to Herodotos (9.57.3), the Persian cavalry had ridden out to harass the Greeks as usual, and finding their positions deserted, had ridden on after them, presumably sending a message back to their commander-in-chief. He, when he learned that the Greeks had gone, and saw their position deserted, first allegedly summoned three Thessalian brothers to ask, mockingly, what they thought of Spartan valour now (9.58), then led his Persian infantry at the double across the Asopos, 'on the track of the apparently fleeing Greeks' (9.58.1). Thereupon, seeing the Persians hurrying off in pursuit of the Greeks, the other contingents of their army hastened after them.

So far, setting aside Herodotos' usual attempt to depict Mardonios as a fire-eater, there is nothing here to suggest that he intended anything more than a 'hot pursuit'. But then Herodotos adds that 'he was hurrying after the Lakedaimonians and Tegeates alone, because he could not see the Athenians, who had turned into the plain, for the hills' (*ibid.*). This ties in with his previous statement that when the two contingents set off, 'the Athenians ... went the opposite way to the Lakedaimonians,[64] for the latter clung to

62 Xenophon, *LP*, 11.

63 Cf., e.g., Burn, 532-4. Green, 262-5, has the most elaborate scheme, whereby the Athenians and Spartans deliberately exposed themselves, apparently isolated, to tempt Mardonios into attacking them. Even Barron, 606, wonders whether Pausanias, in ordering a retreat, was making a virtue of necessity, and hoping to entice Mardonios to attack him.

64 An unnecessary fuss has been made about this part of what Herodotos says. Kirsten (*RE* xx 2.2295f.) actually argued that Herodotos literally meant that the Athenians headed north into the flat land along the Asopos because they, like Amompharetos, refused to 'run away from the strangers', but this is absurd. Stein was clearly right to suggest – *ad.loc.* – that the words 'ἤισαν τὰ ἔμπαλιν ἢ Λακεδαιμόνιοι' should be taken with what follows, i.e. the Athenians 'moved in the opposite way to the Lakedaimonians,' because they turned *down* into the plain, whereas the Lakedaimonians kept to the higher ground.

the hills and the lower slopes of Kithairon, ... whilst the Athenians turned down into the plain' (9.56.2). In other words, Mardonios could not see the Athenian contingent once it was off Pyrgos hill and had begun to march south-eastwards across the plain, since his view was obstructed by the Asopos ridge, but the Lakedaimonians and Tegeates remained in full view, since they kept to higher ground.

One final question remains, then, about Mardonios' strategy. Did he, even at this last moment, intend to do no more than harry the Spartans and those with them back to Kithairon, or did he now think that he had the chance to annihilate the Greeks he could see, whilst they were isolated from the rest? Was he drawn into a battle not of his choosing, by the overeagerness of his men, or did he, too, at this supreme moment 'lose his cool'? We shall never know, but if Herodotos is to be believed, although the Persian cavalry acted as it had been doing for several days, and the Persian foot, even if it followed Mardonios across the Asopos 'at the double' (δρόμῳ: 9.59.1), did not lose its discipline, the rest of the Persian army came hurrying after 'as fast as each man could, in no sort of order or formation' (9.59.2). Perhaps, then, Mardonios, in the end, found himself committed to a battle he had never really wanted.

According to Herodotos (9.57.2), Pausanias and the main force had withdrawn ten stades (c2000m) and then waited for Amompharetos, 'near where the river Moloeis is located and the so-called Argiopian land, where there is also a temple (ἱρόν) of Eleusinian Demeter.' Later (9.62.2) he says that the battle took place 'by the Demetrion itself' and expresses his wonder(9.65.2) that of those who fought beside the grove (ἄλσος) of Demeter, not one Persian either entered or fell in the sacred enclosure (τέμενος). Neither the river Moloeis nor the 'Argiopian land' can be securely located, but it is possible that the temple is to be identified with the two buildings, traces of which have been found at the western foot of the ridge which rises south of the chapel of the Pantanassa, about two kilometres north-east of Kriekouki. Other remains include a terracotta antefix of fifth century date, suggesting the presence of a temple, and two inscriptions relating to the worship of Eleusinian Demeter (*IG* vii 1670 & 1671). This is, however, considerably more than ten stades (c2000m) from the Gargaphian spring, and in any case the ridge above the Pantanassa chapel is probably the site of the ancient Hysiai, which one would think Herodotos would have mentioned if the battle had been fought in its vicinity.[65] Others have gone to the other extreme and looked for the temple of Demeter near the chapel of St. Demetrios,[66] but the coincidence of name means nothing, since Demetrios is a very popular saint, and no trace of an ancient shrine has been found in the vicinity; in any case, this is too near Gargaphia, if that is Retsi.

It is, of course, possible that Herodotos' 'ten stades' is mistaken, but it is no argument that since the Persian cavalry evidently played no part in the actual battle, Pausanias

65 See Fossey, *Topography and Population of Ancient Boiotia* (Chicago, 1988), 112-5, for the location of Hysiai, and for the remains, Pritchett, *AJA* 61 (1957), 12ff., and *Studies in Ancient Greek Topography* i (Berkeley & Los Angeles, 1965), 104f.

66 Grundy, 495-6; J.L.Myres, *Herodotus: Father of History* (Oxford, 1953), 286. But see Pritchett, 1957, 28, and Burn, 535-6. In the Oxford Text, the '10 stades' of Herodotos' MSS is even amended to '4'.

must have got very near Kithairon, where he could protect his flanks and rear.[67] The only evidence for this is in Plutarch's life of Aristeides (11.6-7), and we have already noted how muddled his account of Plataia seems to be (above, n.22).[68] In any case, there is no need to look for somewhere where Pausanias' forces would have been naturally protected from the Persian cavalry. Herodotos clearly believed that the Persian cavalry did catch up with and attack the Greeks before they reached safety (9.57.3 & 9.60.1), but everything we know about warfare at this period shows that Persian cavalry could not ride down unbroken Greek infantry. Having done their job in halting the Greek withdrawal, the cavalry had, sooner or later, to give place to infantry.

It is, thus, not possible to be certain where the battle was fought, on the basis of what Herodotos says. We can ignore his 'ten stades' and accept the proposed location for the temple of Demeter, or we can ignore the latter and try to find a suitable battlefield 'ten stades' from the Retsi spring, or we can try to reconcile the two. A retreat of 2000m from the spring, keeping to high ground, would have meant first moving east for some 400 metres, towards the chapel of St. Demetrios, then swinging south, leaving the hill on which the chapel stands, to the left. A further 1600m or so would have brought the Spartans and their comrades to the relatively flat land north of Kriekouki village. Between this and the site of Kriekouki flows a stream, which might be the river Moloeis, and above it to the northeast is a hill which might be the 'Argiopian land'. Possibly there was another shrine of Demeter here, or perhaps the whole sacred area, the '*temenos*', including temple and grove, stretched a considerable distance from where the temple appears to have been situated.

Amompharetos, if Herodotos is to be believed, had at first thought that Pausanias would never abandon him. But when he realised that the main body had in fact left, he ordered his *lochos* to shoulder arms and led it slowly in pursuit. Herodotos obviously meant the word 'slowly' (βάδην: 9.57.1) to refer to Amompharetos' continued stubborn insubordination, but if, in fact, he was following orders, his measured retreat may rather exemplify the discipline with which the Spartans carried out such manoeuvres. In either case, his timing was perfect, if, as Herodotos says, he and his men rejoined the main body at the moment the whole barbarian cavalry attacked (9.57.3).

Pausanias immediately sent a despatch-rider to ask the Athenians to come to his aid, or, if this was impossible, to send their archers (9.60), but when, on receipt of the message, they started to his assistance, they soon came under attack from the Greeks in Mardonios' army. Thus the Lakedaimonians and Tegeates were left to face Mardonios' Asiatic troops alone. Herodotos says the Greek forces, with the light-armed, numbered 53,000 (9.61.2), but this is because he still persists in thinking that 35,000 helots were present. In reality, there were 11,500 hoplites and probably about the same number of soldier-servants, most of them, no doubt, armed in some fashion, but almost certainly

---

67 Delbrück, 116, citing Ludwig Winter's Berlin dissertation of 1907; Munro, 1904, 163; Ufer, *AS* iv 159-60, cf. 139.

68 Diodoros' is even worse: he has the Greeks move from the foothills after the defeat of the cavalry, and take up a position where there was a high hill on the right and the Asopos on the left, and it is here, in a constricted space, that the battle takes place (11.30.4-31.2). This not only makes nonsense of the second position, but completely omits any mention of the move to the third.

not capable of taking their place in the phalanx. Nevertheless, even though it is very unlikely that Pausanias had planned it this way, he may not have been too dismayed at what had happened. Although his army was still probably larger than any Greek army had ever been, at least it was now of a more manageable size, and almost half its hoplites consisted of his own Spartans. At last he probably knew what he was doing.

A final problem remains before we come to the battle itself. According to Herodotos (9.61.2-3), when the Spartans and their comrades made the customary sacrifice before engaging, the omens proved unfavourable, and, in the meantime, they began to suffer heavy casualties, as the Persians loosed volley after volley of arrows from behind their planted hedge of wicker shields. One of the casualties was Kallikrates, the handsomest man in the Greek army, who, Herodotos later tells us, was hit in the side, as Pausanias was sacrificing, 'sitting in his rank' (9.72.1).[69] This conjures up a marvellous picture of the disciplined Spartans, stolidly sitting as they endured the arrow-storm, perhaps crouched under their shields.

In fact casualties cannot have been too serious, if Herodotos is right in saying (9.70.5) that only 91 Spartans and sixteen Tegeates fell in all. But why did Pausanias risk any casualties at all in this manner? Why not get in close at once? Modern commentators have tended to assume that the bad omens were just an excuse and that Pausanias was waiting until the enemy was committed beyond any possibility of withdrawal,[70] but should we be so cynical? As we saw in the case of the earlier period of eight days' delay allegedly due to bad omens (see above, 228), it is unlikely that a man like Pausanias simply manipulated the state religion for his own purposes. In a crisis-situation like this, it is much more likely that he genuinely wanted to feel that the gods were on his side, and waited until he and his seer became quite convinced that the omens showed they were.

The waiting was finally ended, Herodotos says (9.61.3), when Pausanias looked towards the temple of Hera at Plataia and called upon the goddess' aid: at this moment, first the Tegeates rose to their feet and advanced, and immediately after Pausanias' prayer, the omens came good for the Spartans (9.62.1). Assuming that this is true, if the battle was fought right alongside a temple of Demeter, it is odd that Pausanias should pray to a more distant goddess, and this suggests that he may have been 'looking towards the Heraion' not so much for Hera's help as for that of his centre and left. But it is questionable whether he could have seen Hera's temple from where he stood,[71] and he almost certainly did not know that the centre contingents had gone there (see above, 235). Possibly he had some special, personal regard for Hera, or, if the temple in question was the most important in the area, he may have considered the whole region as under her protection. Again, we do not know why his prayer at this juncture should have had the effect it did, but perhaps, in some way, he received the psychological boost

69 It was this man whom Rider Haggard made the ultimate ancestor of the beloved of She, in his novel of that name.

70 Delbrück, 116; Grundy, 501-2; HW ii 314; Wright, *op.cit.* n.5 above, 68; Hignett, 336; Burn, 538; Green, 266-7. Barron, 608, is the latest: 'With iron determination not to expend his limited forces too soon, Pausanias fell back on his seers, who duly produced unfavourable sacrifices.' Plutarch, typically, elaborates the scene – cf. Jameson, *op.cit.* n.31 above, 207ff.

71 Grundy, 521.

necessary to convince him that the moment had come, and this may be why, suddenly, he saw that the omens were right.

Whatever the truth about this delay, we can surely believe that the Tegeates began to move forwards first, apparently without orders, and presumably Pausanias now had little option, omens or no omens, but to order a general advance. Moreover, whether intended or not, the delay had apparently had the effect of irretrievably committing the Persian infantry to a stand-up fight, and Herodotos' account of the battle, if carefully analysed, enables us to see, quite clearly, how and why the Greeks won. He begins by saying that the Persians had to lay aside their bows (9.62.1), which meant, of course, that they were immediately deprived of the one arm in which they outmatched their opponents. Their one chance of defeating hoplites had always been to stand off and shoot the hoplites down without allowing them to close. Instead, they tried to match them in hand-to-hand combat. This is confirmed by Herodotos' remark that 'the fight began at the [Persian] shields' (9.62.2). In other words, the Persians had abandoned any thought of the fluid fight in which they might well have had the advantage.

'When the shields fell,' Herodotos goes on, 'a tough struggle took place right alongside the shrine of Demeter, for a long time, until they came to shoving (ἐς ὃ ἀπίκοντο ἐς ὠθισμόν), for the barbarians seized the [Greeks'] spears and tried to break them' (9.62.2). Here one should note that 'shoving' (ὠθισμός) was a regular part of hoplite battles. Usually the opposing phalanxes closed to 'within spear-range' (εἰς δόρυ) and then tried to stab each other with their spears. But the press of men in the rear ranks inexorably pushed those in front forward, those in the rear perhaps literally pushing their shields against the backs of those in front, until the opposing front ranks crashed together.[72] At Plataia, the situation was rather different, for the Persians were not hoplites, and, as Herodotos has already explained in his account of Thermopylai (7.211.2), had shorter spears than the Greeks. They were thus at a disadvantage in the preliminary stage, and tried to get round this by grabbing the Greek spears.

But the really interesting passage is Herodotos' next paragraph (9.62.3): 'In spirit and strength the Persians were not inferior, but being unarmoured (ἄνοπλοι),[73] they were also inexperienced (ἀνεπιστήμονες) besides, and not equal to their opponents in skill.' Here Herodotos can hardly mean than the Persians were, in general, untrained and unskilful in comparison with the Greeks, since they were obviously highly skilled in certain respects – archery, for example – and he would have known that most Greek hoplites, the Spartans apart, were basically amateurs. What he meant is clearly explained by the next sentence: 'rushing out in ones and tens and in larger or smaller groups, they fell upon the Spartans and were destroyed.' In other words, firstly, the Persians' lack of skill was in comparison with the *Spartans* – the same point the historian makes in his account of Thermopylai, where the Spartans are described as 'men who knew how to fight amongst men who did not (ἐν οὐκ ἐπισταμένοισι

---

72 Cf. J.F.Lazenby, 'The Killing Zone' in *Hoplites: The classical Greek battle experience*, ed. V.D.Hanson (London, 1991), 96-100.

73 HW ii 314 *ad* 9.62.3 say that 'ἄνοπλοι' 'need only mean "without shields"', though they note that the later phrase 'ἡ ἐσθὴς ἔρημος ἐοῦσα ὅπλων' (9.63.2) implies that the Persian troops were also without cuirasses.

μάχεσθαι ἐπιστάμενοι: 7.211.3).[74] But, secondly and more importantly, Persian lack of skill at Plataia lay precisely in their 'rushing out in ones and tens and in larger or smaller groups,' for this was no way to fight hoplites. Individual courage and skill was useless against an advancing wall of shields, and groups, even of ten or more, would simply be overwhelmed.

Herodotos maintains that while Mardonios was still alive, mounted on his white horse, and surrounded by his picked force of Persian cavalry, the Persians continued to hold and 'felled many of the Spartans' (9.63.1). However, as we saw in the case of the similar claim that the archers inflicted serious casualties before the Spartans advanced (9.61.3), he can only be talking loosely and in relative terms, if the total number of Spartans who fell was only ninety-one. In the event, Mardonios was eventually killed by the Spartan Aeimnestos or Arimnestos (9.64.2), who struck the Persian general on the head with a stone, according to Plutarch (*Aristeides* 19.1), though it is difficult to believe that even in a *mêlée*, a Spartan would have stooped to using such a weapon.

When Mardonios fell, and the troops around him were annihilated, the Persians broke and fled, and Herodotos makes the final comment that 'the principal cause of their destruction was that they were not clad in armour (πλεῖστον γάρ σφεας ἐδηλέετο ἡ ἐσθὴς ἔρημος ἐοῦσα ὅπλων), *for they were were light troops* (γυμνῆτες: literally, 'naked') *trying to make a fight of it against hoplites* (πρὸς γὰρ ὁπλίτας ἐόντες γυμνῆτες ἀγῶνα ἐποιεῦντο: 9.63.2).[75] Again, the whole history of Greek warfare, from the mid-seventh century to the mid-fourth, shows that light troops could not defeat hoplites unless either they caught them in mountainous terrain, or they were in overwhelming numbers, or they were very carefully handled, none of which was true of Plataia.

Herodotos was clearly right to view the main struggle as that between the force under Pausanias and the Persians under Mardonios, but his account makes clear that there was fighting elsewhere, though not all sections of the two armies became involved. He alleges, for example, that Artabazos, who had never wanted a battle in the first place, simply retreated with his force of 40,000 men, when he saw Mardonios' troops in flight (9.66). Modern commentators have suggested that he came late to the field because he and his men had originally been stationed along the Asopos where it bends northwards, and not only had farthest to go, but also had to climb the Asopos ridge.[76] It is going too far, however, to suggest that Artabazos' force was 'marked' by the Corinthians and other troops of the Greek centre as they set off eastwards from the Heraion to join in the fighting to its right.[77]

---

74 HW ii 314 again suggest that the skill of the Spartans may have been shown, as at Thermopylai, by a series of feigned retreats, as Plato (*Laches* 191c) says. But the situations were very different: at Thermopylai it was essential to draw the Persians into hand-to-hand conflict, at Plataia they were already committed to it. In any case, feigning retreat with 11,500 men would have been somewhat different from doing it with 300!

75 Earlier, in his description of the Persian army, Herodotos claims that the Persians themselves wore cuirasses of iron scales (7.61.1), but presumably here, in 9.62.3 and in 9.63.2, he means that the majority of Persian troops enjoyed no such protection.

76 Ufer, *AS* iv 161; Hignett, 337; Burn, 536. Munro, 1904, 165, suggests Artabazos had never been in Boiotia in any case, but this goes too far.

77 Burn, 536.

Of the rest of the Persian army, Herodotos seems to think only the Boiotians were heavily involved. The Theban infantry engaged the Athenians, and lost 300 men in the process (9.67), though they and the other medizing Greeks thus at least prevented the Athenians from joining Pausanias (9.61.1). The Theban cavalry caught the Megarians, Phleiasians and other Greek contingents from the centre as they were crossing the plain by the swiftest route to join Pausanias, and routed them, leaving 600 dead and pursuing the rest to Kithairon (9.69: see 234, Pl. 24). It has been suggested that in fact these troops were trying to come to the aid of the Athenians, and by distracting the Theban cavalry, rendered the Athenians vital service.[78] This may be true, but it is not what Herodotos says, and the argument that we would have expected the Theban cavalry to play its part in the fight with the Athenians, if it had not been distracted, is not cogent, since cavalry usually had no part to play in hoplite battles. Still less is there reason to substitute for Herodotos' statement that the Megarians and the rest set off when they heard that Pausanias and his men had won, a message from Pausanias asking them to come.[79]

As for the Corinthians and the other contingents associated with them, Herodotos says (9.69.1) that they set off along the foothills of Kithairon, heading straight for the temple of Demeter, but he does not tell us whether they actually took part in the fighting. Plutarch (*Moralia* 872d-e) quotes a poem by the contemporary Simonides to the effect that the Corinthians were 'in the centre' (μέσσοι) at Plataia, but this may mean no more than that they were in the middle of the Greek army along the Asopos. The notion that the movement of the Corinthians stopped Artabazos from joining the main struggle is pure hypothesis.[80] All in all, there is little reason to doubt that the battle was essentially fought and won by Pausanias and his 11,500 Lakedaimonians and Tegeates – after all, even the Athenian Aischylos credits the victory to the 'Dorian spear' (*Persai* 817).

When the rout began, Artabazos withdrew to Phokis (9.66.3), the Thebans retreated to their own city (9.67), and those who had been engaged with Pausanias and his men, fled to the stockaded camp, the latter two groups protected by their respective cavalry forces (9.68). Those who reached the camp managed to resist all the efforts of the Spartans to break in, since they allegedly lacked any skill in siege-warfare. But when the Athenians arrived, Herodotos says (9.70.2), they contrived to mount the wall and create a breach for the others. The Athenians are later alleged to have had a skill in siege warfare (Thucydides 1.102.2), but Herodotos may be anachronistic here, for they are not known to have taken part in any significant sieges before Plataia, and it is suspicious that he says the Tegeates were the first to enter. They secured not only Mardonios' tent -probably the one left him by Xerxes (9.82.1) – but the solid bronze manger for his horses, which they later dedicated in the temple of Athena Alea at Tegea (9.70.3).

Of those who had taken refuge in the camp, Herodotos says (9.70.5), not 3000 survived, but although he believed that this meant that in all something like 257,000 Asiatic troops perished, as we have seen, the number is unlikely to have been nearly as large. However, we can well believe that there was a considerable slaughter in the

---

78 Burn, 537.

79 Woodhouse, *op.cit.* n.32 above, 50-1.

80 Cf. n.77 above.

camp, for the Greeks' blood would have been up, and, as Herodotos says (*ibid.*), once the wall had fallen, the enemy were trapped and would not have made much effort to defend themselves. The survivors, including the womenfolk, were either distributed amongst the victors, or sold as slaves. But it is good to record that at least one lady, who had been taken as a concubine from the island of Kos, was rescued by Pausanias, who happened to be a 'guest-friend' (ξένος) of her father's (9.76), and that Pausanias rejected out of hand the suggestion of one Lampon of Aigina that he should impale Mardonios' body, in revenge for the mutilation of Leonidas' after Thermopylai (9.78-9). In the event, Herodotos says (9.84), Mardonios' body disappeared the day after the battle, and he could never find out who took it. That he knew of many who had been rewarded by Mardonios' son for burying it, rings true, though he could not say for certain who it really had been: rumour held that it was one Dionysophanes of Ephesos.

After their victory, the Greeks distributed the booty and then buried their dead. According to Herodotos (9.85), the Spartans had three graves. In one they buried the *eirenes*,[81] including Poseidonios, Amompharetos, Philokyon and Kallikrates, the former three singled out for their bravery in the battle, the last for his unlucky death before he had had a chance to strike a blow (9.71.2, 72). Herodotos himself believed that the bravest man on the field had been Aristodemos, the unfortunate survivor of Thermopylai, who had gone beserk because of the contempt with which he had been treated (9.71.2, cf. 7.231). But he says that the Spartans believed Poseidonios the better man, because he had not wished to die, whereas Aristodemos had wanted to be killed, as a result of his disgrace, and had performed his great deeds 'raging and leaving the line' – the last an unforgiveable crime for a hoplite. This was presumably why Aristodemos was not honoured like the others.

Herodotos believed that the second of the three Spartan graves contained the remainder of the Spartans who had been killed, and the third the helots (9.85.2). But this means either that no *perioikoi* were killed, or that they had no grave, neither of which is likely. It is also, perhaps, slightly odd that the *eirenes* should have been buried separately from the rest of the Spartans. Probably, the truth is that all the Spartans were buried in one grave, the *perioikoi* in the second, and the helots in the third.[82] In addition, Herodotos believed, there were graves for the Tegeates, Athenians and for the Megarians and Phleiasians who had been slaughtered by the Theban cavalry. Pausanias also believed that there was an Athenian tomb at Plataia (9.2.5), and although Thucydides (2.34) says that Athenians who fell in war were buried in Athens, except for those killed at Marathon, he presumably meant that the remains of those who fell in exclusively Athenian conflicts, were brought home, whereas Plataia was a pan-Hellenic triumph.[83]

---

81 The MSS at 9.85.1 and in the next paragraph have 'ἱρέας/-έες' ('priests'), but although this is accepted by, e.g., Burn, 541 and n.78, the *Scholia* clearly read 'ἱρένας/-ες', i.e., probably, young men between the ages of 20 and 30. Burn's argument that Amompharetos could not have commanded a *lochos* when so young, is strong, but there are too many doubts about Amompharetos' position for it to be compelling. It is quite likely that the *eirenes*, who would have been in the front ranks, suffered more heavily than the older Spartans to their rear. The fact that Kallikrates is singled out for his good looks also suggests he was a young man.

82 As HW ii 325 suggest.

83 Cf. HW ii 325 *ad* 9.85.2.

In addition to these graves, Herodotos says the Greeks who had not taken part, also threw up grave-mounds, though they were empty, and singles out, in particular, that of the Aiginetans, which, he claims, was erected ten years after the event by their *proxenos* at Plataia, Kleades (9.85.3). But there may have been no deception intended here: other states may well have lost men in the earlier fighting, but have been unable to recover their bodies, or the bodies may have been buried in a common grave and the states concerned have later erected separate cenotaphs.[84]

Even if this was the case, however, the losses recorded by Herodotos for the main fighting – ninety-one Spartans, sixteen Tegeates and fifty-two Athenians (9.70.5) – seem astonishingly small, and the absence of any *perioikoi* is again remarkable; only the figure of 600 for the Megarians and Phleiasians looks realistic. The figures given by the secondary sources are far larger – more than 10,000 in Diodoros (11.33.1), 1360 in Plutarch (*Aristeides* 19.5) – but the former is certainly too high, and it has been suggested that Plutarch's represents Herodotos' totals rounded up, with the addition of an extra 600 for the rest of the centre contingents.[85] Possibly Herodotos was unable to discover a total for the *perioikoi*, and since Kleidemos claimed (*FGH* 323F22 *ap*. Plut. *Aristeides* 19.6) that all fifty-two Athenians were from the single *phylê, Aiantis*, it has been suggested that Herodotos took the funeral monument of this single *phylê* to be that of all the Athenians.[86] But certainty is obviously not possible.

The least glorious part was played by the men from Mantineia and Elis, if we are to believe Herodotos (9.77). Arriving too late to join in any of the fighting, they were all for pursuing Artabazos, but were forbidden to do so – with some contempt, one would guess – by the Spartans. When their forces returned home, their generals were exiled, and it may have been as a result of this that the Mantineians were not included on the monument erected at Delphi after the war (ML 27), though they had fought at Thermopylai (7.202), whereas the Eleians, who had not, do appear. Perhaps the special position of the latter as the guardians of Olympia, secured them a mention.

The monument in question was one of the thank-offerings Herodotos says were dedicated from the spoils of Plataia, to Apollo at Delphi, Zeus at Olympia and Poseidon at the Isthmus (9.81). The only one that survives is the dedication to Apollo at Delphi: its remains can still be seen in the At-Maidan (the ancient hippodrome) at Istanbul, whither it was taken by Constantine. Herodotos describes it as a triple-headed snake, but it actually takes the form of a bronze column representing three intertwined snakes, though the heads of the snakes eventually dropped off, on 20 October, 1700 AD, apparently as a result of metal-fatigue! Originally it was surmounted by a golden tripod (9.81.1), but this was melted down by the Phokians at the outset of the Sacred War in the fourth century (Pausanias 10.13.5). On the coils of the snakes – again not on the tripod, as Herodotos says (8.82.1) – can still be seen the names of thirty-one Greek peoples, preceded by the simple statement, 'These warred the war' (τοίδε τὸν πόλεμον ἐπολέμεον). There are few nobler – and sadder – sights in the world.

After the funeral rites had been performed, the Greeks decided to move on Thebes and demand the surrender of the 'medizers'. Accordingly, on the eleventh day after the

84 Macan (1908) i 2 772; HW ii 325-6 *ad* 9.85.3.

85 Hignett, 340–1.

86 Hignett, 341.

battle (9.86.2), the army moved north to blockade Thebes, which came to terms after a twenty-day siege. But no attempt was made, at this juncture, to deal with other 'medizing' states, such as Thessaly, though King Leotychidas later campaigned there (6.72). Probably, in many places, the more prominent 'medizers' fled, or were exiled, and one doubts whether any Persian garrisons survived west of Eïon, at the mouth of the Strymon. The last substantial body of Persian troops to leave Greece were those commanded by Artabazos. According to Herodotos (9.89), he fooled the Thessalians into receiving him hospitably by pretending that Mardonios and the rest of the army were close behind, and eventually made his way, not without loss, to Byzantion.

Thus mainland Greece was liberated, and as if this was not enough, far away across the Aegean, on the very same day that Plataia was fought, the Greeks believed (9.90.1), their fleet landed its men on the Mykale peninsula, defeated a Persian army guarding their improvised naval base, stormed the base and burned the beached ships. But although this episode is described by Herodotos, we will, at last, part company with the master here, for Mykale was really the start of something new – the triumphant Greek counter-offensive which was to lead to the liberation of Greek Asia Minor and, eventually, to the creation of the Athenian empire. With the victory of Plataia, the defence of Greece, which is the subject of this book, may be said to have been concluded.

CHAPTER 10

Conclusions

By any reckoning the defeat of Xerxes' invasion was an astonishing achievement. Herodotos no doubt greatly exaggerates the forces arrayed against the Greeks, and he was aware of at least some of the difficulties the Persians faced (cf., e.g., 7.10 2 & 47.2ff.). But we should never forget that the Greek states were tiny, even in ancient terms, whereas the Persian empire was probably then the largest, single, unified state in the world. The Persians, moreover, had conquered their empire in somewhat less than eighty years, in the course of which they had encountered problems at least as difficult as any they were to face in Greece. They had even fought Greeks before, in Asia Minor and in Egypt, and had had no difficulty in defeating them. Marathon should have been a warning, at least against trying to defeat Greek hoplites in set-piece battles, but perhaps Robert Graves was right to imagine that –

'Truth-loving Persians do not dwell upon
The trivial skirmish fought near Marathon.'

All in all, the Delphic Oracle was perfectly justified in advising the Athenians to flee to the ends of the earth rather than try to resist (7.140.2).

So why did the Persians fail? One answer – that it was a case of 'the courage of free men pitted against an oriental despotism'[1] – can be confidently dismissed. It may be of some comfort to those of us who like to think we live in democracies, to assume that free men will always triumph over despotic regimes, but war puts no premium on 'freedom'. In the second World War, for example, although the 'free world' triumphed in the end, we should remember that the USSR had more than a little to do with it, and Soviet Russia was at least as 'despotic' as Nazi Germany or Japan. Nor is it the case that 'subject races' will not fight as hard for their overlords as the troops of the 'master race' itself. Those born under the British Raj would take considerable exception to the idea that Sikhs or Punjabis fought less courageously for the King-Emperor than his British soldiers, and some of the best troops ever to serve the British crown – the Gurkhas – are, strictly speaking, mercenaries.

This is not to deny that the Greeks will have been inspired by the thought that they were fighting for their homes, their families and their whole way of life, as Aischylos, for example, who almost certainly fought at Salamis, makes clear in the 'messenger speech' in the *Persai* (402-5). But there is no reason to believe that the non-Persian subjects of the king of Persia felt any less sense of loyalty, or fought any less fanatically, because they were fighting to conquer Greece for their master, and there is nothing in Herodotos to suggest this. On the contrary, he singles out for praise, for example, the Egyptians at Artemision (8.17), the Samians at Salamis (8.85.2-3) and the

1 N.G.L.Hammond, 1988, 515, referring to Marathon; cf. Green, 36, also referring to Marathon, 'They [the Athenians] were not imperial conscripts, but free men fighting to preserve their freedom.'

Sakai at Plataia (9.71.1). In all armies, at all periods, there are heroes and cowards, slackers and 'workaholics', and the armies of Persia and the Greeks will have been no different.

Nor is the explanation that the Greeks were more highly trained and disciplined than their opponents.[2] This at least gets some backing from Herodotos, who twice, as we have seen, comments on Persian lack of experience and skill in comparison with the Greeks (7.211.3 & 9.62.3). But the first time he is specifically contrasting Persian troops with the Spartans, and the second he is by implication. Spartan soldiers undoubtedly were highly trained to a certain extent, but one doubts whether even they practised more than the simplest drills and manoeuvres, and there is no evidence that the hoplites of other states, at this date, received any training at all. On the contrary, the way in which Greek writers like Thucydides talk about the Spartans (cf., e.g., 5.66ff.), shows that they were still altogether exceptional even later in the fifth century.

Greek hoplites may, however, have been more experienced in at least one aspect of warfare, namely hand-to-hand combat. This was the way hoplites fought, but Persian troops, many of them armed with bows and strong in cavalry, would have been accustomed to a very different kind of combat. Thus they incurred defeat at Marathon and Plataia by allowing themselves to be drawn into a stand-up fight, and also suffered heavy losses at Thermopylai, until they literally found a way round the problem. But Thermopylai, in the end, is a good illustration of the true contrast between Persian professionalism and Greek amateurishness. Once Xerxes learned of the Anopaia path, or, more particularly, probably, acquired a reliable guide, he was immediately able to take advantage of the situation. His troops, moreover, stuck rigidly to the task to which they had been assigned, whereas the Phokians guarding the path forgot what they were supposed to be doing and thought only of defending themselves.

Even more strikingly, at Plataia, the Persians were within an ace of pulling off a spectacular success. Their continual harassing of the Greeks in their second position led to a retreat which went disastrously wrong. If the Persians had kept their distance and their flexibility, they would almost certainly have driven the Greeks back onto Kithairon, even if they had not succeeded in destroying them piecemeal, and the effect on Greek morale would probably have been catastrophic. At Thermopylai the Persians were baffled for two days because the terrain nullified their advantages in numbers and flexibility, but won in the end, when given the chance to play to their strengths. At Plataia the reverse was the case: after the initial hiccup caused by the death of Masistios, the Persians played to their strengths and then forgot what those strengths were.

At sea it is even less likely that the Greeks were superior in skill, despite what Artemisia is supposed to have told Xerxes (8.68-1). Triremes may well have been first used by subjects of the Persian empire, whether Phoenicians or Egyptians,[3] in the last quarter of the sixth century, whereas, according to Thucydides (1.14.2), until shortly before Xerxes' expedition, the navies of mainland Greek states were mostly composed of pentekonters. The Athenian navy constructed at the instigation of Themistokles, was

2 Cf., e.g., Green, 36 & 63.

3 Wallinga, 'The ancient Persian navy and its predecessors' in *Achaemenid History* I (Proceedings of the Groningen 1983 Achaemenid History Workshop, ed. H.Sancisi-Weerdenburg, Leiden, 1987), 47ff.

the first to consist of triremes, and even these were old-fashioned in not being completely decked from side to side (Thucydides 1.14.3). Although the experiments with the reconstructed trireme have shown that a crew can be trained to a competent level in a very short time, one would have expected at least the best ships in the Persian navy to have had the edge, and this is probably what Herodotos means by saying that the Persians thought they had the 'better sailing ships' ([νέας] ἄμεινον πλεούσας: 8.10.1). Indeed, the Athenians assigned twenty ships to the Chalkidians (8.1.2), which does not suggest that the latter would have been highly-trained seamen, and some of their own ships were partly manned by Plataians, though they were 'inexperienced in naval matters' (8.1.1).

But if the Greeks were mostly amateur soldiers and inexperienced seamen, it is also extremely unlikely that they won because of their superior tactics, as is often claimed. On land the crucial battle is Marathon, where the Athenians, under the guidance of Miltiades, are often thought to have employed very sophisticated tactics.[4] But is it likely that an early fifth century Athenian aristocrat, who had spent most of his life in a very different environment from that of the normal city state, could have devised a tactical plan for hoplites which would have done credit to Hannibal? It has been claimed that 'his whole plan [was] based on experience of Persian arms and methods,'[5] but, as we have seen (above, 37) he may never actually have seen Persian troops in action, nor, more importantly, have commanded hoplites against them. His 'experience' was limited to Darius' Skythian expedition, when he had been left behind to guard the Danube bridge (4.137-8), and flight, first from the subsequent Skythian invasion of his fief in the Chersonese (6.40), and then from the Persians themselves (6.41.1). Thus it is much more likely that what happened at Marathon was the result of a series of accidents, and Herodotos implies that the crucial tactical disposition the Athenians made – the thinning of the centre, leaving the wings strong – was intended simply to make their line as long as that of the enemy (6.111.2). In other words, it was purely *defensive*.

At Thermopylai Herodotos singles out for praise the feigned retreats of the Spartans (7.211.3), and Plato, almost certainly wrongly, ascribes the same tactics to them at Plataia (*Laches* 191c). But although such tactics could only have been used by highly trained troops, and no doubt had a limited effectiveness in drawing the Persians into hand-to-hand combat, one cannot believe that they could have been used by more than a handful of men at a time, and one would have thought the enemy would soon have got wise to them. They could only have been effective in terrain like Thermopylai, too constricted to allow the enemy any room to manoeuvre.

As for Plataia, Herodotos' narrative leaves little doubt that this was a true 'soldier's battle'. The alleged exchanging of the wings during the second stage of the campaign may have been the preliminary to some attempt to surprise the enemy by attacking his right, but, if so, nothing came of it, and on the final day, if the truth were told, Pausanias had almost led his army to disaster. Unless we are to believe that the holding back of the Greek advance was due to deliberate manipulation of religious rites, there was really little for him to do at the end. Indeed, in this respect Pausanias was no different from any other hoplite general, as far as we know, down at least to Agis at the first battle of

4 Cf., e.g., Delbrück, 80-1; Macan (1895) ii 245-7; Grundy, 193; Burn, 248ff.; Green, 35-7.

5 Burn, 249.

Mantineia, and it was not really until the Nemea, in 394, that a battle involving hoplites can with any certainty be said to have been won by tactics.

The same is almost certainly true of the naval engagements of 480. Herodotos tells us nothing of any tactics at Salamis, and although both he and Aischylos stress the 'orderliness' (κόσμος: 8.86, cf. *Persai* 399-400) of the Greeks, and the contrasting lack of it among the barbarians, they do not go into detail. Modern 'reconstructions' of the battle have devised the most elaborate tactical plans for the Greeks, but they are purely hypothetical, and again one doubts whether tactics really played any part in an ancient sea-battle before Phormio's first victory in the Corinthian Gulf in the early years of the Peloponnesian War. Down to that time, even a navy like that of Kerkyra – one of the first Greek states to have a substantial number of triremes, according to Thucydides (1.14.2) – still fought in an old-fashioned way, with no manoeuvring (Thucydides 1.49).

The only hint of anything in the naval warfare of 480 that can properly be called tactics is Herodotos' account of what the Greeks did on the first day at Artemision. Whatever precisely he may mean, particularly by his statement that the Greeks 'drew their sterns together into the middle' (ες τὸ μέσον τὰς πρύμνας συνήγαγον: 8.11.1), his reference to the two signals certainly gives the impression that the Greeks were fighting to a carefully rehearsed plan. However, whatever it was, it was clearly very limited in scope. In the first place, the battle was deliberately fought late in the day (8.9), presumably to obviate the possibility of either side's achieving a decisive result. Secondly the Greeks are said to have been 'in a confined space' (ἐν ὀλίγῳ: 8.11.1), either because they had adopted a particular formation, or because the enemy had forced them into it. Thirdly, they are twice said to have been 'bows on' to the enemy (ἀντίπρωροι ... κατὰ στόμα: *ibid.*), which was later thought to be a sign of lack of skill in the steersmen (Thucydides 7.36.5). Almost certainly, then, the tactical plan at Artemision was as defensive as the lengthening of the Athenian line at Marathon.

Strategically, too, the Greeks can hardly have been said to be superior. It is very difficult to believe, in the first place, that the campaign of 480 was all fought to a grand strategic plan, which involved abandoning all northern and central Greece to the enemy, including Attica, and in effect 'refusing' the landward flank, while relying on victory at sea. Apart from the fact that victory at sea would not by itself have meant the defeat of the invasion, as Mardonios' remaining in Greece after Salamis proved, it is very doubtful whether the leaders of any Greek state, even Themistokles, would have thought in these terms so soon after the creation of the first really powerful Greek navy.

Such a strategy would also have been calculated to throw the states of northern and central Greece into the enemy's arms, with the possible exception of places like Athens, Plataia, Thespiai and Phokis, which had their own special reasons for resisting. If the patriotic Greeks had an overall strategic plan, it is far more likely to have been the one Herodotos implies – to hold the enemy as far north as possible. This is why, when appealed to by the Thessalians, they apparently had no hesitation in committing a substantial army as far north as Tempe.

Beyond this their strategy was effectively dictated by what they evidently assumed to be the overwhelming numerical superiority of the enemy, and by the mobility of the enemy's forces, on both land and sea. This meant that they could not hope to defeat them in conventional, set-piece battle in the open, and this in turn limited the number of positions they could occupy with any hope of success. Thus the Tempe pass initially appeared ideal for their army, since it seemed to give the enemy only limited access. But it could too easily be turned both by routes right round the other side of Olympos, and, probably, over the south-eastern corner of the massif itself. It also had no nearby suitable base for the fleet, though this probably seemed less of a problem. There was nowhere between Tempe and the Gulf of Pagasai likely to be known to the Persians, where an army could be landed to 'turn' Tempe from the south, and the Greek fleet presumably remained at Halos, on the western shore of the Gulf of Pagasai, after it had carried the army to Thessaly (7.173.1).

Once Tempe had been abandoned, there was nowhere north of Thermopylai which offered the same chance of success, and here one can well believe that it was only on arrival that Leonidas and his men heard of the Anopaia path (7.175.2). Probably the choice of Artemision was dictated by similarly simplistic considerations – it, too, Herodotos implies (7.176.1), was conceived of as a 'pass'. Possibly in this case, however, the added complication that this 'pass' could so obviously be turned by rounding Euboia to the east, dictated the choice of the Artemision position rather than one even more 'pass-like' and nearer to Thermopylai.

It is Salamis, however, which is crucial to understanding how the Greeks arrived at their strategy. Modern scholars have seen the choice of the island as a base as part of a sophisticated plan to force the Persian navy to fight in adverse conditions, while the army was, in effect, 'refused' behind the Isthmus lines.[6] Herodotos, however, seems to have thought that Salamis became the fleet-base, at least in the first instance, because the Athenians asked for the fleet to put in there while they carried out the evacuation of Attica (8.40). Subsequently he says that when the question where to fight at sea was raised, the majority opinion was to sail to the Isthmus (8.49), and that this decision was confirmed after news of the fall of the acropolis (8.56). It was only the forceful and threatening arguments of Themistokles that got the decision changed (8.57-63). Although these arguments, as represented in Herodotos (8.60), seem to presuppose that if the Greeks remained at Salamis, the Persians would have to fight them there, this is only because either Themistokles himself, or Herodotos, was telescoping a much more hypothetical argument. Logically put, the argument would have been, 'if we fight in open waters, we stand no chance, but if we can induce the enemy to meet us in confined waters, we may stand a chance.' But this would have cut no ice with hard-headed Peloponnesians who needed to be convinced that the very real risks they ran, if they fought at Salamis, were worth taking. So the argument becomes, 'fighting in a confined space, if the results are as usual in war, we shall easily win.'

In any case, whatever the arguments, the Greek position at Salamis certainly did not compel the Persians to fight them there. The Persian army did not depend upon the navy for its supplies, and the Persian navy was probably still large enough both to bottle up the Greek fleet in the Salamis channel, and to turn the Isthmus lines by landing troops elsewhere on the coast of the Peloponnese. Even if it was not large enough to do both, it could still have ignored the Greek fleet and proceeded with operations against the Peloponnese. Faced with this threat, the Greek fleet would, in its turn, have had to choose between ignoring it and coming out to fight, in which latter case it would have

6 Cf., especially, Custance, *War at Sea: modern theory and ancient practice* (Edinburgh & London, 1919), 26-7.

lost the advantage of confined waters. Thus the victory at Salamis was not the result of brilliant strategy, but of luck – or, rather, of a blunder by the Persians, even if this last was induced by Themistokles' famous trick.

As for Plataia, here the strategic roles were reversed. In the end it was the Greeks who took the offensive, and all Mardonios' actions up to the very last moment suggest that he wanted to avoid battle. Up to that moment, too, he had succeeded brilliantly not only in avoiding battle, but also in nearly bringing about a humiliating Greek retreat. Pausanias and his fellow Greek commanders, for their part, seem to have had no idea how to force the battle they wanted, other than by successive advances, first to the Isthmus, then to Eleusis, then to the northern foothills of Kithairon, and finally to the Asopos. Even if Pausanias' strange suggestion that the Spartans and Athenians should swap places is historical and designed, somehow, to bring about a battle on ground of his choosing, it failed, and, in the end, the battle he got was forced upon him when his army was split into three unequal parts and in full retreat.

Nevertheless, in a sense, the war may have been won and lost in the strategic sphere. The Greek strategy, though crude and largely defensive, at least in 480, was at least simple and effective. They managed to avoid any catastrophic defeat on land, and at sea, after holding the enemy to a draw off Artemision, won a decisive victory off Salamis. What is perhaps more to the point is that they *had* a strategy – that is to say, those who were prepared to resist, on the whole worked together to a common plan and under common leadership, so that neither the disaster at Thermopylai, nor the withdrawal from Artemision, nor the capture of Athens, in the end made any difference to the continued resistance.

That the Greeks put up a united resistance, however limited, was undoubtedly the first reason for their success. But one should not exaggerate this unity. It was limited to a minority of states and was always a fragile affair. Even if we add to the thirty-one states which 'warred the war', in the words of the serpent-column, the various states which played some part in the resistance, but whose names do not appear on the monument, we still only get a total of under forty states, and their loyalty was not constant.

The fact that some did not contribute from the first, probably means nothing, since most of those in question – Pale, Leukas, Anaktorion, Ambrakia and Kroton – were distant, and others – Lemnos, Naxos and Tenos – had originally sent their ships to join Xerxes' fleet. Nor can we really blame Opountian Lokris and Phokis for 'medizing', once their territories had been overrun – the latter, in any case, only did so partially and under extreme pressure. The Boiotians, too, may perhaps be excused, since their territory was really indefensible once Thermopylai had fallen At least some Thebans fought at Thermopylai, and possibly not as dishonourably as Herodotos would have us believe. But if the people of Thespiai and Plataia could stay loyal, why could not the Thebans and the others? The failure of the contingents from Elis and Mantineia to arrive in time for Plataia shows that even the core of the alliance – the so-called 'Peloponnesian League' – was fragile, and most shocking of all was the 'medism' of Argos. The Argives were never in any immediate danger of attack, except possibly from the Persian fleet, and although we may understand why they found it so difficult to serve with Spartans, let alone under Spartan leadership, we should remember that the Aiginetans and Athenians were prepared to sink their differences, and the Athenians to serve under Spartans even at sea. One cannot help but feel that Argive behaviour was a disgrace to a city which had once boasted that it had the best soldiers in Greece, when Sparta was only famous for its women.

Nevertheless, for all its fragility, the fact that even so few states managed to form an alliance was the *sine qua non* for success. The core of the alliance was, of course, what we call the 'Peloponnesian League', in ancient terms 'The Lakedaimonians and their Allies'. Of the thirty-nine states which fought the Persians at one time or another, just under half were either probably allies of Sparta, or, in the cases of Poteidaia, Leukas, Anaktorion and Ambrakia, had ties with Sparta's principal ally, Corinth. Although the states which fought Xerxes, formed a new alliance, the fact that so many of them were allies of Sparta and had been accustomed to take common decisions since Sparta initiated the practice of consultation at the end of the sixth century (cf. 5.90ff.), meant that an embryonic structure for the new alliance already existed. More importantly, there could really be no question, from the beginning, about who was to command the allied forces, though it was still immensely to Athens' credit that she did not insist on command at sea (cf. 7.161 & 8.2.2ff.). Eurybiadas and Pausanias may not have been strategic or tactical geniuses, but, like Eisenhower, they managed to hold their heterogenous forces together, sometimes despite the *prima donna*-like behaviour of some of their subordinates, and one only has to remember what happened at Lade to see how important this was.

All this may have come as a considerable shock to the Persians. Admittedly their previous experience of fighting Greeks, in the Ionian revolt, should have taught them that Greeks were capable of uniting, but Lade had suggested that any unity they achieved would not last the course, and what the Persians knew of mainland Greeks might well have given them reason to believe that the latter were even less likely to unite. They had presumably heard, for example, that Athens was at war with Aigina in the 480s, and that at about the time of Marathon the Arcadians had been disaffected from Sparta (6.74.1). They were almost certainly aware that the only state which had actually supported Athens at Marathon had been Plataia, and that for all their talk, the Spartans had arrived too late. They no doubt knew all about such traditional antagonisms as those between Sparta and Argos, Athens and Boiotia and Phokis and Thessaly. The presence at the Persian court of exiles such as the Peisistratidai of Athens and Damaratos of Sparta, would have been a constant reminder of the deep divisions within individual states, and other potential 'quislings' like the Aleuadai of Larisa (7.6.2), and, possibly, men like Timagenidas and Attaginos in Thebes (9.86.1), were also in touch. Thus the Persians may well have believed that treachery such as that which had delivered Eretria into their hands before Marathon (6.101), would again play its part.

Nor need they have been worried about such resistance as they probably thought they were likely to encounter. In the Ionian revolt, after all, they had repeatedly defeated Greek forces on land, including one which had contained Athenians, outside Ephesos, and at sea they had decisively defeated the Ionians off Lade. They may have known something of the prowess of Spartan hoplites, but what could so few achieve? They probably knew, too, that Athens had built a great navy, but could new ships and inexperienced crews match the Phoenicians or the Egyptians? As for walled cities, these were no problem, as victorious sieges from that of Phokaia by Harpagos the Mede

(1.162.2), to that of Eretria, had shown. Mainland Greece was far smaller in area than the Greek parts of Asia Minor and Thrace they had already conquered, and there was nothing to suggest that its conquest would not be just as easy.

Nor will the early stages of the invasion have done anything to shake Persian confidence. The Greek army had not dared to face them at Tempe and had been swept aside with heavy loss at Thermopylai. The Greek navy had put up a spirited fight off Artemision, but, in the end, had been forced to withdraw. Within three months of crossing the Hellespont, Athens, their principal objective, was in their hands. It may, then, have been over-confidence which led them to commit the two fatal blunders, which, as Thucydides evidently saw (1.69.5), were the main reasons for their failure – committing their fleet to battle in confined waters at Salamis, and committing their army to a hand-to-hand encounter at Plataia.

Neither battle was necessary from the Persian point of view. The Greek fleet was effectively bottled up at Salamis, and could have been ignored – indeed, if Herodotos is to be believed, it had decided to withdraw to the Isthmus, where it could either have continued to be ignored, or been brought to battle in at least somewhat more favourable circumstances. If the story of Sikinnos' message is true, moreover, the Persians knew all this, and possibly knew too that a serious split had developed between the Athenians, Megarians and Aiginetans, on the one hand, and the Peloponnesians, on the other. Thus there was everything to be said for leaving dissension to do its work, and, one would have thought, hardly anything for seeking battle in the straits. But news of the divisions amongst the various contingents of the enemy fleet probably fitted in so well with long-held Persian expectations that the temptation to finish the naval part of the job was irresistible.

Plataia, too, was unnecessary. A far surer way of achieving the conquest of the rest of Greece would have been to bring about the collapse of the alliance, and this Mardonios was well on the way to achieving. His initial diplomatic feelers had failed, but Athens' ringing declarations of resistance to the last man had evidently been based on the assumption that the Peloponnesians would take the offensive (cf. 9.7 1), and it had only taken the dashing of these hopes to make the Athenians sing a very different tune (cf. 9.11.1-2). Reluctantly, the Spartans had been forced to take the offensive after all, but had apparently not been able to carry all their Peloponnesian allies with them. No troops came from Mantineia, for example, until too late, though they had been represented at Thermopylai, and though the Tegeates and Orchomenians turned out in greater numbers, there were no hoplites 'from the rest of Arcadia', as there had been at Thermopylai (7.202), so that, in the end, there were actually fewer Arcadians at Plataia than in the former battle.

As day succeeded day in the dusty fields along the Asopos, moreover, even if one does not believe in Plutarch's oligarchic plot among the Athenians, the old strains began to appear. When the order came to retreat, half the army decamped and played little or no further part, and the Athenians again became suspicious of Spartan motives, 'knowing that they thought one thing and said another' (9.54.1). It is doubtful, in short, whether the alliance would have survived a complete withdrawal to the Isthmus, such as was very much on the cards, once the retreat from the Asopos began. Again, the temptation to achieve a spectacular victory was perhaps too great for Mardonios, or perhaps he was forced into a battle not of his choosing, by the overeagerness of his men.

But even if the war was lost by the Persians, it still had to be won by the Greeks, and they did have certain advantages. It is quite clear, in the first place, that Herodotos thought that Greek soldiers were, in two respects, better equipped than their opponents – they had longer spears (7.211.2) and were better protected (9.62.3, 63.2). Some commentators continue to repeat that hoplites still wore bronze armour at this date,[7] but the evidence of vase-painting almost certainly proves them wrong. It strongly suggests that the Athenians, at least, had abandoned plate armour for some kind of more flexible jerkin, made of leather or linen,[8] and this probably means that the other more advanced states had done the same, though old-fashioned armour may have lingered among the more backward. Nevertheless, whatever they were made of, Greek cuirasses seem to have given their wearers better protection than anything worn by most Persian troops, and one should also not forget the greaves worn by hoplites, but by few, if any, of their opponents.

Longer spears and better protective clothing would undoubtedly have given Greek hoplites an advantage in hand-to-hand combat, and the latter would also have provided some protection against arrows, though the story of Kallikrates, assuming that he was wearing some kind of cuirass, shows that an arrow could still penetrate (9.72.1). Probably even better protection against arrows was provided by the hoplite shield. This may be included in Herodotos' remarks about Persian lack of armour (9.62.3 & 9.63.2), but is not specifically mentioned. However, the advantage of a shield over body-armour in protecting a man from arrow-fire is that it is moveable: however fast an arrow flew, a man at the receiving end would have had a split second to react, and even an almost instinctive jerk of the shield might have been just enough. The shield also, of course, offered similar protection against both thrusting and throwing spears, and could itself be used as a weapon, particularly in the 'shoving' stage of a *mêlée*.

Hoplites also enjoyed another advantage when it came to hand-to-hand combat. Even if few of them were in any proper sense trained, and most had had little or no experience, nevertheless this was essentially the only kind of fighting they knew. By the time of Marathon, Greek soldiers had been fighting like this for some 150 years or more, and this long tradition would have given even the most inexperienced a certain quasi-inherited expertise. They *knew* what they had to do, whereas Persian soldiers may have found it difficult to adjust to static, close-quarter combat. This is really what lies behind Herodotos' remarks about Persian lack of 'experience' (ἐπιστήμη) and 'skill' (σοφία) at Plataia (9.62.3).

At sea, however, the situation was almost certainly reversed. Although Herodotos believed that the manoeuvre called the '*diekplous*' was practised by the Ionians at Lade (6.12.1 & 15.2), he rather implies that it was unknown to the mainland Greeks. He says that on the first day at Artemision they wanted to make trial of the Persian 'way of fighting and *diekplous*' (8.9), and he never specifically says the Greeks used the *diekplous* either at Artemision or Salamis. Instead, if what he says about their manoeuvres on the first day at the former really does mean that they formed a circle, they adopted what was later to become the classic counter by an inferior fleet to the *diekplous* of a superior one (cf. Thucydides 2.83.5 & 3.78.).

---

7 Cf., e.g., Burn, 252; Cook, 102; Hammond, 1988, 510; Barron, 608.

8 Cf., e.g., A.M. Snodgrass, *Arms and Armour of the Greeks* (London, 1967), 90f.; P. Connolly, *Greece and Rome at War* (London, 1981), 54f.

Nevertheless, it is possible that the particular circumstances in which Salamis was fought not only nullified the advantages the Persians would have enjoyed in open water, but tipped the balance in favour of the Greeks. Unfortunately, the only evidence for making a detailed comparison between the ships of the two sides is what Plutarch says in his lives of Themistokles and Kimon (14.2 & 12.2), and although this is accepted by some scholars,[9] it is contradicted by Herodotos. In Plutarch it is the Persian ships which are 'heavy in their movements' βαρείας ἐπιφερομένας: *Themistokles* 14.2), the Greek which are built 'for speed and manoeuvre' (πρὸς μὲν τάχος ... καὶ περιαγωγήν: *Kimon* 12.2). But in Herodotos it is the Persians who have the 'better sailing' ships (ἄμεινον πλεούσας: 8.10.1), the Greeks the 'heavier' (βαρυτέρας: 8.60α).

If Herodotos is right, and if the Greek ships were 'heavier' because they were more stoutly constructed, then, as Themistokles is supposed to have claimed (8.60α–β), the confined space in which Salamis was fought would have suited them, just as the 'open sea' would have suited the enemy. In addition to helping to nullify Persian superiority in numbers, narrow waters would have deprived the 'faster sailing' Persian ships of the room to manoeuvre. As we have seen, both Aischylos and Herodotos seem to emphasise the use of the ram at Salamis, and Thucydides' accounts of the battle off Erineus in Achaia, in 413 (7.34), and of the subsequent battles in the 'Grand Harbour' of Syracuse (7.36-8, 40-1, 60-71), make it clear that in a confined space, where there was nothing for it but to ram prow to prow, the more heavily constructed ships came off best.

Aischylos and Herodotos clearly regarded boarding as unimportant at Salamis, though, naturally enough, any Greek captain who rammed one of the enemy was in a position to capture it, if he wanted to, as Polykritos of Aigina evidently did the Sidonian vessel on which his fellow-countrman, Pytheas, had been a prisoner (8.92.1). But boarding may have been more important at Artemision, where the Greeks are said to have 'captured' thirty enemy ships (8.11.2), and the advantages hoplites enjoyed in a *mêlée* on land, would also have stood them in good stead in a fight across the decks. It may also be of significance that the Egyptians are said to have particularly distinguished themselves at Artemision, capturing five Greek ships, for Egyptian marines were conspicuously well armed (7.89.3). They were later taken off their ships to form part of Mardonios' army (9.32). For that matter, it is noticeable that the only ships on the Persian side said to have captured ships at Salamis, apart from the Samothracian vessel with its javelineers (8.90.2), were manned by Ionians (8.85.2), including, presumably, hoplite marines.

But even though the Greeks may have been better equipped for the particular circumstances of the two decisive battles, they still had to be ready to use their equipment, and undoubtedly the final reason for their success was the sheer, stubborn courage they displayed. There have been many 'soldier's battles' in history, but perhaps not so many 'soldier's wars': the Persian wars were clearly an example. Most modern commentators have looked for and found a brilliant strategy and brilliant tactics behind the Greek victories.[10] But nothing in the evidence supports the idea that the Greek

---

9 E.g. Morrison & Coates, 155.

10 Peter Green is, perhaps, the worst offender - cf., e.g., 182, on Salamis, 'The battle of Salamis was *planned* [his italics], down to the last detail'; and 264, on Plataia, 'we can understand

commanders were chosen for their ability, or that they were trained for their task, and it would be very surprising if they all turned out to be born generals and admirals.

This is not, of course, to deny that the Greeks chose their ground, at least in every battle except the last, and that they chose it to their advantage. But it did not require any great strategic flair to know that they stood little or no chance on open ground or in open water, and even here, if Herodotos is to be believed, the majority of the naval commanders, led by Adeimantos of Corinth, was apparently blissfully ignorant of even this simple truth, and one wonders whether Pausanias was much better. Having chosen their ground, however, there was a severe limit to what any commander could do, whether on land or at sea. If one was an Epameinondas or a Hannibal, one might dispose one's forces in new and adventurous ways, and if the enemy behaved as expected, achieve a Leuktra or a Cannae. But there was not much one could do once battle was joined, and changes of formation in the face of the enemy often went disastrously wrong.

In the Persian Wars, there is very little evidence for tactical dispositions or manoeuvring, and too much has been read into what there is. Thus at Marathon the Athenians thinned their centre because they were afraid of being outflanked, not because they were hoping to achieve a double envelopment, and the chances are that whatever it was the two Greek wings did, it was not the result of tactical planning. In particular, it often seems to be forgotten that the Plataians were on the left wing of the Athenian line, and it is extremely unlikely that they could have been integrated into some brilliant tactical scheme in the time available.

Marathon was won because ordinary, amateur soldiers found the courage to break into a trot when the arrows began to fall, instead of grinding to a halt, and when, surprisingly, the enemy wings fled, not to take the easy way out and follow them, but to stop and somehow come to the aid of the hard-pressed centre. There is no need to believe that any orders were given – indeed, one wonders whether they could have been heard through the walls of a bronze helmet, amidst the noise of battle. Instead, during the advance, here and there a courageous man would have broken into a stumbling run, and soon the whole glorious mob would have been at the double, carried along by the sheer exhilaration of the moment. Similarly, when the Persian wings fled, the initial reaction among the Greek hoplites of the wings was probably to stop and get back their breath. But again, it would only have required one or two courageous souls to draw attention to the plight of the centre, to turn the halt into a swing inwards against the Persian flanks. It was never a question of the discipline of Prussian guardsmen, but the determination of ordinary men not to let down their mates.

Similarly, at Thermopylai, one would imagine most of the Greek soldiers found the behaviour of the Spartans just as strange as did Xerxes' scout, and would have stood aghast when, the first time, the Spartan phalanx turned their backs in apparently headlong flight. One would like to think that some of them tried to emulate the Spartans' disciplined fighting skills, but one suspects the fumbling courage of the Phokians who fled in a body to the nearest hill, and prepared to die (7.218.3), was

---

exactly how Pausanias planned his final bid for victory.' But other commentators, from Delbrück to Barron, are prone to use such language.

nearer the mark. Yet something rubbed off if it is true that the men of Thespiai *volunteered* to stay with Leonidas (7.222).

At sea, off Artemision and Salamis, Greek sailors drawn from the poorest men in their states, and some of them, like the Plataians, with little or no experience of the sea, patiently rowed their triremes back and forth, and time and again, when called upon, bent their backs to produce the final, terrifying, ramming speed. Unlike the sailors in Nelson's navy, for example, they can have had little confidence that they were better at their job than the enemy, or that their commanders, with a long tradition of victory at sea behind them, knew exactly what they were doing. But they endured three gruelling fights at Artemision, only to have to row away miserably in the end, with the job still to do, and yet came back for their final, glorious day at Salamis – a day we can still share with them by reading the messenger-speech in Aischylos' *Persai*.

Finally, at Plataia, the average hoplite could have been forgiven for thinking that his commanders were out of their depth, as day followed day and nothing happened, and the situation they found themselves in on the final morning must have been bewildering and frightening. Yet, in all three groups, there were still men prepared to fight – Tegeates who would not wait for the omens to come right, but simply got up and *advanced*; Spartans who stolidly endured the arrow-storm until told to go; Athenians who stood off some of the toughest hoplites in Greece; most typically Megarians and Phleiasians who, albeit incompetently, still marched 'to the sound of the guns'.

Moreover, behind the stubborn courage of these men was something even more remarkable, the moral courage of the citizen-bodies which committed them to the fray. In modern wars, even where democracies are involved, the ordinary soldier has very little, if any, say in whether or not he goes to war, save in so far as he elects the people who make the decisions, in the first place. Similarly, in the Persian Wars, it is unlikely that the rowers in Corinthian or Aiginetan ships had a vote, still less likely that those in Spartan vessels did – they were probably helots. Even on land the 5000 *perioikoi* who fought at Plataia, though 'Lakedaimonians' like the Spartans, would have had no say in the declaration of war. But even at sea most of the 30,000 or so men who rowed for Athens, were Athenian citizens, and could have voted in the assembly, and this was no doubt true of at least some of the other sailors. On land, even in the most oligarchic states, the hoplites probably had a say in decision-making, even if it was only to ratify proposals laid before them by some kind of probouleutic council. So not only Athenian, but Spartan and Corinthian, Plataian and Megarian hoplites, would have been men who had themselves voted to endure the appalling experience of hand-to-hand combat – there was nothing remote about such decisions, no 'them' to blame.

In these wars, too, the decision was not the comparatively easy one of deciding to march out and defend one's own home. When the Plataians decided to go to the aid of the Athenians at Marathon, they were, admittedly, fulfilling a treaty-obligation, but it was still a question of voting to march about eighty kilometres across rough terrain to fight for men who spoke a different dialect, and to obey the orders of another state's generals.[11] Even more remarkable was the willingness of Thespiai apparently to send *all* its hoplites to fight at Thermopylai (cf.9.30). As far as we know, Thespiai had no

11 Burn, in *The Lyric Age of Greece* (London, 1960), 37, conjures up a marvellous picture of what it may have been like when the Plataians voted to march to Marathon.

obligation to Sparta or even Athens, although, like Plataia, there was a tendency for its people to gravitate towards the latter out of hostility towards Thebes. But at this juncture Thebes still adhered, however precariously, to the patriotic cause, and, in any case, no other Greek state sent all its troops to Thermopylai, except Opountian Lokris, which was very much in the 'firing line'. The 400 Theban hoplites who turned out to fight also deserve all honour, even if they represented a pro-Spartan faction which had nothing to lose and everything to gain. One would like to believe that Herodotos' story of their surrender at the end is untrue.

There appears to have been the same sense of duty to something above and beyond their own interests about the commitment of many states to the war at sea. There seems to have been no question of Chalkis, Eretria and Styra, for example, 'medizing' after Thermopylai, and although Ambrakia and Leukas were originally colonies of Corinth, they could, no doubt, have sheltered under the excuse of 'adverse winds', like the Kerkyraians (7.168), to get out of risking their ships at Salamis, and even if Phaÿllos of Kroton and his men were exiles (cf. Pausanias 10.9.1), they were under no compulsion to fight for Greece. Striking, too, is the commitment of the small islands, Kythnos, Seriphos, Siphnos and Melos, even though the latter three could only contribute old-fashioned pentekonters (8.48).

All honour, too, to Antidoros of Lemnos and his crew, who came over to the Greeks at Artemision (8.11.3), to Demokritos of Naxos and his four ships which had been sent to join Xerxes, and joined the Greeks instead (8.46.3), and to Panaitios of Tenos who brought the vital news of Persian movements the night before Salamis (8.82.1). One normally takes a dim view of desertion, even from the 'enemy', but these were men deserting for no promise of reward, as far as we know, though Antidoros was given land on Salamis (*loc.cit.*), and deserting, too, what appeared to be the winning side. There was no guarantee that they would ever be allowed home and even if the usual internal squabbling lay behind their actions, they surely chose 'the better cause'.

But most striking of all is the turn-out for the Plataia campaign. It is true that the vast majority of the hoplites came from Sparta and her allies – 27,300 out of 38,700 – and that a further 1600 came from Corinth's erstwhile colonies. But it was a remarkable effort, all the same, for that day and age. The numbers are striking enough in themselves, but even more impressive is the spread of states which contributed, from Poteidaia in the north to Sparta in the south, and from Styra in the east to Pale on Kephallenia in the west. The majority of these states lay at considerable distances from the battlefield and the logistical problems of getting their hoplites there and then maintaining them would have been horrendous for such relatively primitive communities. Yet we hear of no desertions as the campaign dragged on, unless we count the 'flight' of the centre to Plataia before the final day – rather, according to Herodotos, contingents continued to come in until after the battle was over.

Even more remarkable examples of collective moral courage were the decisions of the peoples of Plataia and Thespiai not to submit even when there was no hope left of defending their homes. Most remarkable of all is the case of Athens. Here we have one of the largest states in Greece, with a population scattered over some 2600km^2, which evacuated almost its entire population, rather than surrender. Even if Herodotos' account of the meeting of the fleet commanders at which Adeimantos of Corinth is supposed to have tried to silence Themistokles by saying that he had no 'country' and was a 'city-less man' (8.61.1), is untrue, it surely gives us an idea of the traumas inherent in such decisions. Yet the Athenians were apparently prepared to go through them not once, but twice. It is difficult to think of a parallel in history for the peoples of states being prepared to carry on a war, even after total evacuation from their homes.

But if one has to choose one incident that best explains why the Greeks won, it should surely be that great moment at Salamis when Polykritos of Aigina, having just rammed a Sidonian galley, looked across the water to see an Athenian racing by in pursuit of another enemy warship, and, recognizing Themistokles' flagship, shouted some taunt about Aiginetan medism (8.92). Here was a man probably at the supreme moment of his life, taking part in the greatest sea-battle the Greeks ever fought, and still he had time time to remember that he was an Aiginetan first, and only a Greek second, and that it would have taken only the slightest twist of fortune to have sent him careering into the Athenian ship instead. Clearly, in the end, such men as Polykritos were, quite simply, irrepressible.

Abbreviations

AAA = *Αρχαιολογικα Αναλεκτα εξ Αθηνων.*
AC = *Antiquité classique.*
ADelt = *Αρχαιολογικον Δελτιον.*
AJA = *American Journal of Archaeology.*
AJAH = *American Journal of Ancient History.*
AJSL = *American Journal of Semitic Languages.*
AM = *Mitteilungen des deutschen archäologischen Instituts, Athenische Abteilung.*
BCH = *Bulletin de correspondance hellénique.*
BICS = *Bulletin of the Institute of Classical Studies*, London.
BSA = *Annual of the British School at Athens.*
CJ = *Classical Journal.*
CPh = *Classical Philology.*
CQ = *Classical Quarterly.*
CR = *Classical Review.*
CSCA = *California Studies in Classical Antiquity.*
CW = *Classical Weekly.*
Ergon = *Εργον της Αρχαιολογικης Εταιρειας.*
GRBS = *Greek, Roman and Byzantine Studies.*
HSCPh = *Harvard Studies in Classical Philology.*
HUCA = *Hebrew Union College Annual.*
JAOS = *Journal of the American Oriental Society.*
JDAI = *Jahrbuch des deutschen archäologischen Instituts.*
JHS = *The Journal of Hellenic Studies.*
JÖAI = *Jahrbuch des österreichischen archäologischen Instituts.*
PAE = *Πρακτικα της Αρχαιολογικης Εταιρειας.*
PCPhS = *Proceedings of the Cambridge Philological Society.*
PP = *La Parola del Passato.*
RA = *Revue archéologique.*
RE = *Pauly's Real-Encyclopädie der classischen Altertumswissenschaft.*
REA = *Revue des études anciennes.*
RFIC = *Rivista di filologia e d'istruzione classica.*
RhM = *Rheinisches Museum für Philologie.*
SEG = *Supplementum Epigraphicum Graecum.*
SO = *Symbolae Osloenses.*
TAPA = *Transactions of the American Philological Society.*

Note also the following:-

AP = *'Αθηναίων Πολιτεία* (*Athênaiôn Politeia*, i.e. 'Constitution of the Athenians'), attributed to Aristotle.
AS iv = *Antike Schlachtfelder* iv, ed. J.Kromayer (Berlin, 1924-31).

CAH = *The Cambridge Ancient History.*

FGH = *Fragmente der griechischen Historiker*, F.Jacoby (Berlin, 1922-).

HCT = *A Historical Commentary on Thucydides*, vols. i-v, A.W.Gomme and others, (Oxford, 1945ff.)

HW = *A Commentary on Herodotus*, vols i & ii, W.W.How & J.Wells (corrected impression, Oxford, 1928).

IG = *Inscriptiones Graecae.*

LP = *Λακεδαιμονίων Πολιτεία (Lakedaimoniôn Politeia*, i.e '*Constitution of the Spartans*'), attributed to Xenophon.

ML = *Greek Historical Inscriptions*, R.Meiggs & D.Lewis (Oxford, 1969).

Bibliography

[Note: not all the works referred to in the notes are in the bibliography and *vice versa*. Other abbreviations are given at the beginning of the relevant entry below, in the form, e.g., 'Burn = Burn, A.R., *Persia and the Greeks* (London, 1962)].

Agard, W.J. 'Boreas at Athens', *CJ* 61 (1966), 241ff.

Allinson, F.G. 'The original Marathon runner', *CW* 24 (1931), 152.

Amandry, P. 'Sur les "épigrammes de Marathon"', *Theoria: Festschrift Schuchhardt* (Baden-Baden, 1960), 1ff.

Armayor, O.K. 'Herodotus' catalogues and the Persian Empire in the light of the monuments and the Greek literary tradition,' *TAPA* 108 (1978), 1ff.

Avery, H.C. 'Herodotus 6.112.2', *TAPA* 103 (1972), 15ff.

Avery, H.C. 'The number of Persian dead at Marathon', *Historia* 22 (1973), 757.

Baelen, J. *L'an 480. Salamine.* (Paris, 1961).

Baillie Reynolds, P.K. 'The shield signal at the Battle of Marathon', *JHS* 49 (1929), 160ff.

Balcer, J.M. 'Athenian politics: the ten years after Marathon', *Panathenaia: Studies in Athenian Life and Thought in the Classical Age* (ed. T.E.Gregory & A.J.Podlecki, Lawrence, 1979), 27ff.

Balcer, J.M. 'Persian occupied Thrace (Skudra)', *Historia* (37 (1988), 1ff.

Balcer, J.M. 'The Persian Wars against Greece', *Historia* 38 (1989), 127ff.

Barron = Barron, J.P. *Cambridge Ancient History* (2nd edition, 1988), chapter 11.

Barth, H. 'Das Verhalten des Themistokles gegenüber dem Gelde, οὐ γὰρ ἐπαύετο πλεονεκτέων (Herodot VIII 12)', *Klio* 43-5 (1965), 30ff.

Bayer, E. 'Psyttaleia', *Historia* 18 (1969), 640.

Beloch = Beloch, K.J. *Griechische Geschichte*,[2] ii. 1 and 2 (Strassburg, 1914 & 1916).

Bengston, H. 'Zur Vorgeschichte der Schlacht bei Salamis,' *Chiron* 1 (1971) 89ff.

Béquignon, Y. 'Un décret de Thémistocle', *RA* 48 (1961), 57ff.

Berthold, R.M. 'Which way to Marathon?', *REA* 78-9 (176-7), 84ff.

Bicknell, P.J. 'The command structure and generals of the Marathon campaign', *AC* 39 (1970), 427ff.

Bicknell, P.J. 'The date of Miltiades' Parian expedition,' *AC* 41 (1972), 225ff.

Bigwood, J.M. 'Ctesias as historian of the Persian Wars', *Phoenix* 32 (1978), 14ff.

Boegehold, A. 'The Salamis epigram', *GRBS* 6 (1975), 176ff.

Boucher, A. 'La bataille de Platées d'après Hérodote,' *RA* 2 (1915), 237ff.

Bovon, A. 'La représentation des guerriers perses et la notion de Barbare dans la Ire moitié du Ve siècle', *BCH* 87 (1963), 579ff.

Brunt, P.A. 'The Hellenic League against Persia', *Historia* 2 (1953), 135ff.

Buck, R.J. 'The reforms of 487 B.C. in the selection of Archons', *CPh* 60 (1965), 96ff.

Buck, R.J. 'Boeotarchs at Thermopylae', *CPh* 69 (1974), 47f.

Burn = Burn, A.R. *Persia and the Greeks* (London, 1962).

Burn, A.R. 'Thermopylae and Callidromos', *Studies Presented to D.M. Robertson on his Seventieth Birthday* I (St. Louis, 1953), 479ff.

Burn, A.R. 'Hammond on Marathon: a few notes', *JHS* 89 (1969), 118.

Burn, A.R. 'Thermopylae revisited and some topographical notes on Marathon and Plataiai', *Greece and the Eastern Mediterranean in Ancient History and Prehistory* (ed. K.H.Kinzl, Berlin, 1977), 89ff.

Burstein, S.M. 'The Recall of the ostracized and the Themistocles Decree', *CSCA* 4 (1971), 93ff.

Bury, J.B. 'The campaign of Artemisium and Thermopylae', *BSA* 2 (1895/6), 83ff.

Bury, J.B. 'The battle of Marathon', *CR* 10 (1896), 95ff.

Bury, J.B. 'Aristeides at Salamis', *CR* 10 (1896), 414ff.

Busolt = Busolt, G. *Griechische Geschichte*,^{2} ii (Gotha, 1895).

Calabi Limentani, I. 'Sull tradizione del consiglio di Temistocle di abbandonare Atene davanti al pericolo persiano', *PP* 22 (1967), 264ff.

Caspari = Caspari (Cary), M.O.B. 'Stray notes on the Persian Wars', *JHS* 31 (1911), 100ff.

Cataudella, M.R. 'Erodoto, Temistocle e il decreto di Trezene', *Athenaeum* 43 (1965). 383ff.

Chambers, M. 'The authenticity of the Themistocles decree', *American Historical Review* 67 (1961/2), 306ff.

Chambers, M. 'The significance of the Themistocles Decree' *Philologus* 111 (1967), 157ff.

Cole, J.W. 'Alexander Philhellene and Themistocles', *AC* 47 (1978), 37ff.

Conomis, N.C. 'A decree of Themistocles from Troezen. A Note', *Klio* 40 (1962), 44ff.

Cook = Cook, J.M. *The Persian Empire* (London, 1983).

Daskalakis, A. *Problèmes historiques autour de la bataille de Thermopyles* (Paris, 1962).

Daskalakis, A. 'Les raisons réelles du sacrifice de Léonidas et l'importance historique de la bataille de Thermopyles', *Studii classice* 6 (1964), 57ff.

Delbrück = Delbrück, H. *History of the Art of War*, vol. i, *Antiquity* (trans. W.J.Renfroe, Jr., Westport, Connecticut, 1975).

Delorme, J. 'Deux notes sur la bataille de Salamine', *BCH* 102 (1978), 87ff.

Demand, N. 'Herodotus and metoikesis in the Persian Wars', *AJPh* 109 (1988), 416ff.

Develin, R. 'Miltiades and the Parian expedition', *AC* 46 (1977), 571ff.

Donlan, W. & Thompson, J. 'The charge at Marathon: Herodotus 6.112', *CJ* 71 (1976), 339ff.

Donlan, W. & Thompson, J. 'The charge at Marathon again', *CW* 72 (1979), 419f.

Dow, S. 'The purported Decree of Themistocles: stele and inscription', *AJA* 66 (1962), 353ff.

Erbse 'Vier Bemerkunden zu Herodot', *RhM* 98 (1955), 117ff.

Evans, J.A.S. 'The final problem at Thermopylae', *GRBS* 5 (1964), 231ff.

Evans, J.A.S. 'Notes on Thermopylae and Artemision', *Historia* 18 (1969), 389ff.

Evans, J.A.S. 'The oracle of the "wooden wall"', *CJ* 78 (1982-3), 24ff.

Evans, J.A.S. 'Herodotus and Marathon', *Florilegium* 6 (1984), 1ff.

Evans, J.A.S. 'Cavalry about the time of the Persian wars: a speculative essay', *CJ* 82 (1986-7), 97ff.

Fehling = Fehling, D. (trans. Howie, J.G.), *Herodotus and his Sources: citation, invention and narrative art* (Leeds, 1989).

Ferrill, A. 'Herodotus and the strategy and tactics of the invasion of Xerxes', *American Historical Review* 72 (1966), 102ff.

Fischer, R. 'Das Zahlenproblem im Perserkriege 480-479 B.C.', *Klio* 25 (1932), 289ff.

Fitton Brown, A.D. 'Notes on Herodotus and Thucydides', *Hermes* 86 (1958), 379ff.

Fornara, C.W. 'The hoplite achievement at Psyttaleia', *JHS* 86 (1966), 51ff.

Fornara, C.W. 'The value of the Themistocles Decree', *American Historical Review* 73 (1967/8), 425ff.

Fornara, C.W. *Herodotos* (Oxford, 1971).

Fornara, C.W. 'Evidence for the date of Herodotus' publication', *JHS* 91 (1971), 25ff.

Fornara, C.W. 'Herodotus' knowledge of the Archidamian War', *Hermes* 109 (1981), 149ff.

Forrest, W.G. 'Herodotos and Athens', *Phoenix* 38 (1984), 1ff.

Fossey, J.M. *Topography and Population of Ancient Boiotia*, vol. i (Chicago, 1988).

Francis, E.D. & Vickers. M. 'The Oenoe painting in the Stoa Poikile, and Herodotus' account of Marathon', *BSA* 80 (1985), 99ff.

Frost, A.J. 'Themistocles and Mnesiphilos', *Historia* 20 (1971), 20ff.

Frost, A.J. 'A note on Xerxes at Salamis', *Historia* 22 (1973), 118f.

Frost, A.J. 'Troizen and the Persian War: some new data', *AJA* 82 (1978), 105ff.

Frost, F.J. 'Scyllias: diving in antiquity', *Greece & Rome* 15 (1968), 180ff.

Frost, F.J. 'The dubious origins of the 'Marathon'', *AJAH* 4 (1979), 159ff.

Garzetti, A. 'Erodoto e il decreto di Milziade ΔΕΙΝ ΕΞΙΕΝΑΙ', *Aevum* 27 (1953), 15ff.

Gillis, D. 'Marathon and the Alcmaeonids', *GRBS* 10 (1969), 133ff.

Gillis, D. *'Collaboration with the Persians'*, (*Historia* Einzelschriften 34, 1979), 1ff.

Gomme, A.W. 'Herodotus and Marathon', *Phoenix* 6 (1952), 77ff.

Goodwin, W. 'The Battle of Salamis', *HSCPh* 17 (1906), 73ff.

Grant, J.R. 'Leonidas' last stand', *Phoenix* 15 (1961), 14ff.

Green = Green, Peter, *The Year of Salamis* (London, 1970).

Grundy = Grundy, G.B. *The Great Persian War* (London, 1901).

Guratzach, C. 'Der Sieger von Salamis', *Klio* 39 (1961), 48ff.

Guarducci, M. 'Nuove osservazioni sul decreto di Temistocle', *RFIC* 39 (1961), 48ff.

Hammond, 1956 = Hammond, N.G.L. 'The battle of Salamis', *JHS* 76 (1965), 32ff.

Hammond, 1968 = Hammond, N.G.L. 'The campaign and battle of Marathon', *JHS* 88 (1968), 13ff.

Hammond, 1973 = Hammond, N.G.L. *Studies in Greek History* (Oxford, 1973).

Hammond, 1982 = Hammond, N.G.L. 'The narrative of Herodotus vii and the decree of Themistocles at Troezen', *JHS* 102 (1982), 75ff.

Hammond, 1988 = Hammond, N.G.L. *Cambridge Ancient History* (2nd edition, 1988), chapters 9 & 10.

Hammond, N.G.L. 'Studies in Greek chronology of the sixth and fifth centuries B.C.', *Historia* 4 (1955), 406ff.

Hammond, N.G.L. 'τὸ Μηδικόν and τὰ Μηδικά', *CR* (NS) 7 (1957), 100f.

Hammond, N.G.L. 'On Salamis', *AJA* 64 (1960), 367f.

Hammond, N.G.L. 'Strategia and Hegemonia in fifth-century Athens', *CQ* (NS) 19 (1969), 111ff.

Hammond, N.G.L. 'Army transport in the fifth and fourth centuries', *GRBS* 24 (1983), 27ff.

Hammond, N.G.L. 'The manning of the fleet in the decree of Themistokles', *Phoenix* 40 (1986), 143ff.

Hands, A.R. 'On strategy and oracles, 480/479 B.C.', *JHS* 85 (1965), 55ff.

Hansen, O. 'On the Athenian decree concerning Salamis', *Hermes* 115 (1987), 499.

Hansen, O. 'The memorial of Kallimachus reconsidered', *Hermes* 116 (1988), 482f.

Hardy, D.A. & Pritchett, W.K. 'Suggested Changes in the Troizen Inscription', *BSA* 59 (1964), 30f.

Harrison, E.B. 'The victory of Kallimachos', *GRBS* 12 (1971), 5ff.

Harrison, E.B 'The south frieze of the Nike temple and the Marathon painting in the Painted Stoa', *AJA* 76 (1972), 353ff., & pls. 73-8.

Hauben, H. 'The King of the Sidonians and the Persian imperial fleet', *Ancient Society* 1 (1970), 1ff.

Hauvette = Hauvette, A. *Hérodote, historien des guerres médiques* (Paris, 1894).

Henderson, R.B. 'Marathon', *JHS* 52 (1932), 302.

Hignett = Hignett, C. *Xerxes' Invasion of Greece* (Oxford, 1963).

Hodge, A.T. 'Marathon. The Persians' voyage', *TAPA* 105 (1975), 155ff.

Hodge, A.T. 'Marathon to Phaleron', *JHS* 95 (1975), 169ff.

Hodge, A.T. & Losada, L.A. 'The time of the shield signal at Marathon', *AJA* 74 (1970), 31ff.

Hooker, G.T.W. 'Their Finest Hour', *Greece & Rome* 7 (1960), 97ff.

Hope Simpson, R. 'Leonidas' decision', *Phoenix* 26 (1972), 1ff.

Hörhager, H. 'Zu den Flotten operationen am Kap Artemision', *Chiron* 3 (1973), 43ff.

How, W.W. 'Cornelius Nepos on Marathon and Paros', *JHS* 39 (1919), 48ff.

How, W.W. 'Arms, tactics and the strategy of the Persian War,' *JHS* 43 (1923), 117ff.

Hudson, H.G. 'The shield signal at Marathon', *American Historical Review* 12 (1937), 443ff.

Huxley, G.L. 'The Medism of Caryae', *GRBS* 8 (1967), 29ff.

Huxley, G.L. 'Kleidemos and the Themistokles Decree', *GRBS* 9 (1968), 313ff.

Istinsky, H.V. 'Herodot und der erste Zug des Mardonius gegen Griechenland', *Hermes* 84 (1956), 477ff.

Jacoby, F. 'Some Athenian epigrams from the Persian Wars', *Hesperia* 14 (19430, 161ff.

Jameson, M.H. 'A Decree of Themistokles from Troizen', *Hesperia* 29 (1960), 198ff.

Jameson, M.H. 'Waiting for the barbarian: new light on the Persian Wars', *Greece & Rome* 8 (1961), 5ff.

Jameson, M.H. 'A Revised text of the decree of Themistokles from Troizen', *Hesperia* 31 (1962), 310ff.

Jameson, M.H. 'The Themistokles Decree: notes on the text', *AJA* 66 (1962), 368.

Jameson, M.H. 'The provisions for mobilization in the decree of Themistokles', *Historia* 12 (1963), 385ff.

Jordan, B. *The Athenian Navy in the Classical Period* (University of California Classical Studies xiii, 1975).

Jordan, B. 'The honours for Themistocles after Salamis', *AJPh* 109 (1988), 547ff.

Karavites, P. 'Realities and appearances, 490-480 B.C.', *Historia* 26 (1977), 129ff.

Kase, E.W. & Szemler, G.J. 'Xerxes' march through Phokis (Her. 8, 31-5)', *Klio* 64 (1982), 353ff.

Keil, J. 'Die Schlacht bei Salamis', *Hermes* 73 (1938),, 329ff.

Kelly, D.H. 'Thucydides and Herodotus on the Pitanate lochos', *GRBS* 22 (1981), 31ff.

Kelly, T. 'Argive foreign policy in the fifth century B.C.', *CP* 69 (1974), 81ff.

Keyser, P. 'Errors of calculation in Herodotus', *CJ* 81 (1986), 230ff.

Kinzl, K.H. 'Miltiades' Parosexpedition in der Geschichtsschreibung', *Hermes* 104 (1976), 280ff.

Kirsten, E. 'Athener und Spartaner in der Schlacht bei Plataiai', *RhM* 86 (1937), 50ff.

Knight, W.F.J. 'The defence of the Acropolis and the panic before Salamis', *JHS* 51 (1931), 174ff.

Koumanoudis, S.N. 'A Marathon', *AAA* 11 (1978), 232ff.

Labarbe, J. 'Chiffres et modes de repartition de la flotte grecque à Artémision et à Salamine', *BCH* 76 (1952), 384ff.

Labarbe, J. 'Un témoignage capital de Polyen sur la bataille de Thermopyles', *BCH* 78 (1954), 1ff.

Labarbe, J. 'Léonidas et l'astre des tempêtes', *Revue belge de philogie* 37 (1959), 69ff.

Labarbe, J. *La Loi Navale de Thémistocle* (Paris, 1957).

Lanzani, C. 'Gli oracoli greci al tempo dell Guerre Persiane', *Rivista storica dell' Antichità* 8 (1968), 241ff.

Last, H. 'Thermopylae', *CR* 57 (1943), 63ff.

Lattimore, R. 'The wise adviser in Herodotus', *CP* 34 (1939), 24ff.

Lazenby, J.F. 'The strategy of the Greeks in the opening campaign of the Persian war', *Hermes* 92 (1964), 264ff.

Lazenby, J.F. 'Aischylos and Salamis', *Hermes* 116 (1988), 168ff.

Lehmann, G.A. 'Bemerkunden zur Themistokles? Inschrift von Troizen', *Historia* 17 (1968), 276ff.

Lenardon = Lenardon, R.J. *The Saga of Themistocles* (London, 1978).

Levy, I. 'L'inscription triomphale de Xerxes', *Revue historique* 185 (1939), 105ff.

Lewis, D.M. 'Notes on the decree of Themistocles', *CQ* (NS) 11 (1961), 61ff.

Lewis, D.M. *Sparta and Persia* (Leiden, 1977).

Loader, W.R. & Stanier, R.S. 'Questions about Marathon', *Greece & Rome* 16 (1947), 17ff. and 133ff.

Lolling. H.G. 'Das Artemision auf Nordeuböa', *AM* 8 (1883), 7ff.

Macan (1895) = Macan, R.W. *Herodotus. The Fourth, Fifth and Sixth Books*, vols. i and ii (London, 1895).

Macan (1908) = Macan, R.W. *Herodotus. The Seventh, Eighth and Ninth Books*, vol. i, parts 1 and 2, and vol. ii (London, 1908).

McCulloch, H.Y. 'Herodotus, Marathon and Athens', *SO* 57 (1982), 35ff.

McGregor, M.F. 'The Pro-Persian party at Athens', *HSCPh* 1 (1940),

Mackay, P.A. 'Procopius' *de Aedificiis* and the topography of Thermopylae', *AJA* 67 (1963), 241ff.

McLeod, W. 'The range of the ancient bow', *Phoenix* 19 (1965), 1ff.

McLeod, W. 'The bowshot and Marathon', *JHS* 90 (1970), 197-8.

McLeod, W. 'The range of the ancient bow: addenda', *Phoenix* 26 (1972), 78ff.

Maddoli, G. 'Il valore storiografico del decreto temistocleo di Trezene' *PP* 18 (1963), 419ff.

Marg, W. 'Herodot über die Folgen von Salamis', *Hermes* 81 (1953), 196ff.

Marg, W. 'Zur Strategie der Schlacht von Salamis', *Hermes* 90 (1962), 116ff.

Marinatos, S. Reports on excavations at Marathon: *AAA* 3 (1970), 63ff., 153ff., 349ff.; *Ergon* 1970, 5ff.; 1971, 5ff.; 1972, 5ff.; *PAE* 1970, 5ff.; 1971, 5ff.; 1972, 5ff.

Mason, H.J. & Wallace, M.B. 'Appius Claudius Pulcher and the Hollows of Euboia', *Hesperia* 41 (1972), 128ff.

Maurice, F. 'The size of the army of Xerxes in the invasion of Greece, 480 B.C.', *JHS* 50 (1930), 210ff.

Maurice, F. 'The campaign of Marathon', *JHS* 52 (1932), 13ff.

Merritt, B.D. 'The Persians at Delphi', *Hesperia* 16 (1947), 58ff.

Merritt, B.D. 'Epigrams from the battle of Marathon', in *The Aegean and the Near East. Studies presented to Hetty Goldman*, ed. S.S.Weinberg (New York, 1956), 268ff.

Merritt, B.D. 'Notes on the text of the decree of Themistocles', *Hesperia* 31 (1962), 413.

Meyer = Meyer, E. *Geschichte des Altertums*,[1] iii 1-417 (Stuttgart, 1901).

Meyer, E. 'Thermopylen', *AM* 71 (1956), 101ff.

Miltner, F. 'Der taktische Aufbau der Schlacht bei Salamis', *JÖAI* 26 (1930), 115ff.

Miltner, F. 'Pro Leonida', *Klio* 28 (1935), 228ff.

Milton, M.P. 'The second message to Xerxes and Themistocles' views on strategy', *Proceedings of the African Clasical Association* 17 (1983), 22ff.

Moretti, L. 'Nota al decreto di Temistocle trovato a Trezene', *RFIC* 88 (1960), 390ff.

Moretti, L. 'Studi sul decreto di Temistocle', *RFIC* 92 (19640, 117ff.

Morrison, J.S. '*Hyperesia* in naval contexts in the fifth and fourth centuries B.C.', *JHS* 104 (1984), 48ff.

Morrison, J.S. 'The Greek ships at Salamis and the *diekplous*', *JHS* 111 (1991), 196ff.

Morrison & Coates = Morrison, J.S. and Coates, J.F., *The Athenian Trireme* (Cambridge, 1986).

Morrison, J.S. & Williams, R.T. *Greek Oared Ships* (Cambridge, 1968).

Müller, D. 'Von Doriskos nach Therme. Der weg des Xerxes-Heeres durch Thrakien und Ostmakedonien', *Chiron* 5 (1975), 1ff.

Munro, 1899 = Munro, J.A.R. 'Some observations on the Persian Wars: 1. The Campaign of Marathon', *JHS* 19 (1899), 185ff.

Munro, 1902 = Munro, J.A.R. 'Some observations on the Persian Wars: 2. The campaign of Xerxes', *JHS* 22 (1902), 294ff.

Munro, 1904 = Munro, J.A.R. 'Some observations on the Persian Wars: 3. The campaign of Plataea', *JHS* 24 (1904), 144ff.

Notopoulos, J.A. 'The slaves at the Battle of Marathon', *AJP* 62 (1941), 352ff.

Ober, J. 'Edward Clarke's Ancient road to Marathon A.D. 1801', *Hesperia* 51 (1982), 453ff.

Obst, E. 'Der Felzug des Xerxes', *Klio* Beiheft xii (1914).

Olmstead, A.T. 'Persia and the Greek frontier problem', *CP* 34 (1939), 305ff.

Olmstead, A.T. *History of the Persian Empire* (Chicago, 1948).

O'Sullivan, J.N. 'On Herodotus 7.183: three sound ships for Salamis', *CQ* (NS) 27 (1977), 92ff.

Papanikolaou, D.A. 'Aischylos über die Flottenstärke bei Salamis', *RhM* 94 (1971), 217ff.

Papastonios, G.A. 'ο μηδισμὸς τῶν Θεσσαλῶν καὶ τῶν Φωκέων', *Platon* 8 (1956), 18ff.

Peek, W.R. 'Zu einem Inschrift-Fragment von Marathon', *AAA* 4 (1971), 413.

Pemberton, E.G. 'The east and west friezes of the temple of Athena Nike', *AJA* 76 (1972), 303.

Philipp, G.B. 'Wie des Gesetz es befahl? Bemerkungen zur einer neuen Leonidaslegende', *Gymnasium* 75 (1968), 1ff.

Podlecki = Podlecki, A.J. *The Life of Themistocles* (Montreal & London, 1975).

Podlecki, A.J. 'Simonides: 480', *Historia* 17 (1968), 262ff.

Prentice, W.K. 'Thermopylae and Artemision', *TAPA* 51 (1920), 5ff.

Pritchett, W.K. 'New light on Plataea', *AJA* 61 (1957), 9ff.

Pritchett, W.K. 'Calendars of Athens again', *BCH* 81 (1957), 278ff.

Pritchett, W.K. 'New light on Thermopylae', *AJA* 62 (1958), 203ff.

Pritchett, W.K. 'Towards a restudy of the Battle of Salamis', *AJA* 63 (1959), 251ff.

Pritchett, W.K. 'Marathon', *University of California Publications in Classical Archaeology* 4, 2 (1960), 137ff.

Pritchett, W.K. 'Xerxes' route over Mount Olympus', *AJA* 65 (1961), 369ff.

Pritchett, W.K. 'Herodotus and the Themistokles Decree', *AJA* 66 (1962), 43ff.

Pritchett, W.K. 'Xerxes' fleet at the 'Ovens', *AJA* 67 (1963), 1ff.

Pritchett, W.K. *Studies in Ancient Greek Topography*, vols. i–v (Berkeley & Los Angeles, 1965–1985).

Pritchett, *GSW* = Pritchett, W.K. *The Greek State at War*, vols. i–v (Berkeley & Los Angeles, 1971–1991).

Pritchett, W.K. 'Plataiai', *AJP* 100 (1979), 145ff.

Raubitschek, A.E. 'Two monuments erected after the victory of Marathon', *AJA* 44 (1940), 53ff.

Raubitschek, A.E. 'The ostracism of Xanthippos', *AJA* 51 (1947), 257ff.

Raubitschek, A.E. 'Herodotus and the inscriptions', *BICS* 8 (1961), 59ff.

Raubitschek, A.E. 'The covenant of Plataea', *TAPA* 91 (1970), 178ff.

Rhodes = Rhodes, P.J. *A Commentary on the Aristotelian* Athenaion Politeia (Oxford, 1981).

Robertson, M. 'Archaeology in Greece 1938–9', *JHS* 59 (1939), 199f.

Robertson, N. 'The Thessalian expedition of 480 B.C.', *JHS* 96 (1976), 100ff.

Robertson, N. 'Timokreon and Themistokles', *AJP* 101 (1980), 61ff.

Robertson, N. 'The decree of Themistocles in its contemporary setting', *Phoenix* 36 (1982), 1ff.

Robertson, N. 'The true meaning of the "Wooden Wall"', *CPh* 82 (1987), 1ff.

Robinson, C.A. 'Medizing Athenian aristocrats', *CW* 35 (1941), 39f.

Sacks, K.K. 'Herodotus and the dating of the Battle of Thermopylae', *CQ* (NS) 26 (1976), 232ff.

Scaife, R. 'Alexander I in the Histories of Herodotos', *Hermes* 117 (1989), 129ff.

Schachermeyr, F. 'Marathon und die persische Politik', *Historische Zeitschrift* 172 (1952), 1ff.

Schachermeyr, F. 'Die Themistokles-Stele und ihre Bedeutung für die Vorgeschichte der Schlacht von Salamis', *JÖAI* 46 (1961-3), 158ff.

Schreiner, J.H. 'The battles of 490 B.C.', *PCPhS* (NS) 16 (1970), 97ff.

Sealey, R. 'Again the siege of the Acropolis, 480 B.C.', *CSCA* 5 (1972), 183f.

Sealey, R. 'The pit and the well. The Persian heralds of 491 B.C.', *CJ* 72 (1976), 13ff.

Shrimpton, G. 'The Persian cavalry at Marathon', *Phoenix* 34 (1980), 20ff.

Sidebotham, S. 'Herodotus on Artemisium', *CW* 75 (1982), 177ff.

Smets, G. & Dorsinfang-Smets, A. 'La bataille de Salamine. Les sources', *Annuaire de l'Istitut de philologie et d'histoire orientales* 12 (1952), 409ff.

Sokolowski, K.F. 'L'attitude de Delphes au moment de l'invasion des Perses', *Przeglad historyczny* 13 (1936), 394ff.

Solmesen, L. 'Speeches in Herodotus' account of the Battle of Plataea', *CP* 39 (1944), 241ff.

Soteriades, G. Reports on excavations at Marathon: *PAE* 1933, 31ff.; 1934, 29ff.; 1936, 41ff.; 1935, 84ff.; 1939, 27ff.

Staes, B. Reports on excavations at Marathon: *ADelt* 1890, 65ff., 123ff.;1891, 34ff. and 97; *AM* 18 (1893), 46ff.

Starr, C.G. 'Why did the Greeks defeat the Persians?', *PP* 17 (1962), 321ff.

Tarn, 1908 = Tarn, W.W. 'The fleet of Xerxes', *JHS* 28 (1908), 202ff.

Themeles, P. 'Μαραθών: τὰ πρόσφατα ἀρχαιολογικὰ εὑρήματα σὲ σχέση μὲ τὴ μάχη', *ADelt* 29 (1974), 226ff.

Thompson, D.B. 'The Persian spoils in Athens', in *The Aegean and the Near East. Studies presented to Hetty Goldman* (ed. S.S.Weinberg, New York, 1956), 281ff.

Treu, M. 'Zur Neuen Themistokles-Inschrift', *Historia* 12 (1963), 47ff.

Tronson, A. 'The Hellenic League of 480 B.C. – fact or ideological fiction', *Acta Classica* 34 (1991), 93ff.

Vanderpool, E. 'An archaic inscribed stele from Marathon', *Hesperia* 11 (1942), 329ff.

Vanderpool, E. 'The deme of Marathon and the Herakleion', *AJA* 70 (1966), 319ff.

Vanderpool, E. ' A monument to the battle of Marathon', *Hesperia* 35 (1966), 93ff.

Vanderpool, E. 'The marble trophy from Marathon in the British Museum', *Hesperia* 36 (1967), 108ff.

Van der Veer, J.A.G. 'The Battle of Marathon. A topographical survey', *Mnemosyne* 34 (1982), 290.

Wace, A.J.B. 'The topography of Pelion and Magnesia', *JHS* 26 (1906), 143ff.

Wallace, M.B. 'Herodotus and Euboia', *Phoenix* 28 (1974), 22ff.

Wallace, P.W. 'Kleomenes, Marathon, the Helots and Arkadia', *JHS* 74 (1954), 32ff.

Wallace, P.W. 'Psyttaleia and the trophies of the Battle of Salamis,' *AJA* 73 (1969), 293ff.

Wallace, P.W. 'The Anopaia Path at Thermopylai', *AJA* 84 (1980), 15ff.

Wallace, P.W. 'Aphetae and the Battle of Artemision', *Studies presented to Sterling Dow on his eightieth birthday* (ed. K.J.Rigsby), *GRBS* Suppl. X (1984), 305ff.

Wallinga, H.T. 'The trireme and its crew', *Actus*. Studies in Honour of H.L.W. Nelson, (ed. J. den Boeft & A.H.M. Kessels, Utrecht, 1982), 463ff.

Wallinga, H.T. 'The Ionian Revolt', *Mnemosyne* 37 (1984), 401ff.

Wallinga, H.T. 'The ancient Persian navy and its predecessors', *Achaemenid History I*, Proceedings of the Groningen 1983 Achaemenid History Workshop (ed. H.Sancisi-Weerdenburg, Leiden, 1987), 47ff.

Wallinga, H.T. 'The trireme and history', *Mnemosyne* 43 (1990), 132ff.

Walters, K.R. 'Four hundred ships at Salamis?', *RhM* 124 (1981), 199ff.

Wardman, A.E. 'Tactics and the tradition of the Persian Wars', *Historia* 8 (1959), 49ff.

Welwei, K.-W. 'Die "Marathon"-Epigramme von der athenischen Agora', *Historia* 19 (1970), 295ff.

Welwei, K.-W. 'Das sogennante Grab der Plataier im Vranatal bei Marathon', *Historia* 28 (1979), 101ff.

West, W.C. 'The trophies of the Persian wars', *CPh* 64 (1969), 7ff.

West, W.C. 'Saviors of Greece', *GRBS* 11 (1970), 271ff.

Westlake, H.D. 'The Medism of Thessaly', *JHS* 56 (1936), 12ff.

Whatley, N. 'On the possibility of reconstructing Marathon and other ancient battles', *JHS* 84 (1964), 119ff.

Whitehead, I. 'Xerxes' fleet in Magnesia: the anchorage at Sepias', *The Mariner's Mirror* 74 (1988), 283ff.

Whitehead, I. 'The periplous', *Greece & Rome* 34 (1987), 178ff.

Wilhelm, A. 'Zur Topographie der Schlacht bei Salamis', *Sitzungsberichte der österreichischen Akademie der Wissenschaften* 211 (1929), 3ff.

Willetts, R.F. 'Herodotos IX 85, 1-2', *Mnemosyne* 33 (1980), 272ff.

Wolski, J., 'ΜΗΔΙΣΜΟΣ et son importance en Grèce à l'époque des Guerres Médiques', *Historia* 22 (1973), 3ff.

Woodhouse, W.J. 'The Greeks at Plataiai', *JHS* 18 (1898), 33ff.

Wright, H.B. *The Campaign of Plataea* (New Haven, 1904).

Wyatt, W.F. 'Persian dead at Marathon', *Historia* 25 (1976), 483f.

Wycherley, R.E. 'Marathon and the Poikile', *PCPhS* (NS) 18 (1972), 78.

Wuest, F.R. 'A decree of Themistokles from Troizen', *Gymnasium* 69 (1961), 233ff.

Young, T.C. Jnr. '480/79 B.C. – a Persian Perspective', *Iranica Antiqua* 15 (1980), 213ff.

Appendix 1: Historical Summary

[NB: references in square brackets are to the Penguin Classics Herodotos].

560-550: Cyrus becomes king of Persia and conquers Medes [85ff.]. Sparta defeats Tegea [65ff.] and begins to form 'Peloponnesian League'.

550-540: Cyrus conquers Lydia in western Asia Minor, and begins subjugation of Asiatic Greek states [67ff., 99ff.]; Athens finally falls under sway of 'tyrant' Peisistratos [61ff.].

540-530: Cyrus conquers Mesopotamia, Lebanon and Palestine [112ff.]; killed fighting Massagetai [122ff.]; Kambyses succeeds (530).

530-520: Miltiades becomes 'tyrant' of Thracian Chersonese (Gallipoli) [401]; Peisistratos of Athens dies; succeeded by Hippias (528); Kambyses conquers Egypt (525) [129, 203ff.]; Spartan naval expedition fails to oust Polykrates, 'tyrant' of Samos (c.525) [220ff.]; Kambyses dies, and, after period of turmoil, is succeeded by Darius (522) [229ff.].

520-510: Darius conquers 'India' (i.e. western Pakistan) [284f.]; crosses Bosporos into Europe, but is defeated north of the Danube by the Skythians (513) [299ff.]; Persians conquer Thrace [341]; Skythian embassy to Sparta [417]; Hippias of Athens' brother, Hipparchos, murdered by Harmodios and Aristogeiton (514) [360]; Hippias' rule becomes more oppressive; Athenian aristocrats, led by Alkmaionidai, secure support of Sparta, and after defeat of Spartan sea-borne expedition by Thessalian cavalry sent to aid Hippias, Spartan army led by Kleomenes I invades Attica; Hippias flees (510) [362f.].

510-500: Democratic reforms of Kleisthenes in Athens, including introduction of 'ostracism', lead to two abortive Spartan attempts to intervene [364ff.]; Sparta summons congress of allies, in effect, creating 'Peloponnesian League' [373], probably comprising all states of Peloponnese, apart from Argos and Achaia, and including Megara and, possibly, Aigina; Persian attack on Naxos (506?) [350ff.].

500-490: Greek states of Asia Minor revolt (499?), and appeal to Sparta and Athens for help; Sparta refuses, Athens and Eretria agree [352ff., 357ff., 379]; Greeks burn Sardis but are defeated outside Ephesos; Athens withdraws forces [380f.]; Darius vows revenge on Athens [382]; Asiatic Greeks defeated at battle of Lade (495?) [390ff.]; fall of Miletos (494) ends so-called 'Ionian Revolt' [394f.]; Themistokles archon 493/2; Miltiades flees from Chersonnese and returns to Athens [401f.]; Mardonios' operations in Thrace end in failure (492?) [402f.]; Darius demands 'earth and water' from Greeks (491?) [404]; *rapprochement* between Athens and Sparta; medism of Aigina leads Kleomenes to intervene and arrest medizers, after securing deposition of fellow-king, Damaratos [404ff.]; Persian expeditionary force attacks Naxos, Karystos and Eretria and lands at Marathon; battle of Marathon (490) [421ff.].

490-481: death of Kleomenes; Leonidas becomes king of Sparta (490?); Athens at war with Aigina; Miltiades' disastrous attack on Paros; Miltiades dies (489?), first ostracisms in Athens; death of Darius and accession of Xerxes (486) [442f.]; revolt of Egypt, Judaea and Babylon (485) [442f.]; Persians begin preparations for invasion of Greece (484) [443ff.]; Aristeides ostracized; Themistokles persuades Athenians to begin building navy (483/2) [490]; Xerxes leaves Sousa on march to west (18 April(?), 481), winters at Sardis [454ff.]; Greeks consult Delphi and hold first congress (autumn) [486ff.]; relations between Athens and Aigina patched up; spies sent to Asia Minor and embassies to Argos, Gelon of Syracuse, Kerkyra (Corfu) and Crete [490ff.].

480: Xerxes leaves Sardis (c.15 April?) [458ff.]; at 2nd Greek congress in spring, Thessalian appeal leads to abortive Greek attempt to defend Tempe pass (May/June?) [502f.]; evacuation of Attica; Xerxes at Hellespont (c.15 May-15 June?); advances to Doriskos, where holds review (end-June?) [464ff.]; march continues to Therma (July?) [478ff.]; Xerxes' sightseeing trip to Tempe; Greeks decide to defend Thermopylai and Artemision [503f.]; Xerxes and army leave Therma (c.10 August?), followed by fleet 11 days later (c.21 August?) [505] - **for detailed summary of following events see 'Diary' p.119**; Greeks defeated at Thermopylai [510ff.]; battles off Artemision lead to Greek withdrawal (end-August?) [525ff.]; Xerxes advances through central Greece to Attica and captures Athens (early September?) [533ff.]; after delay, Persian army moves on Isthmus and wrangling among Greek commanders is resolved by Themistokles' message to Persians, when Peloponnesians threaten to abandon Salamis; Persian navy enters straits and battle of Salamis follows (24 September?) [537ff.]; Greek fleet pursues fleeing Persian ships as far as Andros [559ff.]; eclipse of sun seen by Spartan army at Isthmus (2 October) [580]; Xerxes retreats to Asia Minor (October?), leaving Mardonios and army in Thessaly [562ff.].

480/79 (winter): Artabazos recaptures Olynthos after revolt, but fails to take Poteidaia [566ff.]; Mardonios sends Mys to consult oracles and then Alexander of Macedonia to Athens to offer terms which Athenians reject [569ff.].

479: Greek fleet musters at Aigina (spring) [568f.]; Mardonios moves south; second evacuation of Athens; Mardonios reoccupies city (June?); sends Mourychides to Salamis to offer same terms, which are again rejected; Lykidas and family lynched [577f.]; Spartans finally decide to mobilize (July?) [578ff.]; Mardonios retreats to Boiotia, sending cavalry to try to intercept Greek advance-force on Isthmus [581ff.]; Spartans and allies joined by Athenians at Eleusis [584]; Greeks cross Kithairon and take up position at foot [584]; Persian cavalry beaten off [584ff.]; Greeks move to second position near Asopos [586]; 10-day delay imposed by bad omens broken only by Persian cavalry's attack on Greek supply-lines [593]; Alexander allegedly betrays Mardonios' plans to Greeks [595f.]; Persian harrassing and choking of Gargaphia spring lead to Greek withdrawal and battle of Plataia (August?) [597ff.].

Appendix 2: Glossary of Proper Names and Greek Terms

[NB: I mostly transliterate Greek names'correctly', but some may be more familiar in their Latin spellings; these are given below in brackets.]

Abdera: Greek city in Thrace.
Abydos (Abydus): Greek city on Asiatic side of the Hellespont.
Achaia (Achaea): region west of Sikyon on south side of Gulf of Corinth.
Achaia Phthiotis: region on west coast of Gulf of Pagasai (q.v.).
Achaimenes: Xerxes' brother; satrap of Egypt; admiral in 480 BC.
Acharnai (Acharnae): important Attic deme (q.v.) c.14km north of Athens.
Agatharkides (Agatharcides): geographer of 2nd century BC; works lost.
Aiakos (Aeacus): legendary king of Aigina, grandfather of Aias (Ajax).
Aias (Ajax): legendary hero of Salamis.
Aigaleos (Aegaleus): ridge between Eleusis and Athens.
Aigina (Aegina): island in Saronic Gulf, south-west of Athens.
Aiginetan(s): inhabitants of Aigina.
Aiolis (Aeolis): region of Greek colonisation in north-west Asia Minor.
Aischylos (Aeschylus): Athenian tragedian of 5th century BC.
Aitolia (Aetolia): region of west-central Greece.
Akanthos (Acanthus): Greek city of Chalkidikê in Thrace.
Aleuadai (Aleuadae): principal family of Larissa (q.v.) in Thessaly.
Alkaios (Alcaeus): 7th/6th century BC lyric poet from Lesbos.
Alkmaionidai (Alcmaeonidae): Athenian aristocratic family.
Ambrakia (Ambracia): city of western Greece (now Arta).
Amompharetos (Amompharetus): Spartan officer, commander of *lochos* of Pitana (q.v.), allegedly guilty of disobeying orders before Plataia.
Amphictyonic Council (Αμφικτύονες, *Amphiktyones*): synod of delegates from various Greek states, meeting alternately at Anthele, near Thermopylai, and Delphi, and having charge of latter.
Anaktorion (Anactorium): city on west coast of Greece.
Andros: island south-east of Euboia.
Anopaia (Anopaea): mountain-track by which Persians turned Thermopylai.
Antikyra (Anticyra): town on Gulf of Malis (q.v.).
Aphetai (Aphetae): Persian fleet-base during operations off Artemision.
Aphidna: important deme (q.v.) of north-east Attica.
Apis-bull: sacred bull worshipped at Memphis in Egypt.
Archilochos (Archilochus): Greek lyric poet of 7th century BC.
Areiopagos (Areopagus): hill west of Athenian acropolis; also title of council which met there.

Arginousai (Arginusae): group of islands between Lesbos and Asia Minor, scene of naval battle between Spartans and Athenians in 406 BC.
Argives: people of Argos (see below).
Argolid: peninsula of north-east Peloponnese.
Argos: important city of north-east Peloponnese.
Aristeides (Aristides) (1): Athenian statesman and general, commander of Athenian contingent at Plataia.
Aristeides (Aristides) (2): Greek rhetorician of 2nd century AD.
Aristophanes (1): Athenian comic playwright of 5th/4th century BC.
Aristophanes (2): Boiotian historian of late 5th/4th century BC.
Artabanos (Artabanus): Xerxes' uncle.
Artabazos (Artabazus): Persian general in 480/79 BC.
Artaxerxes I: king of Persia 465-425 BC.
Artaxerxes II: king of Persia 405-359 BC.
Artemisia: queen of Halikarnassos at time of Xerxes' invasion of Greece.
Artemision (Artemisium): temple of goddess Artemis on north coast of Euboia, giving name to Greek fleet-base at time of Thermopylai.
archon (ἄρχων): title of officials in many Greek states, but especially in Athens, where were nine each year, of whom one gave name to year. Since archons held office from July to July, archon-dates are usually given in form, e.g., '493/2'.
Asopos (Asopus): name of several rivers in Greece, of which most famous was in Boiotia; another flowed into sea west of Thermopylai.
Athos: easternmost prong of Chalkidikê (q.v.).
Bakis (Bacis): name of several prophets, of whom most famous was Boiotian. Collections of oracles supposedly delivered by Bakis existed.
Baktria (Bactria): province of Persian empire – (roughly = Afghanistan).
Boiotia (Boeotia): region of central Greece.
Boreas: the north wind.
Caria: region in south-west Asia Minor.
Chalkedon (Chalcedon): city opposite Byzantion (Byzantium) on Bosporos.
Chalkis (Chalcis): city on west coast of Euboia.
Chalkidian(s): inhabitants of Chalkis.
Chalkidikê (Chalcidice): peninsula in northern Aegean (now Chalkidiki).
Charon: early Greek historian from Lampsakos on Hellespont; works lost.
Chersonese (strictly, 'Thracian Chersonese): Gallipoli peninsula.
Chilon: ephor (q.v.) of Sparta, traditionally in 556 BC.
Chios: Greek island off central part of western Asia Minor.
Chiot(s): inhabitants of Chios.
Cicero: Roman orator and statesman (106-43 BC).
Cilicia: area in south-east Asia Minor.
Cornelius Nepos (see 'Nepos').
Cyclades: island group in Aegean, including Naxos, Paros, Andros, etc.
Damaratos (Demaratus): exiled Spartan king; accompanied Xerxes to Greece.
Dekeleia (Decelea): deme (q.v.) north of Athens (now Tatoi or Dhekelia).
Delos: island in central Aegean, sacred to Apollo and Artemis.
Delphi: in Phokis, site of famous temple and oracle of Apollo.

deme (δῆμος, *dêmos*): one of 139 villages or wards into which Attica was divided as result of reforms of Kleisthenes' (q.v.).
Demeter: goddess of agriculture, and, particularly, cereal crops.
Demosthenes: Athenian orator and statesman of 4th century BC. (Where there is doubt about authenticity of speech attributed to him, it is conventional to put his name in square brackets).
Didyma: place on west coast of Asia Minor, south of Miletos.
Diomedes: legendary ruler of Argos.
Dionysios (Dionysius): Greek writer from Halikarnassos; lived in Rome from 29 BC until death in 7 BC; wrote on Roman antiquities, etc.
Diodoros (Diodorus Siculus): Sicilian historian of 1st century BC.
Doriskos (Doriscus): town on coast of Thrace where Xerxes reviewed forces.
drachma(i) (δραχμή): coin; average daily wage of casual labourer.
Eïon: town at mouth of Strymon in Thrace.
eirên, eirenes (εἴρην, εἴρενες): young Spartans, probably in twenties.
Eleusis: town in Attica west of Athens, famous as home of 'Mysteries'.
Elis: city of north-west Peloponnese, in whose territory lay Olympia.
Epameinondas (Epaminondas): Theban general; defeated Spartans at Leuktra.
Ephesos (Ephesus): Greek city on west coast of Asia Minor.
Ephialtes (1): traitor who led Persian troops round Thermopylai.
Ephialtes (2): Athenian statesman, responsible for reforms of 462/1 BC.
ephor(s) (ἔφορος, ἔφοροι): five most important Spartan civic officials.
Ephoros (Ephorus): 4th century BC Greek historian from Kyme in western Asia Minor; works lost, but one of main sources of Diodoros (q.v.).
Eretria: city on west coast of Euboia.
Erineus: place on coast of Achaia (q.v.), scene of naval engagement between Athenians and Corinthians in 413 BC.
Euboia (Euboea): island off east coast of Greece.
Euripos (Euripus): channel between Euboia and mainland.
Eurotas: river on which Sparta lies.
Eurybiadas (Eurybiades): Spartan officer who commanded Greek fleet at Artemision and Salamis.
Eurymedon: river of southern Asia Minor, scene of victory by Athens and allies over Persians in about 466 BC.
Frontinus, Sex. Iulius: Roman author, governor of Britain 75-8 AD.
Gelon: 'tyrant' of Gela 491-485 BC, and then of Gela and Syracuse 485-478.
gerousia (γερουσία): council of elders at Sparta, including kings.
Gonnos (Gonnus): Thessalian town commanding western exit from Tempe pass.
Gyndes: tributary of Tigris, rising in Kurdistan.
Halikarnassos (Halicarnassus): city in south-west Asia Minor (now Bodrum).
Hekataios (Hecataeus): geographer and historian from Miletos; works lost.
Hellanikos (Hellanicus): historian from Lesbos; works lost.
Hellespont: the Dardanelles.
helot(s) (εἱλώτης, –αι): serfs who worked land of Spartans and served as batmen and light troops in war.
Herakleion (Heracleum): shrine of Herakles, or town named after it.

Herakles (Hercules): legendary Greek hero.
Hesiod: late eighth century poet from Boiotia.
hippeis (ἱππεῖς): 'horsemen'; often elite forces such as cavalry drawn from wealthy Athenians; in Sparta unit of young men who fought on foot and acted as 'Royal Guard'.
Histiaia (Histiaea): town on north coast of Euboia, now Oreoi.
homoios (plural *homoioi*): 'equals'; full citizens of Sparta.
hoplite(s) (ὁπλίτης, -αι): Greek heavy infantry.
Iakchos (Iacchus): ritual name for Bacchus, used in Eleusinian Mysteries.
Ikaros: island in central Aegean, now Ikaria.
Imbros: island in northern Aegean.
'Immortals': elite Persian infantry supposedly always 10,000 strong.
Ion: 5th century BC tragedian from Chios; works now lost.
Ionia: central area of Greek settlement in western Asia Minor.
Iphikrates (Iphicrates): Athenian general of 4th century BC.
Isagoras: archon of Athens 508/7 BC; tried to prevent Kleisthenes' reforms.
Isokrates (Isocrates): Athenian orator and pamphleteer (436-338 BC).
Isthmia: sanctuary of Poseidon on east side of Isthmus of Corinth.
Isthmus: unless otherwise specified, Isthmus of Corinth.
Justin: Roman historian of uncertain date, author of history of Macedonia, based on lost work of Pompeius Trogus, historian of Augustus' time.
Kallikrates (Callicrates): handsome Spartan, killed at Plataia.
Kallimachos (Callimachus): Athenian polemarch (q.v.) at time of Marathon.
Kallisthenes (Callisthenes): 4th century BC Greek historian ; works lost.
Kalynda: island in Dodecanese, now Kalymnos.
Karneia (Carnea): Spartan summer festival.
Karyiai (Caryae): town of *perioikoi* (q.v.) north-east of Sparta.
Karystos (Carystus): city at southern end of Euboia.
Kekrops (Cecrops): legendary first king of Athens.
Keos (or Kea): island east of Cape Sounion (Sunium).
Kimon (Cimon): son of Miltiades, Athenian general of 5th century BC.
Kissia (Cissia): area in Persian empire north of head of Persian Gulf.
Kithairon (Cithaeron): mountain separating Attica from Boiotia.
Kleidemos (Clidemus): 4th century BC Athenian historian.
Kleisthenes (Clisthenes): late 6th century BC Athenian political reformer.
Kleombrotos (Cleombrotus): brother of Leonidas, half-brother of Kleomenes.
Kleomenes I: king of Sparta c.520-c.490 BC.
Kopais (Copais): lake in northern Boiotia, now drained.
Kounaxa (Cunaxa): village near Baghdad, scene of victory of Artaxerxes II over brother, Cyrus, in 401 BC.
Krateros (Craterus): 3rd century BC compiler of collection of documents relating to Athenian history, now lost.
Krestonia (Crestonia): region of Macedonia between Axios and Strymon.
Kroton (Croton): Greek colony in southern Italy.

Ktesias (Ctesias): court-physician of Artaxerxes II; author of history of Persia (Περσικά, *Persika*) which survives in epitome made for 9th century AD Byzantine bishop, Photius.
Kylon (Cylon): 6th century BC Athenian who attempted to become 'tyrant'.
Kyme (1): town on north-east coast of Euboia.
Kyme (2): town in north-west Asia Minor, birthplace of Ephoros (q.v.).
Kyme (3) (Cumae): oldest Greek colony on mainland of Italy.
Kynaigeiros (Cynaegirus): brother of Aischylos, killed at Marathon.
Kythera (Cythera): island off south-east corner of Peloponnese.
Kythnos (Cythnus): island in central Aegean.
Lade: island off Miletos; where Persians defeated Asiatic Greeks c.495 BC.
Lakedaimon (Lacedaemon): region in which Sparta lay.
Lakedaimonians (Lacedaemonians): originally, inhabitants of Lakedaimon; usually = 'Spartans', but can refer to all free inhabitants of Spartan territory, including *perioikoi (q.v.).*
lambda (λάμβδα): Greek letter 'l', shaped like inverted 'v' – Λ; possibly used as device on shields of Spartans and *perioikoi* (q.v.), standing for 'Lakedaimonians' (Λακεδαιμόνιοι).
Lamia: town in Spercheios valley.
Lampsakos (Lampsacus): Greek city on Asiatic side of the Hellespont.
Larissa: most important town of northern Thessaly.
Laureion (Laurium): hill in south-east Attica famous for silver-mines.
Lechaion (Lechaeum): sea-port of Corinth on Gulf of Corinth.
Lemnos: island in northern Aegean.
Leotychidas (Leotychides): king of Sparta after deposition of Damaratos.
Leukas (Leucas): island off west coast of Greece.
lochos (λόχος): term for unit of soldiers, varying in size, but usually at least several hundred strong.
Lucian: 2nd century AD Greek author from Syria.
Lycia: area in south-west Asia Minor.
Lydia: kingdom in western Asia Minor conquered by Cyrus 546 BC.
Lygdamis (1): 'tyrant' of Halikarnassos in Herodotos' time.
Lygdamis (2): late 6th century BC 'tyrant' of Naxos.
Lykourgos: famous, possibly legendary, lawgiver of Sparta.
Magnesia: coastal region of Thessaly, south of Tempe (q.v.); also name of several cities.
Maiander (Maeander): river of south-west Asia Minor (now Menderes).
Malea, Cape: eastern 'prong' of Peloponnese.
Malis: region of north-central Greece.
Mantineia (Mantinea): city in eastern Arcadia, near which were fought three battles – first in 418 BC, second in 362, third in 207.
Mardonios (Mardonius): Persian general; commanded in Thrace c.492 BC; defeated and killed at Plataia in 479.
Marsyas: river of south-west Asia Minor.
Mede(s): people of Media; often used by Greeks to mean 'Persians'.
'medism', 'medize': (Μηδίζειν): siding with 'Medes', i.e. Persians.

Megabazos: Persian general responsible for conquest of Thrace.

Megara: city state spanning eastern part of Isthmus of Corinth.

Melos: island in southern Aegean.

Miletos (Miletus): Greek city on coast of Ionia.

Miltiades: Athenian aristocrat, 'tyrant' of Chersonese c.530-493, *stratêgos* at Marathon, and often regarded as architect of victory.

mora: one of six main divisions of Spartan army in Xenophon's time, and possibly earlier.

Myronides: Athenian general of 450s BC.

Mykale (Mycale): promontory north of Miletos, now Samsun Dagi; scene of final victory of Greeks over beached Persian fleet in 479 BC.

Mykenai (Mycenae): famous Bronze Age fortress near Argos; small town at time of Xerxes' invasion.

Mytilene: most important city on island of Lesbos.

Naxos: island in central Aegean.

Nemea: town and river of northern Peloponnese. (The battle of 394 BC usually referred to as 'the Nemea', was actually fought near a river east of the river Nemea, the ancient name of which is unknown).

Nepos, Cornelius: 1st century BC Roman biographer.

nomos: usual Greek term for 'law', but also used for 'district'.

'Old Oligarch': modern term for author of '*Constitution of the Athenians*' attributed to Xenophon, but probably written in 420s BC.

Olynthos (Olynthus): city in Chalkidikê.

Opountian Lokris: area on east coast of Greece, south-east of Thermopylai, so-called after principal town, Opous.

oracle: either shrine, etc., where prophecies were made, especially Delphi, or prophecy emanating from such source.

Orchomenos (Orchomenus) (1): city in north-west Boiotia.

Orchomenos (Orchomenus) (2): city in Arcadia.

Orestheion: place in Arcadia, just over border from Spartan territory.

ostracism (whence 'ostracize', 'ostracisé): political device at Athens, probably introduced by Kleisthenes, whereby Athenian citizens could get rid of someone they disliked by writing name on sherd (*'ostrakon'* in Greek); provided there was a quorum of at least 6000 'votes', the man whose name appeared most frequently had to go into exile for ten years; many such *ostraka* have been found.

Othrys: range of hills between Thessaly and Spercheios valley.

Pagasai (Pagasae), Gulf of: in south-eastern Thessaly, now Gulf of Volo.

Paiania (Paeania): deme (q.v.) of eastern Attica.

paidagôgos (paedagogus): literally, 'boy-conductor'; term used for slave employed to look after young boys.

Paionia (Paeonia): northern Macedonia.

Pale: town on island of Kephallenia, off west coast of Greece.

Pallas: title of goddess Athena.

Pallene: deme (q.v.) in eastern Attica.

Pamphylia: area on south coast of Asia Minor.

Panaitios (Panaetius): captain of ship from Tenos who deserted to Greeks before Salamis.
Paros: island in central Aegean.
Pausanias (1): 2nd century AD Greek author of guidebook to Greece.
Pausanias (2): Spartan prince who commanded Greek army at Plataia.
Peiraeus (or Peiraieus): harbour of Athens.
Peisistratos (Pisistratus): Athenian 'tyrant'; first seized power 561/0 BC; twice expelled; finally won control 546 BC.
Peisistratidai: family of Peisistratos.
Pelasgians (Πελασγοί): name of possibly legendary pre-Greek inhabitants of Greece.
Pelion (Pelium): mountain in central Magnesia (q.v.).
Peloponnesian War: war between Athens and Sparta (431-404 BC), described by Thucydides.
pentekontor: warship with twenty-five oars a-side.
Perikles (Pericles): Athenian statesman of 5th century BC.
perioikoi: free inhabitants of Spartan territory, other than Spartans, who had no political rights, though liable for military service; collectively, *perioikoi* + Spartans, = 'Lakedaimonians' (q.v.).
Persepolis: summer capital of Persian empire.
phalanx: originally line of battle; used of army of hoplites.
Phaleron (Phalerum): bay east of Peiraeus, originally used as fleet-base by Athenians.
Phanias: 4th century Greek philosopher from Lesbos; works lost.
Pharsala (Pharsalos, Pharsalus): city in southern Thessaly.
Philippides (or, possibly, Pheidippides): runner who ran from Athens to Sparta to ask for help before Marathon.
Phleious (Phlius): city in north-east Peloponnese.
Phleiasians: inhabitants of Phleious.
Phoenicia: roughly corresponds to modern Lebanon.
Phokaia (Phocaea): Greek city on coast of western Asia Minor.
Phokis (Phocis): area in central Greece, including Delphi.
Phormio: Athenian admiral; won two victories in Gulf of Corinth in 429 BC.
Phrynichos (Phrynichus): late 6th/early 5th century BC Athenian dramatist.
phylê (plural '*phylai*') (φυλή, φυλαί): term, often translated 'tribe(s)', used particularly of ten divisions into which Athenian citizens were divided by reforms of Kleisthenes.
Pillars of Herakles (Hercules): Straits of Gibraltar.
Pindar: Theban poet (c.522-442 BC), author of odes for victors at Olympia (*Olympians*), Delphi (*Pythians*) and Isthmia (*Isthmians*).
Pitana: one of four 'obes' (villages) making up 'city' of Sparta.
Plataia (Plataea): small city in south-west Boiotia near which Greeks finally defeated Persians in 479 BC.
Plutarch (c.50-c.120 AD): author of lives of prominent Greeks and Romans, and of essays on various themes usually referred to as '*Moralia*'.
polemarch (πολέμαρχος): title of military official in various Greek states; in Athens one of nine archons (q.v.), probably c.-in-c. down to 487/6; at Sparta one of most

senior officers, after king; in time of Xenophon, commander of one of six *morai* (q.v.).

Polyainos (Polyaenus): 2nd century AD author of book on stratagems.

Polybios (Polybius): Greek historian of 2nd century BC (c.204-118).

Polykrates (Polycrates): 6th century 'tyrant' (possibly two!) of Samos.

Poseidon (Neptune): god of the sea.

Poteidaia (Potidea): city of Chalkidikê (q.v.), later Kassandreia.

Priene: town near Miletos in western Asia Minor.

proxenos (-oi) (πρόξενος, πρόξενοι): citizen of one city who looked after interests of another; still Greek term for 'consul(s)'.

Psammmetichos (Psamtik): pharaoh of Egypt 671-617 BC.

Pythia: title given to priestess of Apollo at Delphi.

quinquereme: principal warship of Punic Wars; probably rowed by five files of men from bow to stern a-side, with perhaps two men rowing each oar in two upper banks, and one each oar in lowest bank; invented in 4th century BC.

Royal Road: main highway from Sardis to Sousa.

sagaris (σάγαρις): axe used by Sakai.

Sakai (Persian, 'saka'): inhabitants of Turkmenskaya and Uzbekskaya.

Samos: Greek island off west coast of Asia Minor.

Samothrace: island off coast of Thrace.

Sardis: capital of Lydia and later of satrapy (q.v.) of Ionia.

Saronic Gulf: gulf east of Isthmus of Corinth, between Attica and Argolid.

satrap (σατράπης, Persian *'satrapa'*): governor of Persian province, whence 'satrapy'.

Sepeia (Sepea): place near Nauplion in Argolid, where Spartans defeated Argives in 494 BC.

Sepias: cape at southern end of Magnesia (q.v.).

Seriphos: island in central Aegean.

Sidon: city of Phoenicia (q.v.).

Sikyon (Sicyon): city west of Corinth on Gulf of Corinth.

Simonides: 6th/5th century BC Greek poet from island of Keos.

Siphnos: island in central Aegean.

Siris: Greek colony in southern Italy.

Skamander (Scamander): river near Troy (now Kücük Menderes).

Skiathos (Sciathus): island east of southern end of Magnesia (q.v.).

Skyllias (Scyllias): famous diver who deserted to Greeks at Artemision.

Skyros: island east of Euboia.

Skythian(s) (Scythians) (Σκύθης, Σκύθαι): Greek term for steppe-peoples, particularely those beyond Danube.

Sophokles (Sophocles): 5th century BC Athenian tragedian.

soros (σωρός): grave-mound; particularly that of Athenians at Marathon.

Souda (*Suda*): Byzantine lexicon of c.1000 AD or later, originally ascribed to author called 'Suidas'.

Sounion (Sunium): south-eastern cape of Attica.

Sousa (Susa): winter capital of Persian empire.

Spartiate(s) (Σπαρτιάτης, Σπαρτιάται): 'Spartan(s)', as distinct from other free inhabitants of Spartan territory (cf. 'Lakedaimonians' & '*perioikoi*'); sometimes = '*homoioi*' (q.v.).

Spercheios (Spercheus): river flowing into Gulf of Malis.

Sphakteria (Sphacteria): island off west coast of Peloponnese, where 420 Spartan troops were trapped by Athenian navy in 425 BC.

stade(s) (στάδιον, στάδια): Greek measure of length; = 195•6 metres, but in this book usually rounded up to 200 metres.

Stephanos (Stephanus) of Byzantion (Byzantium): 5th century AD author of geographical lexicon surviving in later epitome.

Stoa Poikile ('Painted Stoa'): colonnade on north side of *agora* at Athens containing painting of battle of Marathon.

Strabo: Greek geographer (c.54 BC-c.24 AD).

stratêgos, stratêgoi (στρατηγός, στρατηγοί): 'general(s)'; in Athens, after reforms of Kleisthenes, ten annually elected officials; possibly originally commanders of ten army-units based on *phylai* (q.v.), later called '*taxeis*' and commanded by '*taxiarchoi*'.

Strymon: river of western Thrace.

Styra: city in southern Euboia.

Sybaris: Greek colony in southern Italy, and daughter of Themistokles.

Sybota: islands between southern Kerkyra (Corfu) and mainland; scene of sea-battle between Kerkyraians and Corinthians in 432 BC.

talent (τάλαντον): fixed weight of silver, = 6000 *drachmai* (q.v.). Euboic or Attic talents weighed c.26 kg, Aiginetan c.43 kg.

taxis, plural, '*taxeis*' (τάξις, τάξεις): unit(s) of troops; in Athens those of a single *phylê* (q.v.).

Tegea: city in eastern Arcadia.

Tegeates (Τεγεάται): inhabitants of Tegea.

temenos (τέμενος): piece of land sacred to god or goddess.

Tempe: narrow defile between Mt. Olympos and Mt. Ossa on coast of Thessaly.

Tenos: island in central Aegean.

Teos: city in Ionia.

Thasos: island in northern Aegean.

Thebes: most important city of Boiotia.

Themistokles (Themistocles): Athenian statesman, commander of Athenian contingent at Salamis.

Themistokles Decree: name given to 3rd century BC inscription from Trozen, purporting to be copy of decree proposed by Themistokles in 481 or 480 BC.

Therma: city on site of present Thessaloniki.

Thespiai: town in south-west Boiotia.

Thouria (Thourioi, Thurii): Greek colony in southern Italy.

Thrace (Θράκη): Greek name for area north of Aegean, extending into Bulgaria.

Thria: plain of Eleusis (q.v.).

Thucydides: celebrated Athenian historian (c.460 – c.398 BC), author of history of Peloponnesian War.

Thyrea, Thyreatis: area disputed between Sparta and Argos; finally passed under Spartan control in 546 BC.

Tigranes: general who commanded Persian forces at Mykale (q.v.).

Timokreon (Timocreon): 5th century poet from Rhodes; works lost.

Torone: city of Chalkidikê.

Trachis: town to west of Thermopylai, north of Asopos and commanding gorge.

triakonter: small ship rowed by 15 oars a-side.

trierarch (τριήραρχος): captain of trireme (see below).

trireme (τριήρης): main warship of Persian Wars; c.35m long by c.5m wide; probably rowed by 85 oars a-side, 31 in top bank, 27 in lower two; also carried deck-crew – later 16 – and marines, perhaps normally 14, but sometimes as many as 40.

Trozen (Troizen, Troezen): city on north-east coast of Peloponnese.

'tyrant' (τύραννος): someone who seized power by force, roughly = dictator, though that was title of perfectly respectable Roman official!

Xanthippos (Xanthippus): Athenian statesman and general; commanded Athenian contingent at Mykale (q.v.); father of Perikles.

Xanthos: historian from Lydia; works lost; also city in Lycia (q.v.).

Xenophon: Athenian soldier and writer works include *Anabasis* (account of adventures as mercenary), history of Greece (*Hellenika*), account of upbringing and life of Cyrus (*Kyropaideia*, *Cyropaedia*), and a 'Constitution of the Lakedaimonians' (*Lakedaimoniôn Politeia*), which some scholars think was written by someone else.

Index